D1461150

Rover 213 & 216 Owners Workshop Manual

Peter G Strasman

Models covered
All Rover 213 & 216 saloons, including special/limited edition models;
1342 cc & 1598 cc

Does not cover Rover 214 & 216 introduced October 1989

(1116-5S6)

ABCDE
FGHIJ
KLMNO
PQRS

2

THE
BOOK

Haynes Publishing Group
Sparkford Nr Yeovil
Somerset BA22 7JJ England

Haynes Publications, Inc
861 Lawrence Drive
Newbury Park
Cailfornia 91320 USA

Acknowledgements

Thanks are due to the Champion Sparking Plug Company Limited who supplied the illustrations showing spark plug conditions, to Holt Lloyd Limited who supplied the illustrations showing bodywork repair, and to Duckhams Oils who provided lubrication data. Certain other illustrations are the copyright of the Austin Rover Group Limited and are used with their permission. Sykes-Pickavant provided some of the workshop tools, and Duckhams Oils provided lubrication data. Lastly special thanks are due to all those people at Sparkford who helped in the production of this manual.

A book in the **Haynes Owners Workshop Manual Series**

Printed by J. H. Haynes & Co. Ltd, Sparkford, Nr Yeovil, Somerset BA22 7JJ, England

ISBN 1 85010 679 7

British Library Cataloguing in Publication Data
Strasman, Peter G., 1923 –
Rover 213 & 216 owners workshop manual.
1. Cars. Maintenance & repair – Amateurs' manuals
I. Title II. Series
629.28'722
ISBN 1-85010-679-7

Restoring and Preserving our Motoring Heritage

Few people can have had the luck to realise their dreams to quite the same extent and in such a remarkable fashion as John Haynes, Founder and Chairman of the Haynes Publishing Group.

Since 1965 his unique approach to workshop manual publishing has proved so successful that millions of Haynes Manuals are now sold every year throughout the world, covering literally thousands of different makes and models of cars, vans and motorcycles.

A continuing passion for cars and motoring led to the founding in 1985 of a Charitable Trust dedicated to the restoration and preservation of our motoring heritage. To inaugurate the new Museum, John Haynes donated virtually his entire private collection of 52 cars.

Now with an unrivalled international collection of over 210 veteran, vintage and classic cars and motorcycles, the Haynes Motor Museum in Somerset is well on the way to becoming one of the most interesting Motor Museums in the world.

A 70 seat video cinema, a cafe and an extensive motoring bookshop, together with a specially constructed one kilometre motor circuit, make a visit to the Haynes Motor Museum a truly unforgettable experience.

Every vehicle in the museum is preserved in as near as possible mint condition and each car is run every six months on the motor circuit.

Enjoy the picnic area set amongst the rolling Somerset hills. Peer through the William Morris workshop windows at cars being restored, and browse through the extensive displays of fascinating motoring memorabilia.

From the 1903 Oldsmobile through such classics as an MG Midget to the mighty 'E' Type Jaguar, Lamborghini, Ferrari Berlinetta Boxer, and Graham Hill's Lola Cosworth, there is something for everyone, young and old alike, at this Somerset Museum.

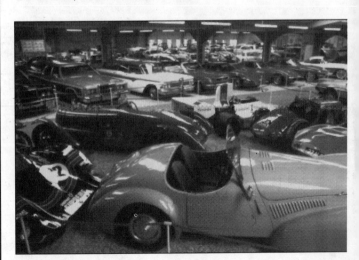

Haynes Motor Museum

Situated mid-way between London and Penzance, the Haynes Motor Museum is located just off the A303 at Sparkford, Somerset (home of the Haynes Manual) and is open to the public 7 days a week all year round, except Christmas Day and Boxing Day.

Contents

Spark plug condition and bodywork repair colour pages between pages 32 and 33

Rover 216 Vitesse EFi

Rover 216 Vanden Plas EFi

About this manual

Its aim

The aim of this manual is to help you get the best value from your vehicle. It can do so in several ways. It can help you decide what work must be done (even should you choose to get it done by a garage), provide information on routine maintenance and servicing, and give a logical course of action and diagnosis when random faults occur. However, it is hoped that you will use the manual by tackling the work yourself. On simpler jobs it may even be quicker than booking the car into a garage and going there twice, to leave and collect it. Perhaps most important, a lot of money can be saved by avoiding the costs a garage must charge to cover its labour and overheads.

The manual has drawings and descriptions to show the function of the various components so that their layout can be understood. Then the tasks are described and photographed in a step-by-step sequence so that even a novice can do the work.

Its arrangement

The manual is divided into thirteen Chapters, each covering a logical sub-division of the vehicle. The Chapters are each divided into Sections, numbered with single figures, eg 5; and the Sections into paragraphs (or sub-sections), with decimal numbers following on from the Section they are in, eg 5.1, 5.2, 5.3 etc.

It is freely illustrated, especially in those parts where there is a detailed sequence of operations to be carried out. There are two forms of illustration: figures and photographs. The figures are numbered in sequence with decimal numbers, according to their position in the Chapter – eg Fig. 6.4 is the fourth drawing/illustration in Chapter 6. Photographs carry the same number (either individually or in related groups) as the Section or sub-section to which they relate.

There is an alphabetical index at the back of the manual as well as a contents list at the front. Each Chapter is also preceded by its own individual contents list.

References to the 'left' or 'right' of the vehicle are in the sense of a person in the driver's seat facing forwards.

Unless otherwise stated, nuts and bolts are removed by turning anti-clockwise, and tightened by turning clockwise.

Vehicle manufacturers continually make changes to specifications and recommendations, and these, when notified, are incorporated into our manuals at the earliest opportunity.

Whilst every care is taken to ensure that the information in this manual is correct, no liability can be accepted by the authors or publishers for loss, damage or injury caused by any errors in, or omissions from, the information given.

Introduction to the Rover 200 Series

The cars in the range are economical and well constructed but, of course, show much evidence of their Japanese influence in design.

There is a sufficiently large number of model variations to suit most demands in respect of engine, transmission and trim specifications. It will be realised that the performance of the smaller-engined versions, especially with automatic transmission, must be limited with such a large body.

From the points of view of servicing and repair, the car should present no problems to the home mechanic.

For modifications, and information applicable to later models, refer to the Supplement at the end of this manual.

General dimensions, weights and capacities

For modifications, and information applicable to later models, see Supplement at end of manual

Dimensions

Overall length	4.156 m (163.8 in)
Overall width	1.623 m (63.8 in)
Overall height (at kerb weight)	1.377 m (54.0 in)
Ground clearance (at kerb weight)	165.0 mm (6.5 in)
Wheelbase	2.45 m (96.5 in)
Track-front	1.4 m (55.0 in)
Track-rear	1.415 m (55.5 in)

Kerb weights up to 1987 (with oil, coolant and full fuel tank)

213 (manual)	860 kg (1896 lb)
213 S:	
Manual	865 kg (1907 lb)
Automatic	876 kg (1932 lb)
213 SE (automatic)	886 kg (1954 lb)
213 Vanden Plas	945 kg (2084 lb)
216 S	940 kg (2073 lb)
216 SE	945 kg (2084 lb)
216 Vanden Plas:	
Manual	954 kg (2104 lb)
Automatic	976 kg (2152 lb)
216 Vitesse	945 kg (2084 lb)

Kerb weights from 1987 (with oil, coolant and full fuel tank)

213	895 kg (1975 lb)
213S:	
Manual	900 kg (1985 lb)
Automatic	910 kg (2010 lb)
213 SE Automatic	925 kg (2040 lb)
213 EX	945 kg (2084 lb)
216 S	975 kg (2150 lb)
216 SE	970 kg (2139 lb)
216 SE EFi and EX:	
Manual	990 kg (2185 lb)
Automatic	1010 kg (2230 lb)
216 Vanden Plas:	
Manual	995 kg (2194 lb)
Automatic	1020 kg (2249 lb)
216 Vitesse	1000 kg (2205 lb)
216 Sprint	960 kg (2117 lb)

Capacities

Engine oil with filter change:	
1.3 models	3.5 litres (6.25 pints)
1.6 models	3.6 litres (6.30 pints)
Manual transmission:	
1.3 models	2.3 litres (4.0 pints)
1.6 models	2.2 litres (3.75 pints)
Automatic transmission (service fluid change):	
Three speed	2.4 litres (4.25 pints)
Four-speed	2.0 litres (3.5 pints)
Refill from dry (includes torque converter):	
Three speed	5.0 litres (8.75 pints)
Four-speed	5.75 litres (10.0 pints)
Cooling system:	
1.3 models up to VIN 800 000 (1985 model year)	4.5 litres (8.0 pints)
1.3 models from VIN 800 000 (1985 model year)	6.4 litres (11.0 pints)
1.6 models	6.4 litres (11.0 pints)
Fuel tank	46.0 litres (10.0 gals)

Jacking, towing and wheel changing

To avoid repetition, the procedure for raising the vehicle, in order to carry out work under it, is not included before each relevant operation described in this Manual.

It is to be preferred, and it is certainly recommended, that the vehicle is positioned over an inspection pit or raised on a lift. Where these facilities are not available, use ramps or jack up the vehicle strictly in accordance with the following guide. Once the vehicle is raised, supplement the jack with axle stands.

Jacking

To lift the front of the car (both wheels) locate the jack under the jacking bracket. Support the car with axle stands placed under the forward jacking points under the sills.

Raise the rear of the car by placing the jack under the rear jacking bracket.

Support the car with axle stands placed under the rearmost jacking points under the sills.

Towing

If the car is being towed, use the hooks provided, but have the ignition key in position (1) so that the steering does not lock. Remember that the brake pedal will require greater effort as the vacuum servo assistance will not be available.

It is permissible to tow a light vehicle using the rear towing hook.

If the car is fitted with automatic transmission it is recommended that the front wheels are raised off the ground when being towed. If this is not possible, restrict the towing speed to 48 km/h (30 mph) and the distance towed to 48 km (30 miles).

Wheel changing

To change a roadwheel, remove the spare wheel from the well in the luggage boot.

Remove the jack, wheelbrace and trim removal lever from the container ahead of the spare wheel.

Prise off the hub cap or roadwheel trim according to model.

Make sure that the handbrake is fully applied and chock the wheel opposite to the one being removed.

Release but do not remove the wheel nuts.

Locate the jack from the tool kit under the reinforced jacking point below the sill nearest to the roadwheel being changed. Do not jack up under the tubular bars adjacent to the jacking points. The correct points of lift are marked with a triangle.

Raise the car, remove the wheel nuts and roadwheel.

Fit the spare wheel, tighten the nuts until the roadwheel cannot be held against rotation.

Lower the jack and tighten the roadwheel nuts fully. Fit the wheel trim or hub cap.

Sill jacking point
A DO NOT jack up or support the car under this box member.
B Correct jacking/support location point.

Front towing hook

Rear towing hook

Front jacking bracket

Rear jacking bracket

Spare wheel stowage

Tool and jack stowage

Prising off wheel centre cap

H.16656

Roadwheel trim plate

Buying spare parts
and vehicle identification numbers

Buying spare parts

Spare parts are available from many sources, for example Austin Rover garages, other garages and accessory shops, and motor factors. Our advice regarding spare part sources is as follows.

Officially appointed Austin Rover garages – This is the best source of parts which are peculiar to your car and are not generally available (eg complete cylinder heads, internal gearbox components, badges, interior trim etc). It is also the only place at which you should buy if your vehicle is still under warranty – non Austin Rover components may invalidate the warranty. To be sure of obtaining the correct parts it will always be necessary to give the storeman your car's vehicle identification number, and if possible, to take the 'old' part along for positive identification. Many parts are available under a factory exchange scheme – any parts returned should always be clean. It obviously makes good sense to go straight to the specialists on your car for this type of part for they are best equipped to supply you.

Other dealers and accessory shops – These are often very good places to buy materials and components needed for the maintenance of your car (eg oil filters, spark plugs, bulbs, drivebelts, oils and grease, touch-up paint, filler paste etc). They also sell general accessories, usually have convenient opening hours, charge lower prices and can often be found not far from home.

Motor factors – Good factors will stock all of the more important components which wear out relatively quickly (eg clutch components, pistons, valves, exhaust systems, brake pipes/seals and pads etc). Motor factors will often provide new or reconditioned components on a part exchange basis – this can save a considerable amount of money.

Vehicle identification numbers

Modifications are a continuing and unpublicised process in vehicle manufacture, quite apart from major model changes. Spare parts manuals and lists are compiled upon a numerical basis, the individual vehicle numbers being essential to correct identification of the component required.

When ordering spare parts, always give as much information as possible. Quote the car model, year of manufacture, body and engine numbers as appropriate.

The vehicle identification number is also stamped into the body – on vehicles up to VIN 886518 in the boot aperture drain channel, and from VIN 886519 in the right-hand side of the bulkhead.

Additionally, a body number plate is welded to the right-hand side of the spare wheel well.

When ordering parts relating to the body, or paint, quote both the VIN and body number.

The engine number on 1.3 models is stamped on the crankcase adjacent to the flywheel housing. On 1.6 models the engine number is stamped on the cylinder block below the spark plugs.

Vehicle identification number

Engine number (1.3)

General repair procedures

Whenever servicing, repair or overhaul work is carried out on the car or its components, it is necessary to observe the following procedures and instructions. This will assist in carrying out the operation efficiently and to a professional standard of workmanship.

Joint mating faces and gaskets

Where a gasket is used between the mating faces of two components, ensure that it is renewed on reassembly, and fit it dry unless otherwise stated in the repair procedure. Make sure that the mating faces are clean and dry with all traces of old gasket removed. When cleaning a joint face, use a tool which is not likely to score or damage the face, and remove any burrs or nicks with an oilstone or fine file.

Make sure that tapped holes are cleaned with a pipe cleaner, and keep them free of jointing compound if this is being used unless specifically instructed otherwise.

Ensure that all orifices, channels or pipes are clear and blow through them, preferably using compressed air.

Oil seals

Whenever an oil seal is removed from its working location, either individually or as part of an assembly, it should be renewed.

The very fine sealing lip of the seal is easily damaged and will not seal if the surface it contacts is not completely clean and free from scratches, nicks or grooves. If the original sealing surface of the component cannot be restored, the component should be renewed.

Protect the lips of the seal from any surface which may damage them in the course of fitting. Use tape or a conical sleeve where possible. Lubricate the seal lips with oil before fitting and, on dual lipped seals, fill the space between the lips with grease.

Unless otherwise stated, oil seals must be fitted with their sealing lips toward the lubricant to be sealed.

Use a tubular drift or block of wood of the appropriate size to install the seal and, if the seal housing is shouldered, drive the seal down to the shoulder. If the seal housing is unshouldered, the seal should be fitted with its face flush with the housing top face.

Screw threads and fastenings

Always ensure that a blind tapped hole is completely free from oil, grease, water or other fluid before installing the bolt or stud. Failure to do this could cause the housing to crack due to the hydraulic action of the bolt or stud as it is screwed in.

When tightening a castellated nut to accept a split pin, tighten the nut to the specified torque, where applicable, and then tighten further to the next split pin hole. Never slacken the nut to align a split pin hole unless stated in the repair procedure.

When checking or retightening a nut or bolt to a specified torque setting, slacken the nut or bolt by a quarter of a turn, and then retighten to the specified setting.

Locknuts, locktabs and washers

Any fastening which will rotate against a component or housing in the course of tightening should always have a washer between it and the relevant component or housing.

Spring or split washers should always be renewed when they are used to lock a critical component such as a big-end bearing retaining nut or bolt.

Locktabs which are folded over to retain a nut or bolt should always be renewed.

Self-locking nuts can be reused in non-critical areas, providing resistance can be felt when the locking portion passes over the bolt or stud thread.

Split pins must always be replaced with new ones of the correct size for the hole.

Special tools

Some repair procedures in this manual entail the use of special tools such as a press, two or three-legged pullers, spring compressors etc. Wherever possible, suitable readily available alternatives to the manufacturer's special tools are described, and are shown in use. In some instances, where no alternative is possible, it has been necessary to resort to the use of a manufacturer's tool and this has been done for reasons of safety as well as the efficient completion of the repair operation. Unless you are highly skilled and have a thorough understanding of the procedure described, never attempt to bypass the use of any special tool when the procedure described specifies its use. Not only is there a very great risk of personal injury, but expensive damage could be caused to the components involved.

Tools and working facilities

Introduction

A selection of good tools is a fundamental requirement for anyone contemplating the maintenance and repair of a motor vehicle. For the owner who does not possess any, their purchase will prove a considerable expense, offsetting some of the savings made by doing-it-yourself. However, provided that the tools purchased meet the relevant national safety standards and are of good quality, they will last for many years and prove an extremely worthwhile investment.

To help the average owner to decide which tools are needed to carry out the various tasks detailed in this manual, we have compiled three lists of tools under the following headings: *Maintenance and minor repair, Repair and overhaul,* and *Special.* The newcomer to practical mechanics should start off with the *Maintenance and minor repair* tool kit and confine himself to the simpler jobs around the vehicle. Then, as his confidence and experience grow, he can undertake more difficult tasks, buying extra tools as, and when, they are needed. In this way, a *Maintenance and minor repair* tool kit can be built-up into a *Repair and overhaul* tool kit over a considerable period of time without any major cash outlays. The experienced do-it-yourselfer will have a tool kit good enough for most repair and overhaul procedures and will add tools from the *Special* category when he feels the expense is justified by the amount of use to which these tools will be put.

It is obviously not possible to cover the subject of tools fully here. For those who wish to learn more about tools and their use there is a book entitled *How to Choose and Use Car Tools* available from the publishers of this manual.

Maintenance and minor repair tool kit

The tools given in this list should be considered as a minimum requirement if routine maintenance, servicing and minor repair operations are to be undertaken. We recommend the purchase of combination spanners (ring one end, open-ended the other); although more expensive than open-ended ones, they do give the advantages of both types of spanner.

Combination spanners - 10, 11, 12, 13, 14 & 17 mm
Adjustable spanner - 9 inch
Engine sump/gearbox drain plug key
Spark plug spanner (with rubber insert)
Spark plug gap adjustment tool
Set of feeler gauges
Brake bleed nipple spanner
Screwdriver - 4 in long x ¼ in dia (flat blade)
Screwdriver - 4 in long x ¼ in dia (cross blade)
Combination pliers - 6 inch
Hacksaw (junior)
Tyre pump
Tyre pressure gauge
Oil can
Fine emery cloth (1 sheet)
Wire brush (small)
Funnel (medium size)

Repair and overhaul tool kit

These tools are virtually essential for anyone undertaking any major repairs to a motor vehicle, and are additional to those given in the *Maintenance and minor repair* list. Included in this list is a comprehensive set of sockets. Although these are expensive they will be found invaluable as they are so versatile - particularly if various drives are included in the set. We recommend the ½ in square-drive type, as this can be used with most proprietary torque wrenches. If you cannot afford a socket set, even bought piecemeal, then inexpensive tubular box spanners are a useful alternative.

The tools in this list will occasionally need to be supplemented by tools from the *Special* list.

Sockets (or box spanners) to cover range in previous list
Reversible ratchet drive (for use with sockets)
Extension piece, 10 inch (for use with sockets)
Universal joint (for use with sockets)
Torque wrench (for use with sockets)
'Mole' wrench - 8 inch
Ball pein hammer
Soft-faced hammer, plastic or rubber
Screwdriver - 6 in long x 56 in dia (flat blade)
Screwdriver - 2 in long x 56 in square (flat blade)
Screwdriver - 1½ in long x ¼ in dia (cross blade)
Screwdriver - 3 in long x ⅛ in dia (electricians)
Pliers - electricians side cutters
Pliers - needle nosed
Pliers - circlip (internal and external)
Cold chisel - ½ inch
Scriber
Scraper
Centre punch
Pin punch
Hacksaw
Valve grinding tool
Steel rule/straight-edge
Allen keys
Selection of files
Wire brush (large)
Axle-stands
Jack (strong trolley or hydraulic type)

Special tools

The tools in this list are those which are not used regularly, are expensive to buy, or which need to be used in accordance with their manufacturers' instructions. Unless relatively difficult mechanical jobs are undertaken frequently, it will not be economic to buy many of these tools. Where this is the case, you could consider clubbing together with friends (or joining a motorists' club) to make a joint purchase, or borrowing the tools against a deposit from a local garage or tool hire specialist.

The following list contains only those tools and instruments freely available to the public, and not those special tools produced by the vehicle manufacturer specifically for its dealer network. You will find occasional references to these manufacturers' special tools in the text of this manual. Generally, an alternative method of doing the job without the vehicle manufacturers' special tool is given. However, sometimes, there is no alternative to using them. Where this is the case and the relevant tool cannot be bought or borrowed, you will have to entrust the work to a franchised garage.

Valve spring compressor
Piston ring compressor
Balljoint separator
Universal hub/bearing puller
Impact screwdriver
Micrometer and/or vernier gauge
Dial gauge
Stroboscopic timing light
Tachometer
Universal electrical multi-meter
Cylinder compression gauge
Lifting tackle
Trolley jack
Light with extension lead

Buying tools

For practically all tools, a tool factor is the best source since he will have a very comprehensive range compared with the average garage or accessory shop. Having said that, accessory shops often offer excellent quality tools at discount prices, so it pays to shop around.

There are plenty of good tools around at reasonable prices, but always aim to purchase items which meet the relevant national safety standards. If in doubt, ask the proprietor or manager of the shop for advice before making a purchase.

Care and maintenance of tools

Having purchased a reasonable tool kit, it is necessary to keep the tools in a clean serviceable condition. After use, always wipe off any dirt, grease and metal particles using a clean, dry cloth, before putting the tools away. Never leave them lying around after they have been used. A simple tool rack on the garage or workshop wall, for items such as screwdrivers and pliers is a good idea. Store all normal wrenches and sockets in a metal box. Any measuring instruments, gauges, meters, etc, must be carefully stored where they cannot be damaged or become rusty.

Take a little care when tools are used. Hammer heads inevitably become marked and screwdrivers lose the keen edge on their blades from time to time. A little timely attention with emery cloth or a grindstone will soon restore items like this to a good serviceable finish.

Working facilities

Not to be forgotten when discussing tools, is the workshop itself. If anything more than routine maintenance is to be carried out, some form of suitable working area becomes essential.

It is appreciated that many an owner mechanic is forced by circumstances to remove an engine or similar item, without the benefit of a garage or workshop. Having done this, any repairs should always be done under the cover of a roof.

Wherever possible, any dismantling should be done on a clean, flat workbench or table at a suitable working height.

Any workbench needs a vice: one with a jaw opening of 4 in (100 mm) is suitable for most jobs. As mentioned previously, some clean dry storage space is also required for tools, as well as for lubricants, cleaning fluids, touch-up paints and so on, which become necessary.

Another item which may be required, and which has a much more general usage, is an electric drill with a chuck capacity of at least 5/16 in (8 mm). This, together with a good range of twist drills, is virtually essential for fitting accessories such as mirrors and reversing lights.

Last, but not least, always keep a supply of old newspapers and clean, lint-free rags available, and try to keep any working area as clean as possible.

Spanner jaw gap comparison table

Jaw gap (in)	Spanner size
0.250	$\frac{1}{4}$ in AF
0.276	7 mm
0.313	$\frac{5}{16}$ in AF
0.315	8 mm
0.344	$\frac{11}{32}$ in AF; $\frac{1}{8}$ in Whitworth
0.354	9 mm
0.375	$\frac{3}{8}$ in AF
0.394	10 mm
0.433	11 mm
0.438	$\frac{7}{16}$ in AF
0.445	$\frac{3}{16}$ in Whitworth; $\frac{1}{4}$ in BSF
0.472	12 mm
0.500	$\frac{1}{2}$ in AF
0.512	13 mm
0.525	$\frac{1}{4}$ in Whitworth; $\frac{5}{16}$ in BSF
0.551	14 mm
0.563	$\frac{9}{16}$ in AF
0.591	15 mm
0.600	$\frac{5}{16}$ in Whitworth; $\frac{3}{8}$ in BSF
0.625	$\frac{5}{8}$ in AF
0.630	16 mm
0.669	17 mm
0.686	$\frac{11}{16}$ in AF
0.709	18 mm
0.710	$\frac{3}{8}$ in Whitworth; $\frac{7}{16}$ in BSF
0.748	19 mm
0.750	$\frac{3}{4}$ in AF
0.813	$\frac{13}{16}$ in AF
0.820	$\frac{7}{16}$ in Whitworth; $\frac{1}{2}$ in BSF
0.866	22 mm
0.875	$\frac{7}{8}$ in AF
0.920	$\frac{1}{2}$ in Whitworth; $\frac{9}{16}$ in BSF
0.938	$\frac{15}{16}$ in AF
0.945	24 mm
1.000	1 in AF
1.010	$\frac{9}{16}$ in Whitworth; $\frac{5}{8}$ in BSF
1.024	26 mm
1.063	$1\frac{1}{16}$ in AF; 27 mm
1.100	$\frac{5}{8}$ in Whitworth; $\frac{11}{16}$ in BSF
1.125	$1\frac{1}{8}$ in AF
1.181	30 mm
1.200	$\frac{11}{16}$ in Whitworth; $\frac{3}{4}$ in BSF
1.250	$1\frac{1}{4}$ in AF
1.260	32 mm
1.300	$\frac{3}{4}$ in Whitworth; $\frac{7}{8}$ in BSF
1.313	$1\frac{5}{16}$ in AF
1.390	$\frac{13}{16}$ in Whitworth; $\frac{15}{16}$ in BSF
1.417	36 mm
1.438	$1\frac{7}{16}$ in AF
1.480	$\frac{7}{8}$ in Whitworth; 1 in BSF
1.500	$1\frac{1}{2}$ in AF
1.575	40 mm; $\frac{15}{16}$ in Whitworth
1.614	41 mm
1.625	$1\frac{5}{8}$ in AF
1.670	1 in Whitworth; $1\frac{1}{8}$ in BSF
1.688	$1\frac{11}{16}$ in AF
1.811	46 mm
1.813	$1\frac{13}{16}$ in AF
1.860	$1\frac{1}{8}$ in Whitworth; $1\frac{1}{4}$ in BSF
1.875	$1\frac{7}{8}$ in AF
1.969	50 mm
2.000	2 in AF
2.050	$1\frac{1}{4}$ in Whitworth; $1\frac{3}{8}$ in BSF
2.165	55 mm
2.362	60 mm

Nut and bolt threads used on the Rover 200 Series may be of metric or UNF depending upon the component.

Conversion factors

Length (distance)

Inches (in)	X	25.4	= Millimetres (mm)	X 0.0394	= Inches (in)
Feet (ft)	X	0.305	= Metres (m)	X 3.281	= Feet (ft)
Miles	X	1.609	= Kilometres (km)	X 0.621	= Miles

Volume (capacity)

Cubic inches (cu in; in³)	X	16.387	= Cubic centimetres (cc; cm³)	X 0.061	= Cubic inches (cu in; in³)
Imperial pints (Imp pt)	X	0.568	= Litres (l)	X 1.76	= Imperial pints (Imp pt)
Imperial quarts (Imp qt)	X	1.137	= Litres (l)	X 0.88	= Imperial quarts (Imp qt)
Imperial quarts (Imp qt)	X	1.201	= US quarts (US qt)	X 0.833	= Imperial quarts (Imp qt)
US quarts (US qt)	X	0.946	= Litres (l)	X 1.057	= US quarts (US qt)
Imperial gallons (Imp gal)	X	4.546	= Litres (l)	X 0.22	= Imperial gallons (Imp gal)
Imperial gallons (Imp gal)	X	1.201	= US gallons (US gal)	X 0.833	= Imperial gallons (Imp gal)
US gallons (US gal)	X	3.785	= Litres (l)	X 0.264	= US gallons (US gal)

Mass (weight)

Ounces (oz)	X	28.35	= Grams (g)	X 0.035	= Ounces (oz)
Pounds (lb)	X	0.454	= Kilograms (kg)	X 2.205	= Pounds (lb)

Force

Ounces-force (ozf; oz)	X	0.278	= Newtons (N)	X 3.6	= Ounces-force (ozf; oz)
Pounds-force (lbf; lb)	X	4.448	= Newtons (N)	X 0.225	= Pounds-force (lbf; lb)
Newtons (N)	X	0.1	= Kilograms-force (kgf; kg)	X 9.81	= Newtons (N)

Pressure

Pounds-force per square inch (psi; lbf/in²; lb/in²)	X	0.070	= Kilograms-force per square centimetre (kgf/cm²; kg/cm²)	X 14.223	= Pounds-force per square inch (psi; lbf/in²; lb/in²)
Pounds-force per square inch (psi; lbf/in²; lb/in²)	X	0.068	= Atmospheres (atm)	X 14.696	= Pounds-force per square inch (psi; lbf/in²; lb/in²)
Pounds-force per square inch (psi; lbf/in²; lb/in²)	X	0.069	= Bars	X 14.5	= Pounds-force per square inch (psi; lbf/in²; lb/in²)
Pounds-force per square inch (psi; lbf/in²; lb/in²)	X	6.895	= Kilopascals (kPa)	X 0.145	= Pounds-force per square inch (psi; lbf/in²; lb/in²)
Kilopascals (kPa)	X	0.01	= Kilograms-force per square centimetre (kgf/cm²; kg/cm²)	X 98.1	= Kilopascals (kPa)
Millibar (mbar)	X	100	= Pascals (Pa)	X 0.01	= Millibar (mbar)
Millibar (mbar)	X	0.0145	= Pounds-force per square inch (psi; lbf/in²; lb/in²)	X 68.947	= Millibar (mbar)
Millibar (mbar)	X	0.75	= Millimetres of mercury (mmHg)	X 1.333	= Millibar (mbar)
Millibar (mbar)	X	0.401	= Inches of water (inH₂O)	X 2.491	= Millibar (mbar)
Millimetres of mercury (mmHg)	X	0.535	= Inches of water (inH₂O)	X 1.868	= Millimetres of mercury (mmHg)
Inches of water (inH₂O)	X	0.036	= Pounds-force per square inch (psi; lbf/in²; lb/in²)	X 27.68	= Inches of water (inH₂O)

Torque (moment of force)

Pounds-force inches (lbf in; lb in)	X	1.152	= Kilograms-force centimetre (kgf cm; kg cm)	X 0.868	= Pounds-force inches (lbf in; lb in)
Pounds-force inches (lbf in; lb in)	X	0.113	= Newton metres (Nm)	X 8.85	= Pounds-force inches (lbf in; lb in)
Pounds-force inches (lbf in; lb in)	X	0.083	= Pounds-force feet (lbf ft; lb ft)	X 12	= Pounds-force inches (lbf in; lb in)
Pounds-force feet (lbf ft; lb ft)	X	0.138	= Kilograms-force metres (kgf m; kg m)	X 7.233	= Pounds-force feet (lbf ft; lb ft)
Pounds-force feet (lbf ft; lb ft)	X	1.356	= Newton metres (Nm)	X 0.738	= Pounds-force feet (lbf ft; lb ft)
Newton metres (Nm)	X	0.102	= Kilograms-force metres (kgf m; kg m)	X 9.804	= Newton metres (Nm)

Power

Horsepower (hp)	X	745.7	= Watts (W)	X 0.0013	= Horsepower (hp)

Velocity (speed)

Miles per hour (miles/hr; mph)	X	1.609	= Kilometres per hour (km/hr; kph)	X 0.621	= Miles per hour (miles/hr; mph)

Fuel consumption*

Miles per gallon, Imperial (mpg)	X	0.354	= Kilometres per litre (km/l)	X 2.825	= Miles per gallon, Imperial (mpg)
Miles per gallon, US (mpg)	X	0.425	= Kilometres per litre (km/l)	X 2.352	= Miles per gallon, US (mpg)

Temperature

Degrees Fahrenheit = (°C x 1.8) + 32   Degrees Celsius (Degrees Centigrade; °C) = (°F - 32) x 0.56

*It is common practice to convert from miles per gallon (mpg) to litres/100 kilometres (l/100km), where mpg (Imperial) x l/100 km = 282 and mpg (US) x l/100 km = 235

Safety first!

Professional motor mechanics are trained in safe working procedures. However enthusiastic you may be about getting on with the job in hand, do take the time to ensure that your safety is not put at risk. A moment's lack of attention can result in an accident, as can failure to observe certain elementary precautions.

There will always be new ways of having accidents, and the following points do not pretend to be a comprehensive list of all dangers; they are intended rather to make you aware of the risks and to encourage a safety-conscious approach to all work you carry out on your vehicle.

Essential DOs and DON'Ts

DON'T rely on a single jack when working underneath the vehicle. Always use reliable additional means of support, such as axle stands, securely placed under a part of the vehicle that you know will not give way.

DON'T attempt to loosen or tighten high-torque nuts (e.g. wheel hub nuts) while the vehicle is on a jack; it may be pulled off.

DON'T start the engine without first ascertaining that the transmission is in neutral (or 'Park' where applicable) and the parking brake applied.

DON'T suddenly remove the filler cap from a hot cooling system – cover it with a cloth and release the pressure gradually first, or you may get scalded by escaping coolant.

DON'T attempt to drain oil until you are sure it has cooled sufficiently to avoid scalding you.

DON'T grasp any part of the engine, exhaust or catalytic converter without first ascertaining that it is sufficiently cool to avoid burning you.

DON'T allow brake fluid or antifreeze to contact vehicle paintwork.

DON'T syphon toxic liquids such as fuel, brake fluid or antifreeze by mouth, or allow them to remain on your skin.

DON'T inhale dust – it may be injurious to health (see *Asbestos* below).

DON'T allow any spilt oil or grease to remain on the floor – wipe it up straight away, before someone slips on it.

DON'T use ill-fitting spanners or other tools which may slip and cause injury.

DON'T attempt to lift a heavy component which may be beyond your capability – get assistance.

DON'T rush to finish a job, or take unverified short cuts.

DON'T allow children or animals in or around an unattended vehicle.

DO wear eye protection when using power tools such as drill, sander, bench grinder etc, and when working under the vehicle.

DO use a barrier cream on your hands prior to undertaking dirty jobs – it will protect your skin from infection as well as making the dirt easier to remove afterwards; but make sure your hands aren't left slippery. Note that long-term contact with used engine oil can be a health hazard.

DO keep loose clothing (cuffs, tie etc) and long hair well out of the way of moving mechanical parts.

DO remove rings, wristwatch etc, before working on the vehicle – especially the electrical system.

DO ensure that any lifting tackle used has a safe working load rating adequate for the job.

DO keep your work area tidy – it is only too easy to fall over articles left lying around.

DO get someone to check periodically that all is well, when working alone on the vehicle.

DO carry out work in a logical sequence and check that everything is correctly assembled and tightened afterwards.

DO remember that your vehicle's safety affects that of yourself and others. If in doubt on any point, get specialist advice.

IF, in spite of following these precautions, you are unfortunate enough to injure yourself, seek medical attention as soon as possible.

Asbestos

Certain friction, insulating, sealing, and other products – such as brake linings, brake bands, clutch linings, torque converters, gaskets, etc – contain asbestos. *Extreme care must be taken to avoid inhalation of dust from such products since it is hazardous to health.* If in doubt, assume that they *do* contain asbestos.

Fire

Remember at all times that petrol (gasoline) is highly flammable. Never smoke, or have any kind of naked flame around, when working on the vehicle. But the risk does not end there – a spark caused by an electrical short-circuit, by two metal surfaces contacting each other, by careless use of tools, or even by static electricity built up in your body under certain conditions, can ignite petrol vapour, which in a confined space is highly explosive.

Always disconnect the battery earth (ground) terminal before working on any part of the fuel or electrical system, and never risk spilling fuel on to a hot engine or exhaust.

It is recommended that a fire extinguisher of a type suitable for fuel and electrical fires is kept handy in the garage or workplace at all times. Never try to extinguish a fuel or electrical fire with water.

Note: *Any reference to a 'torch' appearing in this manual should always be taken to mean a hand-held battery-operated electric lamp or flashlight. It does NOT mean a welding/gas torch or blowlamp.*

Fumes

Certain fumes are highly toxic and can quickly cause unconsciousness and even death if inhaled to any extent. Petrol (gasoline) vapour comes into this category, as do the vapours from certain solvents such as trichloroethylene. Any draining or pouring of such volatile fluids should be done in a well ventilated area.

When using cleaning fluids and solvents, read the instructions carefully. Never use materials from unmarked containers – they may give off poisonous vapours.

Never run the engine of a motor vehicle in an enclosed space such as a garage. Exhaust fumes contain carbon monoxide which is extremely poisonous; if you need to run the engine, always do so in the open air or at least have the rear of the vehicle outside the workplace.

If you are fortunate enough to have the use of an inspection pit, never drain or pour petrol, and never run the engine, while the vehicle is standing over it; the fumes, being heavier than air, will concentrate in the pit with possibly lethal results.

The battery

Never cause a spark, or allow a naked light, near the vehicle's battery. It will normally be giving off a certain amount of hydrogen gas, which is highly explosive.

Always disconnect the battery earth (ground) terminal before working on the fuel or electrical systems.

If possible, loosen the filler plugs or cover when charging the battery from an external source. Do not charge at an excessive rate or the battery may burst.

Take care when topping up and when carrying the battery. The acid electrolyte, even when diluted, is very corrosive and should not be allowed to contact the eyes or skin.

If you ever need to prepare electrolyte yourself, always add the acid slowly to the water, and never the other way round. Protect against splashes by wearing rubber gloves and goggles.

When jump starting a car using a booster battery, for negative earth (ground) vehicles, connect the jump leads in the following sequence: First connect one jump lead between the positive (+) terminals of the two batteries. Then connect the other jump lead first to the negative (–) terminal of the booster battery, and then to a good earthing (ground) point on the vehicle to be started, at least 18 in (45 cm) from the battery if possible. Ensure that hands and jump leads are clear of any moving parts, and that the two vehicles do not touch. Disconnect the leads in the reverse order.

Mains electricity and electrical equipment

When using an electric power tool, inspection light etc, always ensure that the appliance is correctly connected to its plug and that, where necessary, it is properly earthed (grounded). Do not use such appliances in damp conditions and, again, beware of creating a spark or applying excessive heat in the vicinity of fuel or fuel vapour. Also ensure that the appliances meet the relevant national safety standards.

Ignition HT voltage

A severe electric shock can result from touching certain parts of the ignition system, such as the HT leads, when the engine is running or being cranked, particularly if components are damp or the insulation is defective. Where an electronic ignition system is fitted, the HT voltage is much higher and could prove fatal.

Routine maintenance

Maintenance is essential for ensuring safety, and desirable for the purpose of getting the best in terms of performance and economy from your car. Over the years the need for periodic lubrication has been greatly reduced if not totally eliminated. This has unfortunately tended to lead some owners to think that, because no such action is required, the items either no longer exist, or will last forever. This is certainly not the case; it is essential to carry out regular visual examination as comprehensively as possible in order to spot any possible defects at an early stage before they develop into major expensive repairs.

The following service schedules are a list of the maintenance requirements and the intervals at which they should be carried out, as recommended by the manufacturers. Where applicable these procedures are covered in greater detail throughout this manual, near the beginning of each Chapter.

Under-bonnet view – 1.3 model

1 Suspension strut	6 Carburettor	11 Fuel pump	16 Bonnet lock
2 Brake master cylinder	7 Coolant expansion tank	12 Rocker cover	17 Vehicle identification
3 Brake servo	8 Battery	13 Oil filler cap	plate
4 Air cleaner (removed) hot	9 Radiator cap	14 Front left engine mounting	18 Alternator
air intake	10 Distributor	15 Exhaust manifold	19 Windscreen wiper motor
5 Air cleaner (removed) cold			
air intake			

Under-body (rear end) – 1.3 model

1 Exhaust silencer
2 Axle beam
3 Panhard rod
4 Fuel tank
5 Trailing arm
6 Exhaust pipe
7 Handbrake cable
8 Brake hose
9 Fuel filter cover

Underbody (front end) – 1.6 fuel injection model

1 Torsion bar
2 Exhaust pipe
3 Gearbox stabiliser bar
4 Gearchange rod
5 Radius arm
6 Tie-rod balljoint
7 Lower suspension arm
8 Transmission
9 Sump pan
10 Brake caliper
11 Driveshaft
12 Cover plates
13 Anti-roll bar

Under-bonnet view – 1.6 fuel injection model

1 Suspension strut
2 Wiper motor
3 Throttle housing
4 Air cleaner

5 Battery
6 Coolant expansion tank
7 Camshaft cover
8 Timing belt upper cover

9   Washer fluid reservoir
10 Fuel rail
11 Fuel pressure regulator

12 Ignition electronic control
    unit (ECU)
13 Servo

14 Brake master cylinder
15 Distributor
16 Bonnet lock

At weekly intervals or before a long journey

Check the engine oil level
Check the coolant level (Chapter 2, Sec 2)
Check the brake fluid level in the reservoir (Chapter 9, Sec 2)
Check the washer fluid level, adding a screen wash such as Turtle Wax High Tech Screen Wash (Chapter 12, Sec 22)
Check the operation of all lights, horn, direction, indicators and wipers
Check the tyre pressures (Chapter 8, Sec 8)

At the end of the first 1000 miles (1500 km) – new cars

Check the transmission oil level (Chapter 6, Sec 2 or 13, or Chapter 7, Sec 3 or 12)
Check handbrake cable adjustment (Chapter 9, Sec 18)
Check brake hoses and pipelines for leaks (Chapter 9, Sec 13)
Check the condition of the drive shaft gaiters and for leakage of lubricant (Chapter 8, Sec 2)
Check the steering rack gaiters for leakage of lubricant (Chapter 10, Sec 2)
Check the clutch pedal adjustment (Chapter 5, Sec 2) (early models only)
Renew engine oil (1.6 models only) (Chapter 1, Sec 35)
Top up carburettor damper piston (1.6 models) (Chapter 3, Sec 2)
Check coolant level (Chapter 2, Sec 2)
Check idle speed and choke operation (1.3 models) (Chapter 3, Secs 15, 16)
Check idle speed and mixture on fuel injection models (Chapter 3, Sec 36)
Check drivebelts for tension (Chapter 2, Sec 12)

Every 6000 miles (10 000 km) or 6 months – whichever comes first

Check wear and condition of tyres (Chapter 8, Sec 8)
Check disc pads for wear (Chapter 9, Sec 3)
Renew engine oil and filter (1.3 models only) (Chapter 1, Sec 3)
Check transmission oil level (Chapter 6, Sec 2 or 13, or Chapter 7, Sec 3 or 12)
Lubricate all controls, linkages and hinges
Adjust clutch (Chapter 5, Sec 2) (early models only)
Check refrigerant (air conditioned models) (Chapter 2, Sec 23)
Clean and re-gap spark plugs (Chapter 4, Sec 7)

Every 12 000 miles (20 000 km) or annually – whichever comes first

Clean battery terminals and apply petroleum jelly (Chapter 12, Sec 2)

Check drivebelts for tension and condition (Chapter 2, Sec 12)
Renew spark plugs (Chapter 4, Sec 7)
Adjust valve clearances (1.3 models) (Chapter 1, Sec 6)
Renew air filter element (Chapter 3, Secs 3, 29)
Top up carburettor damper piston (1.6 models) (Chapter 3, Sec 2)
Renew engine oil and filter (1.6 models) (Chapter 1, Sec 35)
Renew automatic transmission fluid (1.3 models) at first 12 000 miles (20 000 km), then every 24 000 miles (40 000 km) or two years (Chapter 7, Sec 3)
Check shoe linings for wear (Chapter 9, Sec 6)
Renew wiper blades (Chapter 12, Sec 20)

Every 24 000 miles (40 000 km) or every two years – whichever comes first

Check condition and tension of timing belt (Chapter 1, Sec 7 or 39)
Check valve clearances (1.6 models) (Chapter 1, Sec 38)
Renew automatic transmission fluid (1.6 models) (Chapter 7, Sec 12)
Check condition of exhaust system (Chapter 3, Sec 41)
Check front wheel alignment (Chapter 10, Sec 27)
Check ignition timing (1.3 only) (Chapter 4, Sec 3)
Check headlamp alignment (Chapter 12, Sec 16)
Check steering and suspension for wear (Chapter 10, Sec 2)
Check steering and driveshaft gaiters for condition (Chapters 8 and 10)
Renew PCV valve (Chapter 1, Sec 4)
Renew fuel filter (1.3 models) (Chapter 3, Sec 4)
Renew emission blow-by filter (1.3 models) (Chapter 1, Sec 4)
Renew crankcase breather filter (Chapter 1, Sec 4)
Check condition of all coolant and brake hoses (Chapter 2 and 9)
Clean inside of distributor cap and check rotor for erosion (Chapter 4, Sec 2)
Adjust idle speed and mixture (Chapter 3, Sec 15, 22 or 36)
Adjust handbrake cable if travel excessive (Chapter 9, Sec 18)
Drain manual transmission oil and renew (Chapter 6, Secs 2, 13)
Renew anti-freeze coolant (Chapter 2, Sec 5)
Renew brake hydraulic fluid by bleeding (Chapter 9, Sec 14)
Check hub bearings for wear (Chapter 8, Sec 2)

Every 48 000 miles (80 000 km) or four years – whichever comes first

Renew camshaft belt (Chapter 1, Secs 8, 40)
Renew fuel filter (fuel injection models) (Chapter 3, Sec 31)

1.3 models

H.16668

1.6 models

Recommended lubricants and fluids

Component or system	Lubricant type/specification	Duckhams recommendation
Engine (1)*	Multigrade engine oil, viscosity SAE 10W/30 or 10W/40, to API SF	Duckhams QXR, Hypergrade, or 10W/40 Motor Oil
Manual gearbox (2)*	Multigrade engine oil, viscosity SAE 10W/30 or 10W/40, to API SF	Duckhams QXR, Hypergrade, or 10W/40 Motor Oil
Automatic transmission (3) 1.3 models (refill and top up) 1.3 (top up only) and 1.6 models	Hondamatic Automatic Gearbox Fluid Dexron IID type ATF	Duckhams D-Matic
SU carburettor piston damper (4)	Multigrade engine oil	Duckhams QXR, Hypergrade, or 10W/40 Motor Oil
Brake fluid (5)	Hydraulic fluid to FMVSS DOT 4	Duckhams Universal Brake and Clutch Fluid

*Note: *To meet warranty requirements Austin Rover recommendations include a 10W/40 oil. Duckhams QXR and 10W/40 Motor Oil are available to meet these requirements*

Fault diagnosis

Introduction

The vehicle owner who does his or her own maintenance according to the recommended schedules should not have to use this section of the manual very often. Modern component reliability is such that, provided those items subject to wear or deterioration are inspected or renewed at the specified intervals, sudden failure is comparatively rare. Faults do not usually just happen as a result of sudden failure, but develop over a period of time. Major mechanical failures in particular are usually preceded by characteristic symptoms over hundreds or even thousands of miles. Those components which do occasionally fail without warning are often small and easily carried in the vehicle.

With any fault finding, the first step is to decide where to begin investigations. Sometimes this is obvious, but on other occasions a little detective work will be necessary. The owner who makes half a dozen haphazard adjustments or replacements may be successful in curing a fault (or its symptoms), but he will be none the wiser if the fault recurs and he may well have spent more time and money than was necessary. A calm and logical approach will be found to be more satisfactory in the long run. Always take into account any warning signs or abnormalities that may have been noticed in the period preceding the fault – power loss, high or low gauge readings, unusual noises or smells, etc – and remember that failure of components such as fuses or spark plugs may only be pointers to some underlying fault.

The pages which follow here are intended to help in cases of failure to start or breakdown on the road. There is also a Fault Diagnosis Section at the end of each Chapter which should be consulted if the preliminary checks prove unfruitful. Whatever the fault, certain basic principles apply. These are as follows:

Verify the fault. This is simply a matter of being sure that you know what the symptoms are before starting work. This is particularly important if you are investigating a fault for someone else who may not have described it very accurately.

Don't overlook the obvious. For example, if the vehicle won't start, is there petrol in the tank? (Don't take anyone else's word on this particular point, and don't trust the fuel gauge either!) If an electrical fault is indicated, look for loose or broken wires before digging out the test gear.

Cure the disease, not the symptom. Substituting a flat battery with a fully charged one will get you off the hard shoulder, but if the underlying cause is not attended to, the new battery will go the same way. Similarly, changing oil-fouled spark plugs for a new set will get you moving again, but remember that the reason for the fouling (if it wasn't simply an incorrect grade of plug) will have to be established and corrected.

Don't take anything for granted. Particularly, don't forget that a 'new' component may itself be defective (especially if it's been rattling round in the boot for months), and don't leave components out of a fault diagnosis sequence just because they are new or recently fitted. When you do finally diagnose a difficult fault, you'll probably realise that all the evidence was there from the start.

Electrical faults

Electrical faults can be more puzzling than straightforward mechanical failures, but they are no less susceptible to logical analysis if the basic principles of operation are understood. Vehicle electrical wiring exists in extremely unfavourable conditions – heat, vibration and chemical attack – and the first things to look for are loose or corroded connections and broken or chafed wires, especially where the wires pass through holes in the bodywork or are subject to vibration.

All metal-bodied vehicles in current production have one pole of the battery 'earthed', ie connected to the vehicle bodywork, and in nearly all modern vehicles it is the negative (–) terminal. The various electrical components – motors, bulb holders etc – are also connected to earth, either by means of a lead or directly by their mountings. Electric current flows through the component and then back to the battery via the bodywork. If the component mounting is loose or corroded, or if a good path back to the battery is not available, the circuit will be incomplete and malfunction will result. The engine and/or gearbox are also earthed by means of flexible metal straps to the body or subframe; if these straps are loose or missing, starter motor, generator and ignition trouble may result.

Assuming the earth return to be satisfactory, electrical faults will be due either to component malfunction or to defects in the current supply. Individual components are dealt with in Chapter 12. If supply wires are broken or cracked internally this results in an open-circuit, and the easiest way to check for this is to bypass the suspect wire temporarily with a length of wire having a crocodile clip or suitable connector at each end. Alternatively, a 12V test lamp can be used to verify the presence of supply voltage at various points along the wire and the break can be thus isolated.

If a bare portion of a live wire touches the bodywork or other earthed metal part, the electricity will take the low-resistance path thus formed back to the battery: this is known as a short-circuit. Hopefully a short-circuit will blow a fuse, but otherwise it may cause burning of the insulation (and possibly further short-circuits) or even a fire. This is why it is inadvisable to bypass persistently blowing fuses with silver foil or wire.

A simple test lamp is useful for checking electrical faults

Carrying a few spares may save a long walk!

Crank engine and check for spark. Note use of insulated
tool to hold plug lead

Caution: *Use a spare plug, not one removed from the engine, to avoid fire hazard*

Jump start lead connections for negative earth – connect
leads in order shown

Spares and tool kit

Most vehicles are supplied only with sufficient tools for wheel changing; the *Maintenance and minor repair* tool kit detailed in *Tools and working facilities*, with the addition of a hammer, is probably sufficient for those repairs that most motorists would consider attempting at the roadside. In addition a few items which can be fitted without too much trouble in the event of a breakdown should be carried. Experience and available space will modify the list below, but the following may save having to call on professional assistance:

Spark plugs, clean and correctly gapped
HT lead and plug cap – long enough to reach the plug furthest from the distributor
Distributor rotor
Drivebelt(s) – emergency type may suffice
Spare fuses
Set of principal light bulbs
Tin of radiator sealer and hose bandage
Exhaust bandage
Roll of insulating tape
Length of soft iron wire
Length of electrical flex
Torch or inspection lamp (can double as test lamp)
Battery jump leads
Tow-rope
Ignition water dispersant aerosol
Litre of engine oil
Sealed can of hydraulic fluid
Emergency windscreen
Worm drive clips

If spare fuel is carried, a can designed for the purpose should be used to minimise risks of leakage and collision damage. A first aid kit and a warning triangle, whilst not at present compulsory in the UK, are obviously sensible items to carry in addition to the above.

When touring abroad it may be advisable to carry additional spares which, even if you cannot fit them yourself, could save having to wait while parts are obtained. The items below may be worth considering:

Clutch and throttle cables
Cylinder head gasket
Alternator brushes
Tyre valve core

One of the motoring organisations will be able to advise on availability of fuel etc in foreign countries.

Engine will not start

Engine fails to turn when starter operated

Flat battery (recharge, use jump leads, or push start)
Battery terminals loose or corroded
Battery earth to body defective
Engine earth strap loose or broken
Starter motor (or solenoid) wiring loose or broken
Automatic transmission selector in wrong position, or inhibitor switch faulty
Ignition/starter switch faulty
Major mechanical failure (seizure)
Starter or solenoid internal fault (see Chapter 12)

Starter motor turns engine slowly

Partially discharged battery (recharge, use jump leads, or push start)
Battery terminals loose or corroded
Battery earth to body defective
Engine earth strap loose
Starter motor (or solenoid) wiring loose
Starter motor internal fault (see Chapter 12)

Starter motor spins without turning engine

Flat battery
Starter motor pinion sticking on sleeve

Flywheel gear teeth damaged or worn
Starter motor mounting bolts loose

Engine turns normally but fails to start

Damp or dirty HT leads and distributor cap (crank engine and check for spark) – try moisture dispersant such as Holts Wet Start
No fuel in tank (check for delivery at carburettor)
Excessive choke (hot engine) or insufficient choke (cold engine)
Fouled or incorrectly gapped spark plugs (remove, clean and regap)
Other ignition system fault (see Chapter 4)
Other fuel system fault (see Chapter 3)
Poor compression (see Chapter 1)
Major mechanical failure (eg camshaft drive)

Engine fires but will not run

Insufficient choke (cold engine)
Air leaks at carburettor or inlet manifold
Fuel starvation (see Chapter 3)
Ignition fault (see Chapter 4)

Engine cuts out and will not restart

Engine cuts out suddenly – ignition fault

Loose or disconnected LT wires
Wet HT leads or distributor cap (after traversing water splash)
Coil failure (check for spark)
Other ignition fault (see Chapter 4)

Engine misfires before cutting out – fuel fault

Fuel tank empty
Fuel pump defective or filter blocked (check for delivery)
Fuel tank filler vent blocked (suction will be evident on releasing cap)
Carburettor needle valve sticking
Carburettor jets blocked (fuel contaminated)
Other fuel system fault (see Chapter 3)

Engine cuts out – other causes

Serious overheating
Major mechanical failure (eg camshaft drive)

Engine overheats

Coolant loss due to internal or external leakage (see Chapter 2)
Thermostat defective
Low oil level
Brakes binding
Radiator clogged externally or internally
Electric cooling fan not operating correctly
Engine waterways clogged
Ignition timing incorrect or automatic advance malfunctioning
Mixture too weak

Note: *Do not add cold water to an overheated engine or damage may result*

Low engine oil pressure

Gauge reads low or warning light illuminated with engine running

Oil level low or incorrect grade
Defective gauge or sender unit
Wire to sender unit earthed

Engine overheating
Oil filter clogged or bypass valve defective
Oil pressure relief valve defective
Oil pick-up strainer clogged
Oil pump worn or mountings loose
Worn main or big-end bearings

Note: *Low oil pressure in a high-mileage engine at tickover is not necessarily a cause for concern. Sudden pressure loss at speed is far more significant. In any event, check the gauge or warning light sender before condemning the engine.*

Engine noises

Pre-ignition (pinking) on acceleration

Incorrect grade of fuel
Ignition timing incorrect
Distributor faulty or worn
Worn or maladjusted carburettor
Excessive carbon build-up in engine

Whistling or wheezing noises

Leaking vacuum hose
Leaking carburettor or manifold gasket
Blowing head gasket

Tapping or rattling

Incorrect valve clearances
Worn valve gear
Worn timing belt
Broken piston ring (ticking noise)

Knocking or thumping

Unintentional mechanical contact (eg fan blades)
Worn drivebelt
Peripheral component fault (generator, coolant pump etc)
Worn big-end bearings (regular heavy knocking, perhaps less under load)
Worn main bearings (rumbling and knocking, perhaps worsening under load)
Piston slap (most noticeable when cold)

Chapter 1 Engine

For modifications, and information applicable to later models, see Supplement at end of manual

Contents

Specifications

Part A (1.3 engine)
General

Engine type	Four cylinder overhead camshaft transversely mounted
Code	EV2
Capacity	1342 cc (81.8 cu in)
Bore	74.0 mm (2.91 in)
Stroke	78.0 mm (3.07 in)
Compression ratio	8.7 : 1
Firing order	1 – 3 – 4 – 2 (No. 1 at timing belt end)
Rotational direction of crankshaft	Anti-clockwise (viewed from crankshaft pulley)
Maximum power	53 kW (70 bhp) at 6000 rev/min
Maximum torque	104 Nm (77 lbf ft) at 3500 rev/min
Compression pressure:	
Exceeding	10.3 bar (150 lbf/in²)
Maximum difference between cylinders	1.4 bar (20 lbf/in²)

Cylinder block

Material	Light alloy with cast-iron liners
Bore	74.0 to 74.1 mm (2.9133 to 2.9173 in)
Maximum bore taper	0.05 mm (0.002 in)
Maximum out-of-round	0.05 mm (0.002 in)
Re-bore sizes	0.25 and 0.50 mm (0.010 and 0.020 in)

Crankshaft

Number of bearings	5 (monobloc)
Main journal diameter	49.976 to 50.000 mm (1.9676 to 1.9685 in)
Running clearance	0.024 to 0.07 mm (0.0009 to 0.003 in)
Crankpin diameter	39.976 to 40.000 mm (1.5739 to 1.5748 in)
Running clearance	0.020 to 0.07 mm (0.0008 to 0.003 in)

Maximum journal/crankpin taper or out-of-round	0.010 mm (0.0004 in)
Crankshaft endfloat	0.10 to 0.45 mm (0.004 to 0.018 in)

Connecting rods

Big-end bore diameter	43.0 mm (1.69 in)
Side play (on crankshaft)	0.15 to 0.40 mm (0.006 to 0.016 in)

Pistons

Clearance in cylinder	0.01 to 0.07 mm (0.0004 to 0.003 in)
Piston diameter (skirt):	
Standard	73.96 to 73.97 mm (2.9120 to 2.9122 in)
0.25 mm oversize	74.215 to 74.248 mm (2.9218 to 2.9239 in)
0.50 mm oversize	74.465 to 74.498 mm (2.9317 to 2.9330 in)

Piston rings

Number	Two compression, one oil control
Clearance in groove (compression rings)	0.03 to 0.13 mm (0.0012 to 0.005 in)
End gap:	
Compression	0.15 to 0.6 mm (0.006 to 0.024 in)
Oil control (rails)	0.30 to 1.10 mm (0.012 to 0.043 in)

Gudgeon pins

Interference fit in rod	0.02 to 0.04 mm (0.0008 to 0.0016 in)
* All replacement pins are oversize	

Camshaft

Number of bearings	5
Bearing running clearance	0.05 to 0.15 mm (0.002 to 0.006 in)
Shaft endfloat	0.05 to 0.50 mm (0.002 to 0.020 in)
Cam lobe height:	
Inlet	40.056 mm (1.5770 in)
Exhaust	40.078 mm (1.5779 in)

Rocker gear

Rocker arm to shaft clearance	0.018 to 0.08 mm (0.0007 to 0.003 in)

Cylinder head

Material	Light alloy
Thickness (new)	90.0 mm (3.54 in)
Thickness (minimum after re-surfacing)	89.8 mm (3.53 in)
Maximum surface distortion	0.05 mm (0.002 in)

Valves

Stem diameter:	
Inlet	6.55 to 6.59 mm (0.258 to 0.259 in)
Exhaust	6.52 to 6.56 mm (0.257 to 0.258 in)
Stem to guide clearance:	
Inlet	0.02 to 0.08 mm (0.0008 to 0.003 in)
Exhaust	0.05 to 0.11 mm (0.002 to 0.004 in)
Valve seat angle	45°
Seat width	1.25 to 2.00 mm (0.049 to 0.080 in)
Valve clearances (cold):	
Inlet	0.17 to 0.22 mm (0.007 to 0.009 in)
Exhaust	0.22 to 0.27 mm (0.009 to 0.011 in)
Valve spring free length	46.6 to 47.6 mm (1.83 to 1.87 in)

Valve timing

Inlet valve opens	15° ATDC
Inlet valve closes	15° ABDC
Exhaust valve opens	20° BBDC
Exhaust valve closes	15° BTDC

Lubrication system

Oil pump clearances:	
Outer rotor to body	0.1 to 0.2 mm (0.004 to 0.008 in)
Inner to outer rotor lobe gap	0.14 to 0.2 mm (0.006 to 0.008 in)
Rotor endfloat	0.03 to 0.15 mm (0.001 to 0.006 in)
Oil pressure:	
At 3000 rev/min	3.7 to 4.5 bar (54 to 65 lbf/in²)
At idle	1.45 bar (21 lbf/in²)
Oil capacity, including new filter	3.5 litre (6.25 pint)
Oil type/specification*	Multigrade engine oil, viscosity SAE 10W/30 or 10W/40, to API SF (Duckhams QXR, Hypergrade or 10W/40 Motor Oil)
Oil filter	Champion E101

*Note: *To meet warranty requirements Austin Rover recommendations include a 10W/40 oil. Duckhams QXR and 10W/40 Motor Oil are available to meet these requirements*

Torque wrench settings

	Nm	lbf ft
Camshaft sprocket bolt	38	28
Connecting rod big-end nuts	28	21
Crankshaft main bearing cap bolts	50	37
Crankshaft pulley bolt	115	85
Cylinder head bolts and nuts:		
Stage 1	30	22
Stage 2	60	44
Flywheel bolts	120	89
Oil drain plug	45	33
Oil pressure switch	18	13
Oil pump bolts	12	9
Oil pump cover screws	5	3
Oil pump pick-up bolts	12	9
Oil pump pick-up nuts	25	18
Rocker cover nuts	10	7
Rocker shaft bolts	22	16
Spark plugs	18	13
Sump pan nuts and bolts	12	9
Timing belt tensioner bolt	45	33
Timing belt cover bolts	10	7
Rear mounting bracket bolts to engine	65	48
Transmission bracket bolts to body	39	29
Engine rear mounting bracket to body nuts	22	16
Left-hand mounting to engine nut	39	29
Clutch cover bolts	25	18
Lower suspension arm balljoint to hub carrier nut	44	32
Fuel pump nuts	24	18
Carburettor mounting nuts	20	15
Inlet manifold nuts	24	18
Inlet manifold support bracket bolt	22	16
Exhaust manifold nuts	39	29
Exhaust manifold bracket bolt	24	18
Exhaust downpipe flange nuts	22	16
Flywheel housing to engine bolts	68	50
Gear selector rod bolt	22	16
Torque rod to transmission bolt	9	7
Torque rod bracket to body bolts	22	16
Transmission to engine torque bracket bolts	45	33
Coolant pump bolts	12	9
Starter mounting bolts	45	33
Distributor mounting bolts	24	18
Alternator mounting bolts	45	33
Alternator belt adjuster bolt	24	18
Roadwheel nuts	81	60

Part B (1.6 engine)
General

Engine type	Four cylinder, overhead camshaft, transversely mounted
Code	16H
Capacity	1598 cc (97.5 cu in)
Bore	76.20 mm (3.0 in)
Stroke	87.58 mm (3.448 in)
Compression ratio	9.6 : 1
Firing order	1 – 3 – 4 – 2 (No. 1 at timing belt end)
Rotational direction of crankshaft	Clockwise (viewed from crankshaft pulley)
Maximum power	76 kW (104 bhp) at 6000 rev/min
Maximum torque	139 Nm (102 lbf ft) at 3500 rev/min
Compression pressure:	
Exceeding	10.3 bar (150 lbf/in²)
Maximum difference between cylinders	1.4 bar (20 lbf/in²)

Cylinder block

Material	Cast-iron
Bore	76.20 to 76.30 mm (3.000 to 3.006 in)
Maximum bore taper	0.05 mm (0.002 in)
Maximum out-of-round	0.05 mm (0.002 in)
Re-bore size	0.50 mm (0.020 in)

Crankshaft

Number of bearings	5
Main journal diameter	57.19 to 57.20 mm (2.2516 to 2.2520 in)
Running clearance	0.05 to 0.08 mm (0.002 to 0.003 in)
Minimum regrind diameter	56.19 mm (2.2122)
Crankpin diameter	47.62 to 47.64 mm (1.8748 to 1.8756 in)

Running clearance	0.04 to 0.08 mm (0.0015 to 0.003 in)
Minimum regrind diameter	46.63 mm (1.8359 in)
Maximum journal/crankpin taper or out-of-round	0.010 mm (0.0004 in)
Crankshaft endfloat	0.10 to 0.18 mm (0.004 to 0.007 in)
Endfloat thrust washer thicknesses	2.26 mm (0.089 in), 2.28 mm (0.090 in), 2.31 mm (0.091 in), 2.34 mm (0.092 in)

Connecting rods

Length between centres	148.07 mm (5.830 in)

Pistons

Clearance in cylinder:	
At top	0.07 to 0.11 mm (0.0028 to 0.0044 in)
At bottom	0.03 to 0.05 mm (0.001 to 0.002 in)
Piston oversize	0.51 mm (0.020 in)

Piston rings

Number	Two compression, one oil control
Clearance in groove (compression)	0.03 to 0.08 mm (0.0012 to 0.0032 in)
End gap:	
Compression	0.30 to 0.56 mm (0.012 to 0.022 in)
Oil control (rails)	0.38 to 1.14 mm (0.015 to 0.045 in)

Gudgeon pins

Interference fit in rod	0.02 to 0.04 mm (0.0008 to 0.0015 in)

Camshaft

Number of bearings	3
Bearing running clearance	0.025 to 0.056 mm (0.001 to 0.0022 min)
Camshaft endfloat	0.05 to 0.18 mm (0.002 to 0.007 in)
Cam lobe height:	
Inlet	8.68 to 9.5 mm (0.342 to 0.374 in)
Exhaust	8.58 to 9.5 mm (0.338 to 0.374 in)

Cam followers

Outside diameter	30.14 mm (1.1865 in)
Adjustment shim thicknesses:	

Mark	Thickness
97	2.47 mm (0.097 in)
99	2.52 mm (0.099 in)
01	2.56 mm (0.101 in)
03	2.62 mm (0.103 in)
05	2.67 mm (0.105 in)
07	2.72 mm (0.107 in)
09	2.77 mm (0.109 in)
11	2.83 mm (0.111 in)
13	2.87 mm (0.113 in)
15	2.93 mm (0.115 in)
17	2.98 mm (0.117 in)
19	3.03 mm (0.119 in)
21	3.08 mm (0.121 in)
23	3.13 mm (0.123 in)
25	3.18 mm (0.125 in)
27	3.23 mm (0.127 in)

Cylinder head

Material	Cast-iron
Thickness (new)	84.13 to 84.38 mm (3.312 to 3.322 in)
Thickness (minimum after re-surfacing)	83.87 mm (3.302 in)
Maximum surface distortion	0.05 mm (0.002 in)

Valves

Stem diameter:	
Inlet	7.91 to 7.93 mm (0.3115 to 0.3120 in)
Exhaust	7.89 to 7.92 mm (0.3109 to 0.3114 in)
Oversize	8.46 to 8.47 mm (0.331 to 0.336 in)
Stem to guide clearance	0.038 mm (0.0015 in)
Valve seat angle	45° 15′
Valve head diameter:	
Inlet	38.0 mm (1.5 in)
Exhaust	31.0 mm (1.218 in)
Valve clearances (cold)*:	
Inlet	0.35 to 0.38 mm (0.014 to 0.015 in)
Exhaust	0.43 to 0.46 mm (0.017 to 0.018 in)

* Adjust only if clearance below .... 0.30 mm (0.012 in)
Valve spring free length .... 46.6 to 47.6 mm (1.83 to 1.87 in)

Valve timing

Inlet valve opens .... 17° BTDC
Inlet valve closes .... 59° ABDC
Exhaust valve opens .... 57° BBDC
Exhaust valve closes .... 19° ATDC

Lubrication system

Oil pump clearances:
  Outer rotor to body .... 0.18 to 0.27 mm (0.007 to 0.011 in)
  Inner to outer rotor lobe gap .... 0.03 to 0.15 mm (0.001 to 0.006 in)
  Rotor endfloat .... 0.03 to 0.08 mm (0.001 to 0.003 in)
Oil pressure:
  At 3000 rev/min .... 3.7 to 4.5 bar (54 to 65 lbf/in²)
  At idle .... 1.4 bar (21 lbf/in²)
Oil capacity, including new filter .... 3.6 litre (6.30 pint)
Oil type/specification* .... Multigrade engine oil, viscosity 10W/30 or 10W/40, to API SF
    (Duckhams QXR, Hypergrade or 10W/40 Motor Oil)
Oil filter .... Champion C104

* **Note:** *To meet warranty requirements Austin Rover recommendations include a 10W/40 oil, Duckhams QXR and 10W/40 Motor Oil are available to meet these requirements*

Torque wrench settings

	Nm	lbf ft
Brake servo pipe union	50	37
Camshaft belt tensioner bolt	25	18
Camshaft carrier bolts	25	18
Camshaft cover bolts	8	6
Camshaft pulley bolt	57	42
Connecting rod big-end nuts	45	33
Coolant temperature sender	15	11
Crankshaft pulley bolt	45	33
Cylinder head bolts:		
Stage 1	40	29.5
Stage 2	81	60
Stage 3	Tighten ¼ turn (90°)	
Flywheel bolts (new)	58	43
Transmission adaptor plate bolts:		
M8 bolts	25	18
M10 bolts	45	33
M12 bolts	90	66
Knock sensor	12	9
Main bearing cap bolts	90	66
Oil pump bolts	26	19
Oil pressure switch	25	18
Spark plugs	18	13
Sump pan drain plug	25	18
Sump pan bolts	8	6
Coolant inlet elbow bolts	25	18
Coolant outlet elbow bolts	25	18
Manifold bolts and nuts	22	16
Flywheel housing to engine	90	66
Torque converter housing to engine:		
M10 bolts	45	33
M12 bolts	90	66
Driveplate to crankshaft	110	81
Driveplate to torque converter	32	24
Suspension arm balljoint nut	44	32
Roadwheel nuts	81	60
Alternator mounting bracket bolts	45	33
Alternator belt adjuster link bolt	24	18
Reverse lamp switch	25	18
Starter motor mounting bolts	45	33
Engine/transmission mountings:		
Right-hand:		
Bracket to engine bolts	45	33
Bracket nuts	40	30
Through-bolt	120	89
Left-hand:		
Bracket to transmission bolts	45	33
Mounting to body bolts	40	30
Through-bolt	120	89
Rear mounting:		
Bracket to transmission	90	66
Support plate to bracket	75	55
Mounting to bracket bolts	60	44
Mounting through-bolts	60	44

Part A 1.3 (1342 cc) engine

1   General description

The engine is of four cylinder overhead camshaft type mounted transversely with the transmission at the front of the car.

The cylinder block, crankcase and cylinder head are of light alloy construction with cast-iron cylinder liners.

The crankshaft is supported in five main bearings the caps for which are in the form of a monobloc casting.

Crankshaft endfloat is controlled by semi-circular thrust washers at number four journal.

The pistons are fitted with two compression rings and one oil control ring. The gudgeon pin is of press fit type in the connecting rod small end.

The cylinder head incorporates two inlet valves and one exhaust valve per cylinder. The valves are operated by individual rockers from the single belt-driven camshaft.

The oil pump is driven directly from the crankshaft while the distributor is driven from a dog on the end of the camshaft.

The fuel pump is driven from an eccentric cam on the camshaft.

Crankshaft rotation is anti-clockwise when viewed from the pulley end.

**Fig. 1.1 Cutaway view of 1.3 engine and transmission
(Sec 1)**

Fig. 1.2 External components – 1.3 engine (Sec 1)

1 Distributor holder
2 Fuel pump and insulator
3 Rocker cover and gasket
4 Coolant temperature transmitter
5 Camshaft rear bearing upper bracket
6 Camshaft No.4 bearing upper bracket
7 Camshaft No.3 bearing upper bracket
8 Camshaft No.2 bearing upper bracket
9 Camshaft front bearing upper bracket
10 Crankcase breather
11 Thermostat and seal
12 Coolant outlet housing
13 Thermostat housing
14 Inlet manifold and gasket
15 Coolant connecting pipe
16 Oil pressure switch
17 Cylinder block drain plug
18 Coolant pump
19 Oil pump cover plate
20 Oil pump rotors
21 Oil pump
22 Timing belt cover seal
23 Oil filter
24 Timing belt upper cover
25 Timing belt lower cover
26 Belt tensioner access plug
27 Oil pressure relief valve
28 Crankshaft front oil seal
29 Oil drain plug
30 Oil pump pick-up strainer
31 Engine oil dipstick
32 Sump pan
33 Dipstick guide tube
34 Cover plate
35 Sump pan gasket
36 Cylinder block/crankcase
37 Crankshaft rear oil seal retainer
38 Exhaust manifold and gasket
39 Cylinder head and gasket
40 Crankshaft rear oil seal
41 Heater hose connection
42 Coolant inlet housing
43 Cooling system bleed screw
44 Fuel pump cover
45 Hot air cover

32

Fig. 1.3 Internal components – 1.3 engine (Sec 1)

1 Rocker shaft – exhaust
2 Rocker shaft – inlet
3 Valve clearance adjuster
   screw and locknut
4 Spacer
5 Rocker arm
6 Spring
7 Inlet valves
8 Rocker arm
9 Valve guide
10 Camshaft sprocket
11 Timing belt
12 Alternator drivebelt
13 Timing belt sprocket and
    guide plates
14 Timing belt tensioner
15 Piston rings
16 Tensioner spring
17 Big-end bearing shells
18 Main bearing shell
19 Crankshaft pulley
20 Main bearing caps and oil
    gallery – monobloc
21 Crankshaft thrust washers
22 Flywheel
23 Crankshaft
24 Connecting rod and cap
25 Gudgeon pin
26 Piston
27 Exhaust valve
28 Valve guide
29 Valve spring seat
30 Valve stem oil seal
31 Valve spring
32 Valve spring retainer
33 Split cotters
34 Camshaft

Are your plugs trying to tell you something?

Normal.
Grey-brown deposits, lightly coated core nose. Plugs ideally suited to engine, and engine in good condition.

Heavy Deposits.
A build up of crusty deposits, light-grey sandy colour in appearance.
Fault: Often caused by worn valve guides, excessive use of upper cylinder lubricant, or idling for long periods.

Lead Glazing.
Plug insulator firing tip appears yellow or green/yellow and shiny in appearance.
Fault: Often caused by incorrect carburation, excessive idling followed by sharp acceleration. Also check ignition timing.

Carbon fouling.
Dry, black, sooty deposits.
Fault: over-rich fuel mixture.
Check: carburettor mixture settings, float level, choke operation, air filter.

Oil fouling.
Wet, oily deposits. Fault: worn bores/piston rings or valve guides; sometimes occurs (temporarily) during running-in period.

Overheating.
Electrodes have glazed appearance, core nose very white – few deposits. Fault: plug overheating. Check: plug value, ignition timing, fuel octane rating (too low) and fuel mixture (too weak).

Electrode damage.
Electrodes burned away; core nose has burned, glazed appearance. Fault: pre-ignition. Check: for correct heat range and as for 'overheating'.

Split core nose.
(May appear initially as a crack). Fault: detonation or wrong gap-setting technique. Check: ignition timing, cooling system, fuel mixture (too weak).

WHY DOUBLE COPPER IS BETTER FOR YOUR ENGINE.

Unique Trapezoidal Copper Cored Earth Electrode — 50% Larger Spark Area — Copper Cored Centre Electrode

Champion Double Copper plugs are the first in the world to have copper core in both centre <u>and</u> earth electrode. This innovative design means that they run cooler by up to 100°C – giving greater efficiency and longer life. These double copper cores transfer heat away from the tip of the plug faster and more efficiently. Therefore, Double Copper runs at cooler temperatures than conventional plugs giving improved acceleration response and high speed performance with no fear of pre-ignition.

Champion Double Copper plugs also feature a unique trapezoidal earth electrode giving a 50% increase in spark area. This, together with the double copper cores, offers greatly reduced electrode wear, so the spark stays stronger for longer.

 FASTER COLD STARTING

 FOR UNLEADED OR LEADED FUEL

 ELECTRODES UP TO 100°C COOLER

 BETTER ACCELERATION RESPONSE

 LOWER EMISSIONS

 50% BIGGER SPARK AREA

THE LONGER LIFE PLUG

Plug Tips/Hot and Cold.
Spark plugs must operate within well-defined temperature limits to avoid cold fouling at one extreme and overheating at the other.
Champion and the car manufacturers work out the best plugs for an engine to give optimum performance under all conditions, from freezing cold starts to sustained high speed motorway cruising.
Plugs are often referred to as hot or cold. With Champion, the higher the number on its body, the hotter the plug, and the lower the number the cooler the plug.

Plug Cleaning
Modern plug design and materials mean that Champion no longer recommends periodic plug cleaning. Certainly don't clean your plugs with a wire brush as this can cause metal conductive paths across the nose of the insulator so impairing its performance and resulting in loss of acceleration and reduced m.p.g.
However, if plugs are removed, always carefully clean the area where the plug seats in the cylinder head as grit and dirt can sometimes cause gas leakage.
Also wipe any traces of oil or grease from plug leads as this may lead to arcing.

DOUBLE COPPER

1 This photographic sequence shows the steps taken to repair the dent and paintwork damage shown above. In general, the procedure for repairing a hole will be similar; where there are substantial differences, the procedure is clearly described and shown in a separate photograph.

2 First remove any trim around the dent, then hammer out the dent where access is possible. This will minimise filling. Here, after the large dent has been hammered out, the damaged area is being made slightly concave.

3 Next, remove all paint from the damaged area by rubbing with coarse abrasive paper or using a power drill fitted with a wire brush or abrasive pad. 'Feather' the edge of the boundary with good paintwork using a finer grade of abrasive paper.

4 Where there are holes or other damage, the sheet metal should be cut away before proceeding further. The damaged area and any signs of rust should be treated with Turtle Wax Hi-Tech Rust Eater, which will also inhibit further rust formation.

5 *For a large dent or hole* mix Holts Body Plus Resin and Hardener according to the manufacturer's instructions and apply around the edge of the repair. Press Glass Fibre Matting over the repair area and leave for 20-30 minutes to harden. Then ...

5A ... brush more Holts Body Plus Resin and Hardener onto the matting and leave to harden. Repeat the sequence with two or three layers of matting, checking that the final layer is lower than the surrounding area. Apply Holts Body Plus Filler Paste as shown in Step 5B.

5B *For a medium dent*, mix Holts Body Plus Filler Paste and Hardener according to the manufacturer's instructions and apply it with a flexible applicator. Apply thin layers of filler at 20-minute intervals, until the filler surface is slightly proud of the surrounding bodywork.

5C *For small dents and scratches* use Holts No Mix Filler Paste straight from the tube. Apply it according to the instructions in thin layers, using the spatula provided. It will harden in minutes if applied outdoors and may then be used as its own knifing putty.

6 Use a plane or file for initial shaping. Then, using progressively finer grades of wet-and-dry paper, wrapped round a sanding block, and copious amounts of clean water, rub down the filler until glass smooth. 'Feather' the edges of adjoining paintwork.

Protect adjoining areas before spraying the whole repair area and at least one inch of the surrounding sound paintwork with Holts Dupli-Color primer.

Fill any imperfections in the filler surface with a small amount of Holts Body Plus Knifing Putty. Using plenty of clean water, rub down the surface with a fine grade wet-and-dry paper – 400 grade is recommended – until it is really smooth.

Carefully fill any remaining imperfections with knifing putty before applying the last coat of primer. Then rub down the surface with Holts Body Plus Rubbing Compound to ensure a really smooth surface.

Protect surrounding areas from overspray before applying the topcoat in several thin layers. Agitate Holts Dupli-Color aerosol thoroughly. Start at the repair centre, spraying outwards with a side-to-side motion.

If the exact colour is not available off the shelf, local Holts Professional Spraymatch Centres will custom fill an aerosol to match perfectly.

To identify whether a lacquer finish is required, rub a painted unrepaired part of the body with wax and a clean cloth.

If *no* traces of paint appear on the cloth, spray Holts Dupli-Color clear lacquer over the repaired area to achieve the correct gloss level.

The paint will take about two weeks to harden fully. After this time it can be 'cut' with a mild cutting compound such as Turtle Wax Minute Cut prior to polishing with a final coating of Turtle Wax Extra.

When carrying out bodywork repairs, remember that the quality of the finished job is proportional to the time and effort expended.

HAYNES No1 for DIY

Haynes publish a wide variety of books besides the world famous range of *Haynes Owners Workshop Manuals*. They cover all sorts of DIY jobs. Specialist books such as the *Improve and Modify* series and the *Purchase and DIY Restoration Guides* give you all the information you require to carry out everything from minor modifications to complete restoration on a number of popular cars. In addition there are the publications dealing with specific tasks, such as the *Car Bodywork Repair Manual* and the *In-Car Entertainment Manual*. The *Household DIY* series gives clear step-by-step instructions on how to repair everyday household objects ranging from toasters to washing machines.

Whether it is under the bonnet or around the home there is a Haynes Manual that can help you save money. Available from motor accessory stores and bookshops or direct from the publisher.

2 Lubrication system

1 The oil pump is of trochoid type and supplies oil under pressure to a full-flow cartridge type oil filter which incorporates a bypass valve.
2 Oil then flows through the galleries and drillings to all the engine bearings and moving parts. Oil flow from the cylinder block to the cylinder head is regulated by a control orifice.

3 Engine oil and filter

1 At the intervals specified in Routine Maintenance, the engine oil and filter should be renewed.
2 With the engine hot, place a container under the sump pan, remove the dipstick and oil filler cap.
3 Unscrew the sump pan drain plug and allow the oil to drain completely. While this is happening, unscrew and discard the oil filter cartridge. Be prepared for some oil to run out. To remove the filter, the use of a removal tool will probably be required. Alternatively, drive a large screwdriver right through the filter casing (not too close to its base otherwise the threaded connecting sleeve may be damaged) and use the screwdriver as a lever to unscrew it (photos).
4 Clean the filter mounting ring on the crankcase and smear the rubber seal on the filter with engine oil. Screw on the new filter using hand pressure only, not a tool (photo).
5 Wash the filler cap in petrol or paraffin to clean its gauze and shake it dry.
6 Refit and tighten the sump pan drain plug.
7 Refill the engine with the correct quantity of specified oil.
8 Start the engine, the oil warning lamp will take a few seconds to go out. This is normal and is due to the new filter filling with oil.
9 Switch off, check the oil level and top up to the MAXIMUM notch on the dipstick.

4 Crankcase ventilation system

1 This is of the positive crankcase ventilation (PCV) valve type. The purpose of the system is to extract blow-by gases which have passed the piston rings and collected in the crankcase together with oil fumes and draw them into the intake manifold where they are burned during the normal combustion processes.
2 The following servicing should be carried out at the intervals specified in Routine Maintenance.
3 Remove the air cleaner as described in Chapter 3.
4 Release the clip which secures the PCV valve hose to the carburettor insulator and disconnect the hose.

5 Remove the valve and hose assembly from the breather chamber, release the clip and disconnect the hose from the valve.
6 Renew the valve and connect the hose to its small end. Fit the securing clip and fit the large end of the valve in the breather chamber. Fit the other end of the hose to the carburettor insulator. Refit the clip and the air cleaner.
7 Unscrew the wing nut and disconnect the clips and remove the air cleaner cover and lift out the element.
8 Remove the blow-by filter after extracting the screws which hold it to the side of the air cleaner.
9 Renew the filter and fit it by reversing the removal operations.

5 Major operations possible without removing the engine

1 All major operations can be carried out with the engine in the car except for removal and refitting of the crankshaft and main bearings.
2 · Attention to the flywheel and to the crankshaft rear oil seal is possible once the transmission has been removed as described in Chapter 6.

3.3A Sump pan oil drain plug

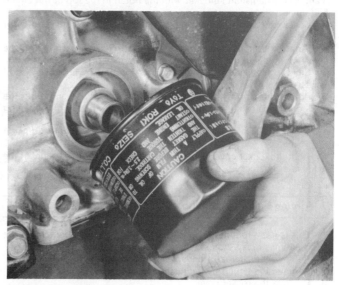

3.4 Fitting a new oil filter

3.3B Unscrewing oil filter

Fig. 1.4 Adjusting a valve clearance (Sec 6)

   1 Camshaft sprocket timing marks
   3 Inlet valve rocker arm
   4 Exhaust valve rocker arm

6 Valve clearances – adjustment

1   Disconnect the spark plug leads, the earth lead and the rocker cover breather hose. Remove the rocker cover.
2   Apply a spanner to the crankshaft pulley bolt and turn the crankshaft in an anti-clockwise direction. Alternatively, engage top gear, raise one front roadwheel and turn it in the forward direction of travel. Keep turning until the UP mark on the camshaft sprocket is uppermost and the marks on the sprocket are parallel with the upper surface of the cylinder head.
3   Check the valve clearances on number one cylinder. Viewed from the camshaft sprocket, inlet valves are on the right and exhaust valves on the left. Remember that the inlet and exhaust valve clearances are different.
4   Insert the feeler blade of appropriate thickness between the end of the valve stem and the rocker arm. It should be a stiff sliding fit, if not, release the adjuster screw locknut and turn the screw as necessary. Tighten the locknut.
5   Rotate the crankshaft through 180° anti-clockwise and align the mark on the camshaft sprocket with the notch in the top of the timing belt cover.
6   Check the valve clearances for number three cylinder, adjust if necessary.
7   Rotate the crankshaft through 180° anti-clockwise and align the camshaft sprocket marks with the upper surface of the cylinder head.
8   Check the valve clearances for number four cylinder, adjust if necessary.
9   Rotate the crankshaft through 180° anti-clockwise and align the mark on the camshaft sprocket with the notch in the top of the timing belt cover.
10 Check the valve clearances for number two cylinder, adjust if necessary.
11 Refit the rocker cover using a new gasket if necessary, connect the leads and breather hose.

Fig. 1.5 Camshaft sprocket timing mark and belt cover notch (Sec 6)

7 Timing belt – tensioning

1   This is not a routine operation and it should only be required if the belt becomes noisy. Adjust when the engine is cold.
2   Remove the alternator drivebelt (Chapter 12).
3   Remove the timing belt adjuster bolt access plug (photo).
4   Remove the rocker cover.
5   Turn the crankshaft by means of its pulley bolt in an anti-clockwise

7.3 Removing timing belt adjuster bolt plug

7.5 Camshaft sprocket TDC marks

7.6 Slackening timing belt tensioner

direction until No. 1 piston is at TDC on its compression stroke. This will be indicated when the UP mark on the camshaft sprocket is uppermost and the timing marks parallel with the top face of the cylinder head (photo).

6   Slacken the timing belt tensioner adjuster bolt (photo).

7   Turn the crankshaft pulley bolt in an anti-clockwise direction to move the timing belt the distance of three teeth of the sprocket. This action will tension the belt automatically by means of the spring-loaded tensioner.

8   Tighten the tensioner bolt to the specified torque.

9   Refit the tensioner bolt access plug.

10 Fit the alternator drivebelt and tension it.

8   Timing belt – removal and refitting

1   Disconnect the battery.

2   Remove the air cleaner (Chapter 3).

3   Disconnect the spark plug leads, the earth lead and breather hose from the rocker cover.

4   Remove the rocker cover and timing belt upper cover.

5   Remove the alternator drivebelt (Chapter 12).

6   Raise the car and securely support the front end. Remove the left-hand front roadwheel and the splash panel.

7   Set No. 1 piston to TDC as described in the preceding Section.

8   Engage a low gear and with an assistant fully applying the footbrake, unscrew the crankshaft pulley bolt.

9   Withdraw the crankshaft pulley and key.

10 Remove the timing belt lower cover.

11 Slacken the belt tensioner bolt, retract the tensioner and re-tighten the bolt.

12 Remove the timing belt and the guide plate from the front of the crankshaft. *Do not turn the sprockets while the belt is off or the valve heads will contact the pistons.*

13 If the belt is to be used again, mark it with the direction of rotation.

14 Check that the sprockets are still set at No. 1 TDC, then fit the belt to the sprockets (photo).

15 Fit the guide plate to the crankshaft, convex side to the belt (photo).

16 Fit the belt lower cover, key and crankshaft pulley. Screw in and tighten the bolt to the specified torque again holding the crankshaft against rotation as previously described. Note that the key is of wedge section. Make sure that the wider face goes into the crankshaft key way (photos).

8.14 Fitting timing belt

8.15 Timing belt outer guide plate

8.16A Tightening timing belt lower cover bolt

8.16B Crankshaft pulley and Woodruff key

8.16C Tightening crankshaft pulley bolt

17 Tension the belt as described in the preceding Section.
18 Fit the splash guard panel, roadwheel and lower the car to the floor.
19 Refit the belt upper cover, rocker cover, leads, hose and alternator drivebelt (photos).
20 Refit the air cleaner and connect the battery.

9 Camshaft front oil seal – renewal

1   Remove the rocker cover.
2   Remove the timing belt upper cover.
3   Hold the camshaft sprocket still with a tool or rod passed through its spokes and release its retaining bolt.
4   Slacken the belt tensioner bolt and retract the tensioner.
5   Slip the timing belt from the camshaft sprocket, then withdraw the sprocket and key. Do not move the position of the camshaft.
6   Using a suitable tool, extract the camshaft oil seal.
7   Apply a smear of jointing compound to the oil seal recess in the housing, apply oil to the seal lips and drive it squarely home so that its lips face inwards.

8.19A Fitting belt upper cover

8.19B Tightening timing belt upper cover bolts

8   Refit the key and sprocket. Tighten the pulley bolt to the specified torque.
9   Refit the timing belt and tension it as described in Section 7.
10 Refit the rocker cover and belt upper cover.

10 Crankshaft front oil seal – renewal

1   Remove the timing belt as described in Section 8. Do not rotate the crankshaft while the belt is off.
2   Using two screwdrivers, remove the crankshaft sprocket and inner guide plate. Prise out the oil seal.
3   Smear the inside of the oil seal housing recess with gasket cement and the seal lips with oil and drive the seal squarely into position. Fit the belt guide plate and sprocket.
4   Fit the timing belt and tension it as described in earlier Sections.

11 Rocker shafts – removal and refitting

1   Remove the air cleaner.
2   Disconnect the spark plug leads, the earth lead and breather hose. Then remove the rocker cover.
3   Set No. 1 piston to TDC as described in Section 7.
4   Unscrew and remove the rocker shaft bracket bolts and lift the rocker assemblies from the cylinder head.
5   Dismantling may be carried out as necessary for the renewal of worn components.
6   Unscrew the rocker shaft lockbolts and slide off the springs, arms and collar.
7   Refitting is a reversal of removal. Check that the shaft collars are not trapped in the shaft bearing caps.
8   Before tightening the rocker shaft fixing bolts, slacken the valve clearance screw locknuts and the screws.
9   Tighten the shaft bolts to the specified torque working in diagonal sequence from the centre bolts towards each end.

10 Check and adjust the valve clearances as described in Section 6.
11 Refit the rocker cover, air cleaner and reconnect the leads and hoses.

12 Camshaft – removal and refitting

1   Remove the rocker shafts as described in the preceding Section.
2   Remove the fuel pump (Chapter 3).
3   Remove the distributor (Chapter 4) and its holder.
4   Disconnect the timing belt as described in Section 9.
5   Remove the camshaft sprocket.
6   Unbolt the camshaft rear bearing upper bracket. Remove all the upper brackets (bearing caps), keeping them in order and the right way round.
7   Lift the camshaft from the cylinder head.
8   Refitting is a reversal of removal. Note that the camshaft bearing caps are numbered 1 to 5 from the timing end of the engine. Numbers 2 and 4 should have their arrows pointing to the timing cover. Read all numbers from the inlet manifold side. Apply RTV sealant at the cylinder head joint faces of Nos 1 and 5 camshaft pedestals.
9   Fit a new camshaft oil seal, tension the timing belt (Section 7) and adjust the valve clearances (Section 6).

13 Cylinder head – removal and refitting

1   The cylinder head should only be removed from a cool engine, below 38°C (100°F).
2   Disconnect the battery negative lead.
3   Drain the cooling system, retaining the coolant for further use.
4   Remove the air cleaner (Chapter 3).
5   Disconnect the brake servo vacuum hose from the inlet manifold. Also remove the coolant bypass hose.
6   Disconnect the radiator top hose from the cylinder head.
7   Disconnect the hoses from the fuel pump and plug them.
8   Disconnect the throttle and choke controls from the carburettor.

Fig. 1.6 Rocker gear components (Sec 11)

1 Inlet valve rocker shaft (eight oil holes)	6 Rocker arm
2 Camshaft centre bearing upper bracket	7 Spacer and spring
3 Rocker arm	8 Exhaust valve rocker shaft (four oil holes)
4 Camshaft front bearing upper bracket	9 Camshaft No.4 bearing upper bracket
5 Camshaft No.2 bearing upper bracket	10 Camshaft rear bearing upper bracket

9 Unscrew the bolts which secure the support bracket to the inlet manifold and the crankcase (photo).
10 Disconnect the leads from the carburettor, ignition coil and coolant sender unit.
11 Detach the air cleaner hot air duct.
12 Remove the radiator heat baffle plate.
13 Remove the centre splash guard panel.
14 Remove the hot air collector cover from the exhaust manifold.
15 Disconnect the exhaust downpipe and unbolt the exhaust manifold steady brackets.
16 Remove the rocker cover.
17 Remove the timing belt upper cover.
18 With a socket on the crankshaft pulley bolt, turn the crankshaft in an anti-clockwise direction until the UP mark on the camshaft sprocket is uppermost and the timing marks on the sprocket are parallel with the top face of the cylinder head. No. 1 piston is now at TDC on its compression stroke.
19 Remove the alternator drivebelt (Chapter 12).
20 Slacken the belt tensioner adjusting bolt, retract the tensioner and slip the timing belt from the camshaft sprocket.
21 Do not rotate the crankshaft while the belt is off the sprocket.
22 Progressively slacken the cylinder head bolts and nuts, half a turn at a time in the reverse order of tightening (Fig. 1.7).
23 Remove the bolts and nuts and lift the cylinder head from the block. It is permissible to lever the head up if it is stuck, but use a suitable tool only between the lugs provided not in the gasket joint. Positioning dowels are fitted so lift the head straight up when removing it (photo).
24 Dismantling and decarbonising of the cylinder head is covered in Section 24.
25 Before refitting the cylinder head, make sure that all carbon and old gasket material has been removed from the cylinder head and block mating surfaces.
26 Check that the positioning dowels are fully located in the top of the block.
27 Place a new gasket on the cylinder block. Check that the timing marks are set as described in paragraph 18 (photo).
28 Carefully lower the head onto the block, insert the bolts (threads clean and lightly oiled) and screw the nuts onto the studs (photo).
29 Tighten the bolts and nuts to the specified torque working in the sequence shown in Fig. 1.7. First tighten to half the tightening torque and then to full tightening torque.
30 Connect the timing belt to the camshaft sprocket with the timing marks correctly positioned as described in paragraph 18.
31 Tension the belt as described in Section 7.
32 If the valve gear has not been disturbed, then the valve clearances will not require checking or adjusting.
33 Fit the rocker cover and the timing belt upper cover.
34 Reconnect all hoses, control cables and electrical leads.
35 Reconnect the exhaust pipe, refit the hot air collector cover,

13.9 Inlet manifold support bracket

13.23 Cylinder head prising lug on block

13.27 New cylinder head gasket in position

13.28 Tightening a cylinder head bolt

Fig. 1.7 Cylinder head bolt tightening sequence (Sec 13)

radiator heat baffle plate and splash guard plate.
36 Fill and bleed the cooling system.

14 Sump pan – removal and refitting

1 Drain the engine oil.
2 Disconnect the exhaust downpipe from the manifold.
3 Refer to Chapter 8 and disconnect the left-hand driveshaft from the transmission.
4 Unbolt and remove the stiffener bracket from between the engine and transmission (photo).
5 Progressively unscrew the six nuts and twelve bolts which hold the sump pan to the crankcase.
6 Remove the cover plate from the lower part of the flywheel housing (photo).
7 Remove the sump pan and peel off the one-piece gasket.
8 Before refitting, wipe the crankcase and sump pan mating surfaces clean and apply a bead of gasket cement between the studs and the main bearing cap, also to both sides of the gasket where it seats at the main bearing cap.
9 Position the new gasket and then offer the sump pan onto the studs and tighten all nuts and bolts to the specified torque. Refit the flywheel housing cover (photos).
10 Refit the stiffener bracket, reconnect the driveshaft and the exhaust downpipe, and refill the engine with oil.

14.4 Engine/transmission stiffener bracket

14.6 Flywheel housing cover plate

14.9A Sump pan gasket

14.9B Tightening sump pan bolts

15 Oil pump – removal and refitting

1   Remove the air cleaner and rocker cover.
2   Remove the timing belt upper cover.
3   Remove the alternator drivebelt (Chapter 12).
4   Drain the engine oil.
5   Disconnect the exhaust downpipe from the manifold.
6   Raise and support the front end of the car, remove the left-hand roadwheel and the centre and left-hand splash guard panels.
7   Refer to Chapter 8 and disconnect the left-hand driveshaft from the transmission.
8   Set No. 1 piston to TDC with the camshaft sprocket timing marks aligned as described in Section 13.
9   Select a low gear and with an assistant applying the brakes fully, unscrew the crankshaft pulley bolt. Remove the pulley and Woodruff key.
10 Remove the crankshaft sprocket timing belt guide plate, the timing belt and then pull off the crankshaft sprocket with the inner belt guide plate. Note that the Woodruff key is combined with the sprocket.
11 Remove the stiffener bracket from between the engine and transmission.
12 Unbolt and remove the flywheel housing cover plate and the sump pan.
13 Extract the split pin, withdraw the collar spring and oil pressure relief valve.
14 Remove the oil pump strainer.
15 Extract the oil pump fixing screws and withdraw the pump from the front end of the crankshaft.
16 Before refitting the oil pump, smear gasket cement to the mounting face. All other operations are a reversal of removal. Always renew the O-ring seal (photos).
17 Note that the crankshaft pulley key is of tapered section. Make sure that the widest face is in the crankshaft key-way.
18 Refer to Section 14 for details of refitting the sump pan.
19 Refer to Section 7 for details of tensioning the timing belt.
20 Make sure that the driveshaft is fully engaged in the differential side gear with the spring clip positively locked.
21 Refill the engine with oil.

16 Connecting rod big-end bearings and piston rings – renewal

1   These operations will normally be carried out at the time of complete engine overhaul, but the work may be done without removing the engine from the car where it is necessary to reduce oil consumption and to improve the oil pressure.
2   Refer to Section 14 and remove the sump pan.
3   Inspect the big-end caps for identification. They should be marked 1 to 4 from the crankshaft pulley end of the side nearest to the exhaust manifold. If not, mark them, with a centre punch on the cap and the adjacent surface of the connecting rod. Do not confuse the bearing shell code numbers (see Section 25).
4   Unscrew the big-end cap nuts, remove the cap with its shell bearing. This is difficult owing to the monobloc construction of the main bearing caps. It can be done however if the crankshaft is rotated gently in both directions and the big-end cap removed through the monobloc apertures.
5   Push each connecting rod slightly upwards and remove the upper shell half. Only move the connecting rod upwards when the big-end is at the lowest point of its throw, otherwise if the piston is at TDC it might be possible for the top piston ring to pop out of the top of the cylinder.
6   If only new shells are to be fitted, fit them in matched pairs making sure that their recesses in both the rod and cap are perfectly clean (see Section 25 regarding shell coding).
7   If the piston rings are to be renewed owing to heavy oil consumption, it is recommended that proprietary oil control sets are fitted.
8   Remove the cylinder head as described in Section 13.
9   Push the piston connecting rod assembly up and out of the top of the cylinder bore. If a heavy wear ridge is evident at the top of the bore, it will have to be carefully removed with a ridge reamer or by scraping in order to allow the ring to pass.

15.16A Fitting oil pump

15.16B Tightening the oil pump bolts

10 Remove the piston rings from the top of the piston. To avoid breaking a ring either during removal or refitting, slide two or three old feeler blades at equidistant points behind the top ring and slide it up them. Remove the other rings in a similar way (photo).
11 Clean carbon from the ring grooves, a segment of old piston ring is useful for this purpose.
12 Clean out the oil return holes in the piston ring grooves and fit the new piston rings. The top ring will be supplied stepped so that it does not impinge on the wear ridge.
13 Insert each piston ring in turn squarely into its bore and check the ring end gap. If it is not within the specified tolerance, carefully grind the end-face of the ring.
14 Now check each compression ring in its groove and measure the clearances with a feeler gauge. If it is tight the ring may be rubbed flat on a sheet of wet and dry paper laid flat on a piece of plate glass (photo).
15 Fit the rings to the piston using the feeler blade method as described for removal. Work from the top of the piston, fitting the oil control ring first.
16 Locate the compression ring gaps at 90° to each other on the thrust side (towards the dipstick guide tube). The expander of the oil control ring should have its gap on the opposite side to the gap in the second compression ring. The gaps in the rails of the oil control ring should be

16.10 Method of removing and refitting piston rings

16.14 Checking piston ring clearance in groove

on either side of the expander gap. Repeat all the operations on the remaining pistons.

17 The cylinder bore should now be de-glazed using a glaze buster or fine glasspaper to enable the new rings to bed in.

18 Take care to remove all debris and then oil the bores and piston rings liberally.

19 Fit a piston ring compressor to the first piston and insert the rod complete with shell bearing into the bore so that the compressor stands flat on the block (photo).

20 Check that with the oil hole in the connecting rod towards the inlet manifold side of the block, the valve head cut-outs in the piston crowns are on the exhaust valve side of the engine, irrespective of the fact there are two inlet valves in the combustion chamber.

21 Place the wooden handle of a hammer on the piston crown and tap the hammer head with the hand to drive the piston into the cylinder bore. The compressor will remain on the face of the block.

22 Lubricate the shell in the cap, fit the cap to its correctly numbered rod, and screw on the cap nuts to the specified torque (photos).

23 Fit the remaining piston/connecting rods in a similar way.

24 Refit the cylinder head (Section 13) refit the sump pan (Section 14).

25 Refill the engine with oil and coolant. Avoid high engine speeds during the first few hundred miles to allow the components to bed in.

16.19 Fitting a piston into cylinder bore

16.22A Fitting a big-end cap

16.22B Tightening a big-end cap nut

Fig. 1.8 Engine/transmission mountings showing tightening sequence (Sec 17)

Stage 1: Lightly tighten nuts/bolts 1 to 4 (encircled) in numerical sequence
Stage 2: Fully tighten the nuts/bolts 5 to 8 in numerical sequence to their specified torque wrench settings

17 Engine/transmission mountings – renewal

1   The mountings may be renewed with the engine/transmission in the car provided the weight of the engine or transmission is taken on a hoist or using a workshop jack with a block of wood as an insulator (photos).

2   Before removing the rear mounting, disconnect the rear gear-change (selector) rod from the transmission.

3   Tighten all nuts and bolts to the specified torque.

17.1A Right-hand front engine mounting bracket

17.1B Rear engine mounting bracket

17.1C Left-hand front engine mounting bracket

17.1D Rear engine mounting

18 Engine – method of removal

The engine should be removed upwards from the engine compartment complete with the transmission.

19 Engine/manual transmission – removal and separation

1   Open the bonnet. Mark the position of the hinges with masking tape.
2   Unbolt the hinges and with the help of an assistant, lift away the bonnet and place it in a safe place where it will not be scratched.
3   Remove the battery and its tray.
4   Drain the engine oil.
5   Remove the air cleaner (Chapter 3).
6   Disconnect the brake servo vacuum hose from the inlet manifold.
7   Disconnect the carburettor controls, the leads from the ignition coil, the engine wiring harness multi-plug connector and the engine and transmission earth cables. Also disconnect the leads from the oil pressure and temperature switches (photo).
8   Disconnect the leads from the starter motor, the tachometer drive, speedometer drive cable and the reverse lamp switch leads. Take care not to remove the speedometer pinion housing or the pinion may drop into the gearbox.
9   Disconnect the clutch release cable from the release lever.
10 Disconnect the fuel feed hose from the fuel pump and plug the hose.
11 Drain the cooling system.
12 Disconnect the radiator top hose from the engine, followed by the lower hose.
13 Disconnect the heater hoses.
14 Raise the front of the car and support it securely and remove the front roadwheels. Place stands under the body members.
15 Using a hoist or other suitable lifting gear, attached to the engine and transmission lifting hooks, take the weight of the engine.
16 Support the suspension lower arms, unscrew the balljoint taper pin nuts and using a suitable splitter tool, disconnect the balljoints from both hub carriers. Take care that the arms do not jump off the jack.
17 Remove the splash guard panels.
18 Turn the steering to full right-hand lock and then disconnect the right-hand driveshaft from the transmission. Do this by inserting a lever between the inboard driveshaft joint and the transmission casing and prising against spring pressure of the shaft retaining clip.
19 Now turn the steering to full left-hand lock and disconnect the left-hand driveshaft.
20 Disconnect the gear selector and torque rods from the transmission.
21 Disconnect the exhaust downpipe from the manifold.

17.1E Right-hand front engine mounting

19.7 Temperature switch and lead

Fig. 1.9 Engine lifting lug (Sec 19)

Fig. 1.10 Transmission lifting lug (Sec 19)

22 Check that the weight of the engine is still being taken by the hoist and disconnect the engine/transmission mountings.
23 Raise the engine transmission slightly and check that everything has been disconnected.
24 Lift the unit out of the engine compartment.
25 Remove all external dirt by steam cleaning or by using a water soluble solvent.
26 Support the engine and remove the starter motor and the cover plate from the face of the flywheel housing.
27 Unscrew and remove the flywheel housing to engine connecting bolts and withdraw the transmission from the engine, supporting its weight so that it does not hang upon the input shaft while the shaft is engaged in the hub of the clutch driven plate.

20 Engine/automatic transmission – removal and separation

1   Removal operations are very similar to those described in the preceding Section for cars with manual transmission, but of course ignore reference to the clutch cable and gear selector. Disconnect the selector cable and kick-down cable.
2   Disconnect and plug the oil cooler pipes.
3   Disconnect the leads from the reverse lamp/inhibitor switch.
4   To separate the transmission from the engine, remove the starter and the cover plate from the face of the torque converter housing.
5   Unscrew the three bolts which hold the driveplate to the torque converter. These are accessible through the starter motor aperture, but the crankshaft will have to be rotated to bring each bolt into view.
6   Unscrew the transmission to engine connecting bolts. It will be found that some of the bolts cannot be completely removed until the transmission has been partially withdrawn.
7   With the engine supported in the vertical position, withdraw the transmission, at the same time holding the torque converter in full engagement within the converter housing otherwise there will be fluid loss and damage to the oil seal. The transmission is very heavy so carry out the work with the help of an assistant or use a trolley jack or hoist.
8   While the transmission is out of the car, make up a plate which can be bolted to the front of the torque converter housing to prevent the torque converter from falling out.

21 Engine – dismantling (general)

1   Stand the engine on a strong bench so as to be at a comfortable working height. Failing this it can be stripped down on the floor, but at least stand it on a sheet of hardboard.

2   During the dismantling process, the greatest care should be taken to keep the exposed parts free from dirt. As the engine is stripped, clean each part in a bath of paraffin.
3   Never immerse parts with oilways in paraffin, e.g. the crankshaft, but to clean, wipe down carefully with a paraffin dampened rag. Oilways can be cleaned out with a piece of wire. If an air line is available, all parts can be blown dry and the oilways blown through as an added precaution.
4   Re-use of old gaskets is false economy and can give rise to oil and water leaks, if nothing worse. To avoid the possibility of trouble after the engine has been reassembled always use new gaskets throughout.
5   Do not throw the old gaskets away as it sometimes happens that an immediate replacement cannot be found and the old gasket is then very useful as a template. Hang up the gaskets on a suitable nail or hook as they are removed.
6   To strip the engine, it is best to work from the top downwards. The engine oil sump proves a firm base on which the engine can be supported in an upright position. When the stage is reached where the pistons are to be removed, turn the engine on its side. Turn the block upside down to remove the crankshaft.
7   Wherever possible, replace nuts, bolts and washers finger-tight from wherever they were removed. This helps avoid later loss and muddle. If they cannot be replaced then lay them out in such a fashion that it is clear from where they came.

22 Engine ancillary components – removal

1   Before complete engine dismantling begins, remove the following ancillary components.

Distributor (Chapter 4)
Inlet manifold and carburettor (Chapter 3)
Fuel pump (Chapter 3)
Exhaust manifold and hot air collector (Chapter 3)
Alternator (Chapter 12)
Clutch (Chapter 5)
Oil filter cartridge and dipstick
Engine mounting brackets

23 Engine – complete dismantling

1   Remove the rocker cover.
2   Remove the timing belt, Section 8.
3   Refer to Section 13 and remove the cylinder head.
4   Remove the timing belt tensioner.

5 Refer to Chapter 2 and remove the coolant pump.
6 Lock the flywheel starter ring gear teeth and unbolt and remove the flywheel (or driveplate – automatic transmission). Renew the bolts and clean the threads in their holes.
7 Remove the crankcase breather.
8 Turn the engine upside down and remove the sump pan (Section 14 and the oil pump (Section 15).
9 Unbolt and remove the crankshaft rear oil seal retainer. Remove the dipstick guide tube.
10 Lay the engine on its side and remove the piston/connecting rods as described in Section 16.
11 Stand the engine on its block face and unbolt and remove the main bearing caps. These are in the form of a monobloc casting. Note the thrust washers located at No. 4 main bearing.
12 Lift the crankshaft from the crankcase. If the bearing shells are to be used again, identify them with their original crankcase or cap recesses.

24 Cylinder head – dismantling and decarbonising

1 With the cylinder head removed to the bench, dismantle in the following way.
2 Unscrew and remove the spark plugs.
3 If not already done, unbolt and remove the inlet manifold with the carburettor and the exhaust manifold with the hot air collector. Remove the thermostat housing and coolant distribution tube.
4 Remove the fuel pump.
5 Remove the distributor and distributor holder.
6 Remove the camshaft sprocket and key.
7 Extract the camshaft front oil seal (Section 9).
8 Remove the rocker shaft assemblies (Section 11).
9 Lift the camshaft from the cylinder head.
10 Using a valve spring compressor, compress the first valve spring and remove the split collets.
11 Gently release the compressor and remove it.
12 Take off the spring retainer, the spring and the spring seat.
13 Remove all the other valves in a similar way keeping them in their original fitted sequence together with their associated components. Remove and discard the valve stem oil seals.
14 Bearing in mind that the cylinder head is of light alloy construction and is easily damaged use a blunt scraper or rotary wire brush to clean all traces of carbon deposits from the combustion spaces and the ports. The valve head stems and valve guides should also be freed from any carbon deposits. Wash the combustion spaces and ports down with paraffin and scrape the cylinder head surface free of any foreign matter with the side of a steel rule, or a similar article.
15 If the engine is installed in the car, clean the pistons and the top of the cylinder bores. If the pistons are still in the block, then it is essential that great care is taken to ensure that no carbon gets into the cylinder bores as this could scratch the cylinder walls or cause damage to the piston and rings. To ensure this does not happen, first turn the crankshaft so that two of the pistons are at the top of their bores. Stuff rag into the other two bores or seal them off with paper and masking tape. The waterways should also be covered with small pieces of masking tape to prevent particles of carbon entering the cooling system and damaging the coolant pump.
16 Press a little grease into the gap between the cylinder walls and the two pistons which are to be worked on. With a blunt scraper carefully scrape away the carbon from the piston crown, taking great care not to scratch the aluminium. Also scrape away the carbon from the surround lip of the cylinder wall. When all carbon has been removed, scrape away the grease which will now be contaminated with carbon particles, taking care not to press any into the bores. To assist prevention of carbon build-up the piston crown can be polished with a metal polish. Remove the rags or masking tape from the other two cylinders and turn the crankshaft so that the two pistons which were at the bottom are now at the top. Place rag in the cylinders which have been decarbonised, and proceed as just described.
17 Examine the head of the valves for pitting and burning, especially the heads of the exhaust valves. The valve seatings should be examined at the same time. If the pitting on the valve and seat is very slight, the marks can be removed by grinding the seats and valves together with coarse, and then fine, valve grinding paste.
18 Where bad pitting has occurred to the valve seats it will be necessary to recut them and fit new valves. This latter job should be

entrusted to the local agent or engineering works. In practice it is very seldom that the seats are so badly worn. Normally it is the valve that is too badly worn for refitting, and the owner can easily purchase a new set of valves and match them to the seats by valve grinding.
19 Valve grinding is carried out as follows. Smear a trace of coarse carborundum paste on the seat face and apply a suction grinder tool to the valve head. With a semi-rotary motion, grind the valve head to its seat, lifting the valve occasionally to redistribute the grinding paste. When a dull matt even surface is produced on both the valve seat and the valve, wipe off the paste and repeat the process with fine carborundum paste, lifting and turning the valve to redistribute the paste as before. A light spring placed under the valve head will greatly ease this operation. When a smooth unbroken ring of light grey matt finish is produced, on both valve and valve seat faces, the grinding operation is complete. Carefully clean away every trace of grinding compound, take great care to leave none in the ports or in the valve guides. Clean the valves and valve seats with paraffin soaked rag, then with a clean rag, and finally, if an air line is available, blow the valve, valve guides and valve ports clean.
20 Check that all valve springs are intact. If any one is broken, all should be renewed. Check the free height of the springs against new ones. If some springs are not within specifications, replace them all. Springs suffer from fatigue and it is a good idea to renew them even if they look serviceable.
21 The cylinder head can be checked for warping either by placing it on a piece of plate glass or using a straight-edge and feeler blades. If there is any doubt or if its block face is corroded, have it re-faced by your dealer or motor engineering works.
22 Test the valves in their guides for side to side rock. If this is any more than almost imperceptible new guides must be fitted, again a job for your dealer.
23 Examine the camshaft for wear or scoring of the journals or cam lobes. Any wear or scoring in the camshaft bearings will mean renewal of the cylinder head as the bearings are line-bored and cannot be replaced independently. It may be possible to have worn cam lobes reprofiled by a specialist firm.
24 Check the rocker shafts and arms and renew any components which are worn.
25 Commence reassembly by oiling the stem of the first valve and pushing it into its guide which should have been fitted with a new oil seal. The valve stem oil seals on the inlet valve guides have a bright metal clip while those for the exhaust valve guides have a black clip (photo).
26 Fit the spring seat, the valve spring so that the closer coils are towards the cylinder head and then the spring retaining cap (photos).
27 Compress the valve spring and using a little grease locate the split cotters in the valve stem cut-out (photo).

24.25A Valve components
1 Valve
2 Valve spring seat
3 Valve stem oil seal
4 Valve spring
5 Valve spring cap
6 Split cotters

46

24.25B Fitting a valve

24.25C Fitting a valve stem oil seal

24.26A Fitting valve spring seat

24.26B Fitting valve spring

24.26C Fitting valve spring cap

24.27 Compressing valve spring and fitting split cotters

28 Gently release the compressor, checking to see that the collets are not displaced.

29 Fit the remaining valve in the same way.

30 Tap the end of each valve stem with a plastic or copper-faced hammer to settle the components.

31 Oil the camshaft bearings in the cylinder head. Lower the camshaft into position (photos).

32 Fit the camshaft bearing cap/pedestals in their numbered sequence with arrows towards the timing belt. Tighten the rear bearing cap bolts (photos).

33 Fit the rocker shaft assemblies complete with rocker arms, springs and spacers. Tighten the bolts to the specified torque (photo).

34 Fit a new camshaft oil seal, the Woodruff key and the camshaft sprocket and then tighten its bolt to the specified torque (photos).

35 Refit the distributor holder, tighten the bolts (photos).

36 Refit the fuel pump.

37 Fit the distributor (Chapter 4).

38 Screw in the spark plugs, clean and correctly gapped.

39 Bolt on the inlet and exhaust manifold using new gaskets.

24.31 Fitting the camshaft

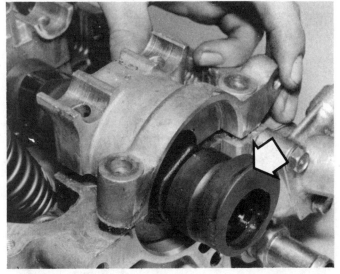

24.32A Fitting a camshaft bearing cap. Fuel pump eccentric arrowed

24.32B Tightening camshaft bearing cap bolt

24.33 Tightening a rocker shaft bolt

24.34A Camshaft oil seal

24.34B Camshaft sprocket Woodruff key

24.34C Camshaft sprocket bolt

24.34D Tightening camshaft sprocket bolt

24.35A Fitting the distributor holder

24.35B Tightening distributor holder bolts

25 Engine components – examination and renovation

1   With the engine stripped down and all parts thoroughly clean, it is now time to examine everything for wear. The following items should be checked and where necessary renewed or renovated as described in the following Sections.

Cylinder block and crankcase
2   Clean away all old gasket material and then examine the casting for cracks particularly about bolt holes. If any are found, specialist welding or cold repair will be required.
3   Clean out the oilways and galleries with compressed air or wire.
4   If the cylinder bores are worn, this will be evident by the emission of exhaust smoke and general deterioration in engine performance together with increased oil consumption. A good way to test the condition of the engine is to have it at normal operating temperature with the spark plugs removed. Screw a compression tester (available from most modern accessory stores) into the first plug hole. Hold the accelerator pedal fully depressed and crank the engine on the starter motor for several revolutions. Record the reading. Zero the tester and check the remaining cylinders in the same way. All four compression

figures should be approximately equal and within the tolerance given in the Specifications. If they are all low, suspect piston ring or cylinder bore wear. If only one reading is down, suspect a valve not seating.
5   The cylinder bores must be checked for taper, ovality, scoring and scratching. Start by examining the top of the cylinder bores. If they are at all worn, a ridge will be felt on the thrust side. This ridge marks the limit of piston ring travel.
6   An internal micrometer or dial gauge can be used to check bore wear and taper against Specifications, but this is a pointless operation if the engine is obviously in need of reboring as indicated by excessive oil consumption.

Pistons and connecting rods
7   If the cylinders have been rebored, then the reconditioner will supply the oversize pistons, rings and the gudgeon pins. Give the job of fitting the new pistons to the connecting rods to him.
8   The gudgeon pin is an interference fit in the connecting rod small end and removal or refitting and changing a piston is a job best left to your dealer or engine reconditioner. This is owing to the need for a press and jig and careful heating of the connecting rod.
9   Removal and refitting piston rings is described in Section 16.

Crankshaft
10   Examine the surfaces of the journals and crankpins; if scored or when measured with a micrometer prove to be oval or tapered then the manufacturer's recommendation is to renew the crankshaft and the colour-coded bearing shells. However, by consulting a specialist crankshaft grinder it may be possible for him to recondition the original crankshaft and supply undersize shells.
11   If the crankshaft is in good condition, but it is decided to renew the main and big-end bearing shells, use the following formula to select them.

Main bearings
12   Match the letter on the cylinder block with the number on the crankshaft web adjacent to each bearing (photo).

Big-end bearings
13   Match the number on the connecting rod with the letter on the crankshaft web adjacent to each bearing.
14   The resulting main bearing or big-end shell will be colour coded on its edge in accordance with the following table.

	A	B	C	D
1	Red	Pink	Yellow	Green
2	Pink	Yellow	Green	Brown
3	Yellow	Green	Brown	Black
4	Green	Brown	Black	Blue

Cylinder head, camshaft and rockers
15   Refer to Section 24.

Timing belt, tensioner and sprockets
16   If the timing belt shows signs of cracking or tooth wear, renew it. If it has been in operation for 80 000 km (50 000 miles) or more, it should be renewed as a matter of routine.
17   If the sprockets have tooth wear, renew them.
18   The tensioner pulley should spin smoothly and quietly. If it is rough or worn on its spindle, renew it.

Flywheel (or driveplate)
19   Check the clutch mating surface of the flywheel. If it is deeply scored (due to failure to renew a worn driven plate) then it may be possible to have it surface ground provided the thickness of the flywheel is not reduced too much.
20   If lots of tiny cracks are visible on the surface of the flywheel then this will be due to overheating caused by slipping the clutch or 'riding' the clutch pedal.
21   With a pre-engaged type of starter motor it is rare to find the teeth of the flywheel ring gear damaged or worn, but if they are, then the ring gear will have to be renewed.
22   To remove the ring gear, drill a hole between the roots of two teeth taking care not to damage the flywheel and then split the ring with a sharp cold chisel.
23   The new ring gear must be heated to 350°C (662°F). If you do not have facilities for obtaining these temperatures, leave the job to your dealer or engine reconditioner.
24   Where such facilities are available, then the ring gear should be either pressed or lightly tapped gently onto its register and left to cool naturally, when the contraction of the metal on cooling will ensure that it is a secure and permanent fit. Great care must be taken not to overheat the ring gear, as if this happens its temper will be lost. A clutch input shaft pilot bearing is not fitted on this engine.
25   If the ring gear on the driveplate is worn, renew the plate complete.

Oil pump
26   Check that the oil relief valve slides freely in its housing.
27   If the pump has been in use for a long time carry out the following checks for wear outside the specified tolerance (see Specifications).
28   Extract the pump rear plate screws. An impact driver will probably be required for this (photo).
29   Remove the rear plate, remove the inner and outer rotors, identifying the faces which are in contact with the rear plate so that they can be refitted the same way round (photos).
30   Clean all components and reassemble the rotors.

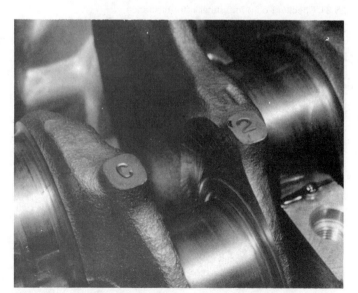
25.12 Main and big-end bearing code number and letter

25.28 Extracting oil pump rear plate screws

25.29A Oil pump outer rotor showing face 'up' dimple

25.29B Oil pump inner rotor showing face 'up' dimple

31 Check the clearance between the outer rotor and the oil pump body using feeler gauges (photo).
32 Check the clearance between the inner rotor lobe tip and the outer rotor lobe tip (photo).
33 Place a straight-edge across the runs of the oil pump housing and insert feeler blades between the rotors and the straight-edge (photo).
34 If any clearance is outside that specified, renew the worn components or the pump complete.

Oil seals and gaskets

35 It is recommended that all gaskets and oil seals are renewed at major engine overhaul. Sockets are useful for removing or refitting oil seals. An arrow is moulded onto some seals to indicate the rotational direction of the component which it serves. Make sure that the seal is fitted the correct way round to comply with the arrow.

26 Engine reassembly – general

1 To ensure maximum life with minimum trouble from a rebuilt engine, not only must every part be correctly assembled, but everything must be spotlessly clean, all the oilways must be clear,

25.31 Checking oil pump outer rotor clearance

25.32 Checking oil pump rotor lobe tip clearance

25.33 Checking oil pump rotor endfloat

locking washers and spring washers must always be fitted where indicated and all bearing and other working surfaces must be thoroughly lubricated during assembly. Before assembly begins renew any bolts or studs whose threads are in any way damaged; whenever possible use new spring washers.

2 Apart from your normal tools, a supply of non-fluffy rag, an oil can filled with engine oil, a supply of new spring washers, a set of new gaskets and a torque wrench should be collected together.

27 Engine – complete reassembly

1 Set the cylinder block on the bench with the crankcase uppermost.
2 Wipe out the main bearing shell recesses in the crankcase and insert the selected shells or if the original ones are being used again, return them to their original locations (photo).
3 Oil the shells liberally and then stick the semi-circular thrust washers on either side of No. 4 main bearing in the crankcase using some thick gease. Make sure that the oil grooves on the thrust washers are visible when the thrust washers are fitted (photos).

4 Lower the crankshaft into the crankcase taking care not to displace the thrust washers (photo).
5 Wipe out the main bearing shell recesses in the main bearing cap monobloc and fit the selected shells or if the original ones are being used again, return them to their original locations (photo).
6 Oil the crankshaft journals and crankpins and fit the cap monobloc (photo).
7 Fit the cap bolts and tighten to the specified torque (photo).
8 Now check the crankshaft endfloat either using a dial gauge or by inserting a feeler blade between the machined shoulder of a crankshaft web and the thrust washers. If the endfloat is outside the specified tolerance then the thrust washer thickness must be incorrect (photo).
9 Lay the engine on its side and fit the piston/connecting rods as described in Section 16.
10 Fit the oil pump having smeared its mounting face with jointing compound.
11 Fit the oil pick-up tube and strainer using a new gasket at its mounting flange (photos).
12 Using a new gasket and seals, fit the sump pan as described in Section 14.
13 Tighten all bolts and nuts to the specified torque.

27.2 Main bearing shell in crankcase

27.3A Oiling main bearing shells

27.3B Crankshaft thrust washer

27.4 Lowering crankshaft into position

27.5 Main bearing shell in monobloc

27.6 Fitting monobloc

27.7 Tightening main bearing monobloc bolts

27.8 Checking crankshaft endfloat

27.11A Oil pick-up tube gasket

27.11B Oil pick-up tube and brackets

14 Bolt on the crankshaft rear oil seal retainer complete with new seal and having applied jointing compound to its mounting face (photos).
15 Fit the cylinder head complete with camshaft and rocker shaft as described in Section 13.
16 Refit the flywheel (or driveplate – automatic transmission), tightening new bolts to the specified torque and having applied locking fluid to their threads (photos).
17 Refer to Chapter 2 and fit the coolant pump. Bolt on the thermostat housing using a new gasket. Use a new O-ring and connect the coolant tube between the pump and thermostat housing (photos).
18 Fit the timing belt tensioner (photo).
19 Fit the belt inner guide, the crankshaft sprocket and key, the timing belt and the belt outer guide, convex side to belt (photos).
20 Fit the belt lower cover, the crankshaft pulley and bolt. Set the crankshaft so that the pulley and cover timing marks are in alignment.
21 Fit the crankcase breather and the oil dipstick guide tube (photo).
22 Connect the timing belt to the camshaft and coolant pump sprockets as described in Section 8 and tension the belt as described in Section 7.
23 Fit the timing belt upper cover triangular-shaped backing plate and then the upper cover (photo).
24 Check and adjust the valve clearances.
25 Fit the rocker cover using a new gasket (photo).
26 Tighten the domed nuts, but do not overtighten them (photo).

27.14A Crankshaft rear oil seal retainer

27.14B Tightening crankshaft rear oil seal retainer bolts

27.16A Applying thread locking fluid to flywheel bolts

27.16B Tightening flywheel bolts

27.17A Bolting on the thermostat housing

27.17B Coolant tube and O-ring

27.18 Timing belt tensioner

27.19A Timing belt inner guide

27.19B Crankshaft sprocket with integral key

27.21 Crankcase breather (oil separator)

27.23 Timing belt upper cover backing plate (arrowed)

27.25 Rocker cover gasket

27.26 Tightening rocker cover nuts

28 Engine ancillary components – refitting

1 Refit and centralise the clutch (Chapter 5).
2 Bolt on the engine mounting brackets.
3 Screw on a new oil filter cartridge and insert the dipstick.
4 Fit the manifolds to the cylinder head using new gaskets. Fit the hot air collector to the exhaust manifold.
5 Fit the carburettor to the inlet manifold.
6 Fit the fuel pump (Chapter 3).
7 Fit the alternator (Chapter 12).
8 Fit the distributor (Chapter 4).

29 Engine/manual transmission – reconnection and refitting

1 Support the engine in an upright position.
2 Apply a smear of grease to the gearbox input (clutch) shaft.
3 Offer the transmission to the engine and slide the input shaft

through the splined hub of the driven plate until the flywheel housing mates with the rear face of the crankcase. If any difficulty is experienced, it may be due to the clutch driven plate not having been correctly centralised or the shaft and hub splines not being aligned. If the latter, have an assistant turn the crankshaft pulley bolt slightly while pushing on the gearbox (photo).
4 Insert the connecting bolts and tighten to the specified torque.
5 Bolt on the starter motor and the flywheel housing cover plate.
6 Attach the lifting gear to the engine/transmission and hoist it up, then down into the engine compartment. Take care that nothing is damaged during the lowering process particularly the radiator and brake master cylinder (photo).
7 Reconnect the engine and transmission mountings.
8 Connect the exhaust downpipe.
9 Connect the gear selector rod and the torque rod.
10 With the steering in full left-hand lock, connect the left-hand driveshaft making sure that the shaft securing clip snaps positively into engagement in the differential side gear.
11 Turn the steering to full right-hand lock and connect the right-hand driveshaft.

29.3 Connecting transmission to engine

29.6 Lowering engine/transmission into engine compartment

29.12A Front splash guard panel

29.12B Side splash guard panel

12 Fit the splash guard panels (photos).
13 Reconnect the suspension lower arm balljoints to the hub carriers.
14 Remove the lifting hoist.
15 Fit the front roadwheels and remove the safety stands.
16 Reconnect the heater and coolant hoses (photo).
17 Reconnect the fuel feed hose to the pump.
18 Connect the clutch cable.
19 Connect the speedometer drive cable to the transmission, also the tachometer drive (if fitted).
20 Connect the reverse lamp switch leads.
21 Connect the leads to the rear of the alternator.
22 Connect the carburettor controls including the wiring harness plug.
23 Connect the HT and LT leads to the coil.
24 Connect the vacuum hoses.
25 Connect the brake servo vacuum hose.
26 Connect the transmission and engine earth cables (photos).
27 Fit the battery and its tray and connect the leads.
28 Fit the air cleaner and connect the vacuum hoses to it. Also fit the air intake duct to the inlet on the wing valance.
29 With the help of an assistant fit the bonnet.
30 Fill the engine with oil and the cooling system with antifreeze mixture. Refill the transmission with oil if it was drained (photo).

30 Engine/automatic transmission – reconnection and refitting

1 Support the engine in an upright position.
2 Check that the torque converter is pushed fully into its housing.
3 Offer the transmission to the engine, insert the connecting bolts and tighten them. Remember that some bolts including those at the base of the torque converter housing must be inserted into their holes in the transmission casing before the engine and transmission are fully connected.
4 Insert the driveplate to torque converter bolts. The crankshaft will have to be turned to align the bolt holes and screw in the bolts one at a time through the starter motor aperture.
5 Bolt on the starter motor and converter housing cover plate.
6 The refitting operations are similar to those described in the preceding Section for cars with manual transmission, but ignoring reference to the clutch and gear selector controls.
7 Connect the transmission fluid cooler pipes.
8 Connect the reverse lamp/inhibitor switch leads.
9 Connect the kickdown cable and selector cable and check their adjustment (Chapter 7).
10 Check and top up the transmission fluid.

29.16 Heater and coolant hoses at thermostat housing

29.26A Engine earth bonding cable

29.26B Transmission earth bonding cable

29.30 Filling the engine with oil

31 Initial start up after major overhaul

1 Before starting the engine, check that all hoses, controls and electrical leads have been connected.
2 Make sure that tools and rags have been removed from the engine compartment.
3 Starting may take a little longer than usual as the fuel pump and carburettor must first fill with fuel.

4 Have the throttle speed screw turned in an extra turn to increase the engine idle speed. This will help to offset the stiffness of the new engine components.
5 Check the ignition timing.
6 If the majority of internal components have been renewed, treat the engine as a new one and restrict speed for the 1000 km (600 miles).
7 It is recommended that the engine oil is renewed at the end of the first 1000 km (600 miles). Also the tension of the drivebelts should be checked and the idle speed and mixture adjusted if necessary.

32 Fault diagnosis – 1.3 engine

Symptom	Reason(s)
Engine will not crank or cranks very slowly	Discharged battery Poor battery connections Starter motor fault
Engine cranks but will not start	No fuel Ignition circuit fault Fuel system fault Leak in PCV lines Leak in intake manifold Leak in hot idle compensator line
Engine stalls or rough idle	Leak in PCV line Leak in intake manifold Leak in hot idle compensator line Very weak mixture Incorrect valve clearances
Hesitation or poor acceleration	Incorrectly adjusted mixture Clogged air cleaner Incorrect valve clearances
Excessive oil consumption	Worn piston rings or cylinder bores Worn oil seals or leaking gaskets
Excessive mechanical noise from engine	Incorrect valve clearances General internal wear
Pinking on acceleration	Ignition too advanced Fuel octane too low Overheating Carbon build up in engine Excessive oil vapour being drawn into crankcase breather system Upper cylinder lubricant being used Weak mixture

Part B 1.6 (1598 cc) engine

33 General description

The engine is of four-cylinder, in-line camshaft type, mounted transversely at the front of the car.

The crankshaft is supported in five shell-type main bearings. Thrust washers are fitted to the centre main bearing in the crankcase to control crankshaft endfloat.

The connecting rods are attached to the crankshaft by horizontally split shell-type big-end bearings, and to the pistons by interference fit gudgeon pins. The aluminium alloy pistons are of the slipper type and have their gudgeon pins offset to the thrust side to reduce piston slap. Two compression rings and a three-piece oil control ring are fitted to each piston.

The overhead camshaft is mounted in a carrier attached to the cylinder head and is driven via a toothed belt by the crankshaft. The camshaft operates the valves through inverted bucket type tappets which are also housed in the camshaft carrier. Tappet adjustment is by shims fitted between the valve stems and the tappet buckets.

Fig. 1.11 Cut-away view of the 1.6 engine fitted with fuel injection (Sec 33)

Fig. 1.12 External components — 1.6 engine (Sec 33)

1   Cylinder block/crankcase
2   Cylinder head gasket
3   Cylinder head
4   O-ring seal
5   Hollow dowel
6   Cylinder head bolt with threaded extension
7   Cylinder head bolt
8   Camshaft carrier
9   Cover gaskets
10 Camshaft cover
11 Camshaft cover
12 Gasket
13 Coolant outlet elbow
14 Thermostat
15 Coolant thermistor
16 Thermostat housing
17 Coolant inlet elbow
18 Oil filler cap
19 Oil filler tube
20 Spark plug
21 Transmission adaptor plate
22 Crankshaft rear oil seal
23 Dipstick guide tube
24 Oil dipstick
25 Crankshaft sensor
26 Knock sensor
27 Sump pan gasket
28 Sump pan
29 Oil separator
30 Drain plug
31 Oil pick-up strainer
32 Main bearing cap
33 Main bearing shells
34 Coolant pump
35 Timing belt tensioner
36 Oil filter
37 Oil pressure switch
38 Crankshaft front oil seal
39 Oil pump
40 Oil pressure relief valve
41 Drive belt
42 Crankshaft pulley
43 Timing belt lower cover
44 Timing belt upper cover

Fig. 1.13 Internal components (1.6 engine) (Sec 33)

1 Timing belt
2 Camshaft sprocket
3 Camshaft front oil seal
4 Camshaft locating plate
5 Camshaft
6 Gudgeon pin
7 Pistons rings and piston
8 Connecting rod and cap
9 Big-end bearing shell
10 Crankshaft
11 Main bearing shell
12 Woodruff key
13 Belt guide plate
14 Crankshaft sprocket
15 Crankshaft pulley
16 Pulley bolt and washer
17 Timing belt tensioner
18 Tappet (cam follower) and shim
19 Inlet valve, oil seal, spring, cap, cotters
20 Exhaust valve
21 Piston/connecting rod
22 Crankshaft thrust washers

The inlet and exhaust valves are mounted at an angle in the cylinder head and are each closed by a single valve spring.

The oil pump, pressure relief valve and full-flow oil filter are located in a housing attached to the front of the cylinder block. The rotor type oil pump is driven directly by the crankshaft.

The distributor rotor is driven directly by the camshaft whereas the fuel pump is operated by an eccentric camshaft lobe. The toothed timing belt also drives the coolant pump and a separate drivebelt is used for the alternator, driven by a sprocket on the crankshaft.

34 Lubrication system

1 The oil pump is of rotor type and the oil pump housing incorporates an oil pressure relief valve.
2 The full-flow canister type oil filter is screwed onto the oil pump housing.
3 Pressurised oil is supplied to the crankshaft and camshaft bearings through oil galleries and drillings.

35 Engine oil and filter

Refer to Part A, Section 3.

36 Crankcase ventilation system

Refer to Part A, Section 4.

37 Major operations possible without removing the engine

Refer to Part A, Section 5.
Warning: *vehicles equipped with air conditioning:*

Whenever overhaul of a major nature is being undertaken to the engine and components of the air conditioning system obstruct the work and such items of the system cannot be unbolted and moved aside sufficiently far within the limits of their flexible connecting pipes, to avoid such obstruction the system should be discharged by your dealer or a competent refrigeration engineer.

As the system must be completely evacuated before recharging, the necessary vacuum equipment to do this is only likely to be available at a specialist.

The refrigerant fluid is Freon 12 and although harmless under normal conditions, contact with the eyes or skin must be avoided. If Freon comes into contact with a naked flame, then a poisonous gas will be created which is injurious to health.

38 Valve clearances – adjustment

1 This is not a routine servicing job and will normally only be required after a high mileage has been covered, overhaul has been carried out or the engine becomes noisy.
2 To check the valve clearances, disconnect the battery negative terminal then undo the retaining bolts and lift off the camshaft carrier covers. Note which bolts also secure cable and hose retaining clips.
3 Using a feeler gauge, check the clearance between the cam lobe and the tappet bucket of each valve in the order given in the following table and record each clearance. The engine may be turned using a spanner or socket on the crankshaft pulley bolt. If necessary remove the access panel from under the right-hand wheel arch to provide greater access to the pulley bolt (photo).

Check No 1 tappet with No 8 valve fully open
Check No 3 tappet with No 6 valve fully open
Check No 5 tappet with No 4 valve fully open
Check No 2 tappet with No 7 valve fully open
Check No 8 tappet with No 1 valve fully open
Check No 6 tappet with No 3 valve fully open
Check No 4 tappet with No 5 valve fully open
Check No 7 tappet with No 2 valve fully open

4 Once the readings have been tabulated for all valves it should be noted that, unless new parts have been fitted or the valve seats reground, adjustment of the valve tappet clearance to the standard setting is only necessary if the clearance of either inlet or exhaust is less than 0.30 mm (0.012 in).
5 If adjustment is necessary, refer to Section 43 and remove the camshaft and tappets (cam followers).
6 Remove the adjusting shim from each maladjusted tappet bucket in turn and note its thickness. The shim reference number is engraved on the face of the shim – see Specifications. By using the following calculation, determine the thickness of the new shim required to give the correct tappet clearance: (photo)

A = clearance measured in paragraph 3
B = thickness of existing shim
C = correct clearance
New shim thickness required = $A + B - C$

7 With new shims obtained as necessary, refer to Section 43 and refit the camshaft and tappets.

38.3 Checking a valve clearance

38.6 Valve clearance adjusting shim

39.1A Removing timing belt upper cover

39.1B Timing belt lower cover (screws arrowed)

39 Timing belt – tensioning

1   Remove both Sections of the timing belt cover (photos).
2   Slacken the tensioner fixing bolts and then engage a torque wrench with a 9.5 mm (3/8 in) square drive in the tensioner bracket hole (photo).
3   Apply torque in a clockwise direction until the following figure is obtained:

    Used belt   *14 Nm (10.3 lbf ft)*
    New belt   *20 Nm (15 lbf ft)*

4   Keep the specified torque applied while the tensioner bracket bolts are tightened.
5   If there is any possibility that the timing sprockets were rotated while the belt was slack, check that when the crankshaft pulley timing marks are in alignment, the camshaft sprocket marks are in alignment. If this is not the case, slacken and reposition the belt and then retension it again.

40 Timing belt – removal and refitting

1   Jack up the front of the car and support it on axle stands.
2   Remove the right-hand front roadwheel and the access panel under the wheel arch.
3   Disconnect the battery negative terminal.
4   Slacken the alternator pivot mounting bolt and the adjustment arm bolts. Move the alternator towards the engine and remove the drivebelt from the pulleys (photo).
5   Lift off the timing belt upper cover then undo the screws and remove the lower cover.
6   Using a socket or spanner on the crankshaft pulley bolt, turn the engine over until the dimple on the rear face of the camshaft sprocket is aligned with the notch on the camshaft carrier. Check also that the notch on the crankshaft pulley is aligned with the timing mark on the oil pump housing (photos).
7   Slacken the two timing belt tensioner retaining bolts and move the tensioner away from the engine (photo).
8   Slip the timing belt off the three sprockets and remove it from the engine (photo). Do not turn the camshaft sprocket while the belt is off.
9   If the original belt is to be reused, mark it with chalk to indicate its direction of rotation and also its outer facing edge. Store the belt on its edge while off the engine.
10 Refitting the timing belt is a reversal of removal. Tension the belt as described in the preceding Section.

39.2 Adjusting timing belt tension

Fig. 1.14 Timing belt tensioner (Sec 39)

1 *Timing belt*   3 *3/8in. drive adjuster hole*
2 *Tensioner securing bolts*

40.4 Alternator drivebelt

40.6A Camshaft sprocket timing marks

40.6B Crankshaft pulley timing marks

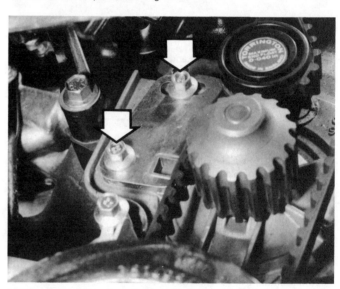
40.7 Timing belt tensioner bolts (arrowed)

40.8 Slipping timing belt from camshaft sprocket

41 Camshaft oil seals – renewal

Front oil seal
1 Remove the timing belt upper cover.
2 Remove the timing belt lower cover.
3 Turn the crankshaft pulley bolt in a clockwise direction until the pulley TDC marks are in alignment. Also check that the camshaft sprocket dimple aligns with the notch.
4 Retract the belt tensioner and slip the belt from the camshaft sprocket.
5 Lock the camshaft sprocket and unscrew its securing bolt. Remove the sprocket.
6 Using a suitable tool, prise out the oil seal.
7 Oil the lip of the new seal and fit it so that the lip is inwards.
8 Refit the sprocket and tighten the bolt.
9 Check that the timing marks are in alignment and fit the belt.
10 Adjust the belt tension as described in Section 39.
11 Refit the belt covers.

Rear oil seal
12 Remove the distributor cap, rotor arm and shield (Chapter 4).
13 Prise out the oil seal and discard it.

41.7 Fitting camshaft front oil seal

41.14 Fitting camshaft rear oil seal

14 Oil the lip of the new seal and fit it with its lip inwards (photo).
15 Refit the distributor, rotor arm and shield.

42 Crankshaft front oil seal – renewal

1 Remove the timing belt as described in Section 40.
2 Engage a low gear and have an assistant apply the brakes hard. Unscrew the crankshaft pulley bolt (photo).
3 Remove the crankshaft pulley and belt guide plate (photo).
4 Remove the crankshaft sprocket and inner guide plate (photos).
5 Using a suitable tool, extract the oil seal.
6 Grease the seal lips and tape the shoulder on the crankshaft to prevent damage to the lips and press it into its seat. Remove the tape.
7 Fit the belt inner guide plate, the crankshaft sprocket, the outer guide plate and pulley.
8 Prevent the crankshaft from rotating and tighten the pulley bolt.
9 Refit the timing belt (Section 40).
10 Tension the belt (Section 39).

42.2 Crankshaft pulley bolt and washer

42.3 Removing crankshaft pulley

42.4A Removing crankshaft sprocket

42.4B Crankshaft sprocket inner belt guide plate

43.6 Camshaft carrier cover

43 Camshaft and tappets (cam followers) – removal and refitting

1   Disconnect the battery negative lead.
2   Remove the air cleaner.
3   Remove the timing belt (Section 40).
4   Remove the fuel pump (Chapter 3).
5   Remove the distributor cap, rotor arm and shield.
6   Undo the retaining bolts and lift off the two camshaft carrier covers. Note the position of the cable and hose clips on the cover bolts (photo).
7   Using a suitable socket, or spanner, undo the camshaft sprocket retaining bolt. Engage a stout screwdriver or bar through the sprocket holes and in contact with the carrier to prevent the camshaft turning.
8   Remove the sprocket retaining bolt and washer then withdraw the sprocket from the camshaft. Carefully ease it off using two levers if it is tight.
9   Using pliers, withdraw the camshaft locating plate from the carrier (photo).

43.9 Camshaft locating plate

10   Progressively slacken the camshaft carrier retaining bolts and, when all tension on the bolts has been relieved, remove them.
11   Raise the camshaft carrier slightly and push down the tappet buckets until the cam lobes are clear.
12   Move the camshaft towards the rotor arm end until sufficient clearance exists to enable the oil seal at the sprocket end to be removed. Hook the seal out using a screwdriver.
13   Now move the camshaft towards the sprocket end and remove the remaining oil seal in the same way.
14   The camshaft can now be carefully removed from the rotor arm end of the carrier (photo).
15   Lift out each of the tappet buckets in turn and keep them in strict order. Make sure that the small adjustment shim has remained in place inside the bucket (photo).
16   Withdraw the camshaft carrier from the cylinder head noting the location of the O-ring oil seal (photo).

Refitting

17   Smear the tappet shims with petroleum jelly and then locate the shims in the recesses of their respective tappet buckets.
18   Place the camshaft carrier in position on the cylinder head and fit the tappet buckets to their locations in the carrier.
19   Lift the carrier slightly, push the tappet buckets down and carefully

43.14 Removing camshaft from carrier

43.15 Removing cam follower

43.16 Removing camshaft carrier from cylinder head

insert the camshaft. Fit the camshaft locating plate to the carrier front bearing journal.

20 Fit the camshaft carrier retaining bolts and progressively tighten them to the specified torque.

21 Before proceeding further the valve clearances should be checked and adjusted using the procedure described in Section 38. For the purpose of valve clearance checking the camshaft may be turned using an adjustable wrench on the square protrusion between No 6 and 7 camshaft lobe (photo).

22 With the tappet clearance checked and the correct new shims obtained as necessary, remove the camshaft, camshaft carrier and the tappet buckets (if not already done).

23 Locate a new O-ring seal in the carrier recess then fill the carrier peripheral groove with Loctite 574 sealant (photo).

24 Place the carrier in position on the cylinder head once more and insert the tappet buckets in their respective locations (photos).

25 Lift the carrier slightly, push down the tappet buckets and slide the camshaft into the carrier. Refit the camshaft locating plate.

26 Fit the camshaft carrier retaining bolts and progressively tighten them to the specified torque.

27 Thoroughly lubricate the lips of new camshaft front and rear oil seals and carefully locate them over the camshaft journals and into their position in the carrier. Tap the seals squarely into the carrier.

28 Place the camshaft sprocket on the camshaft and use the retaining bolt and washer to draw the sprocket fully home. Tighten the retaining bolt to the specified torque (photo).

29 Locate the one-piece rubber gaskets in the camshaft carrier covers using new gaskets if necessary.

30 Apply a continuous bead of RTV sealant to the cover mating faces in the camshaft carrier.

31 Fit the two covers, retaining bolts and brackets, where applicable.

32 Tighten the cover bolts progressively to the specified torque.

44 Cylinder head – removal and refitting

All models

1 Disconnect the battery negative lead.

2 Drain the cooling system (Chapter 2).

43.21 Camshaft flats (arrowed) for turning with spanner

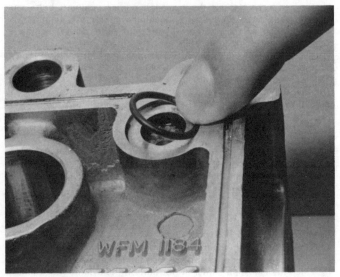

43.23 O-ring in camshaft carrier recess

43.24A Lowering camshaft carrier onto cylinder head

43.24B Cam followers in their bores

43.28 Refitting camshaft sprocket

Carburettor models

3   Disconnect the fuel inlet hose from the carburettor. Unbolt the fuel pump and place it to one side with the hoses still attached (photo).
4   Disconnect the air temperature sensor hose from the air temperature control.
5   Disconnect the brake servo vacuum hose from the inlet manifold.

Fuel injection models

6   Disconnect the fuel inlet and return hoses from the fuel rail pipes. Plug the hoses and pipes.
7   Disconnect the vacuum hoses from the inlet chamber and the multi-plug from the air valve stepper motor (photo).
8   Disconnect the multi-plugs from the fuel injectors, the fuel temperature switch and the coolant temperature thermistor.
9   Disconnect the throttle cable from the throttle lever and the abutment bracket.
10 Disconnect the air inlet hose from the throttle housing.

All models

11 Release the dipstick guide tube from the camshaft front cover, and the oil filler tube support bracket from the cylinder head.

44.3 Removing fuel pump with hoses attached

44.7 Carburettor stepping motor wiring plug

12 Disconnect the coolant hoses from the thermostat housing, the heater inlet elbow and the inlet manifold (photos).

Carburettor models
13 Disconnect the fuel drain pipe from the carburettor and manifold.
14 Disconnect the throttle control cable and the breather and vacuum pipes from the carburettor. If automatic transmission is fitted disconnect the kickdown cable from the carburettor throttle lever.
15 Disconnect the multi-plugs from the starting and economy devices.

All models
16 Disconnect the spark plug leads and the coil HT lead from the distributor cap.
17 Extract the screws and remove the distributor cap, rotor arm and shield.

Carburettor models
18 Disconnect the inlet manifold heater, heater thermostat and coolant sensor leads.

All models
19 Disconnect the support struts and the exhaust downpipe from the manifold (photo).
20 On manual transmission models, release the clutch cable from its clips.
21 Refer to Chapter 12 and remove the alternator and its bracket. Remove the camshaft covers (photo).
22 Set the timing marks in alignment then remove the timing belt covers. Then retract the timing belt tensioner and slip the timing belt from the camshaft sprocket.
23 Support the weight of the engine on a hoist or with a jack and block of wood placed under the sump pan and then remove the through-bolt from the right-hand engine mounting. Remove the nuts

which hold the mounting to the engine and remove the mounting.
24 Unscrew the cylinder head bolts progressively starting with the centre ones and working towards each end of the head.
25 Lift the head straight up off its locating dowels. If it needs to be prised, use the lugs provided, never insert a tool in the gasket joint.
26 Peel off the gasket.
27 Refer to Section 24, Part A for details of dismantling and decarbonising.

Refitting
28 Ensure that the cylinder block and head mating faces are perfectly clean and free from any traces of oil, grease or water.
29 Place a new head gasket in position over the cylinder block dowels (photo).
30 Check that the camshaft TDC marks are aligned (all valves closed).
31 Lower the cylinder head into position and, with their threads lightly oiled, refit the retaining bolts (photo).
32 Tighten the cylinder head bolts in the sequence shown in Fig. 1.15. Tighten to the 1st stage tightening torque, then to the 2nd stage torque. Finally tighten each bolt in sequence by a further 90° (quarter turn).
33 Connect the right-hand engine mounting and remove the hoist or jack.
34 Fit the alternator mounting bracket, tightening the cylinder block screw before those which go into the cylinder head.
35 Fit the timing belt and tension it as described in Sections 40 and 39.
36 Fit the timing belt lower cover and then check that the camshaft locating plate is free in its slot. Turn the camshaft if necessary to free it.
37 Fit the timing belt upper cover.
38 Locate new gaskets in the camshaft cover grooves, having smeared the groove with jointing compound first (photo).
39 Fit the camshaft covers (photo).
40 Refit the alternator and tension the drivebelt (Chapter 12).

44.12A Thermostat housing hoses

44.12B Coolant inlet elbow hoses

44.19 Manifold support strut bolt

44.21 Alternator mounting bracket bolts (arrowed)

44.29 Cylinder head gasket in position

44.31 Lowering cylinder head onto block

Fig. 1.15 Cylinder head bolt tightening sequence (Sec 44)

44.38 Camshaft carrier cover and sealing strips

44.39 Camshaft carrier covers in position showing cable clips

41 Connect the throttle cable, dipstick guide tube and fit the oil filler tube.
42 Reconnect the clutch cable (manual transmission models) and connect the exhaust pipe and manifold support struts.
43 Connect all electrical leads, multi-plugs, hoses and control cables according to the fuel system type fitted by reversing the removal operations described in earlier paragraphs of this Section.
44 Fill the cooling system and connect the battery.

45 Sump pan – removal and refitting

1 Drain the engine oil.
2 Disconnect the crankcase breather hose from the oil separator. Remove the oil separator from the sump pan (photo).
3 Unscrew the bolts which hold the sump connecting plate to the gearbox adaptor plate. Slacken the extension bolts then remove the manifold support stay bolt (photo).
4 Disconnect the alternator wiring harness (photo).
5 Remove the sump pan fixing screws, remove the sump pan and gasket (photo).

45.2 Removing oil separator from sump pan

45.3 Sump pan to adaptor plate bolts

45.4 Alternator wiring harness clips (arrowed)

45.5 Removing the sump pan

6 Before refitting the sump pan, make sure that the crankcase and sump pan mating faces are clean.

7 Apply a bead of RTV sealant to the centre of the semi-circular joint flanges allowing the bead to extend 12.5 mm (0.5 in) beyond the ends of the semi-circular profile (photo).

8 Fit a new gasket, offer up the sump pan and tighten the fixing screws evenly and progressively.

9 Refit and reconnect the disturbed components.

10 Refill the engine with oil.

46 Oil pump – removal and refitting

1 Remove the timing belt (Section 40).

2 Remove the sump pan (Section 45).

3 Disconnect the lead from the oil pressure switch.

4 Unbolt and remove the oil pick-up tube.

5 Unscrew the oil filter cartridge.

6 Undo the bolt securing the crankshaft pulley to the crankshaft, engage 1st gear (manual transmission) and firmly apply the footbrake to prevent crankshaft rotation as the bolt is undone. On automatic transmission models it is necessary to remove the starter motor (Chapter 12) and prevent the crankshaft from turning by inserting a suitable bar into the driveplate ring gear. If the engine is on the bench refit two of the clutch pressure plate retaining bolts to the crankshaft and engage a stout bar between them (photo).

7 Withdraw the crankshaft pulley followed by the crankshaft sprocket and guide plate.

8 Undo the pump retaining bolts, noting their lengths and locations, and also the retaining plate fitted under the top centre bolt.

9 Withdraw the oil pump housing and recover the gasket.

Refitting

10 Make sure that the mating faces of the pump and cylinder block are clean then place a new gasket in position on the pump housing.

11 Wrap some insulating tape around the end of the crankshaft to protect the oil seal as the pump is fitted.

12 Liberally lubricate the lips of the oil seal and the insulating tape with engine oil.

13 Position the flats of the pump inner rotor to correspond with the flats on the crankshaft and carefully fit the pump to the cylinder block (photo).

14 Remove the tape.

15 Refit the pump retaining bolts. The top centre bolt also secures the coolant pump (photo).

16 Tighten the bolts evenly to the specified torque.

45.7 Applying RTV sealant to sump pan joint

46.6 One method of locking crankshaft

46.13 Fitting the oil pump

46.15 Oil pump fixing bolts

46.17A Oil pick-up tube O-ring

46.17B Oil pick-up tube and strainer

17 Refit the oil pick-up tube (photos).
18 Screw on the oil filter cartridge.
19 Refit the sump pan.
20 Refit and tension the timing belt.

47 Transmission adaptor plate – removal and refitting

1 This operation can only be carried out after removal of the transmission.
2 Remove the clutch and flywheel (manual transmission) or driveplate (automatic transmission).
3 Remove the sump pan (Section 45).
4 Remove the oil filler tube.
5 Remove the crankshaft sensor.
6 Undo the bolts securing the adaptor plate to the cylinder block.
7 Tap the adaptor plate using a soft-faced mallet to free it from the locating dowels and remove it from the engine. Remove the two sump retaining bolts and gearbox retaining bolt from their captive recesses in the adaptor plate (photo).
8 Ensure that the mating faces of the cylinder block and adaptor plate are thoroughly clean then apply a bead of RTV sealant to the adaptor plate face (photo).

47.7 Sump pan bolts in transmission adaptor plate

47.8 Applying RTV sealant to transmission adaptor plate

47.9 Sealant application point on gearbox retaining bolt head (arrowed)

47.10 Fitting adaptor plate to cylinder block

9 Make sure that the two sump retaining bolts and the gearbox retaining bolt are fitted in their adaptor plate locations and apply additional sealant to their bolt heads (photo).
10 Liberally lubricate the lips of the crankshaft rear oil seal in the adaptor plate then carefully fit the adaptor plate to the cylinder block (photo).
11 Refit the retaining bolts and tighten them evenly to the specified torque.
12 Refit the components described in paragraphs 2 to 5 of this Section.

48 Connecting rod big-end bearings and piston rings – renewal

1 These operations will normally be carried out at the time of complete engine overhaul, but the work may be done without removing the engine from the car where it is necessary to reduce oil consumption and to improve the oil pressure.
2 Refer to Section 45 and remove the sump pan. If new piston rings are being fitted, remove the cylinder head as described in Section 44.
3 Inspect the big-end caps for identification. They should be marked 1 to 4 from the crankshaft pulley and on the side nearest to the oil dipstick guide tube. If not, mark them with a centre-punch or a file.
4 Renewal of the bearing shells and piston ring is as described in Section 16, but ignore the reference to shell coding. As the shells are being renewed with identical ones, the size will be marked on the back of each shell.
5 The compression rings have their upper faces marked TOP.
6 Stagger the piston ring end gaps so that those for the compression rings are at 90° on the non-thrust side of the piston. The end gaps of the oil control rails and expander should be located over the gudgeon pin.
7 Check that with the piston/rod assembly in its bore, the mark on the piston crown which may be FRONT, A or an arrow is pointing to the crankshaft pulley.
8 Refit the sump pan and cylinder head (Sections 45 and 44).

49 Engine/transmission mountings – renewal

1 The mountings may be renewed with the engine/transmission in the car provided the weight of the engine or transmission is taken on a hoist or using a workshop jack with a block of wood as an insulator.
2 Tighten all nuts and bolts to the specified torque. Disconnect and renew one mounting at a time.

Fig. 1.16 Piston rings (Sec 48)

1   *Compression ring markings*
2   *Compression ring end gaps (90° on non-thrust side of piston)*
3   *Oil control rails and expander*

Fig. 1.17 Engine/transmission mountings (Sec 49)

1 to 7 = Bolt tightening sequence

50 Engine – method of removal

The engine should be removed upwards from the engine compartment complete with the transmission.

51 Engine/manual transmission – removal and separation

1 With the help of an assistant, remove the bonnet as described in Chapter 11.
2 Disconnect and remove the battery and the battery tray.
3 Drain the cooling system.
4 Drain the engine oil, then unscrew and remove the oil filter cartridge.
5 Remove the air cleaner and intake duct.
6 On fuel injection models, depressurise the fuel system and then disconnect all the electrical plugs and fuel connections described in Chapter 3 and paragraphs 6 to 10 in Section 44 in this Chapter. Release the fuel pump relay connector from its bracket.
7 Disconnect the multi-plug and remove the ignition ECU from its bracket. Release the earth cable from behind the bracket.
8 Disconnect the crankshaft sensor wiring plug then undo the two starter motor retaining bolts. Remove the starter, crankshaft sensor bracket (photos).
9 Disconnect the wiring plug at the knock sensor on the front face of the cylinder block (photos).
10 Spring back the clip and disconnect the wiring plug at the rear of the alternator.

51.8A Crankshaft sensor

51.8B Crankshaft sensor wiring plug

51.9A Knock sensor

51.9B Knock sensor wiring plug

11 Disconnect the wiring plug from the coolant temperature thermistor in the thermostat housing (photo).

12 Disconnect the inlet manifold induction heater lead at the wiring connector and the two wires at the inlet manifold induction temperature sensor (photo).

13 Disconnect the wire at the oil pressure switch adjacent to the crankshaft pulley (photo).

14 Disconnect the wiring plug at the carburettor stepping motor and the two leads at the fuel shut-off valve solenoid (photo).

15 Release the retaining clip and remove the fuel inlet hose from the fuel pump. Plug the hose after removal.

16 Pull the float chamber vent hose off the carburettor outlet and remove the hose and pipe from the engine (photo).

17 Detach the crankcase breather hoses at the carburettor, oil filter cap and oil separator, then remove the hose assembly.

18 Disconnect the vacuum hose from the inlet manifold banjo union, undo the union bolt and recover the two washers. Place the servo vacuum hose to one side.

19 Disconnect the throttle linkage.

20 Slacken the retaining clips and disconnect the heater hoses at the inlet manifold.

51.11 Coolant temperature thermistor wiring plug

51.12 Induction temperature sensor leads at the manifold

51.13 Oil pressure switch

51.14 Fuel shut-off solenoid

51.16 Float chamber vent hose (A) and crankcase breather hose (B)

21 Slacken the retaining clips and disconnect the heater hose and radiator bottom hose from the water inlet elbow followed by the expansion tank hose, radiator top hose and heater hose from the water outlet elbow and thermostat housing.
22 Refer to Chapter 5 and detach the clutch cable from the operating lever and gearbox bracket. Disconnect the reverse lamp switch leads (photo).
23 Undo and remove the bolt securing the speedometer cable to the gearbox. Withdraw the cable and pinion assembly and place them aside (photo).
24 Disconnect the gearchange linkage from the transmission.
25 Raise the front of the car and support it securely then remove the two front roadwheels.
26 Disconnect the exhaust downpipes from the manifold.
27 Fit an engine lifting bracket to the extended threads of the cylinder head studs nearest to the distributor cap.
28 Attach a suitable hoist and support the weight of the engine.
29 Place jacks under the front suspension lower suspension (track control) arms.
30 Unscrew the balljoint taper pin nuts and using a suitable splitter tool, disconnect the balljoint from the hub carrier. As they are released,

take care that the car is well supported under the body members with safety stands.
31 Remove the splash guard panels.
32 Turn the steering to full right-hand lock and release the inboard end of the right-hand driveshaft by prising with a lever inserted between the transmission housing and the shaft joint.
33 Release the left-hand driveshaft in a similar way after having turned the steering to full left-hand lock.
34 Unbolt the engine rear mounting bracket from the transmission casing.
35 Remove the through-bolt from the right-hand engine mounting and the bolts which hold the mounting bracket to the engine. Remove the mounting.
36 Remove the left-hand mounting from the transmission in a similar way.
37 Lift the engine/transmission slowly to clear the rear mounting bracket and remove the engine compartment.
38 Remove all external dirt by steam cleaning or by using a water soluble solvent.
39 Remove the cover plate from the face of the flywheel housing.
40 Unscrew and remove the flywheel housing to engine connecting

51.22 Reverse lamp switch leads

51.23 Speedometer drive cable and pinion

bolts and withdraw the transmission from the engine, supporting its weight so that it does not hang upon the input shaft while the shaft is engaged in the hub of the clutch driven plate (photo).

52 Engine/automatic transmission – removal and separation

1   Removal operations are very similar to those described in the preceding Section for cars with manual transmission, but of course ignore reference to the clutch cable and gear selector.
2   Select P and release the selector cable trunnion screw and then extract the screws which hold the abutment bracket to the transmission casing.
3   Disconnect the kickdown cable.
4   Carry out the operations described in Section 20, paragraphs 3 to 8.
5   Drain the cooling system and then disconnect the coolant hoses from the fluid cooler.

53 Engine dismantling – general

Refer to Part A, Section 21.

54 Engine ancillary components – removal

If the engine has been removed from the car for major overhaul or repair, the externally-mounted ancillary components given in the following list, should first be removed. Removal is straightforward, but where necessary reference should be made to the relevant Chapters of the manual as indicated. The removal sequence need not necessarily follow the order given.

Alternator (Chapter 12)
Timing belt covers –
Fuel pump (Chapter 3)
Distributor cap and rotor arm (Chapter 4)
Oil filler tube
Thermostat, housing and coolant inlet elbow (Chapter 2)
Alternator mounting bracket
Knock sensor
Crankshaft sensor (Chapter 4)
Spark plugs (Chapter 4)
Inlet and exhaust manifolds and carburettor (Chapter 3)
Clutch and flywheel assembly (Chapter 5)
Coolant pump (Chapter 2) – after removal of the timing belt
Oil filter
Dipstick
Fuel injection equipment (Chapter 3)

55 Engine – complete dismantling

1   Remove the timing belt (Section 40).
2   Remove the cylinder head (Section 44).
3   Remove the camshaft and tappets (cam followers) (Section 43).
4   Remove the sump pan (Section 45).
5   Remove the oil pump (Section 46).
6   Remove the transmission adaptor plate (Section 47).
7   Check the big-end caps for identification marks. If necessary use a centre punch on the caps and rods to identify them; mark them 1 to 4 on the dipstick tube side to ensure correct refitting. **Note** that No 1 is nearest to the crankshaft pulley end of the engine (photo).
8   Turn the crankshaft so that No 1 crankpin is at its lowest point. Using a suitable socket, undo the two nuts securing the connecting rod cap to the rod.
9   Withdraw the cap, complete with bearing shell.
10 Using the handle of a hammer, carefully push the piston and connecting rod up through the bore and withdraw it from the top of the cylinder block.
11 If there is a severe wear ridge at the top of the cylinder bore it may require removing using a ridge reamer or scraper to enable the piston rings to pass over it.

51.40 Withdrawing manual transmission from the engine

55.7 Big-end cap and rod match marks

12 Keep the bearing shells with their cap or rod if the shells are to be used again.
13 Remove the remaining pistons and rods in a similar way.
14 Check the crankcase and main bearing caps for identification marks and if no marks are present use a centre punch to mark them (photo).
15 Undo the bolts securing the main bearing caps and remove the caps, complete with bearing shells.
16 Before removing the crankshaft, check that the endfloat is within the specified limits by inserting feeler blades between No 4 crankshaft web and the thrust washers. If the clearance is not as specified, new thrust washers will be required for reassembly (photo).
17 Lift the crankshaft out of the crankcase then remove the main bearing shell upper halves and the thrust washers. Keep the main bearing shells in order with their respective caps (photos).

56 Cylinder head – dismantling and decarbonising

1   Remove the exhaust manifolds and carburettor (or fuel injection components).
2   Remove the distributor cap, rotor arm and shield (photos).

55.14 Main bearing cap and crankcase match marks

55.16 Checking crankshaft endfloat

55.17A Removing crankshaft from crankcase

55.17B Crankshaft thrust washer showing oil grooves

56.2A Distributor cap and shield

56.2B Removing rotor arm screw

3   Remove the thermostat housing and coolant inlet elbow.
4   Remove the camshaft and tappets (cam followers).
5   Removal of the valves, valve grinding procedure and other renovation operations are as described in Section 24 (photos).
6   When reassembling note the valve stem oil seal identification ring (Fig. 1.18) (photos).

57 Engine components – examination and renovation

1   All oil seals, gaskets and O-rings should be renewed as a matter of course and also main and big-end shell bearings unless they have had little wear and are in perfect condition.
2   With the engine completely dismantled, clean all the components and examine them for wear. Each part should be checked and where necessary renewed or renovated, as described in Section 25, but with the following differences.

Oil pump
3   Remove the oil filter from the pump housing if not already done.
4   Undo the six screws and lift off the pump backplate (photo).

56.5A Valve spring compressed showing split collets

56.5B Removing a valve

56.5C Removing a valve stem oil seal

Fig. 1.18 Valve stem oil seal identification (Sec 56)

A   Standard with one flange ring   B   Oversize with two flange rings

56.6A Fitting a valve stem oil seal

56.6B Valve spring and cap

57.4 Oil pump backplate screws

5   Lift out the two rotors from the pump body (photo).
6   Unscrew the pressure relief valve cap using a wide-bladed tool and remove the spring and plunger (photos).
7   Clean all the parts in paraffin or a suitable solvent and dry with a lint-free cloth. Examine the components for signs of scoring, wear ridges or other damage and renew the pump as a complete assembly if any of these conditions are apparent.

8   If the pump is satisfactory so far, refit the rotors to the pump body and check the rotor lobe clearance, outer rotor-to-body clearance and the outer rotor endfloat using feeler gauges and a straight-edge (photos).
9   Renew the pump if any of the clearances are outside the figures given in the Specifications.
10 If the pump is serviceable, renew the crankshaft front oil seal in the

57.5 Oil pump rotors

57.6A Unscrewing oil pump pressure relief valve cap

57.6B Relief valve components

57.8A Checking the oil pump rotor lobe clearance

57.8B Checking rotor to body clearance

57.8C Checking oil pump rotor endfloat

Fig. 1.19 Oil pump (Sec 57)

1 Oil pressure switch
2 Outer rotor
3 Pump backplate
4 Inner rotor
5 Pressure relief valve
   plunger
6 Pressure relief valve
   spring
7 Pressure relief valve cap
8 Oil pump body
9 Crankshaft front oil seal

Fig. 1.20 Oil pump lobe clearance measuring point (Sec 57)

pump housing. Tap the old seal out from the inside using a punch and fit a new seal using a tube, block of wood or socket by tapping it squarely into the housing (photos).

11 Lubricate the pressure relief valve plunger with clean engine oil and refit plunger followed by the spring and cap. Tighten the cap securely.

12 Liberally lubricate the two rotors with clean engine oil and place them in position in the pump housing.

13 Refit the pump backplate and secure with the six screws.

Camshaft and tappets (cam followers)

14 The camshaft itself should show no signs of wear, but if very slight score marks on the cams are noticed, they can be removed by gently rubbing down with very fine emery cloth or an oilstone. *The greatest care must be taken to keep the cam profiles smooth.*

15 Carefully examine the camshaft bearing surfaces for wear and, if evident, the camshaft must be renewed.

16 Check the fit of the camshaft in the carrier and if excessive bearing journal clearance is apparent a new carrier must be obtained. The camshaft bearings run directly in the machined journals of the carrier; renewable bearings are not used.

17 The faces of the tappet buckets which bear on the camshaft lobes should exhibit no signs of pitting, scoring, cracks or other forms of wear and should be a smooth sliding fit in the carrier. Slight scuffing and blackening of the tappet bucket sides is normal, providing this is not accompanied by scoring or wear ridges.

18 The small shims found inside the tappet bucket should show no signs of indentation from contact with the valve stem. Renew the shim with one of an identical size if wear has taken place. Make sure that each shim is kept with its tappet bucket and not interchanged.

Crankshaft and main bearings

19 The crankshaft may be reground and undersize bearings fitted as given in the Specifications.

58 Engine reassembly – general

1   To ensure maximum life with minimum trouble from a rebuilt engine, not only must everything be correctly assembled, but it must also be spotlessly clean. All oilways must be clear, and locking washers

57.10A Crankshaft front oil seal in oil pump body

57.10B Fitting a new seal to the oil pump

and spring washers must be fitted where indicated. Oil all bearings and other working surfaces thoroughly with engine oil during assembly.

2   Before assembly begins, renew any bolts or studs with damaged threads.

3   Gather together a torque wrench, oil can, clean rags and a set of engine gaskets and oil seals, together with a new oil filter.

4   A tube of Loctite 574 sealant will be required for the camshaft carrier to cylinder head joint face and an RTV silicone sealant for the remainder of the joint faces that do not have gaskets. These compounds, together with conventional gasket jointing compound, are available from BL dealers or motor factors.

59 Engine – complete reassembly

1   Clean the backs of the bearing shells and the bearing recesses in both the cylinder block and main bearing caps.

2   Press the main bearing shells into the cylinder block and caps and oil them liberally (photo).

3   Using a little grease, stick the thrust washers to each side of No 4

main bearing with their oilways facing away from the bearing.

4   Lower the crankshaft into position, then fit the main bearing caps in their previously noted locations (photo).

5   Insert and tighten evenly the main bearing cap bolts to the specified torque. Check that the crankshaft rotates freely, then check that the endfloat is within the specified limits by inserting a feeler blade between the crankshaft web and the thrust washers.

6   Clean the backs of the bearing shells and the recesses in the connecting rods and big-end caps.

7   Fit the big-end bearing shells into their connecting rod and cap locations and oil them liberally.

8   Position a piston ring compressor around No 1 piston then insert the connecting rod and piston into No 1 cylinder. With No 1 crankpin at its lowest point, drive the piston carefully into the cylinder with the wooden handle of a hammer, and at the same time guide the connecting rod onto the crankpin. Make sure that the mark FRONT, A or an arrow on the piston crown is towards the crankshaft pulley end of the engine (photo).

9   Fit the big-end cap in its previously noted position, then screw on the nuts and tighten them to the specified torque (photos).

59.2 Crankcase main bearing shell

59.4 Fitting front main bearing cap

59.8A Using piston ring compressor to fit piston/connecting rod

59.8B Piston crown marking

59.9A Fitting a big-end cap

59.9B Tightening big-end cap nuts

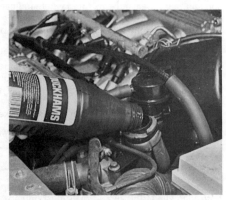

61.8 Refilling the engine with oil

10 Check that the crankshaft turns freely.
11 Repeat the procedures given in paragraphs 3 to 5 for No 4 piston, then turn the crankshaft through half a turn and repeat the procedure on No 2 and No 3 piston.
12 Refit the sump and oil pick-up tube, and the cylinder head with reference to the relevant Sections and Chapters of this manual.
13 Refit the transmission adaptor plate (Section 47).
14 Refit the oil pump (Section 46).
15 Refit the sump pan (Section 45).
16 Refit the camshaft and tappets (cam followers) (Section 43).
17 Refit the cylinder head (Section 44).
18 Refit and adjust the timing belt (Sections 39, 40).
19 Adjust the valve clearances (Section 38).

60 Engine ancillary components – refitting

Reverse the removal operations for the components listed in Section 54.

61 Engine/manual transmission – reconnection and refitting

1 The operations are a reversal of those for removal and separation described in Section 51, but observe the following special points.
2 Once the engine/transmission is lowered into position, fit the left-hand mounting and the right-hand mounting. Tighten the left-hand bracket to gearbox bolts. Do not tighten the right-hand mounting to engine bracket or left-hand mounting to valance bolts nor the mounting through-bolts.
3 Check the alignment of the rear moounting bracket to the gearbox, adjusting the height of the engine/transmission as necessary, and then tighten the bracket to transmission bolts.
4 Tighten the left-hand and right-hand mounting through-bolts.
5 Check the rear mounting rubber. If it is distorted forwards or rearwards, slacken the bracket to mounting bolts, re-align the

mounting rubbers and tighten the bolts.
6 Finally tighten the right-hand mounting to engine nuts and the left-hand mounting to valance bolts.
7 Make sure that the driveshaft circlips are positively engaged in the differential side gears.
8 Refill the cooling system with antifreeze mixture and the engine with oil (photo).

62 Engine/automatic transmission – reconnection and refitting

1 Reverse the removal and separation operations described in Section 52 and Section 20 paragraphs 3 to 8.
2 When connecting the selector cable, set the hand control lever in P and press the lever on the transmission casing fully downwards (anticlockwise). Insert the selector cable into the trunnion and secure the support bracket to the transmission casing. Tighten the trunnion screw. Check that the starter motor only operates in N or P selector positions.
3 Reconnect and adjust (Chapter 7) the kickdown cable.
4 Reconnect the coolant hoses to the fluid cooler.
5 Check and top up the transmission fluid.

63 Initial start-up after major overhaul

Refer to Part A, Section 31.

64 Fault diagnosis – 1.6 engine

1 The symptoms and reasons for engine faults are essentially as listed in Section 32 of Part A, but refer also to Fault Diagnosis in Chapters 3 and 4 as all models are equipped with programmed electronic ignition and some models have a fuel injection system.

Chapter 2
Cooling, heating and air conditioning systems

Contents

Specifications

System type ....
Front mounted radiator, with expansion tank, timing belt driven coolant pump and electric fan. Fresh air heater/ventilation with air conditioner option on certain models

Pressure cap rating (1.3 models) ....
0.7 to 0.9 bar (11 to 14 lbf/in²)

Pressure cap rating (1.6 models) ....
1.035 bar (15 lbf/in²)

Thermostat (1.3 models)
Starts to open ....
76 to 78°C (169 to 173°F)
Fully open ....
91°C (196°F)
Valve lift ....
8.0 mm (0.31 in)

Thermostat (1.6 models)
Starts to open ....
76 to 80°C (169 to 176°F)
Fully open ....
88°C (190°F)
Valve lift ....
8.0 mm (0.32 in)

Fan thermoswitch
Cuts in ....
88.5 to 91.5°C (191 to 196°F)
Cuts out ....
82.0 to 88.0°C (180 to 190°F)

Coolant capacity
1.3 models up to VIN 800 000/1985 model year ....
4.5 litre (8.0 pint)
1.3 models from VIN 800 000/1985 model year ....
6.4 litre (11.0 pint)
1.6 models ....
6.4 litre (11.0 pint)

Coolant type/specification ....
Soft water and ethylene glycol based antifreeze (Duckhams Universal Antifreeze and Summer Coolant)

Torque wrench settings	Nm	lbf ft
1.3 models		
Timing belt tensioner bolt	45	33
Coolant temperature transmitter	28	20
Crankshaft pulley bolt	45	33
Cylinder block drain plug	32	23
Thermostatic switch	23	17
Thermostat housing bolts	12	9
Coolant pump bolts	12	9

Torque wrench settings (continued)

1.6 models

	Nm	lbf ft
Thermostat housing	18	13
Coolant pump bolts	12	9
Coolant temperature transmitter	15	11
Compressor mounting bolts	45	33
Drivebelt tensioner puller nut	45	33
Pipe unions:		
5/8 in	32	23
1/2 in	22	16
3/8 in	17	12

1 Description and operation

1   The type of cooling system used will depend upon the engine and date of production.

1.3 models up to VIN 800 000/1985 model year

2   The system employs a vertical flow radiator with pressure cap, a coolant pump driven by the timing belt and a thermostat.

3   Circulation is by thermosyphon action and coolant pump impeller assistance.

4   The radiator is cooled by the ram effect of air when the car is in forward motion and has supplementary cooling by an electric fan which is actuated by a thermostatic switch.

5   The expansion tank, although not pressurised, accepts displaced coolant which is forced out past the radiator drawn back into the system as it cools. A vacuum is prevented from occurring by the opening of the vacuum valve in the radiator cap.

1.3 models from VIN 800 000/1985 model year and all 1.6 models

6   On these models, a crossflow aluminium radiator is fitted with an expansion tank to which is fitted a pressure cap.

Fig. 2.1 Cooling system (1.3 models up to VIN 800 000/1985 model year) (Sec 1)

1	Radiator drain plug	4	Pressure cap	7	Thermostat housing
2	Radiator	5	Thermostatic (fan) switch	8	Coolant flow control valve
3	Fan motor	6	Expansion tank	9	Bleed screw

Fig. 2.2 Cooling system (1.3 models from VIN 800 000/1985 model year) (Sec 1)

1 Coolant flow control valve
2 Thermostat housing
3 Expansion tank cap

4 Radiator bottom hose
5 Fan motor
6 Bleed screw

7 Radiator
8 Radiator top hose
9 Fan thermostatic switch

Fig. 2.3 Cooling system (1.6 models with carburettor) (Sec 1)

1 Heater connection
2 Expansion tank filler cap

3 Coolant pump
4 Fan thermostatic switch

5 Radiator
6 Radiator top hose

7 Fan, motor and cowl
8 Thermostat housing

Fig. 2.4 Cooling system (1.6 fuel injection models) (Sec 1)

1   Heater connection
2   Expansion tank filler cap
3   Coolant pump
4   Fan thermostatic switch
5   Radiator
6   Radiator top hose
7   Fan, motor and cowl
8   Thermostat housing

7   A coolant pump is driven by the timing belt and a thermostat is incorporated in the system.

8   An electric radiator cooling fan is fitted which is controlled by a thermostatic switch.

Operation

9   On models with a vertical flow radiator the system operates in the following way. While the engine is warming up the thermostat is shut with the bypass valve open to allow coolant to circulate through the coolant pump to the cylinder block and inlet manifold. When the engine has warmed up, the thermostat opens and the bypass valve closes. Coolant is then drawn from the radiator bottom tank and circulates through the thermostat to the coolant pump and cylinder block.

10 On models with a crossflow radiator, coolant is drawn from the base of the left-hand radiator tank then passes through the coolant pump to the cylinder block. As the engine temperature increases and the thermostat opens, the coolant flows to the radiator right-hand tank and then across the radiator matrix to the left-hand tank.

11 As the coolant temperature rises, so it expands and the level in the expansion tank rises. When the system cools, a partial vacuum is created, but a valve in the expansion tank cap allows atmospheric pressure to enter thus forcing the coolant back into the system.

12 On all models a heater and ventilation system of fresh air type is fitted.

13 On certain models an air conditioner can be specified as a factory-fitted option.

2   Maintenance

General

1   As all models are fitted with a cooling system expansion tank, in theory, topping up should never be required.

2   If anything more than very occasional additions of coolant are required, check for a leak, probably at a hose clip. If no external leaks are evident, suspect an internal leak from a faulty cylinder head gasket. Water may show on the engine oil dipstick.

1.3 models up to VIN 800 000/1985 model year

3   At the weekly maintenance check, open the bonnet and check the coolant level in the expansion tank. This should be at or near the MAX mark.

4   Top up the tank if necessary, using water to which anti-freeze has been added in the same proportion as the original coolant. Refit the tank cap.

1.3 models from VIN 800 000/1985 model year and all 1.6 models

5   At the weekly maintenance check, open the bonnet and preferably with the engine cold, remove the expansion tank pressure cap.

6   If the engine is hot, cover the cap with a cloth to prevent escaping steam scalding. Unscrew the cap to the first stop to allow pressure to escape, depress again, turn the cap and remove it.

7   Check the coolant level which should be between the minimum and maximum points on the level indicator inside the tank.

8   If necessary, top up to the maximum level using coolant containing anti-freeze in the same proportion as the original mixture.

9   Refit the expansion tank pressure cap.

All models

10 Regularly check the security of the coolant hose clips and inspect the hoses for deterioration.

11 At the specified intervals (see Routine Maintenance) check the drivebelt tension and renew the coolant.

3   Cooling system – draining and refilling

1.3 models up to VIN 800 000/1985 model year

1   With the cooling system cold, remove the radiator pressure cap.

2   Set the heater temperature lever to maximum.

3   Remove the radiator and cylinder block drain plugs, allow the coolant to drain. Catch the coolant in a suitable receptacle if it is to be used again. Drain and clean the expansion tank.

Fig. 2.5 Expansion tank coolant level indicator (Sec 2)

1   Cap   3   Maximum
2   Minimum

4   If the cooling system has been well maintained, with regular changes of anti-freeze, then there should be no evidence of rust or sediment and it may be refilled immediately. If the system has been neglected, then it should be flushed through with a cold water hose. In severe cases, reverse flushing of the radiator may be required or even the use of a cooling system cleanser such as Holts Radflush or Holts Speedflush, used strictly in accordance with the manufacturer's instructions.

5   Refit the drain plugs and refill the expansion tank to the maximum mark with anti-freeze mixture (see Section 5).

6   Slacken the air bleed screw adjacent to the coolant outlet elbow (photo).

7   Fill the radiator slowly to the bottom of the filler neck, tightening the bleed screw as soon as coolant is ejected from it.

8   Do not fit the radiator cap yet, but run the engine to normal operating temperature, allowing the electric cooling fan to cut in twice.

9   Top up to the bottom of the filler neck and refit the radiator cap.

1.3 models from VIN 800 000/1985 model year and all 1.6 models

10 With the cooling system cold, set the heater temperature control lever to maximum.

11 Unscrew and remove the cap from the expansion tank.

12 Disconnect the radiator bottom hose and allow the coolant to drain. Catch the coolant in a suitable receptacle if it is to be used again.

3.6 Slackening air bleed screw

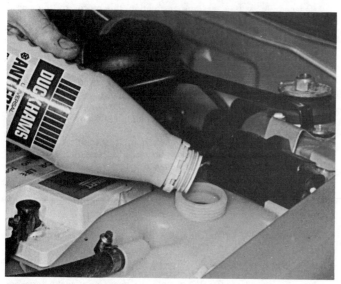

3.15 Filling the expansion tank with coolant

13 Remove, drain and clean the expansion tank. Refer to paragraph 4.
14 Reconnect the radiator bottom hose and on 1.3 models, unscrew the bleed screw. Refit and connect the expansion tank.
15 Fill the system slowly through the expansion tank using the specified anti-freeze mixture (see Section 5). Continue filling until the level is just below the maximum mark (1.6 models) or coolant flows from the bleed screw (1.3 models). Tighten the bleed screw (photo).
16 Run the engine to normal operating temperature. switch off and allow to cool.
17 Remove the expansion tank cap and top up with anti-freeze mixture to the maximum point on the level indicator.

4 Pressure cap

1 This may be fitted to either the radiator or the expansion tank depending upon the model.
2 A faulty pressure cap can cause coolant loss and it is a wise precaution to have it tested at regular intervals by your dealer or service station.

3 If the cap is found to be faulty, renew it with one which is marked with the identical pressure rating.

5 Coolant mixtures

1 Plain water should never be used in the engine cooling system. Apart from giving protection against freezing, an antifreeze mixture protects the engine internal surfaces and components against corrosion. This is especially important in respect of the 1.3 all alloy engine.
2 Always use a top quality glycol based antifreeze which is suitable for mixed metal engines.
3 Ideally, a 50% mixture of antifreeze and soft or demineralised water should be used to maintain protection against freezing and corrosion. On no account use less than 30% antifreeze.
4 Renew the coolant at the specified intervals as the inhibitors contained in the antifreeze gradually lose their effectiveness.
5 Even when operating in climates where antifreeze is not necessary, never use plain water, but add a corrosion inhibitor to it.

6 Thermostat – removal, testing and refitting

1.3 models
1 Remove the radiator filler cap, taking the necessary precautions (see Section 2) if the engine is hot.
2 Drain the cooling system as described in Section 3.
3 Remove the thermostat cover and the thermostat. Extract the seal (photos).
4 To check the thermostat, its valve plate should be fully closed when cold. Now suspend the thermostat in a saucepan of water which is being heated. Prevent the thermostat from contacting the container which is being heated. Use a thermometer to check that the thermostat valve plate begins to open and is fully open at the specified temperature levels.
5 If the thermostat does not perform correctly, fit a new one.
6 Fit the thermostat using a new seal and make sure that the jiggle pin is uppermost. Bolt on the thermostat housing cover.
7 Fill the cooling system as previously described in Section 3.

1.6 models
8 The operations are very similar to those just described for 1.3 models, but note that the opening temperatures differ slightly.
9 Always use a new gasket on clean mating surfaces when refitting the thermostat housing cover.

6.3A Removing thermostat housing cover

6.3B Removing thermostat

7.1 Radiator removed (early 1.3 model)

7 Radiator cooling fan (1.3 models up to VIN 800 000/1985 model year) – removal and refitting

The fan and motor can only be removed after the radiator has been withdrawn as described in Section 10 (photo).

8 Radiator cooling fan (1.3 models from VIN 800 000/1985 model year and all 1.6 models) – removal and refitting

1   Disconnect the battery.
2   Unscrew the lower screw from the bonnet lock platform support.
3   Disconnect the wiring plug from the fan motor.
4   Unscrew the three retaining nuts and release the cowl from the radiator.
5   Withdraw the fan/cowl assembly from the engine compartment.
6   To dismantle the fan, extract the circlip and pull the fan hub from the motor shaft. The motor can be separated from the cowl after drilling out the rivets.

7   Reassembly will necessitate re-riveting the motor to the cowl. Refitting is a reversal of removal.

9 Fan thermostatic switch – testing, removal and refitting

1.3 models up to VIN 800 000/1985 model year
1   If there is any doubt about the radiator cooling fan cutting in when the coolant temperature is high, test in the following way.
2   Disconnect the leads from the thermostatic switch which is screwed into the radiator bottom tank.
3   Join the leads together and switch on the ignition. If the fan operates then the switch is faulty and must be renewed. To do this, drain the cooling system and unscrew the switch. Use a new sealing washer when refitting.
4   If as a result of the test, the motor stil does not operate, first check for a blown fuse or a broken lead, otherwise the motor must be faulty and it should be renewed or repaired.

1.3 models from VIN 800 000/1985 model year and all 1.6 models
5   The testing operations are very similar to those just described for earlier 1.3 models but note that the switch is retained to the radiator by means of a swivel type lockplate. Always use a new sealing washer when refitting the switch.

10 Radiator (1.3 models up to VIN 800 000/1985 model year) – removal, repair and refitting

1   Drain the cooling system as described in Section 3.
2   Disconnect the leads from the cooling fan motor and the thermostatic switch (photo).
3   Place the car over an inspection pit or raise the front end on stands, support it securely and then remove the undershield.
4   Disconnect the expansion tank and radiator coolant hoses (photo).
5   On cars fitted with automatic transmission, disconnect the transmission fluid (cooler) pipes from the unions on the radiator side tank and plug or cap them to prevent the entry of dirt.
6   Unscrew and remove the radiator mounting bolts from the bonnet release catch panel. Also remove the lower bolt from the bonnet release catch.
7   Unscrew and remove the bolts which hold the release catch panel to the bonnet platform and move the panel aside. Remove the centre support (photo).
8   Release the radiator from the lower platform and withdraw the radiator complete with fan and cowl from the car (photo).
9   The radiator cannot be satisfactorily repaired by the home mechanic and any work should be left to specialists or an exchange

10.2 Cooling fan and thermostatic switch connections

10.4 Expansion tank hose at radiator

10.7 Removing bonnet release catch panel

10.8 Removing the radiator

unit obtained. Minor leaks from the radiator can be cured using Holts Radweld. Extensive damage should be repaired by a specialist or the unit exchanged for a new or reconditioned radiator. Before parting with the old radiator remove the fan and cowling thermostatic switch, radiator mounting blocks and filler neck and cap.
10 Refitting is a reversal of removal, but use new O-ring seals at the filler neck and the thermostatic switch. Refill the cooling system as described in Section 3.
11 On cars with automatic transmission, check the transmission fluid level and top up if necessary.

11 Radiator (1.3 models from VIN 800 000/1985 model year and all 1.6 models) – removal, repair and refitting

1 Disconnect the battery.
2 Drain the cooling system as previously described in Section 3.
3 Remove the radiator grille as described in Chapter 11.
4 Unscrew the bolts which hold the radiator top mounting brackets to the bonnet lock platform.
5 Remove the top rail panel.
6 On 1.6 models, remove the bolt from the bonnet lock support strut.
7 Disconnect the radiator hoses and the electrical leads from the thermostatic switch and the cooling fan motor.
8 On 1.3 models fitted with automatic transmission, disconnect the fluid cooler hoses and plug them.
9 Remove the radiator top mounting brackets. If the car is equipped with an air conditioner, take care not to damage the condenser.
10 Lift out the radiator assembly.
11 The radiator cannot be satisfactorily repaired by the home mechanic and any work should be left to specialists or an exchange unit obtained. Minor leaks from the radiator can be cured using Holts Radweld. Extensive damage should be repaired by a specialist or the unit exchanged for a new or reconditioned radiator. Before parting with the old radiator, remove the fan and cowling, the thermostatic switch, top mounting brackets and flexible blocks.
12 Refitting is a reversal of removal. Use a new seal at the thermostatic switch.
13 Refill the cooling system as described in Section 3.
14 On 1.3 models fitted with automatic transmission, check and top up the transmission fluid.

12 Drivebelts

1 The coolant pump is driven by the toothed timing belt and tensioning is covered in Section 13 and 14.
2 Tensioning and renewal of the Vee drivebelt for the alternator is described in Chapter 12.

3 Tensioning and renewal of the Vee drivebelt for the air conditioner compressor is described in Section 24 of this Chapter.

13 Coolant pump (1.3 models) – removal and refitting

1 Disconnect the battery.
2 Drain the cooling system as described in Section 3.
3 Refer to Chapter 12 and remove the alternator drivebelt.
4 Remove the air cleaner and the rocker cover. Also remove the left-hand roadwheel and splash panel, having raised the car and supported it securely.
5 Apply a spanner to the crankshaft pulley bolt and turn the crankshaft anti-clockwise until the UP mark on the camshaft pulley is uppermost and the timing marks on the camshaft pulley rear face are aligned with the surface of the cylinder head.
6 Unscrew the crankshaft pulley bolt and withdraw the pulley. In order to prevent the crankshaft from rotating while the bolt is being unscrewed, engage a low gear and have an assistant apply the footbrake hard. Alternatively, remove the starter motor and jam the flywheel teeth with a suitable tool.
7 Unbolt and remove the two sections of the timing belt cover.
8 Slacken the belt tensioner bolt, retract the tensioner and re-tighten the bolt.
9 Mark the rotational direction of the timing belt and slip it from the sprockets together with the belt guide plate.
10 Do not rotate the camshaft or crankshaft while the belt is off.
11 Unbolt and remove the coolant pump and discard the O-ring seal.
12 Repair of the coolant pump is not possible and if the pump is leaking or faulty it must be renewed.
13 Bolt the new pump into position using a new O-ring seal (photos).
14 Check that the camshaft sprocket timing marks are still in alignment with the cylinder head. Also, by temporarily refitting the belt lower cover and pulley, check that the crankshaft pulley timing marks are in alignment.
15 Fit the timing belt in its original rotational direction.
16 Fit the timing belt guide plate (convex side to belt) and the belt lower cover.
17 Fit the crankshaft pulley and bolt. Hold the crankshaft against rotation as previously described while the bolt is tightened to the specified torque.
18 Tension the belt by releasing the tensioner bolt and then turning the crankshaft pulley in an anti-clockwise direction so that the camshaft sprocket moves through three teeth. Tighten the tensioner bolt to the specified torque.
19 Fit the belt upper cover and rocker cover.
20 Refit and tension the alternator drivebelt.
21 Refit the air cleaner and reconnect the battery.
22 Refill the cooling system.
23 Refit the roadwheel and splash panel.

13.13A Fitting coolant pump

13.13B Tightening coolant pump bolts

14 Coolant pump (1.6 models) – removal and refitting

1   Disconnect the battery.
2   Drain the cooling system as previously described.
3   Unbolt and remove both sections of the timing belt cover.
4   Apply a spanner to the crankshaft pulley bolt and turn the crankshaft until the timing mark on the rear face of the camshaft sprocket is in alignment with the notches on the camshaft carrier and the crankshaft pulley. The TDC notch is aligned with the cast mark on the oil pump.
5   Unbolt and remove the timing belt tensioner.
6   Move the timing belt aside and unbolt and remove the coolant pump.
7   Clean off all traces of dirt and sealant from the pump mounting face of the engine.
8   The coolant pump cannot be repaired and if it is leaking or faulty it must be renewed.
9   Apply an even bead of RTV type sealant (instant gasket) around the pump mounting face on the engine and bolt the new coolant pump into position. Tighten the bolts to the specified torque.
10 Check that the camshaft and crankshaft timing marks are still in alignment and then bolt the tensioner into position, but with the bolts finger tight.
11 Engage a suitable torque wrench with $^3/_8$ in (9.5 mm) adaptor in the square hole of the tensioner plate, apply the specified torque of 20 Nm (15 lbf ft) and tighten the tensioner bolts while holding the applied torque.
12 Fit the timing belt covers, refill the cooling system and reconnect the battery.

15 Heating and ventilation system – description

1   The system consists of a heater matrix inside a casing, a three-speed blower and a manually-operated control unit, together with all the necessary ducting and outlet grilles. On 1.3 models, a coolant flow control valve is included in the system.
2   Fresh, outside air enters the heater casing through the grille at the base of the windscreen and passes over the matrix to either absorb heat, or not, according to the control valve setting. The air is then ducted as required according to the setting of the distribution levers on the control panel.
3   The blower motor can be set to either recirculate air inside the car or to boost the volume of outside air passing through the heater.
4   Stale air from the car interior is extracted through grilles at each side of the rear window (photo).

Fig. 2.6 Coolant pump bolts (1.6 models) (Sec 14)

1   Coolant pump   3   Coolant pump bolts
2   Belt tensioner bolts   4   Clamp plate

16 Heater – removal and refitting

1   Disconnect the battery.
2   Drain the cooling system (Section 3).
3   Refer to Chapter 11 and remove the facia lower access panel, glovebox and frame and the facia panel (photo).
4   Working within the engine compartment, disconnect the heater hoses at the bulkhead.
5   Remove the nut from the large stud in the centre of the engine compartment rear bulkhead.

Fig. 2.7 Heater unit (Sec 15)

1	Blower casing	5	Gasket	8	Duct	11	Control unit
2	Fan fixing nut	6	Blower motor	9	Duct joint	12	Matrix
3	Fan	7	Blower motor cover	10	Heater casing	13	Matrix cover
4	Fan casing						

15.4 Air extraction grille

16.3 Glovebox frame

16.6 Heater blower motor plug

16.8 Heater control cables

6   Carefully prise out the plastic pins which hold the air duct to the blower motor and heater casings and withdraw the air duct. Disconnect the blower motor wiring plug (photo).

7   Release the recirculation control outer cable from its fixing clip and the inner cable from the operating lever.

8   Disconnect the remaining control cables in a similar way (photo).

9   Release the wiring harness from its clip.

10 Unscrew and remove the two upper heater mounting bolts, pull the heater from the bulkhead and lift it away.

11 The casing may be dismantled for access to the matrix. If the matrix is clogged, try reverse flushing it. If the matrix is leaking, leave repairs to a specialist or exchange it for a new one.

12 Refitting is a reversal of removal. Adjust the control cables as described in Section 21.

13 Refill the cooling system, reconnect the battery.

17 Heater blower – removal and refitting

1   Disconnect the battery.

2   Refer to Chapter 11 and remove the glovebox and frame.

3   Carefully prise out the plastic pins which hold the air duct to the blower motor and heater casings, withdraw the air duct.

4   Disconnect the multi-plugs from the motor casings and the blower motor.

5   Disconnect the recirculation control cable.

6   Unscrew the three nuts and withdraw the blower motor and casing.

7   Disconnect the corrugated hose from the blower motor.

8   Unscrew the motor cover screws and then withdraw the motor/fan assembly.

9   If dismantling is necessary, unscrew the fan nut and pull the fan from the motor shaft. Retrieve the washer.

10 Refitting is a reversal of removal, but use a new gasket on the motor mounting flange.

11 Adjust the recirculation control as described in Section 21. Reconnect the battery.

18 Heater control panel – removal and refitting

1   Disconnect the battery.

2   Refer to Chapter 11 and remove the glovebox frame and the facia lower access panel.

3   Release the steering column upper mounting bracket and lower clamp plate and lower the column.

4   Extract the choke knob fixing screw and pull off the knob.

5   Unscrew the choke control bezel nut and release the choke control from the facia panel.

6   Prise the knobs from the blower motor and heater controls (photo).

7   Prise out the heater control escutcheon plate (photo).

8   Refer to Chapter 12 and remove the radio.

9   Unscrew the nut and release the blower motor switch from the control unit panel.

10 Release the recirculation control cable from the blower motor casing and the control arm.

11 Disconnect the other control cables in a similar way.

12 Extract the heater control panel fixing screws, withdraw the panel and disconnect the multi-plug from the rear of the panel (photo).

13 Refitting is a reversal of removal. Adjust the control cables as described in Section 21.

14 Reconnect the battery.

18.6 Pulling off heater control knob

18.7 Heater control escutcheon plate

18.12 Heater control panel screws (arrowed)

19 Blower motor switch – removal and refitting

1 Remove the control panel as described in the preceding Section.
2 Disconnect the leads and remove the switch.
3 Refitting is a reversal of removal.

20 Coolant flow control valve (1.3 models) – removal and refitting

1 Drain the cooling system.
2 Remove the plastic cover from the coolant control valve (photo).
3 Disconnect the cable from the valve lever.
4 Disconnect the hoses from the valve.
5 Extract the fixing screws and remove the valve from its mounting bracket.
6 Refitting is a reversal of removal.
7 Refill the cooling system.

21 Heater control rods and cables – removal, refitting and adjustment

1 The removal and refitting of all rods and cables is simply a matter of unclipping and releasing from the control lever and operating arm.
2 It is important to adjust each control rod or cable carefully in the following way if it has been disturbed or operation is incorrect.

Recirculation control cable
3 With the glovebox and frame removed (Chapter 11) to give access to the cable, disconnect the inner cable from the lever on the heater.

Fig. 2.8 Coolant flow control valve (1.3 models) (Sec 20)

1 Control cable	4 Valve	
2 Operating lever	5 Mounting bracket	
3 Heater hoses		

20.2 Heater coolant control valve

Fig. 2.9 Heater control rods and cables (Sec 21)

1   Air distribution control outer cable clip
2   Air distribution control outer cable
3   Rear intermediate lever
4   Operating lever
5   Front intermediate lever
6   Air distribution control operating lever spigot
7   Air distribution control inner cable
8   Air distribution flap control rod clip
9   Air distribution flap control rod
10 Air distribution flap control rod clip
11 Air distribution flap control rod
12 Heater flap control rod
13 Heater flap control rod clip
14 Intermediate lever
15 Intermediate lever spigot
16 Temperature control inner cable
17 Temperature control inner cable clip
18 Temperature control outer cable
19 Heater flap control arm
20 Control arm spigot
21 Heater valve inner cable (1.3 models)
22 Outer cable clip (1.3 models)
23 Heater valve outer cable (1.3 models)
24 Lower flap operating lever
25 Upper flap operating lever

Fig. 2.10 Recirculation control cable (Sec 21)

1   Inner cable
2   Operating lever
3   Outer cable (conduit)

4 Set the facia recirculation hand control lever fully to the left and the lever on the heater fully towards the bulkhead.
5 Re-set the position of the outer cable in its clip so that the inner cable eye will drop over the lever spigot at the heater without any need to adjust either lever.
6 Check that the cable operates over its full range and the flap valve opens and closes correctly.
7 Refit the glovebox and frame.

Temperature control cable
8 Disconnect the battery and remove the facia lower access panel.
9 Release the inner cable from the spigot on the intermediate lever.
10 Move the temperature control hand lever to COLD.
11 Release the heater flap control rod from its clip on the intermediate lever and then pull the spigot on the lever fully towards the rear.
12 Adjust the position of the temperature control outer cable in its securing clip until the inner cable eye will drop over the spigot on the intermediate lever without having to move the position of either lever.
13 On 1.3 models, disconnect the coolant flow valve cable from the spigot on the flap control arm and push the arm fully towards the bulkhead.
14 Fix the heater flap control rod to the clip on the intermediate lever.
15 Move the temperature control hand lever to HOT.
16 On 1.3 models, remove the plastic cover from the coolant flow control valve and push the operating lever fully towards the bulkhead. Adjust the position of the valve outer control cable until the eye of the inner cable will drop over the spigot on the float control arm without having to alter the setting of lever or arm. Refit the valve plastic cover.
17 Check for correct operation of the flap valve.
18 Refit the facia lower access panel.
19 Reconnect the battery.

Air distribution control cable
20 Disconnect the battery and remove the facia lower access panel.

21 Pull the cable from spigot on the operating lever at the heater and then move the hand control lever to the left (face level position).
22 Disconnect the flap control rods from the intermediate levers.
23 Pull the spigot on the operating lever at the heater to the rear move the outer cable in its clip until the inner clip can be dropped onto the lever spigot without having to move either lever.
24 Move the air distributor control fully to the right ensuring that the lug on the operating lever is at the top of the slot in the rear instrument lever.
25 Pull the upper flap control arm forwards and connect the control rod to the clip on the rear intermediate lever.
26 With the control lever still held fully to the right, check that the lug on the operating lever is at the bottom of the slot in the front intermediate lever.
27 Pull the lower flap operating lever forwards and connect the control rod to the clip on the front intermediate lever.
28 Check the flaps open and close correctly when the control lever is operated.
29 Refit the facia lower access panel and reconnect the battery.

22 Air conditioning system – description

1 Air conditioning is an option on certaiin models and consists of a belt-driven compressor, a condenser mounted ahead of the radiator, a receiver dryer and an evaporator.

Compressor
2 This circulates refrigerant through the system and incorporates an electro-magnetic clutch to engage or disengage the compressor according to pressure and temperature requirements.
3 While the compressor is running, the idle control solenoid permits vacuum to be applied on the idle boost diaphragm which moves the

Fig. 2.11 Air conditioning system (Sec 22)

1 Idle control solenoid
2 Idle boost diaphragm
3 Blower unit
4 Evaporator, expansion valve, thermostat
5 Heater/air conditioner control panel
6 Condenser
7 Low pressure switch
8 Sight glass
9 Receiver drier
10 Compressor
11 Charge and discharge valves
12 Tensioner pulley

throttle linkage to compensate for the increased engine load at idle speed.

Condenser

4   This receives vaporised refrigerant from the compressor and by cooling it, converts the vapour into liquid.

Receiver drier

5   This is located at the side of the condenser and collects moisture from the system to prevent freezing of the components.

Evaporator

6   From the receiver drier, the refrigerant flows through the sight glass to give an indication of refrigerant charge.
7   The refrigerant is then vaporised by the pressure drop as it passes through an expansion valve and passes into the evaporator. Air flow through the fins of the evaporator is cooled before it is distributed inside the car. The refrigerant is then drawn back into the compressor to start a new cycle.

23 Air conditioner – precautions and maintenance

1   Refer to *Warning* in Chapter 1, Section 37.
2   Periodically check the condition of the system hoses and for leaks at the unions.
3   During the winter or when the unit is not in regular use, run it for ten minutes every week.
4   Never switch on the air conditioner before starting the engine.
5   When ascending a long hill with the air conditioner on, if the temperature gauge starts to indicate a high reading, switch off the air conditioner until the gauge shows a normal level.
6   Keep the compressor drivebelt correctly tensioned and in good condition as described in the next Section.
7   Periodically check the refrigerant charge as follows.
8   Run the engine at a fast idle for a few minutes with the air conditioning switched on. Inspect the sight glass: it should appear clear, with perhaps a few bubbles. This shows that the charge is correct.
9   If the sight glass displays a constant stream of bubbles, foam, streaking or cloudiness, switch off the air conditioning immediately and do not use it again until the system has been checked by a dealer or refrigeration specialist.
10 Gradual loss of refrigerant is a normal feature of air conditioning systems. It is recommended that the system be professionally inspected, and recharged if necessary, at least every two years.

Fig. 2.12 Air conditioning sight glass (arrowed) (Sec 23)

24 Compressor drivebelt – tensioning and renewal

1   Slacken the tensioner pulley nut and move the pulley by turning the adjusting bolt until the tension is correct. This is when the total deflection at the mid-point of the longest run is between 7.0 and 9.0 mm (0.28 and 0.35 in).
2   Tighten the tensioner pulley nut to the specified torque.
3   If the compressor drivebelt is to be renewed, slacken the tensioner

pulley and ease the belt over the rim of the pulley. If it is difficult to remove, apply a spanner to the crankshaft pulley bolt, turn it while prising the belt up and over the pulley rim.
4   Fit the new belt, again turning the crankshaft pulley while prising the belt over the pulley rim and into its groove.
5   Tension the belt, run the engine for five minutes and then re-tension it as described in paragraph 1.

25 Air conditioning system components – removal and refitting

Warning: *Before removing or refitting any component have the system discharged by your dealer or refrigerant engineer. Once a component has been removed, cap the ends of open pipelines or couplings to prevent the entry of moisture.*

Compressor

1   Disconnect the battery and the compressor clutch stator lead.
2   Disconnect the compressor hoses and plug all openings.
3   Remove the drivebelt as described in Section 24.
4   Unscrew and remove all the mounting bolts and lift the compressor from the engine compartment.
5   If a new compressor is being fitted, then 30 cc (1.0 fl. oz) of refrigerant oil must be added to the low pressure fitting on the compressor.
6   Refitting is a reversal of removal. Tension the drivebelt as previously described and have the system charged by your dealer or refrigeration engineer.

Condenser

7   Disconnect the battery.
8   Refer to Chapter 11 and remove the front bumper.
9   Disconnect the high pressure pipe from the receiver and the low pressure hose from the condenser. Plug the openings.
10 Disconnect the condenser fan switch leads, remove the condenser mounting bolts and lift the condenser from the car. If required, the condenser fan can be detached from the condenser.
11 If a new condenser is being fitted, pour 10 cc (0.33 fl. oz) of refrigerant oil into the condenser.
12 Refitting is a reversal of removal. Have the system charged by your dealer or refrigeration engineer.

Evaporator, expansion valve and thermostat

13 Disconnect the battery.
14 Disconnect the low pressure hose and the receiver pipe from the evaporator. Extract the O-ring seals and then plug or cap all openings.
15 Remove the protective sleeve from the low pressure hose. Also remove the grommet and retainer plate.
16 Refer to Chapter 11 and remove the glovebox and glovebox frame.
17 Refer to Section 17 and remove the blower unit. Slacken the sealing band which secures the evaporator to the heater.
18 Disconnect the drain hose and the electrical leads.
19 Unscrew the mounting bolts and lift away the evaporator assembly.
20 Release the fixing clips and remove the bottom half of he eveporator casing.
21 If the expansion valve must be removed, take off the tape and release the capillary tube from the low pressure pipe. Then remove the expansion valve and extract the O rings. Plug or cap all openings.
22 If the thermostat must be removed, withdraw the capillary tube from the evaporator fins and remove the thermostat.
23 The evaporator can be withdrawn from its casing after extracting the screws from the casing upper section.
24 If a new evaporator is being fitted, pour 30 cc (1.0 fl oz) into it.
25 Refitting is a reversal of removal. Apply sealant around the bulkheadd grommet.
26 Reconnect the battery, have the system charged by your dealer or refrigeration engineer.

26 Coolant temperature gauge and sender unit

1   If the reading on the temperature gauge is suspect, test in the following way.

2 Disconnect the lead from the transmitter unit and earth the lead.
3 Switch on the ignition. The gauge needle should move to HOT. Do not leave the ignition on for more than five seconds. If the need does not move as indicated. check the fuse and connecting wires and if these are alright, then the gauge is faulty.
4 If the needle does move to HOT then the transmitter is faulty and should be renewed.
5 If the fuel and temperature gauges indicate FULL and HOT at the same time, then they are faulty and should be renewed.
6 The test the transmitter unit have the engine cold and disconnect the lead from the transmitter.
7 Run the engine until the coolant temperature reaches 50°C

(122°F). This can be checked by inserting a thermometer in the radiator filler neck (1.3 models) or in the end of the expansion tank hose (later 1.3 and 1.6 models) after having disconnected it from the tank.
8 Using an ohmmeter, measure the resistance between the terminal of the transmitter unit and the engine (earth). The resistance should be between 135 and 176 ohms.
9 Continue running the engine until the coolant temperature reaches 80°C (176°F), at which point the resistance should be between 47.6 and 56.9 ohms.
10 If the readings are not as specified, renew the transmitter unit.

27 Fault diagnosis – cooling, heating and air conditioning

Symptom	Reason(s)
Cooling	
Overheating	Insufficient coolant in system
	Radiator blocked either internally and externally
	Kinked or collapsed hose causing coolant flow restriction
	Thermostat not working properly
	Engine out of tune
	Ignition timing retarded or auto advance malfunction
	Cylinder head gasket blown
	Engine not yet run-in
	Exhaust system partially blocked
	Engine oil level too low
	Brakes binding
Engine running too cool	Faulty, incorrect or missing thermostat
Loss of coolant	Loose hose clips
	Hoses perished or leaking
	Radiator leaking
	Filler/pressure cap defective
	Blown cylinder head gasket
	Cracked cylinder block or head
	Leak into transmission fluid (automatic transmission)
Heater	
Heater gives insufficient output	Engine overcooled (see above)
	Heater matrix blocked
	Heater controls maladjusted or broken
	Heater control valve jammed or otherwise defective
Air conditioner	
Bubbles observed in sight glass of receiver drier	Leak in system
	Low refrigerant level
No cooling	No refrigerant
Expansion valve frosted over on evaporator	Faulty or clogged expansion valve
	Thermal bulb leaking
Insufficient cooling	Faulty expansion valve
	Air in refrigerant circuit
	Clogged condenser
	Receiver drier clogged
	Faulty compressor or slack drivebelt
	Compressor overfilled with oil

Chapter 3 Fuel and exhaust systems

For modifications, and information applicable to later models, see Supplement at end of manual

Contents

Specifications

Part A (Models with carburettor)
Fuel pump (1.3 models)

Type .... Mechanically operated by camshaft
Delivery pressure .... 0.19 to 0.26 bar (2.7 to 3.8 lbf/in²)

Fuel pump (1.6 models)

Type .... Electric, five vane
Delivery pressure .... 0.3 bar (4.0 lbf/in²)

Air cleaner element (1.3 models) .... Champion W183

Air cleaner element (1.6 models) .... Champion W114

Carburettor (1.3 models)

Type	Keihin dual-barrel fixed jet with manual choke
Float level	35.4 to 37.4 mm (1.39 to 1.47 in)
Accelerator pump stroke	18.5 to 19.5 mm (0.73 to 0.77 in)
Idle speed	700 to 800 rev/min
CO at idle	not exceeding 1%
Fast idle speed	1500 to 2500 rev/min

Carburettor (1.6 models)

Type	SU HIF 44E with electronic mixture control
Idle speed	700 to 800 rev/min
CO at idle	2.0 to 3.5%
Fast idle speed	1150 to 1300 rev/min
Float level	1.0 to 1.5 mm (0.04 to 0.062 in)
Piston damper oil type/specification	Multigrade engine oil (Duckhams QXR, Hypergrade, or 10W/40 Motor Oil)

Fuel tank capacity

46.0 litres (10.0 gal)

Fuel octane rating (minimum)

1.3 models	Leaded (91 RON) or Unleaded (95 RON)
1.6 models	Leaded (97 RON)

Part B (Models with fuel injection system)
Fuel pump

Type	Electric
Delivery pressure	4.1 bar (60 lbf/in²)
Pressure regulator range	2.5 to 1.8 bar (36 to 26 lbf/in²)

Fuel temperature switch closes

90°C (195°F)

Idle speed

Controlled by electronic control unit	710 ± 50 rev/min
With air valve closed	650 to 680 rev/min

CO at idle

1.0 to 1.5%

Air cleaner element

Champion W114

Fuel tank capacity

46.0 litre (10.0 gal)

Fuel octane rating

Four-star (97 RON)

Torque wrench settings
1.3 models

	Nm	lbf ft
Carburettor mounting nuts	20	15
Fuel pump nuts	24	18
Inlet manifold support bracket nuts	22	16
Inlet manifold fixing nuts	22	16
Manifold support bracket bolt	45	33
Exhaust manifold fixing nuts	39	29
Exhust manifold to downpipe nuts	55	41

1.6 models with carburettor

Carburettor mounting nuts	20	15
Inlet manifold fixing nuts/bolts	22	16
Manifold electric heater sensor	18	13
Exhaust manifold fixing nuts	25	18

All models

Fuel tank mounting strap bolts	22	16

Warning: *Many of the procedures in this Chapter entail the removal of fuel pipes and connections which may result in some fuel spillage. Before carrying out any operation on the fuel system refer to the precautions given in Safety First! at the beginning of this manual and follow them implicity. Petrol is a highly dangerous and volatile liquid and the precautions necessary when handling it cannot be over-stressed.*

Part A (Models with carburettor)

1 General description

The fuel system on carburettor models consists of a fuel tank which is mounted forward of the rear suspension, a fuel pump mechanically operated on 1.3 models, electric on 1.6 versions and a carburettor and temperature controlled air cleaner.

The air cleaner contains a disposable paper filter element and incorporates an automatic air temperature control system. The system is controlled by a flap valve located at the junction of the air cleaner hot and cold air intakes. The flap is operated by inlet manifold vacuum acting on a thermac unit in conjunction with a temperature-sensitive thermac switch. The system allows hot or cold air to be delivered to the carburettor, depending on the position of the flap valve which varies according to engine temperature and load.

The carburettor on 1.3 models is of dual barrel fixed jet type while on 1.6 models, it is of variable venturi type with an electronic mixture control system.

Fig. 3.1 Fuel system (1.3 models) (Sec 1)

1	Fuel pump	4	Fuel feed line	7	Fuel pick-up unit	10 Breather hose
2	One-way valve	5	Fuel return line	8	Fuel filter	11 Fuel transmitter unit
3	Carburettor	6	Fuel tank	9	Two-way valve	

2 Maintenance and inspection

1   Regularly inspect the fuel hoses for security and condition .
2   Renew the air cleaner element and (on 1.3 models) the fuel filter at
the specified intervals (all Routine Maintenance).
3   The engine idle speed and mixture setting (CO content of exhaust
emission) should also be checked at the specified intervals.
4   Inspect the exhaust system periodically for leaks or severe
corrosion.
5   With SU carburettors keep the damper hollow piston rod topped up
with engine oil.

3 Air cleaner – servicing, removal and refitting

1.3 models
1   Unscrew the wing nut and remove the cover. Lift out the filter
element (photos).
2   Wipe out the casing, fit the new element and cover.
3   To remove the air cleaner, first identify all hoses, pipes and ducts
and disconnect them from the air cleaner casing (photos).
4   Unscrew the cover wing nut and the casing mounting bolt and lift
the air cleaner from the engine (photo).

H.16657

Fig. 3.2 SU carburettor damper. Oil level arrowed (Sec 2)

3.1A Air cleaner element

3.1B Air cleaner casing

3.3A Air cleaner cold air intake. Note auxiliary lamp relay

3.3B Cold air intake bracket screw

3.3C Hot air intake hose at air cleaner

3.3D Crankcase vent hose at air cleaner

3.4 Air cleaner casing mounting bracket

1.6 models

5   Release the clips and take off the air cleaner cover.
6   Remove the soiled filter element, wipe out the casing and fit the new element.
7   Refit the cover and secure it with the toggle clips.
8   To remove the air cleaner, first disconnect the cold air pipe from the air temperture control and then release the clip which secures the inlet hose to the plenum chamber.
9   Unscrew the bolts from the air cleaner mounting bracket, then disconnect the hot air pipe and vacuum hose from the air temperature control.
10 Withdraw the air cleaner and air temperature control assembly.
11   Refitting of both types of air cleaner is a reversal of removal

4   Fuel filter (1.3 models) – renewal

Warning: *Take adequate fire precautions during this procedure*

1   Disconnect the battery.
2   Raise the rear end of the car and support it securely on axle stands.
3   Remove the fuel filter cover and release the filter bracket.
4   Disconnect the hoses from the filter and plug the hose ends to prevent fuel leakage.
5   Remove and discard the old filter and fit the new one by reversing the removal operations.

Fig. 3.3 Air cleaner (1.6 with carburettor) (Sec 3)

1 Top cover	5 Thermac unit	10 Gasket	13 Hot air box
2 Paper element	6 Adaptor sleeve	11 Connecting tube	14 Cold air intake hose adaptor
3 Air cleaner body	7 Cold air intake hose	12 Hot air duct	15 Gasket
4 Air cleaner mounting bracket	8 Plenum chamber		
	9 Support bracket		

5.6 Fuel pump

5.7 Fuel pump cover and drain tube

5.8 Unscrewing fuel pump fixing nuts

5 Fuel pump (1.3 models) – testing, removal and refitting

Warning: *Take adequate fire precautions during this procedure*

1 Disconnect the fuel supply hose from the carburettor and insert its open end in a suitable container.
2 Disconnect the negative (blue) LT lead from the ignition coil and then have an assistant turn the ignition key to actuate the starter motor.
3 Fuel should be ejected in regular well defined spurts from the fuel hose.
4 If this is not the case then the fuel pump must be renewed as the pump is of sealed type and cannot be repaired or even cleaned.
5 To remove the pump, disconnect the battery.
6 Disconnect the fuel lines from the pump and plug the ends to prevent loss of fuel.
7 Unscrew the bolt which secures the coolant hose support bracket and fuel pump cover and remove the cover/drain tube complete (photo).
8 Unscrew the pump fixing nuts and remove the pump, insulator block and gaskets (photo).
9 Clean the old gasket from the flanges, locate a new gasket on each side of the insulator block and refit the pump (photo).
10 Tighten the fixing nuts to the specified torque.
11 Fit the pump cover/support bracket and locate the drain hose in its clip.
12 Reconnect the fuel lines and the battery.

6 Fuel pump (1.6 models) – testing, removal refitting and precautions

Warning: *Take adequate fire precautions during this procedure*

1 Raise the left-hand rear of the car and support it securely.
2 Disconnect the outlet hose from the pump and fit a substitute hose, the open end being inserted into a glass bottle.
3 Have an assistant turn on the ignition switch. The pump should operate and eject fuel into the bottle. If this does not happen, check the inertia switch (Section 26), then remove the pump and fit a new one in the following way.
4 Disconnect the battery.
5 Drain the fuel tank by syphoning the fuel into a container which can be sealed.
6 Disconnect the wiring plug from the pump.
7 Disconnect the two hoses from the pump.
8 Unscrew the fixing nuts and remove the pump and mounting bracket.
9 Release the fuel pump from its insulating rubber.

5.9 Fuel pump insulator

Fig. 3.4 Fuel pump (1.6 model with carburettor) (Sec 6)

10 When refitting, use a new rubber insulator and locate the pump and insulator so that the wiring plug socket will be towards the outside of the car.

11 The remaining refitting operations are reversals of removal, remember to fit a rubber and flat washer under each nut.

Precautions

12 Do not leave the ignition switched on for more than a few minutes without the engine running.

13 Do not switch on the ignition (pump operational) with an empty fuel tank.

7 Fuel tank (1.3 models) – removal, repair and refitting

Warning: *Take adequate fire precautions during this procedure*

1 Disconnect the battery.

2 Unscrew the tank drain plug and drain the fuel into a container which can be sealed (photo).

3 Raise the rear end of the car, support it securely and remove the left-hand rear roadwheel.

4 Remove the fuel filter cover and release the fuel filler hose access panel.

5 Disconnect the filler and vent hoses from the neck of the fuel filler.

6 Disconnect the electrical leads from the fuel level transmitter unit.

7 Support the tank on a jack with a block of wood as an insulator. Slacken the mounting strap nuts and move the straps aside (photo).

8 Lower the tank slowly until the hoses can be released from the pick-up unit and the two-way valve.

9 Remove the two-way valve from the top of the tank and then withdraw the tank from under the car.

10 If the fuel tank is leaking, have it repaired by specialists. *Never attempt to weld or solder a fuel tank. Residual fuel vapour cannot be satisfactorily removed unless the tank is steamed or boiled out for several hours.*

11 If the reason for tank removal was to remove sediment or water, remove the transmitter unit as described in Section 9. Pour in some paraffin and shake the tank vigorously, then drain. Repeat as necessary, giving a final rinse with clean fuel.

12 Refitting is a reversal of removal.

8 Fuel tank (1.6 models) – removal, repair and refitting

Warning: *Take adequate fire precautions during this procedure*

The operations are very similar to those described in the preceding Section except that a tank drain plug is not fitted and the fuel must therefore be syphoned or pumped out.

9 Fuel level transmitter – removal, testing and refitting

Warning: *Take adequate fire precautions during this procedure*

1 Remove the fuel tank as previously described.

2 Unscrew the transmitter unit retaining ring using a suitable tool to engage with the ring lugs.

3 Carefully withdraw the transmitter unit taking care not to bend the float arm.

4 Discard the sealing ring.

5 If an ohmmeter is available, the transmitter can be tested by measuring the resistance between the terminals.

Float in fully lowered (empty) positon 105 to 110 ohms
Float in half full positon 25.5 to 39.5 ohms
Float fully up (full) position 2.0 to 5.0 ohms

6 If the readings are not as indicated, renew the transmitter, if they are, then the fuel gauge is faulty, refer to the next Section.

7 Refitting the transmitter is a reversal of removal, use a new sealing ring.

10 Fuel gauge – testing

1 Disconnect the leads from the fuel tank level transmitter.

2 Connect the leads together using a bridging wire.

3 Switch on the ignition. The needle of the fuel gauge should move to FULL. Do not leave the ignition switched on for more than five

7.2 Fuel tank drain plug

7.7 Fuel tank mounting strap

seconds. If the gauge does not indicate FULL and it has been established that the wiring is in good order, renew the gauge as described in Chapter 12.

4 If the gauge does operate correctly then the fault must be in the transmitter.

11 Throttle cable – adjustment and renewal

1 When correctly adjusted, the throttle cable should have a slight slackness at the carburettor. Cable deflection should be between 4.0 and 10.0 mm (0.16 to 0.40 in).

2 Adjustment is carried out using the locknuts at the cable bracket (photo).

3 With the help of an assistant, check that idle and full throttle positions are obtainable with the accelerator pedal released or fully depressed.

4 To remove the throttle cable, release the cable bracket locknuts. If the cable inner is secured to the throttle quadrant by a clamp screw, slacken the screw.

Fig. 3.5 Throttle cable at carburettor (Sec 11)

1 Cable	4 Cable deflection
2 Locknut	5 Throttle lever
3 Locknut	

11.2 Throttle cable locknuts

5   Slip the cable end fitting from the carburettor throttle quadrant and the cable from its support bracket.
6   Working inside the car, disconnect the cable from the accelerator pedal by slipping the cable end fitting from the hole in the pedal arm (photo).
7   Withdraw the cable assembly through the bulkhead grommets.
8   Refitting is a reversal of removal. Adjust the cable as previously described.

12 Choke cable (1.3 models) – adjustment, removal and refitting

1   Remove the air cleaner.
2   With the choke control knob pushed fully in on the facia panel, check that the choke valve plate in the carburettor is fully open. In this position, the choke cable at the carburettor should have 5.0 mm (0.20 in) deflection under finger pressure. If not, adjust the cable setting at the choke valve plate lever connection.
3   To remove the choke cable, disconnect it from the carburettor.
4   Working inside the car, extract the choke knob retaining screw and pull off the knob (photos).
5   Unscrew the bezel nut and release the cable from the facia panel.
6   Lower the cable slightly until the leads can be disconnected from the choke warning lamp switch.
7   Withdraw the choke cable through the bulkhead grommet.
8   Fitting the new cable is a reversal of removal. Adjust as previously described.

11.6 Throttle cable at accelerator pedal arm

12.4A Extracting choke knob screw

12.4B Choke cable bezel nut

13.2 Accelerator pedal return spring

13 Accelerator pedal – removal and refittting

1   Disconnect the throttle cable as described in Section 11.
2   Working inside the car under the facia panel, extract the split pin and take off the washer from the accelerated pedal pivot rod. Disconnect the pedal return spring (photo).
3   Remove the pedal.
4   Refitting is a reversal of removal.

14 Carburettor (1.3 models) – description

1   The carburettor is of dual barrel, fixed jet type of Keihin manufacture.
2   The carburettor incorporates four inter-related systems: a primary slow-running system, a primary main system, a secondary slow and a secondary main.
3   A manually operated choke is fitted.
4   A fuel cut-off solenoid valve is fitted to prevent running on after the ignition is switched off.
5   The accelerator pump is of diaphragm type.

15 Carburettor (1.3 models) – idle speed and mixture adjustment

1   If a tachometer is not fitted, connect a reliable instrument in accordance with the manufacturer's instructions.
2   Have the engine at full working temperature with the radiator fan cutting in.
3   Make sure that all electrical equipment is switched off.
4   Clear the intake manifold by gradually increasing the engine speed to 2500 rev/min and holding it there for thirty seconds.
5   Check the idle speed. If outside the Specification, turn the throttle stop screw (photo).
6   The mixture is set during production and will not normally require adjustment. However, after carburettor overhaul or if the engine characteristics change due to wear or carbon build up, the mixture can be adjusted in the following way.
7   Ideally, the mixture should be adjusted using an exhaust gas analyser. Turn the mixture screw in until the CO level in the exhaust gas is at the specified level.
8   Where an exhaust gas analyser is not available, unscrew the mixture screw until the idle speed is at its highest point and then turn the screw in until the idle speed drops by 50 rev/min.

Fig. 3.6 Adjustment screws on Keihin carburettor (Sec 15)

1   Tamper proof plug   3   Throttle speed screw
2   Mixture screw

9   Re-adjust the idle speed to the specified level.
10 During the foregoing adjustments, clear the manifold at three minute intervals as described in paragraph 4.

16 Carburettor (1.3 models) – choke adjustments

Choke relief valve
1   Normally, the hook of the tension spring should be engaged in the rear notch as shown in Fig. 3.7.

15.5 Keihin carburettor idle speed screw (arrowed)

Fig. 3.7 Choke relief valve adjustment (Sec 16)

1 Forward notch (richer)   2 Rear notch (normal)

2   In severe weather, if the engine is difficult to start or is hesitant when driving away, it is acceptable to move the spring to the forward notch. Return it to its original setting when milder conditions resume.

Fast idle speed
3   If the choke control cable has been correctly set, then when the choke cable knob is pulled out to its first detent the marks on the choke valve plate lever and the carburettor body should be in alignment. If not, make a slight adjustment to the choke outer cable.
4   At cold start with the choke knob pulled fully out, the fast idle speed should be between 2600 and 2800 rev/min. Any adjustment required may be made by opening or closing the fork gap on the fast idle lever.

17 Carburettor (1.3 models) – accelerator pump stroke adjustment

1   Refer to Fig. 3.9 and measure the gap between the tab on the pump lever and the stop plate on the carburettor body. This represents the accelerator pump lever travel.

Fig. 3.8 Choke fast idle setting (Sec 16)

1 Choke lever
2 Carburettor body alignment mark
3 Fast idle lever
4 Fork gap

Fig. 3.9 Accelerator pump lever travel (Sec 17)

1 Pump lever
2 Stop plate
3 Pump lever travel (stroke)

2   If the travel is not as shown in Specifications, carefully bend the stop plate.

18 Carburettor (1.3 models) – throttle damper adjustment

1   Have the engine running at 3500 rev/min holding it at this level by means of the carburettor throttle lever.
2   Release the throttle lever suddenly. The damper arm should fully extend during a period of between one and four seconds.
3   If the period is not as specified, small adjustments may be made to the fork slot on the opener lever (Fig. 3.10).
4   Failure to correct matters may be due to a leaking diaphragm hose or a faulty diaphragm unit.

19 Carburettor (1.3 models) – removal and refitting

1   Disconnect the battery.
2   Remove the air cleaner.
3   Disconnect the throttle and choke control cables from the carburettor.
4   Disconnect the electrical lead from the fuel cut-off solenoid valve.
5   Disconnect the fuel supply hose.
6   Unscrew the carburettor mounting nuts and lift the carburettor from the inlet manifold.
7   Refitting is a reversal of removal. Use a new flange gasket on clean mounting surfaces and adjust the throttle and choke control cables as described in Sections 11 and 12.

20 Carburettor (1.3 models) – overhaul

1   It is usually sufficient to overhaul a carburettor by removing the top cover, mopping out the fuel from the float chamber and extracting and cleaning the jets (photo).
2   Obtain a gasket and seal set for use during reassembly.
3   If a carburettor has been in use for a long time and is obviously well worn, with slackness in the throttle valve spindle bores, it will probably be more economical to purchase a new or rebuilt unit.
4   However, for those wishing to completely dismantle the carburettor, proceed in the following way.
5   With the unit removed from the car, clean away external dirt using paraffin and a brush.
6   Disconnect the accelerator pump arm from the top cover.

Fig. 3.10 Throttle damper (Sec 18)

1   *Diaphragm unit*   3   *Opener lever*
2   *Fork slot*

7   Extract the screws and remove the top cover and the gasket (photo).
8   Carefully tap out the float pivot pin and remove the float.
9   Unscrew the float adjusting screw and take off the O-ring. Remove the filter gauze and the fuel inlet needle valve.
10 Remove the primary slow, main and secondary main air jets and emulsion tubes.
11 Remove the slow fuel jet plug, turn the carburettor upside down to eject the slow fuel jet.
12 Remove the main jet retainer, the power valve, the primary and secondary main jets. Take off the O-rings.
13 Remove the accelerator pump diaphragm cover, the diaphragm, spring and O-rings.
14 Clean all jets, passages and orifices with air from a tyre pump. On

20.1 Secondary throttle opener vacuum unit on Keihin carburettor

20.7 Top cover on Keihin carburettor

Fig. 3.11 Exploded view of Keihin carburettor (Sec 20)

1 Choke valve spindle	11 Accelerator pump diaphragm	21 Secondary main air jet
2 Float adjusting screw	12 Insulator	22 Primary main air jet
3 Fuel inlet needle valve	13 O-ring	23 Primary main fuel jet
4 Accelerator pump lever	14 Carburettor body	24 Secondary main fuel jet
5 Primary throttle damper diaphragm unit	15 Secondary throttle spindle	25 Slow fuel jet plug
6 Throttle speed screw	16 Throttle lever	26 Primary slow air jet
7 Fuel cut-off solenoid valve	17 Primary slow emulsion tube	27 Power valve
8 Non-return valve	18 Slow fuel jet	28 Float
9 Mixture adjusting screw	19 Secondary emulsion tube	29 Gasket
10 Primary throttle spindle	20 Primary emulsion tube	30 Secondary throttle opener diaphragm

no account probe them with wire or this will ruin their calibration.

15 This should be the limit of dismantling.

16 Before reassembling, obtain the appropriate repair kit which will contain all the necessary seals and gaskets.

17 Reassembly is a reversal of dismantling, but adjust the float in the following way.

18 Locate the fuel inlet needle valve, O-rings and filter gauze and

screw in the float adjusting screw a turn or two.

19 Fit the float and its pivot pin.

20 Hold the top cover vertically so that the float hangs downwards under its own weight.

21 With the top cover gasket in position, measure the dimension (A) (Fig. 3.12) which should be as given in the Specifications. Turn the float adjusting screw in or out to achieve this (photo).

Fig. 3.12 Keihin carburettor float setting (Sec 20)

1   Float arm/needle valve contact point
2   Float adjusting screw
A   Float setting (measured from gasket) 35.4 to 37.4 mm
    (1.39 to 1.47 in)

20.21 Float level adjusting screw on Keihin carburettor

21 Carburettor (1.6 models) – description

1   The SU HIF (Horizontal Integral Float chamber) carburettor is of
the variable choke, constant depression type incorporating a sliding
piston which automatically controls the mixture of air and fuel supplied
to the engine with respect to the throttle valve position and engine
speed. In addition the carburettor is equipped with an electronically-
operated mixture control device. This alters the mixture strength and
engine speed when starting and during slow running, and also
controls the operation of a fuel shut-off valve when decelerating or
descending a hill.
2   The carburettor functions as follows. When the engine is started
and is allowed to idle, the throttle valve passes a small amount of air.
Because the piston is in a low position it offers a larger restriction and
the resultant pressure reduction draws fuel from the jet, and
automisation occurs to provide a combustible mixture. Since the inside
section of the tapered needle is across the mouth of the jet, a relatively
small amount of fuel is passed.
3   When the throttle valve is opened, the amount of air passing
through the carburettor is increased, which causes a greater depression
beneath the sliding piston. An internal passageway connects this
depression with the suction chamber above the piston, which now
rises. The piston offers less of a restriction where the forces of
depression, gravity, and spring tension balance out. The tapered needle
has now been raised, and more fuel passes from the jet.
4   Incorporated in the jet adjusting (mixture) screw mechanism is a
bi-metal strip which alters the position of the jet to compensate for
varying fuel densities resulting from varying fuel temperatures.
5   Fuel enrichment for cold starting is by an internal valve which
admits more fuel into the airstream passing through the carburettor.
This valve is operated by a stepping motor which also controls the
engine idling speed. An electronic control unit (ECU) which is a small
microprocessor receives input from the coolant temperature sensor,
ambient air temperature sensor, accelerator pedal switch and ignition
coil and adjusts the engine idle speed and mixture accordingly. The

Fig. 3.13 SU carburettor (Sec 21)

1   Damper and oil reservoir   8   Throttle disc
2   Atmospheric pressure port   9   Idling fuel port
3   Needle and jet   10 Float
4   Bi-metal jet lever   A   Atmospheric pressure
5   Piston and return spring   B   Continuous depression
6   Depression transfer port   C   Manifold depression
7   Mixture enrichment port

Fig. 3.14 SU carburettor electronic mixture control circuit (Sec 21)

1 Carburettor	6 Ignition coil negative	9 Temperature gauge	A From ignition switch
2 Fuel cut-off valve	terminal	10 Accelerator pedal switch	B To programmed ignition
3 Stepper motor	7 Ambient air temperature	11 Coolant thermistor	electronic control unit
4 Vacuum switch	sensor	12 Fuel pump	
5 Fuel electronic control unit	8 Inertia (fuel cut-off) switch		

Wiring colour code

B Black	K Pink	S Slate	W White
G Green	O Orange	U Blue	Y Yellow
LG Light green			

ECU also controls the operation of a fuel shut-off valve which comes into operation when decelerating or descending a hill. If, during these conditions, the engine speed is in excess of 1300 rpm, the ambient air temperature and engine temperature are above a predetermined value, and the accelerator pedal switch is closed (pedal released) the valve will be opened and closed at half second intervals. This introduces a partial vacuum to the top of the float chamber thus weakening the mixture. The fuel shut-off circuit is deactivated if the engine speed suddenly stops, ie when declutching. When accelerating, a vacuum-operated switch acts upon the mixture control, allowing more fuel to be drawn through, resulting in the necessary richer mixture.

6 The air intake temperature is controlled by a vacuum-operated flap at the base of the air cleaner to blend the supply of hot and cold air. The flap is controlled by the thermac switch which is located in the plenum chamber adjacent to the carburettor.

7 An inertia cut-off switch is fitted in the fuse box as a means of isolating the fuel pump in the event of forward impact.

8 The overall effect of this type of carburettor is that it will remain in tune during the lengthy service intervals and also under varying

operating conditions and temperature changes. The design of the unit and its related systems ensure a fine degree of mixture control over the complete throttle range, coupled with enhanced engine fuel economy.

22 Carburettor (1.6 models) – in-car adjustments

Note: *Before carrying out any carburettor adjustment, ensure that the spark plug gaps, valve clearances and the ignition timing are correctly set. To carry out the following adjustments an accurate tachometer will be required. The use of an exhaust gas analyser (CO meter) is also preferable, although not essential.*

1 Remove the air cleaner and the plenum chamber.

2 Unscrew and remove the piston damper from the suction chamber.

3 Undo and remove the three securing screws and lift off the suction chamber, complete with piston and piston spring. After removal avoid rotating the piston in the suction chamber.

4 Invert the suction chamber assembly and drain the oil from the

hollow piston rod. Check that the needle guide is flush with the piston face and is secure. Do not be concerned that the needle appears loose in the guide, this is perfectly normal.

5   Observe the position of the jet in relation to the jet guide located in the centre of the carburettor venturi. The jet will probably be slightly below the top face of the jet guide. Turn the mixture adjusting screw until the top of the jet is flush with the top of the jet guide. Now turn the ajdusting screw two complete turns clockwise. If the mixture adjusting screw is covered by a small blue or red tamperproof plug, hook this out with a small screwdriver and discard it.

6   Refit the piston and suction chamber assembly, taking care not to turn the piston in the suction chamber any more than is necessary to align the piston groove with its guide. If the piston is turned excessively the spring will be wound up and the assembly will have to be dismantled, as described in Section 24.

7   Check that the piston is free to move in the suction chamber by lifting it and allowing it to drop under its own weight. A definite metallic click should be heard as the piston falls and contacts the bridge in the carburettor body. If this is not the case, dismantle and clean the suction chamber, as described in Section 24. If satisfactory, top up the damper oil with engine oil to the top of the hollow piston rod and refit the damper and plenum chamber.

8   Check that the throttle linkage operates smoothly and that there is a small amount of free play in the accelerator cable.

9   Connect a tachometer to the engine in accordance with the manufacturer's instructions, and also a CO meter if this is to be used.

10 Reconnect the vacuum hoses to the air cleaner and plenum chamber and lay the unit alongside the carburettor.

11 Start the engine and run it at a fast idle speed until it reaches its normal operating temperature. Continue to run the engine for a further

five minutes before commencing adjustment.

12 Increase the engine speed to 2500 rpm for 30 seconds and repeat this at three minute intervals during the adjustment procedure. This will ensure that any excess fuel is cleared from the inlet manifold.

13 Disconnect the coolant thermistor wiring plug (see Chapter 2 if necessary) and join the two plug terminals together using a suitable length of wire. This will ensure that the mixture control stepping motor is not actuated during adjustment.

14 If the cooling fan is running, wait until it stops then turn the idle speed adjustment screw as necessary until the engine is idling at the specified speed.

15 Switch off the engine.

16 Check the clearance between the fast idle pushrod and fast idle adjustment screw using feeler gauges (position B in Fig. 3.15). Turn the fast idle adjustment screw as necessary to obtain the specified clearance.

17 Check the throttle lever lost motion gap using feeler gauges (position A in Fig. 3.15) and, if necessary, turn the throttle lever adjustment screw to obtain the specified clearance.

18 Start the engine and slowly turn the mixture adjustment screw clockwise (to enrich) or anti-clockwise (to weaken) until the fastest idling speed which is consistent with smooth even running is obtained. If a CO meter is being used, adjust the mixture screw to obtain the specified idling exhaust gas CO content.

19 Reset the idling speed, if necessary, using the idle speed adjustment screw then switch off the engine once more.

Fig. 3.15 SU carburettor setting diagram (Sec 22)

1 Piston damper oil level	3 Throttle cable	5 Fast idle screw	A Clearance 1.55 to 2.05 mm
2 Throttle speed adjusting	4 Throttle lever adjusting	6 Fast idle push rod	(0.06 to 0.08 in)
screw	screw	7 Mixture adjusting screw	B Clearance 0.13 mm (0.005
			in) minimum

20 Remove the wire connecting the coolant thermistor wiring plug terminals together, but leave the plug disconnected.

21 Start the engine again. The mixture control stepping motor should move the fast idle pushrod to the fast idle position. Compare the engine fast idle speed with the specified setting and if necessary adjust by turning the fast idle adjustment screw as required.

22 Switch off the engine and reconnect the coolant thermistor wiring plug. **Note:** after carrying out this adjustment, ensure that the specified minimum clearance still exists between pushrod and screw, as described in paragraph 16. Adjust the screw if the clearance is less than specified.

23 Make a final check that the idling speed and mixture are correct after refitting the air cleaner and plenum chamber then switch off the engine and disconnect the instruments.

24 On cars equipped with an air conditioner, idle boost adjustment must be carried out in the following way after the system has been recharged with refrigerant.

25 Have the engine at normal operating temperature and idling.

26 Switch on the air conditioner and have the temperature control in the BLUE position and the air distribution and recirculation control set to the left-hand side. Set the fan switch to maximum speed.

27 When the radiator cooling fan cuts in, check the idle speed with the air conditioner switch off. Adjust to the specified speed if necessary.

28 Now turn the fan switch off and again check the idle speed. Adjust if necessary.

29 Turn the switch off and on several times, the engine idle speed should not alter.

23 Carburettor (1.6 models) – removal and refitting

1 Disconnect the battery.
2 Disconnect all electrical leads, ducts and hoses from the carburettor and thermac switch (photos).
3 Disconnect the fuel supply hose and plug its open end.
4 Disconnect the throttle cable.
5 Unscrew the carburettor fixing nuts and lift the carburettor from the

inlet manifold. Remove the flange insulating block and gaskets. Separate the carburettor from the plenum chamber.
6 Refitting is a reversal of removal. Use a new gasket on each side of the insulating block and adjust the throttle cable as described in Section 11.

24 Carburettor (1.6 models) – overhaul

1 Remove the carburettor, as described in the previous Section.
2 Clean off the exterior of the carburettor using paraffin, or a suitable solvent and wipe dry.

23.2B Stepping motor connecting plug

23.2A Fuel cut-off (anti run on) valve on carburettors

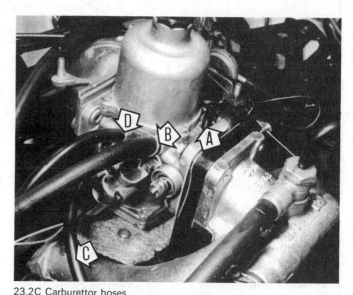

23.2C Carburettor hoses
A   Ignition vacuum advance   C   Fuel inlet
B   Crankcase breather   D   Float chamber vent

Fig. 3.16 Exploded view of SU HIF carburettor (Sec 24)

1   Damper piston
2   Jump ring
3   Suction chamber
4   Air valve piston
5   Spring
6   Needle retaining screw
7   Needle bias spring
8   Jet needle
9   Needle guide
10 Throttle adjusting screw
11 Seal

12 Mixture adjusting screw
13 Fuel cut-off valve
14 Valve solenoid
15 Spindle nut and lockplate
16 Seal
17 Throttle valve plate and
    screw
18 Throttle valve plate spindle
19 Carburettor body
20 Vacuum capsule and seal

21 Mixture control stepper
    motor
22 Fast idle pushrod
23 Jet bearing
24 Jet bearing nut
25 Jet assembly
26 Float needle seat
27 Float needle
28 Bi-metal jet lever
29 Float

30 Jet retaining screw and
    spring
31 Float chamber cover seal
32 Float chamber cover
33 Plain washer
34 Progressive throttle lever
    and return spring
35 Lost motion link/throttle
    stop and spring
36 Fast idle lever and return
    spring

3 Unscrew the damper from the suction chamber and drain the oil from the piston rod (photo).

4 Unscrew the three retaining screws and lift off the suction chamber and piston assembly (photo).

5 Push the piston up to expose the retaining circlip. Extract the circlip and withdraw the piston and spring assembly (photo).

6 Unscrew the needle guide locking screw and withdraw the needle guide and spring (photo).

7 Mark the relationship of the float chamber cover to the carburettor body. Unscrew the four retaining screws and lift off the cover and O-ring seal (photo).

8 Unscrew the jet adjusting lever retaining screw and withdraw the jet and adjusting lever assembly. Disengage the jet from the lever (photo).

9 Unscrew the float pivot screw and lift out the float and fuel needle valve. Unscrew the needle valve seat from the base of the float chamber (photos).

10 Unscrew the jet bearing locking nut and remove the jet bearing (photos).

11 Undo the three retaining screws and remove the fuel shut-off valve and solenoid assembly. Recover the gasket (photo).

24.3 Withdrawing damper

24.4 Carburettor suction chamber and air valve piston

24.5A Piston rod circlip

24.5B Removing air valve piston and spring

24.6 Needle locking screw (arrowed) and needle partially withdrawn

24.7 Lifting off float chamber cover

24.8 Jet and adjuster lever

24.9A Float pivot screw

24.9B Fuel inlet needle valve

24.9C Unscrewing needle valve seat

24.10A Jet bearing locknut

24.10B Removing jet bearing

24.11 Fuel shut off (anti run on) solenoid valve

12 Dismantling the remaining components is not recommended, as these parts are not available separately. If the throttle levers, linkage or spindle appear worn, or in any way damaged, it will be necessary to renew the complete carburettor. **Do not** remove the mixture control stepping motor or vacuum switch. These components are set to each individual carburettor during manufacture and may not operate correctly if disturbed.
13 Check the condition of the float needle valve and seat and renew these components if there is any sign of pitting or wear ridges particularly on the needle. Ensure that the filter in the seat assembly is clean (photo).
14 Examine the carburettor body for cracks and damage, and ensure that the brass fittings and piston guide are secure.
15 Clean the inside of the suction chamber and the outer circumference of the piston with a petrol-moistened rag and allow to air dry. Insert the piston into the suction chamber without the spring. Hold the assembly in a horizontal position and spin the piston. If there is any tendency for the piston to bind, renew the piston and dashpot assembly.
16 Connect a 12 volt supply to the terminals of the fuel shut-off valve solenoid and ensure that the valve closes. If not, renew the solenoid.

17 Check the piston needle and jet bearing for any signs of ovality, or wear ridges.
18 Shake the float and listen for any trapped fuel which may have entered through a tiny crack or fracture.
19 Check the condition of all gaskets, seals and connecting hoses and renew any that show signs of deterioration.
20 Begin reassembly by refitting the jet bearing and retaining nut to the carburettor body.
21 Refit the fuel needle valve and seat, followed by the float and float pivot screw.
22 Allow the float to close the needle valve under its own weight and measure the distance from the centre of the float to the face of the carburettor body, as shown in Fig. 3.17. If the measured dimension is outside the float level height setting given in the Specifications, carefully bend the brass contact pad on the float to achieve the required setting.

Fig. 3.17 SU carburettor float setting diagram (Sec 24)

A   1.0 to 1.5 mm (0.039 to 0.059 in)

24.13 Fuel needle valve seat filter

Fig. 3.18 SU carburettor needle arrangement (Sec 24)

24.26 Needle, spring and guide

23 Engage the jet with the cut-out in the adjusting lever, ensuring that the jet head moves freely. Position the jet in the jet bearing and, at the same time, engage the slot in the adjusting lever with the protruding tip of the mixture adjustment screw. Secure the assembly with the retaining screw.
24 Turn the mixture adjustment screw as necessary to bring the top of the jet flush with the jet bearing upper face when viewed from above. Now turn the adjustment screw two complete turns clockwise to obtain an initial mixture setting.
25 Fit a new O-ring seal to the float chamber cover. Fit the cover with the previously made marks aligned and secure with the four retaining screws.
26 Refit the piston needle, spring and needle guide to the piston ensuring that the needle guide is flush with the underside of the piston and the triangular etch mark on the guide is between the two transfer holes in the piston. Refit and tighten the locking screw (photo).
27 Temporarily refit the piston and dashpot to the carburettor body without the spring. Engage the piston in its guide and, with the suction chamber in its correct position relative to the retaining screws, mark the piston-to-suction chamber relationship. Remove the suction chamber and piston.
28 Fit the spring to the piston, align the previously made marks and slide the suction chamber over the piston and spring. Avoid turning the piston in the suction chamber, otherwise the spring will be wound up.
29 Push the piston rod up and refit the circlip to the piston rod.
30 Refit the piston and suction chamber, and secure with the three retaining screws tightened evenly. Fill the piston damper with engine oil up to the top of the piston and refit the damper.
31 Refit the fuel shut-off valve using a new gasket, if necessary, and secure the unit with the three screws.

25 Thermac switch – removal and refitting

1 The thermac switch can be removed independently of the carburettor or air cleaner.
2 Prise the sensor and grommet from the plenum chamber. Remove the seal and disconnect both vacuum hoses.
3 Reassemble the new switch to the grommet and secure it with the spring clip.
4 When installed, check that the switch is firmly held in the grommet.
5 Apply suitable sealant to the grommet and fit the switch assembly into the plenum chamber so that the switch is in the horizontal plane. Reconnect both vacuum hoses.

26 Inertia switch (1.6 models) – removal and refitting

1 Open the cover of the fuse box and remove the bolt from the inertia (fuel cut-off) switch mounting bracket.

Fig. 3.19 Thermac switch (Sec 25)

1 Plenum chamber
2 Grommet and switch
3 Air flap hose (large bore)
4 Manifold hose (small bore)
5 Carburettor

2 Withdraw the switch and disconnect the multi-plug.
3 To check the action of the inertia switch, depress the button and then strike the front of the switch against the hand which will cause the button to lock in the raised position.
4 Once the switch is fitted, depress the button to set it.

Part B (Models with fuel injection)

27 Description and operation

1 The system consists of a fuel tank located ahead of the rear suspension, an electrically operated fuel pump, a temperature controlled air cleaner and a Lucas electronic fuel injection system.
2 The main components of the fuel injection system are shown in Fig. 3.20 and their function is described in the following paragraphs.

Fig. 3.20 Location of fuel injection system components (Sec 27)

1 Fuel pump
2 Fuel electronic control unit
3 Fuel filter
4 Main relay
5 Fuel pump relay and pump ballast resistor
6 Air flow meter
7 Coolant temperature thermistor
8 Fuel injector and clip
9 Engine speed resistor
10 Speed transducer
11 Throttle housing
12 Air valve stepper motor
13 Throttle potentiometer
14 Fuel cut-off switch
15 Fuel pressure regulator
16 Fuel temperature switch
17 Fuel feed pipe
18 Fuel spill return pipe
19 Fuel tank

Fig. 3.21 Schematic layout of electronic fuel injection system (Sec 27)

1 Fuel tank pick-up strainer	11 Base idle speed and mixture adjustment screw	18 Engine harness multi-plug	27 Coolant temperature thermistor
2 Fuel spill return swirl pot	12 Air valve stepper motor	19 Inertia (fuel cut-off) switch	28 Knock sensor
3 Fuel pump	13 Throttle housing – coolant and crankcase ventilation ports	20 Ignition ECU	29 Crankshaft sensor
4 Fuel pump ballast resistor		21 Fuel temperature switch	A Regulated fuel pressure
5 Fuel filter	14 Inlet manifold	22 Speed sensor	B Spill return low pressure fuel
6 Fuel pressure regulator	15 To main harness multi-plug	23 Fuel pump relay	C Inlet air flow
7 Injector	16 Main relay	24 Engine speed resistor	D Manifold depression
8 Air flow meter	17 Fuel ECU	25 Ignition coil	
9 Throttle potentiometer		26 Distributor cap and spark plug leads	
10 Throttle speed screw			

3 Directly associated with the system are the ignition electronic control unit, the injection coil and the speed sensor.

Fuel electronic control unit
4 This is located under the front left-hand seat and is the control centre for the fuel injection system.

Fuel injectors
5 The fuel injectors are solenoid operated and are located between the pressurised fuel rail and the inlet manifold. The injector nozzles are designed to give good fuel atomisation.

Engine coolant temperature thermistor
6 This is located in the coolant inlet elbow on the cylinder head. The thermistor is a resistive device, its resistance varying with temperature changes.

Air flow meter
7 This is of hot wire type over which the intake air flows. A proportion of the air flows through a bypass in which a sensing and compensating element are located.

Throttle potentiometer
8 This is mounted at the rear of the throttle housing and is directly coupled to the throttle shaft. Movement of accelerator pedal and in consequence the throttle shaft, rotates the arm in the potentiometer to vary the resistance which is then monitored by the fuel control unit.

Air valve stepper motor
9 This is screwed into the top of the throttle housing and has directional control windings so that the air valve can be opened or closed as directed by the fuel control unit.

Throttle housing
10 This is attached directly to the inlet manifold and incorporates the throttle speed screw, base idle speed screw and the mixture adjusting screw.

Fuel pump

11 This is located on the left-hand side of the fuel tank and is of self-priming centrifugal type. The pump supplies fuel under pressure through an in-line filter to the fuel rail and pressure regulator.

Fuel pressure regulator

12 This is a mechanical device which controls fuel rail pressure by means of manifold vacuum pressure. The regulator is located on the fuel rail. Under normal driving conditions, the fuel rail pressure is maintained at 2.5 bar (36 lbf/in²) above manifold vacuum to ensure that the pressure difference across the injector nozzles remains constant.

Relays

13 These are located on the air cleaner housing mounting bracket (photo). The main relay is energised with the ignition on and provides a feed to the fuel ECU. The fuel pump relay is energised by the ECU briefly when the ignition is switched on, and continuously when the engine is running.

27.13 Fuel injection system relay

Fuel temperature switch

14 This is a bi-metallic switch which when the temperature in the fuel rail rises above 90°C (194°F), the switch closes and the engine coolant temperature thermistor signal is bypassed. This action is sensed by the fuel control unit which then increases the opening period of the injectors during hot starting to reduce the effects of fuel vaporisation. At hot start, it is normal for the coolant temperature gauge and warning lamp to indicate high temperature.

Fuel cut-off inertia switch

15 This is a safety switch mounted on the steering column bracket behind the facia panel. In the event of a collision, the switch shuts off the control unit and the fuel pump relay. The switch is reset by depressing the button inside the fuse box.

Speed transducer

16 This is mounted on the engine compartment rear bulkhead, its purpose being to provide the fuel system control unit with road speeds.

Operation

17 When the ignition is switched on, voltage is applied through the fuel cut-off switch to the fuel pump relay, the fuel and ignition system electronic control units. The fuel rail is pressurised and voltage is applied to the air flow meter, the fuel injectors and the ignition control unit.

18 When the ignition switch is turned to the start position, the fuel control unit receives data from the transducer, thermistor, potentiometer air flow meter and ignition pulses to determine fuel injector opening time and fuel enrichment.

19 Once the engine fires, the fuel control unit regulates the injector

opening and consequently the volume of fuel injected, varying this as the engine temperature rises.

20 Constant engine idle speed is maintained by the control unit regulating the air valve position.

21 If while the engine is idling, engine load is increased through the alternator having to supply a greater output, because of electrical accessories being switch on, then the stepper motor will be energised and the air valve opened by the control unit to maintain a constant engine idle speed.

22 During normal driving, the control unit continually monitors road speed, air flow engine temperature, throttle opening and engine speed. All changes in these parameters are monitored to vary the injector opening times to suit all monitoring conditions. An electronic memory is used as a basis for engine speed/load fuel requirement computations.

23 During engine overrun conditions, the control unit cuts off the fuel, provided certain conditions apply regarding the engine coolant temperature, which should be above 36°C (96.8°F), the throttle in idle position and the engine speed in excess of 1400 rev/min.

24 As the engine speed falls below 110 rev/min and the accelerator pedal depressed, fuel is again supplied for smooth take up.

25 At full throttle conditions, the fuel electronic control unit provides more fuel for full load enrichment by holding the injectors open for a longer period.

26 The fuel electronic control unit signals the ignition control unit during idling to ensure that the ignition timing is held at 20° BTDC so that the idle speed is held steady.

28 Maintenance and inspection

1 At the intervals given in Routine Maintenance at the beginning of this Manual, carry out the following service operations to the fuel system components.

2 With the car over a pit, raised on a vehicle lift, or securely supported on axle stands, carefully inspect the fuel pipes, hoses and unions for chafing, leaks and corrosion. Renew any pipes that are severely pitted with corrosion or in any way damaged. Renew any hoses that show signs of cracking or other deterioration. Only use specially supplied cut to length fuel injection hoses as they have a special lining to resist the high temperature and pressure of the fuel.

3 Always position the hose clips 3.0 mm (0.12 in) from the end of the hoses, never flush with the end.

4 Examine the fuel tank for leaks, particularly around the fuel gauge sender unit, and for signs of corrosion or damage.

5 Check condition of exhaust system, as described in Section 41.

6 From within the engine compartment, check the security of all fuel hose attachments and inspect the fuel hoses and vacuum hoses for kinks, chafing or deterioration.

7 Renew the air cleaner element and clean the air cleaner body and cover.

8 Check the operation of the accelerator linkage and lubricate the linkage, cable and pedal pivot with a few drops of engine oil.

9 Check the fuel injection system idle speed and mixture settings, as described in Section 36 where necessary.

10 Renew the fuel filter as described in Section 31.

29 Air cleaner – servicing, removal and refitting

1 To renew the air cleaner element, spring back the retaining clips and lift off the air cleaner cover (photo).

2 Withdraw the element then wipe clean the inside of the air cleaner housing and cover.

3 Fit a new element, locate the cover on the air cleaner housing and secure with the retaining clips.

4 To remove the air cleaner and bracket first disconnect and remove the battery (Chapter 12).

5 Slacken the clip and detach the cold air intake hose from the air cleaner housing.

6 Disconnect the small vacuum hose from the centre of the air cleaner cover (photo).

7 Disconnect the air flow meter wiring plug, undo the bolts and remove the air flow meter from the air cleaner. Move the meter to one side, with the hose still attached, or disconnect the hose to the throttle

Fig. 3.22 Air cleaner (fuel injection system) showing vacuum pipe (Sec 29)

29.1 Air cleaner casing and element

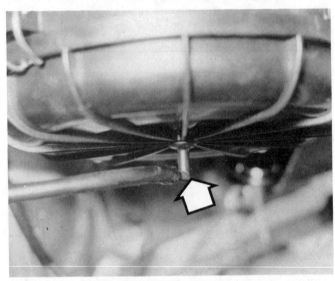

29.6 Air cleaner cover vacuum hose

29.7A Disconnecting the air flow meter wiring plug

29.7B Removing the air flow meter

29.8 Main and fuel pump relays clipped to air cleaner bracket

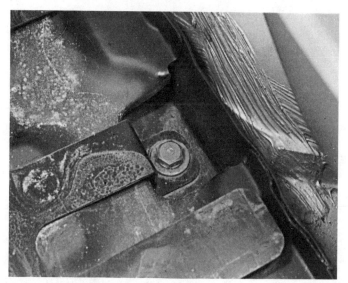

29.11 Close up of bracket securing bolt

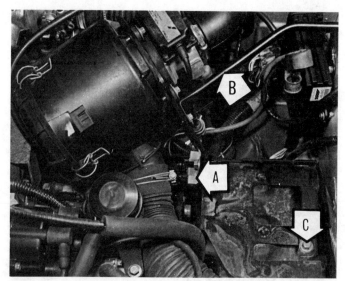

29.12 General view of air cleaner and bracket showing resistor (A), support tube (B) and bracket securing bolt (C)

housing and remove the air flow meter (photos).

8 Pull the two relays, with their sockets, from the air cleaner bracket and place them to one side, still connected (photo).

9 Disconnect the two wires to the fuel pump ballast resistor, marking them for correct refitting.

10 Remove the bolts from the air cleaner bracket support tube and remove the tube.

11 Remove the bolt securing the air cleaner bracket to the battery tray and lift out the air cleaner and bracket (photo).

12 Refitting is a reversal of removal, ensuring that the relay caps are uppermost (photo).

30 Fuel system – depressurising

Warning: *Take adequate fire precautions during this procedure*

1 The fuel system must be depressurised before any part of the fuel line between the fuel pump and fuel regulator is disconnected.

2 Disconnect the fuel pump relay and then disconnect the blue/red lead from the starter solenoid. This will prevent the fuel pump from operating. As a safety measure, if it is not wished for the engine to run, disconnect the HT lead from the ignition coil. Do not disconnect the LT lead.

3 Crank the engine for at least ten seconds or allow it to run until it stops.

4 Disconnect the battery and then uncouple the fuel line or component. Be prepared for some fuel to drain out.

5 On completion of work, reconnect the relay, HT lead and battery.

31 Fuel filter – renewal

Warning: *Take adequate fire precautions during this procedure*

1 Depressurise the fuel system as described in the preceding Section.

2 Slacken the clips on the air intake elbow at the flow meter and on the fuel intake hose at the throttle housing.

3 Remove the air intake hose with elbow.

4 Slacken the fuel filter clamp bracket, ease the filter forward and out of its bracket. Release the filter from the fuel inlet hose (photo).

5 Refit the new filter by reversing the removal operations, but make sure that the arrow on the filter points towards the fuel outlet hose.

32 Fuel pump – removal and refitting

Warning: *Take adequate fire precautions during this procedure*

1 Depressurise the fuel system as described in Section 30 then disconnect the battery negative terminal.

2 Syphon, or hand pump all the fuel from the fuel tank.

3 Jack up the rear of the car and support it on axle stands.

4 Disconnect the wiring connectors at the fuel pump which is located to the rear of the fuel tank, just above the rear axle transverse member (photo).

5 Undo the two nuts and washers securing the pump retaining strap to the mounting bracket.

6 Ease the strap studs out of the mounting bracket, then manoeuvre the pump down between the rear axle member and the spare wheel well.

7 Position a suitable bowl beneath the pump and disconnect the inlet and outlet hoses from the pump nozzles. Plug the hoses after removal. **Note:** *a quantity of fuel will be released during this operation.*

8 Note the fitted relationship of the pump terminals to the strap studs and push the pump out of the strap support rubbers. Free the pump from the rubbers if adhesive has been used for retention.

9 To refit the pump apply adhesive to the strap rubbers and insert the pump into the strap. Position the pump in the strap as noted during removal so that the terminals will be vertical when the pump is installed.

10 Reconnect the inlet and outlet hoses to the pump nozzles.

11 Fit the plain washers to the strap mounting studs, manoeuvre the pump into position and secure with the plain washers and nuts.

12 Reconnect the pump wiring and lower the car to the ground.

13 Reconnect the fuel relay circuit, reconnect the battery and fill the fuel tank.

33 Fuel tank – removal, repair and refitting

The operations are as described in Section 8 of Part A.

34 Fuel level transmitter and gauge

Refer to Part A, Sections 9 and 10.

35 Throttle cable and accelerator pedal

Refer to Part A, Sections 11 and 13. Note that the cable is attached to the lever on the throttle housing.

31.4 Fuel filter

Fig. 3.23 Fuel pump (fuel injection system) (Sec 32)

36 Idle speed and mixture – adjustment

See Chapter 13, Section 4

Note: *Idle speed is controlled by the fuel ECU and should not normally need adjusting. Idle mixture may need adjusting after long periods of service. The complete procedure described here would be used after major component renewal, and may require special equipment – see paragraph 6.*

Some adjustment screws may be protected by tamperproof caps. Satisfy yourself that you are not breaking local or national anti-pollution laws before removing such caps; fit new caps on completion when required by law.

1 Bring the engine to normal operating temperature (cooling fan having operated at least once). Switch off all electrical equipment.
2 Connect an accurate tachometer (rev counter) to the engine in accordance with the maker's instructions.
3 Set the air valve in the closed position as follows:

(a) With the ignition on, disconnect the air valve stepper motor multi-plug. Switch the ignition off, wait five seconds and reconnect the multi-plug

(b) Switch the ignition on, wait five seconds and repeat paragraph (a)

(c) Switch the ignition on, wait five seconds and disconnect the multi-plug

4 Turn the throttle by-pass screw fully clockwise. (This screw is not present on later models).
5 Start the engine and allow it to idle. The idle speed should be within the limits given with the air valve closed (see Specifications). Turn the base idle screw if necessary to bring the idle speed within limits.
6 If the base idle screw has been disturbed, the throttle potentiometer must now be adjusted by a Rover dealer or other competent specialist using dedicated test equipment.
7 Reconnect the air valve stepper motor multi-plug. Run the engine and check that the idle speed (now controlled by the ECU) is as specified.
8 Connect an exhaust gas analyser in accordance with its maker's instructions.
9 Read the exhaust CO level at idle and compare it with that specified. If adjustment is necessary, turn the mixture screw clockwise to increase the CO level, anti-clockwise to reduce it (photo).

10 If the radiator cooling fan cuts in during adjustment, wait until it stops before proceeding.
11 Stop the engine, disconnect the test gear and (when applicable) fit new tamperproof caps.

Fig. 3.24 Fuel injection system adjustment screws (Sec 36)

A   Mixture screw   C   Throttle by-pass screw (early
B   Base idle screw   models only)

36.9 Adjusting the mixture screw

37.2 Air flow meter

37.5 Stepper motor plug (arrowed)

37.13 Fuel pressure regulator union nuts (A), vacuum hose (B) and retaining nut (C)

37 Fuel injection system components – removal and refitting

Air flow meter
1 Disconnect the air flow meter wiring plug.
2 Release the retaining clip and detach the intake air hose from the air flow meter (photo).
3 Undo the two bolts securing the meter to the air cleaner bracket and withdraw the unit from the bracket and air cleaner body.
4 Refitting is the reverse sequence to removal. Make sure that the hose clip is fitted squarely.

Air valve stepper motor
5 Slide back the rubber cover and disconnect the stepper motor multi-plug (photo).
6 Using a 32 mm spanner, unscrew the stepper motor from the throttle housing.

7 To refit the stepper motor, fit a new sealing washer and apply a thread sealant to the stepper motor threads.
8 Screw the unit in finger tight then carefully tighten with the spanner.
9 Refit the multi-plug and the rubber cover.

Fuel temperature switch
10 Disconnect the wiring multi-plug and unscrew then switch from the top of the fuel rail.
11 Refit the switch using the reverse sequence of removal.

Fuel pressure regulator
Warning: *Take adequate fire precautions during this procedure*

12 Depressurise the fuel system as described in Section 30 then disconnect the battery negative terminal.
13 Place absorbent rags beneath the regulator, unscrew the union nuts and remove the two fuel hoses (photo).

14 Disconnect the vacuum hose from the rear of the regulator.

15 Undo the retaining nut and washer then withdraw the unit from its support bracket.

16 Refitting is the reverse sequence of removal. After fitting reconnect the fuel relay circuit as described in Section 30 and reconnect the battery.

Fuel rail

Warning: *Take adequate fire precautions during this procedure*

17 Depressurise the fuel system as described in Section 30 then disconnect the battery negative terminal.

18 Place absorbent rag beneath the fuel rail.

19 Unscrew the fuel pressure regulator to fuel rail hose union at the regulator. Plug the hose and regulator after removal.

20 Slacken the fuel pressure regulator retaining nut, slide the regulator out of its support bracket and place it one side.

21 Unscrew the fuel inlet hose union at the fuel rail, remove the hose and plug its end (photos).

22 Disconnect the wiring multi-plug at each fuel injector (photo).

23 Extract the clips securing the fuel injectors to the fuel rail.

24 Undo the two bolts securing the fuel rail to the manifold, holding the injectors to prevent displacement, and remove the fuel rail.

25 Before refitting the fuel rail, renew the O-ring seals on each fuel injector.

26 Refitting the fuel rail is the reverse sequence of removal. After fitting reconnect the fuel relay circuit as described in Section 30 and reconnect the battery.

Fuel injectors

Warning: *Take adequate fire precautions during this procedure*

27 Slacken the fuel pressure regulator retaining nut, slide the regulator out of its support bracket and lay it on the manifold with hoses still attached.

28 Undo the two bolts securing the fuel rail to the manifold. Lift up the fuel rail and at the same time ease the injectors out of their seatings in the manifold. Lay the injectors over the engine wiring harness.

29 Switch on the ignition, wait ten seconds, then switch off. The fuel pump will operate for approximately three seconds while the ignition is switched on and will pressurise the injectors.

30 Observe each injector and renew any that leak more than two drops of fuel per minute.

31 To check the injector spray pattern, disconnect all the injector multi-plugs except the one on the injector to be tested.

32 Place a glass jar under the connected injector so that the sprayed fuel can be contained, but the pattern still observed.

33 Ensure that the ignition is switched off then disconnect the wiring multi-plug from the fuel system ECU. The ECU is located under the carpet above the passenger's footwell.

34 Using suitable connectors, connect pin No 1 and pin No 16 in the ECU multi-plug connector to earth. Ensure that the connectors do not touch any of the pins in the plug. Observe the fuel spray which will now be emitting from the injector. The spray pattern should be regular and at a rate of 185cc/min. If this is not the case the injector should be renewed.

35 After testing, remove the earth connector from the ECU multi-plug. Reconnect the multi-plug to the next injector to be tested and position it in the jar. Remove the multi-plug from the previously tested injector then repeat the test as described in paragraph 34.

36 After all the injectors have been tested, renew any that are faulty. To do this, depressurise the fuel system and then disconnect the battery.

37 Disconnect the wiring multi-plug at the fuel temperature switch and the multi-plug at each fuel injector.

38 Lift the fuel rail up and at the same time ease the injectors out of their locations in the manifold. Extract the retaining clip(s) and withdraw the injector(s) from the fuel rail.

39 To refit the injector(s), wipe clean the injector and manifold seating areas and fit a new O-ring seal to the base of each injector. Fit a new O-ring seal to the top of any injector that was removed from the fuel rail.

40 Fit the injectors to the fuel rail and secure with the retaining clips.

41 Align the injectors with their seatings in the manifold and press them fully into position.

42 Refit the two fuel rail retaining bolts and tighten securely.

43 Reconnect the fuel temperature switch and fuel injector multi-plugs.

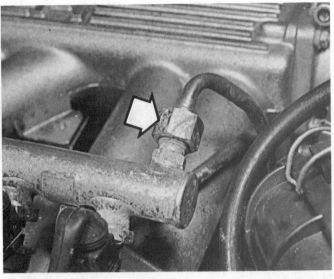

37.21A Fuel rail union nut (arrowed)

37.21B Fuel rail

37.22 Fuel injector plug

Fig. 3.25 Fuel injector (Sec 37)

1 Fuel injector
2 O-ring seal
3 O-ring seal

4 Fuel rail
5 Injector retaining clip

44 Slide the fuel pressure regulator back into its support bracket and tighten the retaining nut.
45 Reconnect the fuel relay circuit as described in Section 30 then reconnect the battery.

Throttle housing

46 Disconnect the battery negative terminal.
47 Disconnect the wiring multi-plug at the end of the throttle potentiometer lead.
48 Slide back the rubber cover and disconnect the wiring multi-plug at the air valve stepper motor.
49 Slacken the retaining clip and detach the intake air hose from the throttle housing.
50 Slacken the retaining screw and release the accelerator cable from the connector on the throttle housing linkage.
51 On models with automatic transmission, disconnect the kickdown cable.
52 Unscrew the cooling system expansion tank filler cap to release all pressure in the cooling system. Remove the cap slowly if the system is hot.
53 Disconnect the air and vacuum hoses at the rear of the throttle housing, noting their location.
54 Undo the bolts securing the throttle housing to the manifold and ease the unit off the flange.
55 Disconnect the coolant and crankcase breather hoses from beneath the housing and remove the housing from the engine. Plug the coolant hose.
56 The air valve stepper motor may be removed from the throttle housing by simply unscrewing it using a 32 mm spanner, it is advisable to leave the throttle potentiometer undisturbed so as not to lose its set fitted position. If the potentiometer is disturbed, recalibration by a BL dealer will be necessary.
57 Refitting the throttle housing is the reverse sequence of removal bearing in mind the following points:

(a) Ensure that the throttle housing and manifold mating faces are perfectly clean and if necessary use a new gasket
(b) Reconnect the accelerator cable
(c) Top-up the cooling system if necessary to the level indicated on the expansion tank.

Fuel cut-off inertia switch

58 Unbolt the switch mounting bracket from below and to the right of the heater unit.
59 Disconnect the wiring plug from the switch.
60 Unscrew the two through-bolts and disconnect the switch from its bracket.
61 Refitting is a reversal of removal.

Electronic control unit

62 Disconnect the battery.
63 Remove the left-hand front seat.
64 Disconnect the multi-plug from the control unit and unbolt the control unit mounting bracket.
65 Refitting is a reversal of removal.

Speed transducer

66 Disconnect the multi-plug from the speed transducer (photo).
67 Unscrew the speedometer cable from the speed transducer.
68 Unscrew the nut which holds the speed transducer mounting bracket to the engine compartment rear bulkhead and lift away the speed transducer and bracket.
69 Refitting is a reversal of removal.

37.66 Speed transducer

Part C (Manifolds, exhaust systems and Fault diagnosis)

38 Manifolds (1.3 models) – removal and refitting

Inlet manifold

1 The inlet manifold is coolant-heated and is of light alloy construction.
2 To remove the manifold, drain the cooling system and then disconnect all hoses from the manifold.
3 Disconnect all leads, hoses and control cables from the carburettor and remove it.
4 Unbolt the manifold support bracket (photo).
5 Unscrew the manifold fixing nuts and withdraw the manifold. Discard the gasket (photo).

Exhaust manifold

6 The exhaust manifold is of cast iron construction and incorporates a hot air collecting shroud.

38.4 Wiring harness support clip at inlet manifold

38.5 Unscrewing inlet manifold nuts

7   To remove the manifold, disconnect the battery, raise the front of the car and support it securely.
8   Remove the centre undershield.
9   Disconnect he exhaust downpipe from the manifold. Retrieve the sealing ring (photo).
10 Disconnect the weathershield from the front panel and disconnect the hot air duct from the manifold shroud.
11 Remove the hot air shroud and the manifold support bracket (photos).
12 Unscrew the fixing nuts and lift the manifold from the cylinder head. Discard the gasket (photo).
13 Refitting both manifolds is a reversal of removal. Use new gaskets fitted to clean mating surfaces and tighten all nuts and bolts to the specified torque (photo).
14 If the inlet manifold was removed, refill the cooling system (Chapter 2).
15 Reconnect the battery.

Fig. 3.26 Inlet manifold (1.3 models) (Sec 38)

1 Gasket   3 Support bracket
2 Manifold

Fig. 3.27 Exhaust manifold (1.3 models) (Sec 38)

1 Gasket   3 Manifold
2 Hot air collecting shroud   4 Support bracket

38.9 Exhaust manifold to downpipe flange support bracket
(arrowed)

38.11A Exhaust manifold hot air collector

38.11B Exhaust manifold with hot air collector removed

38.12 Exhaust manifold gaskets

38.13 Inlet manifold gasket

39 Manifolds (1.6 carburettor models) – removal and refitting

1   The inlet manifold incorporates an electric heater which operates as soon as the ignition switch is turned on. Its purpose is to reduce cold start enrichment. The manifold is also coolant-heated and as the temperature of the coolant rises a temperature sensor reduces and then switches off the electric heater.

2   To reduce the manifolds, first disconnect the battery.

3   Remove the air cleaner (Section 3).

4   Remove the carburettor (Section 23).

5   Drain the cooling system.

6   Disconnect all hoses and leads from the inlet manifold.

7   Raise the front of the car and support it securely. Disconnect the exhaust downpipe from the manifold.

8   Unbolt the inlet manifold support struts.

9   Unbolt and remove the heat shield from the inlet manifold and the hot air shroud from the exhaust manifold.

10 Unscrew all fixing nuts and bolts and lift the manifolds from the cylinder head. Discard the gasket.

11 Refitting is a reversal of removal. Use a new gasket on clean mating surfaces and tighten all nuts and bolts to the specified torque.

Fig. 3.28 Manifold (1.6 models with carburettor) (Sec 39)

1	Gasket	6	Exhaust heater
2	Heat shield	7	Hot air collecting shroud
3	Inlet manifold	8	Support strut
4	Induction temperature sensor	9	Support strut
5	Induction heater		

12 Refill the cooling system.
13 Reconnect the battery.

40 Manifolds (1.6 fuel injection models) – removal and refitting

1   Depressurise the fuel system as described in Section 30.
2   Disconnect the battery.
3   Disconnect the vacuum hoses from the inlet chamber and the multi-plug from the air valve stepper motor.
4   Disconnect the wiring plugs from the fuel injectors and fuel temperature switch.
5   Disconnect the spill return hose from the fuel regulator valve. be prepared for some loss of fuel.
6   Release the fuel rail from the manifold and place the fuel rail to one side.
7   Release the throttle cable from its support bracket.
8   Disconnect the throttle housing from the flange on the inlet manifold.
9   Extract the two screws which hold the heater rail to the inlet manifold.
10 Slacken all manifold fixing nuts and bolts which are accessible from above. Remember the nut under the thermostat housing.
11 Slacken the manifold support strut bolts.
12 If the inlet and exhaust manifolds are to be removed, then disconnect the exhaust downpipe from the manifold.
13 Unscrew the remaining manifold and support strut nuts and bolts from underneath the car.
14 Withdraw the manifolds and discard the gaskets.

Fig. 3.29 Manifolds (1.6 models with fuel injection) (Sec 40)

1	Gasket	4	Support strut (RH)
2	Inlet manifold	5	Support strut (LH)
3	Exhaust manifold	6	Throttle cable bracket

15 Refitting is a reversal of removal. Use new gaskets on clean mating surfaces. Tighten all nuts and bolts to the specified torque.

41 Exhaust system – inspection, removal and refitting

1   The exhaust system should be examined for leaks, damage and security at regular intervals (see Routine Maintenance). To do this, apply the handbrake and in a well ventilated area, allow the engine to idle. Lie down on each side of the car in turn, and check the full length of the exhaust system for leaks while an assistant temporarily places a wad of cloth over the end of the tailpipe. If a leak is evident, stop the engine and use a proprietary repair kit to seal. If the leak is excessive, or damage is evident, renew the section. Check the rubber mountings for deterioration, and renew them, if necessary. Holts Flexiwrap and Holts Gun Gum exhaust repair systems can be used for effective repairs to exhaust pipes and silencer boxes, including ends and bends. Holts Flexiwrap is an MOT approved permanent exhaust repair. Holts Firegum is suitable for the assembly of all exhaust system joints.
2   On 1.3 models, a single downpipe is used while on 1.6 versions, a dual downpipe is used.
3   All systems are of three section type using a flexible joint with bolts and coil springs, or ball couplings with tension springs according to vehicle model, to absorb the flexing of the engine on its mountings (photos).
4   If only one section of the system requires renewal, it is recommended that the complete exhaust is withdrawn from under the car to make separation easier. Do this by disconnecting the downpipe from the manifold and releasing the flexible mountings (photos).
5   When reassembling the system, do not tighten the clamps until the exhaust has been attached to the car. Once the pipe and silencer have been correctly aligned and they are not likely to knock against any adjacent suspension or body components, fully tighten the clamps.

41.3A Spring-loaded exhaust joint

41.3B Exhaust system support at transmission (1.3 shown)

41.3C Exhaust support bracket at transmission (1.3 models)

41.4A Exhaust system fixed joint

41.4B Exhaust system centre mounting

41.4C Exhaust silencer flexible mounting

42 Fault diagnosis – fuel system

Unsatisfactory engine performance, bad starting and excessive fuel consumption are not necessarily the fault of the fuel system or carburettor. In fact they more commonly occur as a result of ignition and timing faults. Before acting on the following, it is necessary to check the ignition system first. Even though a fault may lie in the fuel system, it will be difficult to trace unless the ignition system is correct. The faults below, therefore, assume that, where applicable, this has been attended to first. If during the fault diagnosis procedure it is suspected that the carburettor electronic mixture control or any of its related systems may be at fault, it is recommended that the help of a reputable BL dealer is sought. Accurate testing of the system and its components entails the use of a systematic checking procedure using specialist equipment and this is considered beyond the scope of the average home mechanic.

Sympton	Reason(s)
Models with carburettor	
Smell of petrol when engine is stopped	Leaking fuel lines or unions Leaking fuel tank
Smell of petrol when engine is idling	Leaking fuel line unions between pump and carburettor Overflow of fuel from float chamber due to wrong level setting, ineffective needle valve or punctured float
Difficult starting when cold	Faulty electronic mixture control system or related component Carburettor piston sticking (SU) Fuel tank empty or pump defective Incorrect float chamber fuel level Manual choke maladjusted (Keihin) Weak mixture
Difficult starting when hot	Faulty electronic mixture control system or related component Air cleaner choked Carburettor piston sticking (SU) Float chamber flooding or incorrect fuel level Fuel tank empty or pump defective Carburettor idle mixture adjustment incorrect Accelerator pedal pumped before starting
Excessive fuel consumption	Leakage from tank, pipes, pump or carburettor Air cleaner choked Carburettor idle mixture adjustment incorrect Carburettor float chamber flooding Faulty fuel shut-off solenoid or control system Carburettor worn Excessive engine wear or other internal fault Tyres underinflated Brakes binding Worn jets (Keihin) Choke maladjusted (Keihin)
Fuel starvation	Fuel level flow Leak on suction side of pump Fuel pump faulty Float chamber fuel level incorrect Fuel tank breather restricted Fuel tank inlet or carburettor inlet filter blocked
Poor performance, hesitation or erratic running	Carburettor idle mixture adjustment incorrect Faulty carburettor vacuum switch (SU) Carburettor piston damper oil level low (SU) Leaking manifold gasket Fuel starvation Carburettor worn Excessive engine wear or other internal fault Faulty accelerator pump (Keihin) Blocked jets (Keihin) Slack in throttle cable
Engine runs on	Fuel cut-off valve stuck open

Models with electronic fuel injection

Owing to the complexity of the electronic circuitry and the nature of the computer controlled operation, special test equipment has been developed for fault diagnosis on the fuel injection system. Therefore any suspected faults on the system or its related components should be referred to a suitably equipped BL dealer.

Chapter 4 Ignition system

For modifications, and information applicable to later models, see Supplement at end of manual

Contents

Specifications

Part A 1.3 models
System type .... Electronic (breakerless)

Distributor
Firing order .... 1 – 3 – 4 – 2
Rotor rotation .... Clockwise

Ignition timing (at idle speed, vacuum pipe connected) .... 15 to 19° BTDC
Centrifugal advance (crankshaft degrees BTDC, vacuum disconnected) ....

28 to 32° at 5500 rev/min
22 to 25° at 4000 rev/min
18 to 21° at 3000 rev/min
8 to 12° at 2000 rev/min
0 to 4° at 1200 rev/min
No advance below 800 rev/min

Vacuum advance:
    Starts .... 55 to 85 mm Hg (2.2 to 3.3 in Hg)
    Finishes .... 220 to 280 mm Hg (8.7 to 11.0 in Hg)
Maximum advance .... 9 to 11°

Spark plugs
Type/gap .... Champion RN9YCC or RN9YC/1.0 mm (0.040 in)

HT leads .... Champion CLS 13, boxed set

Ignition coil
Primary winding resistance .... 1.24 to 1.46 ohms at 20°C (68°F)
Secondary winding resistance .... 8000 to 12 000 ohms at 20°C (68°F)

Part B 1.6 models
System type .... Programmed electronic
Firing order .... 1 – 3 – 4 – 2
Rotor rotation .... Anti-clockwise

Ignition timing
Carburettor engine at 1400 rev/min:
Vacuum disconnected from ECU	13° BTDC
Vacuum connected to ECU	40° BTDC

Fuel injection engine at 750 rev/min:
Vacuum disconnected from ECU	20° BTDC
Vacuum connected to ECU	20° BTDC

Spark plugs
Type/gap:

Carburettor and fuel injection engines .... Champion RC9YCC or RC9YC/0.8 mm (0.032 in)

HT leads .... Champion CLS 5, boxed set

Ignition coil
Primary resistance at 20°C (68°F) .... 0.71 to 0.81 ohms

Part C All models

Torque wrench settings
	Nm	lbf ft
Spark plugs	18	13
Distributor mounting bolts	24	18

Part A 1.3 models

1 General description

The ignition system on 1.3 models is of electronic, breakerless type and incorporates a distributor driven from the rear of the camshaft, an igniter module mounted on the distributor body and a coil.

The distributor contains a reluctor mounted on its shaft and a magnet and stator fixed to the baseplate.

Ignition advance is controlled in the conventional way mechanically by centrifugal weights and a diaphragm unit for vacuum advance.

Instead of the conventional method of interrupting the low tension circuit to generate high tension voltage in the coil by means of a mechanical contact breaker, when the electronic ignition is switched on the switching of the transistors in the igniter module prevents current flow in the coil primary windings.

Once the crankshaft rotates, the reluctor moves through the magnetic field created by the stator and when the reluctor teeth are in alignment with the stator projections a small AC voltage is created. The module amplifies this voltage and applies it to switch the transistors and so provide an earth path for the primary circuit.

As the reluctor teeth move out of alignment with the stator projections the AC voltage changes, the transistors in the module are switched again to interrupt the primary circuit earth path. This causes a high voltage to be induced in the coil secondary winding.

A time control circuit in the module controls the charging time for the coil according to engine speed. This reduces consumption at low engine speeds and also prevents secondary voltage drop at high engine speeds.

2 Maintenance

1 Compared with a mechanical breaker type distributor, maintenance operations are simple and include the following.
2 Remove the battery and take off the distributor cap (two screws) and pull off the rotor (photo).
3 Wipe the cap clean and inspect it for hair cracks, erosion of the terminals and a worn centre carbon brush. If any of these faults are found, renew the cap.
4 The contact end of the rotor may be cleaned up carefully using very fine 'wet and dry' paper.
5 It is unlikely that the air gaps between the reluctor and stator will be unequal but if there is any doubt, check them with a feeler gauge and re-set them by releasing the stator screws and moving the position of the stator, until all four air gaps are equal.
6 Check the distributor cap seal and renew if necessary.

3 Ignition timing

1 The valve clearances and spark plug gaps should be correctly set

2.2 Removing distributor cap

Fig. 4.1 Distributor air gaps (Sec 2)

1 Stator	*3 Reluctor*
2 Stator fixing screws	*4 Air gaps*

and the carburettor in perfect tune.
2 Have the engine at normal operating temperature. Do not disconnect the distributor vacuum hose.
3 Connect a stroboscope in accordance with the manufacturer's instructions. With the engine idling, point the light from the stroboscope at the timing marks on the front of the engine.
4 The red mark on the crankshaft pulley should be aligned with the timing mark on the oil pump cover. If necessary, increase the contrast of the red (BTDC) pulley mark with a dab of white paint (photo).
5 If the marks are not in alignment, release the distributor mounting screws and rotate the distributor in either direction until they are.
6 Tighten the mounting screws switch off the engine and remove the stroboscope.

4 Distributor – removal and refitting

1 To provide clearance, remove the battery and take off the distributor cap and place it to one side.
2 Disconnect the hose from the distributor vacuum advance unit.
3 Disconnect the primary (low tension) leads by pulling off the coil rubber cap and unscrewing the terminal nuts.

4 Scribe a line across the joint between the distributor mounting flange and the drive housing (holder).
5 Unscrew and remove the distributor mounting bolts and withdraw the distributor.
6 When refitting the distributor, note that the drive dog is offset so that the rotor cannot be set incorrectly (180° out) (photo).
7 Push the distributor into its drive housing, align the scribed marks and insert and tighten the fixing bolts (photos).
8 Reconnect the vacuum hose, low tension lead and fit the distributor cap.

5 Distributor – overhaul

1 With the distributor removed from the engine, clean away external dirt.
2 Remove and discard the O-ring from the distributor mounting shoulder.
3 Take off the rotor.
4 Remove the reluctor from the distributor shaft. Do this by prising it upwards using two screwdrivers held at opposite points.
5 Retrieve the roll pin.

3.4 Crankshaft pulley timing marks

4.6 Distributor offset dog

4.7A Fitting distributor. Note O-ring seal

4.7B Tightening distributor mounting bolt

Fig. 4.2 Exploded view of the distributor (Sec 5)

1 Distributor cap	11 Vacuum unit link arm pivot	20 Counterweights	31 Distributor cap seal
2 Rotor	stud	21 Pivot pins	32 Distributor body
3 Module cover screw.	12 Baseplate screw	22 Distributor shaft	33 C-clip
4 Reluctor roll pin	13 Baseplate	23 Circlip	34 Vacuum advance unit
5 Reluctor	14 Rubber cap	24 Screw	35 Screw
6 Pick-up coil fixing screw	15 Distributor shaft screw	25 Thrust washer	36 O-ring
7 Pick-up coil unit	16 Washer	26 Thrust plate	37 Thrust washer
8 Magnet screw	17 Distributor upper shaft	27 Bearing	38 Drive dog
9 Stator	18 C-clip	28 Module cover	39 Pin retainer
10 Magnet	19 Counterweight governor	29 Module (igniter)	40 Pin
	springs	30 Oil seal	

6 Extract the screws which hold the module cover, remove the cover (photo).

7 Pull the igniter away from the distributor body. Use two screwdrivers as levers if necessary (photos).

8 Extract the screws which hold the pick-up coil and remove the coil.

9 Knock out the drive dog pin, remove the dog having marked its offset in relation to the shaft. Retrieve the thrust washer.

10 Extract the C-clip which secures the vacuum unit link rod and release the rod from the stud.

11 Remove the fixing screws and withdraw the vacuum unit from the distributor body.

12 Remove the vacuum unit link rod stud, stator, magnet set and baseplate.

13 Remove the advance counterweights, springs and shaft upper section.

14 Withdraw the distributor shaft from the distributor body and retrieve the thrust washer.

15 Remove the thrust plate, bearing and oil seal.

5.6 Distributor module cover

5.7A Removing distributor igniter

5.7B Distributor igniter removed

16 Inspect all components for wear, cracks or damage and renew as necessary.
17 Reassembly is a reversal of dismantling, but observe the following points.
18 Renew the shaft circlip, oil seal and O-ring. Also remove the drive dog pin.
19 Apply a smear of molybdenum disulphide grease to the distributor shaft and counterweight pivots.
20 When fitting the reluctor, make sure that the gap in the roll pin faces away from the distributor shaft.
21 Adjust the air gap so that they are equal.

6 Ignition coil

1 The coil is of special type designed for use with the electronic ignition system. Never substitute a coil from a mechanical breaker system. The coil is mounted on the right-hand wing valance.
2 To check a coil, disconnect the coil high tension lead from the distributor (pull off rubber cap complete with lead) and earth it. Using a voltmeter, check that there is a voltage of between 1 and 3 volts between the coil positive ($+$) and negative ($-$) terminals when the engine is being cranked on the starter (photo).

6.1 Ignition coil (1.3 models)

6.2 Removing coil cover and HT lead

3 Always connect the coil LT leads correctly, black/yellow to positive and blue to negative.

7 Spark plugs and high tension leads

1 The correct functioning of the spark plugs is vital for the correct running and efficiency of the engine. It is essential that the plugs fitted are appropriate for the engine, and the suitable type is specified at the beginning of this chapter. If this type is used and the engine is in good condition, the spark plugs should not need attention between scheduled replacement intervals. Spark plug cleaning is rarely necessary and should not be attempted unless specialised equipment is available as damage can easily be caused to the firing ends.
2 To remove the plugs, open the bonnet, and pull the HT leads from them. Grip the rubber end fitting, not the lead, otherwise the connection to the end fitting may fracture.
3 Brush out any accumulated dirt or grit from the spark plug recesses in the cylinder head otherwise it may drop into the combustion chamber when the plug is removed.
4 Unscrew the spark plugs with a deep socket or a box spanner. Do not allow the tool to tilt otherwise the ceramic insulator may be cracked or broken.
5 Examination of the spark plugs will give a good indication of the condition of the engine.
6 If the insulator nose of the spark plug is clean and white, with no deposits, this is indicative of a weak mixture, or too hot a plug (a hot plug transfers heat away from the electrode slowly, a cold plug transfers heat away quickly).
7 If the tip and insulator nose are covered with hard black-looking deposits, then this is indicative that the mixture is too rich. Should the plug be black and oily, then it is likely that the engine is fairly worn, as well as the mixture being too rich.
8 If the insulator nose is covered with light tan to greyish brown deposits, then the mixture is correct and it is likely that the engine is in good condition.

9 The spark plug gap is of considerable importance, as, if it is too large or too small, the size of the spark and its efficiency will be seriously impaired. For the best results the spark plug gap should be set in accordance with the Specifications at the beginning of this Chapter.
10 To set it, measure the gap with a feeler gauge and then bend open, or close, the outer electrode until the correct gap is achieved. The centre electrode should never be bent as this may crack the insulation and cause plug failure if nothing worse.
11 Special spark plug electrode gap adjusting tools are available from most motor accessory stores.
12 Screw each plug in by hand. This will ensure that there is no chance of cross-threading.
13 Tighten to the specified torque. If a torque wrench is not available, just lightly tighten each plug. It is better to undertighten than strip the threads from the light alloy cylinder head.
14 When reconnecting the spark plug leads, make sure that they are refitted in their correct order, 1 – 3 – 4 – 2, No 1 cylinder being at the timing belt end of the engine (photo).
15 The spark plug leads require no routine attention other than being kept clean by wiping them regularly.
16 In order to minimise corrosion in the distributor cap lead sockets, smear the HT cable end fittings with a light coating of petroleum jelly.

Part B 1.6 models

8 General description

1 These models are fitted with a programmed ignition system in which timing is controlled electronically instead of by centrifugal weights and a vacuum unit, as is the case in a conventional distributor system.
2 The normal method of high tension voltage distribution is retained using a rotor and distributor cap, but not the distributor body. The rotor is driven from the rear end of the camshaft.
3 Information in respect of engine speed and crankshaft position is

Fig. 4.3 HT lead sequence at distributor cap (1.3 models)
(Sec 7)

7.14 Spark plug leads

Fig. 4.4 Ignition circuit (1.6 model with carburettor) (Sec 8)

Wiring colour code

B	Black	L	Blue
G	Green	LG	Light green
GR	Grey	W	White
K	Pink	Y	Yellow

3	Battery	381	Knock sensor	A	Tachometer	D	Pin 5 Fuel ECU inertia switch and fuel cut-off solenoid
19d	Fuse No. 4	382	Crankshaft sensor and reluctor disc	B	Pin 11 Fuel ECU		
38	Ignition switch			C	Pin 17 Fuel ECU and coolant thermistor		
39	Ignition coil	393	Electronic control unit (ECU)				
40	Distributor cap						

Fig. 4.5 Ignition circuit (1.6 model with fuel injection) (Sec 8)

Wiring colour code

B	Black	L	Blue
G	Green	LG	Light green
GR	Grey	W	White
K	Pink	Y	Yellow

3	Battery	40	Distributor cap	393	Electronic control unit (ECU)	C	Pin 10 Fuel ECU and coolant thermistor
19d	Fuse No. 4	381	Knock sensor	A	Tachometer	D	Inertia switch
38	Ignition switch	382	Crankshaft sensor and reluctor disc	B	Pin 13 Fuel ECU	E	Pin 20 Fuel ECU
39	Ignition coil						

Fig. 4.6 Programmed ignition system components (carburettor engine shown) (Sec 8)

1 Coolant temperature thermistor
2 Ignition ECU
3 Ignition coil
4 Distributor cap
5 Reluctor disc
6 Crankshaft sensor
7 Knock sensor

8.6 Crankshaft sensor

8.9 Knock sensor

8.14 Electronic control unit (ECU)

transmitted to the electronic control unit by the crankshaft sensor. This ensures that there is no variation in timing due to wear in mechanical components.

4   The purpose of the main components of the system is described in the following paragraphs.

Reluctor disc

5   The disc is mounted on the flywheel and takes the form of a toothed rotor. The rotor has 34 teeth spaced at 10° intervals but having two spaces 180° apart which correspond to two TDC positions.

Crankshaft sensor

6   This is an inductive device located on the transmission adaptor plate. It runs betwen the reluctor disc teeth (photo).

7   When the crankshaft is turning, the sensor produces a pulse every time a tooth passes it. These problems are monitored by the electronic control unit which recognises the 10° pulsations and the absence of a pulse which represents TDC. These signals provide the basis of the electronic control unit timing.

Coolant temperature thermistor

8   This device responds to changes in engine coolant temperature and relays them to the electronic control unit to permit temperature corrections to be taken into account during ignition timing computations.

Knock sensor

9   This sensor allows the engine to run close to the limit of engine advance without the possibility of pre-ignition and engine damage (photo).

10   The device is located in the cylinder block between number 2 and 3 cylinders. It is sensitive to engine noise and vibration resulting from pre-ignition and relays this to the electronic control unit which in turn adjusts the ignition advance.

Ignition coil

11   This is similar in appearance, but totally different in characteristics, from ignition coils used in other systems. It is located in front of the battery.

Pressure transducer

12   This is located in the electronic control unit and is connected to the inlet manifold by a vacuum pipe.

13   Its purpose is to monitor engine load and signal the electronic control unit which then determines the optimum switching times of the coil.

Electronic control unit

14   This is basically a printed circuit board upon which the electronic components are mounted (photo).

Distributor cap and rotor

15   The rotor is mounted on a vibration damped stub shaft driven directly from the camshaft.

16   The distributor cap is secured to the camshaft carrier by two screws.

9   Maintenance and inspection

1   The only components of the system which require periodic maintenance are the distributor cap, HT leads and spark plugs. The spark plugs and HT leads should be treated in the same way as for 1.3 litre models, as described in Section 7. Attend to the distributor cap and rotor arm as described in Section 2.

2   On this system, dwell angle and ignition timing are a function of the electronic control unit and there is no provision for adjustment. It is

possible to check the ignition advance using a stroboscopic timing light, but this should only be necessary as part of a fault finding procedure. Further details will be found in Section 3.

10 Distributor cap and rotor arm – removal and refitting

1   Undo the two screws and lift the cap off the camshaft carriers. Thoroughly clean the cap inside and out with a dry lint-free rag. Examine the four HT lead segments inside the cap. If the segments appear badly burned or pitted, renew the cap. Make sure that the carbon brush in the centre of the cap is free to move and stands proud of its holders. If renewal of the cap is necessary, mark the position of the HT leads then pull them off. Transfer the leads to a new cap, fitting them in the same position (photo).
2   To remove the rotor arm, undo the retaining screw using a suitable Allen key and withdraw the rotor arm from the end of the camshaft. If necessary remove the rotor arm shield (photos).
3   Refitting the shield, rotor arm and distributor cap is the reverse sequence to removal. It is advisable to clean the rotor arm retaining screw threads in the camshaft using an M6 tap to remove all traces of old thread-locking compound. If this is not done, it is possible for the screw to seize in position rendering subsequent removal impossible.

11 Ignition coil – description and testing

1   The coil is located under the cold air intake duct for the air cleaner. It should be cleaned occasionally to prevent high tension (HT) voltage loss (photo).
2   To ensure correct HT polarity at the spark plugs, the LT coil leads must always be connected correctly ie white lead to the coil **positive** terminal and white/black lead to the coil **negative** terminal. Incorrect connections can cause bad starting, misfiring and short spark plug life.
3   Accurate checking of the coil output requires special equipment and for the home mechanic the easiest test is by substitution of a new unit.
4   If a new coil is to be fitted, ensure that it is of the correct type, specifically for use on the programmed electronic ignition system. Failure to do so could cause irreparable damage to the electronic control unit.
5   To remove the coil, disconnect the HT and LT wiring, undo the two retaining bolts and lift away the coil. Refitting is the reverse sequence to removal.

10.1 Extracting a distributor cap screw

10.2A Rotor arm with socket headed fixing screw

10.2B Distributor shield

11.1 Ignition coil (1.6 models)

Part C All models

12 Ignition switch – removal and refitting

1 The ignition switch is the same on all models.
2 Disconnect the battery and remove the steering column shrouds (Chapter 10).

3 Insert the ignition key into the lock.
4 Disconnect the wiring harness plug.
5 Extract the two switch fixing screws and remove the switch from the lock.
6 Refitting is a reversal of removal, but make sure that as the switch is fitted to the lock, the tang on the lock barrel enters the recess in the switch.

13 Fault diagnosis – ignition system

Symptom	Reason(s)
1.3 models	
Engine fails to start	Faulty or disconnected leads
	Faulty spark plug
	Air gap incorrect
	Fault in ignition coil
	Fault in pick-up or control unit
Engine starts and runs but misfires	Incorrect timing
	Fouled spark plug
	Incorrectly connected HT leads
	Crack in distributor cap or rotor
	Poor battery, engine and earth connections
Engine overheats, lacks power	Seized distributor weights
	Perforated vacuum pipe
	Incorrect ignition timing
Engine 'pinks'	Timing too advanced
	Advance mechanism stuck in advanced position
	Broken distributor weight spring
	Low fuel octane
	Upper cylinder oil used in fuel
	Excessive oil vapour from crankcase ventilation system or worn piston rings

1.6 models

Problems associated with the programmed electronic ignition system can usually be grouped into one of two areas, those caused by the more conventional HT side of the system such as spark plugs, HT leads, rotor arm and distributor cap, and those caused by the LT circuitry including the electronic control unit and its related components.

Apart from checking the wiring and terminal connections, testing the system components should be left to your dealer or automotive electrician as special equipment will be required. If you are in possession of a voltmeter and ohmmeter then the following tests will be possible.

Programmed ignition system test procedure
Engine fails to start

Test	Remedy
1 Connect a voltmeter across pins 9(+) and 12(−) of the electronic control unit (ECU) wiring connector. Does the voltmeter indicate battery voltage 10 seconds after switching on the ignition?	Yes: Proceed to test 2 No: Check the wiring between the ignition switch and pin 9, and between pin 12 and earth. Rectify as required
2 Connect a voltmeter across pins 10(+) and 12(−) of the ECU wiring connector. Does the voltmeter indicate battery voltage 10 seconds after switching on the ignition?	Yes: Proceed to test 3 No: Check the wiring between the ignition switch and coil (+) terminal and between pin 10 and the coil (−) terminal. Rectify as required
3 Connect an ohmmeter across the coil terminals. If the coil primary winding resistance between 0.7 amd 0.81 ohms?	Yes: Proceed to test 4 No: Renew the coil
4 Connect a voltmeter between the battery (+) terminal and the coil (−) terminal. Does the reading on the voltmeter increase when the engine is cranking?	Yes: Engine should start. If not check ignition HT components, fuel system and engine internal components No: Proceed to test 5
5 Switch ignition off and connect an ohmmeter across terminals 4 and 6 of the ECU. Does the ohmmeter register 1.5 k ohms approximately?	Yes: Probable ECU fault No: Check crankshaft sensor wiring and connections. If satisfactory, sensor is suspect

Engine misfires and performance is unsatisfactory

Test	Remedy
1 Highlight ignition timing marks (notch on crankshaft pulley, corresponding notch on water pump bracket) with white chalk, connect a stroboscopic timing light, disconnect ECU vacuum pipe at manifold and start engine. Does the pulley mark advance as engine speed is increased?	Yes: Proceed to test 2 No: Probable ECU fault
2 With the engine operating as in test 1 above, apply suction to the end of the disconnected ECU vacuum pipe. Does the pulley mark advance as suction is applied?	Yes: Ignition system is satisfactory, fault lies elsewhere No: Check for leaks in vacuum pipe and connections. If satisfactory, ECU is faulty.

Chapter 5 Clutch

For modifications, and information applicable to later models, see Supplement at end of manual

Contents

Specifications

Type .... Single dry plate, diaphragm spring, cable actuation

1.3 models

Driven plate diameter .... 195.0 mm (7.5 in)
Release arm free play .... 4.0 to 5.0 mm (0.157 to 0.196 in)
Pedal free play:
    Up to VIN 800 014/1985 model year .... 16.0 to 21.0 mm (0.63 to 0.83 in)
    From VIN 800 015/1985 model year .... 12.0 to 18.0 mm (0.47 to 0.70 in)

1.6 models

Driven plate diameter .... 200.0 mm (7.87 in)
Pedal free play .... 12.0 to 28.0 mm (0.47 to 1.10 in)

Torque wrench settings

	Nm	lbf ft
Clutch bellhousing to engine bolts:		
(1.3)	68	50
(1.6)	90	66
Clutch cover to flywheel bolts:		
(1.3)	26	19
(1.6)	23	17

1 General description

The clutch is of simple dry plate type with a diaphragm spring pressure plate.

The driven plate used on 1.3 models incorporates rubber torsional dampers while they are of coil spring type on 1.6 models.

The clutch release bearing is of sealed ball type.

Clutch actuation is by means of a cable. The clutch cable is self-adjusting on all 1.6 models, but only from VIN 800014 on 1.3 versions.

2 Clutch cable (1.3 up to VIN 800014) – adjustment

1 The clutch pedal free play on the 1.3 model up to 1985 model year should be maintained at between 16.0 and 21.0m (0.63 to 0.83 in). The free play is the amount of movement felt when the pedal is depressed with the fingers from the fully released position to the point where diaphragm spring pressure can be felt.

Fig. 5.1 Clutch components (1.3 models) (Sec 1)

1 Release arm and shaft   3 Release fork   5 Clutch cover/pressure plate   7 Flywheel
2 Release arm spring   4 Release bearing   6 Driven plate

Fig. 5.2 Clutch components (1.6 models) (Sec 1)

1 Reluctor ring   5 Pressure plate   8 Retaining spring   11 Cable seat
2 Flywheel   6 Release bearing   9 Release shaft   12 Rubber pad
3 Lockplate   7 Release fork   10 Shaft seal   13 Clutch cable
4 Driven plate

movement felt when the pedal is depressed with the fingers from the fully released postion to the point where diaphragm spring pressure can be felt.

2   Adjust by turning the cable adjusting nut at the support bracket within the engine compartment (photo).

3   Clutch cable (manually adjustable type) – renewal

1   Slacken the cable adjuster nut right off.
2   Disconnect the inner cable from the release arm on the clutch bellhousing.
3   Detach the outer cable from the gearbox and servo brackets.
4   Working under the facia panel, release the cable from the clutch pedal arm.
5   Withdraw the clutch cable assembly from the bulkhead into the engine compartment.
6   Refitting is a reversal of removal. Adjust the pedal free movement as described in the preceding Section.

4   Clutch cable (automatically adjustable type) – renewal

1   Working within the engine compartment, disconnect the clutch outer cable from its support clips.
2   Pull out the C-clip from the self-adjuster coil spring.
3   Disconnect the end of cable from the release arm.
4   Withdraw the cable through the gearbox support bracket, the rubber retainer will have to be disengaged from the guide sleeve.
5   Working within the car, unhook the cable from the clutch pedal and then withdraw the cable through the bulkhead into the engine compartment.
6   Refitting the new cable is a reversal of removal of the old one, but observe the following.
7   When passing the cable through the bulkhead, smear the inside of the cable abutment tube with rubber grease or petroleum jelly. Press the rubber bush fully into the tube so that the steel washer is fully up against the tube.
8   Once the cable is connected to both pedal and release lever, pull on the outer cable, compress the coil spring and fit the C-clip.

2.2 Clutch cable adjuster (early 1.3 models)

9   Now set the initial automatic adjustment. To do this, hold the adjuster mechanism in the bulkhead tube at the same time pulling the outer cable until resistance can be felt.

5   Clutch pedal – removal and refitting

1   Working inside the car, remove the facia lower access panel (Chapter 11).
2   Disconnect the clutch cable from the pedal as previously described.
3   Disconnect the pedal return spring.

Fig. 5.3 Clutch cable (manually adjustable) (Sec 3)

1   Pedal   2   Cable   3   Adjuster nut   4   Release arm

Fig. 5.4 Clutch cable (automatically adjustable) (Sec 4)

1 Release arm	3 Rubber pad	5 C-clip	7 Support at bulkhead
2 Cable seat	4 Support at gearbox	6 Self-adjuster coil spring	8 Clutch pedal

4   Unscrew the nut from the pivot bolt which serves the brake and clutch pedals and withdraw it until the clutch pedal can be removed.
5   The pedal bushes can be renewed if worn.
6   Grease the bushes and pivot bolt when refitting.
7   Adjust the clutch cable as described in earlier Sections.

6 Clutch – removal

1   Disconnect the battery.
2   Refer to Chapter 6 and remove the gearbox.
3   Unscrew each of the clutch cover bolts progressively until the diaphragm spring pressure is relieved. Lock the flywheel with a tool inserted in the starter ring gear teeth to prevent it rotating.
4   Remove the bolts and take the cover/pressure plate from the locating dowels on the flywheel. Catch the driven plate as it drops out.

7 Clutch – inspection

1   Slipping of the clutch will probably have been the reason for overhaul and the driven plate will show that the linings have worn down to the rivets.
2   The clutch cover should also be renewed, as clutch overhaul is normally carried out so infrequently it is not worthwhile putting the old one back. This will certainly be the case if the diaphragm spring fingers are stepped due to wear by contact with the release bearing.
3   Renew the driven plate and the cover/pressure plate assembly with complete units.
4   If there is any evidence of oil leaking within the bellhousing, this will probably be due to a worn crankshaft rear oil seal or the gearbox input shaft oil seal. Renew the faulty seal and clean away all the oil residue.
5   Examine the face of the flywheel. If it is grooved or deeply scored or is covered in tiny cracks, caused by overheating, it may be possible to

Fig. 5.5 Typical flywheel locking tool (Sec 6)

have it surface ground. If it is not possible to refinish the flywheel, it will have to be renewed.
6   Lastly, renew the clutch release bearing as a matter of routine. Removal and refitting of the bearing is described in the next Section.

8.1 Unscrewing clutch release fork lockbolt

8.3 Removing clutch release bearing and fork

8 Clutch release mechanism – removal and refitting

The engine and gearbox must be separated for access to the clutch release mechanism.

1.3 models

1 Remove the release fork lock bolt from inside the clutch bellhousing (photo).
2 Withdraw the release shaft complete with arm from the bellhousing.
3 Take out the release fork complete with bearing and spring (photo).
4 Release the spring and separate the bearing/holder from the fork (photo).
5 The clutch release bearing is a grease-sealed unit, never immerse it in solvent of any kind.
6 Refit the new bearing by reversing the removal operations. Apply a little molybdenum disulphide grease to the release shaft bushes and to the bearing and guide sleeve sliding surfaces.

1.6 models

7 Prise the retaining spring legs apart and withdraw the release bearing and its carrier.
8 Fit the new bearing and make sure that the legs of the retaining spring are located behind the release fork.

8.4 Release bearing spring arrangement

9 Clutch – refitting

1 Clean the friction surfaces of the flywheel and pressure plate, but do not remove the protective coating from the clutch cover.
2 Offer the driven plate to the flywheel so that the side with the greater projecting hub is away from the flywheel and towards the gearbox (photo). The driven plate may be marked 'FLYWHEEL SIDE'.
3 Offer the clutch cover onto the flywheel dowels so that it sandwiches the driven plate between it and the flywheel.
4 Screw in the clutch cover bolts finger tight.
5 The driven plate must now be centralised so that when the gearbox is offered to the engine, the input shaft splines will pass smoothly through the splines in the driven plate hub.
6 Centralisation can be carried out using a clutch alignment tool, an old input shaft or simply a round bar. Insert the tool into the driven plate hub and move the plate up or down or sideways until the splined hub is absolutely concentric with the ends of the circle of diaphragm spring fingers (photo).
7 Tighten the clutch cover bolts evenly to the specified torque again locking the flywheel against rotation. Withdraw the centralising tool (photo).
8 Refit the gearbox (Chapter 6).
9 Reconnect the battery.

9.2 Offering clutch to flywheel

9.6 Centralising the clutch driven plate

9.7 Tightening a clutch cover bolt

10 Fault diagnosis – clutch

Symptom	Reason(s)
Judder when taking up drive	Loose engine or gearbox mountings Badly worn friction linings or contaminated with oil Worn splines on gearbox input shaft or driven plate hub
*Clutch spin (failure to disengage) so that gears cannot be meshed	Incorrect release bearing to pressure plate clearance Rust on splines (may occur after vehicle standing idle for long periods) Damaged or misaligned pressure plate assembly Cable stretched or broken
Clutch slip (increase in engine speed does not result in increase in vehicle road speed – particularly on gradients)	Incorrect release bearing to pressure plate finger clearance Friction linings worn out or oil contaminated
Noise evident on depressing clutch pedal	Dry, worn or damaged release bearing Incorrect pedal adjustment Weak or broken pedal return spring Excessive play between driven plate hub splines and input shaft splines
Noise evident as clutch pedal released	Distorted driven plate Broken or weak driven plate cushion coil springs or dampers Incorrect pedal adjustment Weak or broken clutch pedal return spring Distorted or worn input shaft Release bearing loose on retainer hub

*This condition may also be due to the driven plate being rusted to the flywheel or pressure plate. It is possible to free it by applying the handbrake, engaging top gear, depressing the clutch pedal and operating the starter motor. If really badly corroded, then the engine will not turn over, but in the majority of cases the driven plate will free. Once the engine starts, rev it up and slip the clutch several times to clear the rust deposits.

Chapter 6 Manual transmission

For modifications, and information applicable to later models, see Supplement at end of manual

Contents

Specifications

Part A 1.3 models

Type .... Five forward speeds and reverse. Synchromesh on all forward speeds. Differential/final drive integral with transmission. Unit mounted on right-hand side of car transversely in line with engine.

Ratios
1st	2.916:1
2nd	1.764:1
3rd	1.181:1
4th	0.846:1
5th	0.714:1
Reverse	2.916:1
Final drive	4.428:1

Gear endfloats and gearbox clearances
1st speed gear .... 0.03 to 0.18 mm (0.001 to 0.007 in) Adjustment by selective thrust washer

Washer thickness .... 1.89 to 1.92 mm (0.074 to 0.076 in)
1.92 to 1.95 mm (0.076 to 0.077 in)
1.95 to 1.98 mm (0.077 to 0.078 in)

2nd, 3rd, 4th speed gears .... 0.05 to 0.18 mm (0.002 to 0.007 in) Adjustment by selective spacer collars

Collar thickness .... 28.01 to 28.04 mm (1.103 to 1.104 in)
28.04 to 28.07 mm (1.104 to 1.105 in)
28.07 to 28.10 mm (1.105 to 1.106 in)
28.10 to 28.13 mm (1.106 to 1.107 in)

5th gear endfloat .... 0.05 to 0.4 mm (0.002 to 0.016 in)
Reverse idler shaft running clearance .... 0.4 mm (0.016 in)
Selector fork clearance in synchro groove 1st/2nd, 3rd/4th and 5th .. 1.0 mm (0.040 in)
Reverse gear to fork (max) .... 0.7 mm (0.028 in)
Reverse shaft fork:
    End gap .... 6.9 to 7.0 mm (0.27 to 0.28 in)
    Groove width .... 7.05 to 7.25 mm (0.278 to 0.285 in)

Fork to shaft clearance (max)	0.5 mm (0.020 in)
Finger thickness (minimum)	6.0 mm (0.236 in)
Shaft arm to dog clearance (maximum)	0.15 mm (0.006 in)
Final drive crownwheel to pinion backlash	0.073 to 0.25 mm (0.0029 to 0.010 in)
Differential pinion gear backlash	0.05 to 0.15 mm (0.002 to 0.006 in) Adjustment by selective thrust washers
Washer thickness	0.7 mm (0.028 in)
	0.8 mm (0.031 in)
	0.9 mm (0.035 in)
	1.0 mm (0.039 in)
Differential side clearance	0.10 to 0.15 mm (0.004 to 0.006 in) Adjustment by selective circlip
Circlip thickness	2.45 mm (0.096 in)
	2.55 mm (0.100 in)
	2.65 mm (0.104 in)
	2.75 mm (0.108 in)
	2.85 mm (0.112 in)
	2.95 mm (0.116 in)

Oil capacity   2.3 litre (4.0 pint)

Oil type/specification*   Multigrade engine oil, viscosity SAE 10W/30 or 10W/40, to API SF
(Duckhams QXR, Hypergrade or 10W/40 Motor Oil)

*Note: *To meet warranty requirements Austin Rover recommendations include a 10W/40 oil. Duckhams QXR and 10W/40 Motor Oil are available to meet these requirements*

Part B 1.6 models

Type   Five forward speeds and reverse. Synchromesh on all forward speeds. Differential/final drive integral with transmission. Unit mounted on left-hand side of car transversely in line with engine

Ratios

	Carburettor models	Fuel injection models
1st	2.92:1	3.25:1
2nd	1.75:1	1.89:1
3rd	1.15:1	1.33:1
4th	0.87:1	1.04:1
5th	0.66:1	0.85:1
Reverse	3.00:1	3.00:1
Final drive	4.1:1	3.87:1

Gear endfloats and gearbox clearances

Mainshaft endfloat	0.14 to 0.21 mm (0.006 to 0.008 in) Adjustment by selective circlips circlips
Circlip thickness	0.50 mm (0.020 in)
	0.55 mm (0.022 in)
	0.60 mm (0.024 in)
	0.65 mm (0.026 in)
	0.70 mm (0.028 in)
	0.75 mm (0.030 in)
	0.80 mm (0.032 in)
	0.85 mm (0.034 in)
	0.90 mm (0.036 in)
	0.95 mm (0.038 in)
	1.00 mm (0.040 in)
	1.05 mm (0.042 in)
	1.10 mm (0.044 in)
	1.15 mm (0.046 in)
Countershaft gear endfloat	0.1 to 0.35 mm (0.004 to 0.014 in) Adjustment by selective collars and shims
Collar availability	28.99 mm (1.142 in)
	29.04 mm (1.144 in)
Shim thicknesses	1.96 mm (0.077 in)
	1.99 mm (0.078 in)
	2.02 mm (0.080 in)
	2.05 mm (0.081 in)
	2.08 mm (0.082 in)
Baulk ring to gear cone clearance (minimum)	0.40 mm (0.016 in)
Reverse idler gear to shaft clearance (maximum)	0.14 mm (0.006 in)
Fork to synchro sleeve groove clearance (maximum)	1.0 mm (0.040 in)
Reverse gear to fork clearance (maximum)	0.7 mm (0.028 in)
Final drive pinion to crownwheel backlash	0.07 to 0.14 mm (0.003 to 0.005 in)
Planet gear backlash	0.05 to 0.15 mm (0.002 to 0.006 in) Adjustment by selective thrust washers

Washer thickness .... 0.70 mm (0.028 in)
                                                              0.75 mm (0.030 in)
                                                              0.80 mm (0.031 in)
                                                              0.85 mm (0.033 in)
                                                              0.90 mm (0.035 in)
                                                              0.95 mm (0.037 in)
                                                              1.00 mm (0.039 in)
                                                              1.05 mm (0.041 in)
Differential side clearance .... 0.15 mm (0.006 in) Adjustment by selective circlip
Circlip thickness .... 2.45 mm (0.096 in)
                                                              2.55 mm (0.100 in)
                                                              2.65 mm (0.104 in)
                                                              2.75 mm (0.108 in)
                                                              2.85 mm (0.112 in)
                                                              2.95 mm (0.116 in)

Oil capacity .... 2.2 litres (3.75 pints)
Oil type/specification* .... Multigrade engine oil, viscosity SAE 10W/30 or 10W/40, to API SF
                                                              (Duckhams QXR, Hypergrade or 10W/40 Motor Oil)

*Note: *To meet warranty requirements Austin Rover recommendations include a 10W/40 oil. Duckhams QXR and 10W/40 Motor Oil are available to meet these requirements*

Torque wrench settings	Nm	lbf ft
Part A 1.3 models		
Countershaft nut	110	81
Crownwheel bolts	103	76
Oil drain plug	40	30
Oil filler/level plug	45	33
Gear selector remote control rod pivot bolt	22	16
Reverse gear fork nut	24	18
Selector arm holder bolts	12	9
Detent plugs	22	16
Selector fork lock bolts	17	13
Torque rod to body bolts	22	16
Torque rod to transmission	9	7
Transmission to engine torque bracket bolts	45	33
5th speed gear housing bolts	12	9
Transmission casing to flywheel housing bolts	28	21
Flywheel housing to engine bolts	68	50
Rear mounting bracket bolts	65	48
Right-hand mounting to body bolts	39	29
Rear mounting bracket nuts	22	16
Left-hand mounting bracket nuts	39	29
Suspension arm balljoint nut	44	32
Driveshaft nut	185	137
Part B 1.6 models		
Gearchange shaft detent plug	22	16
Gearchange holder screw:		
M8	28	21
M6	14	10
Reverse fork bracket screws	14	10
Crown wheel bolts	110	81
Countershaft nut	110	81
Transmission casing to flywheel housing bolts	27	20
Breather pipe bracket bolt	27	20
Reverse idler shaft bolt	67	49
Reverse lamp switch	25	18
Drain plug	40	30
Oil level/filler plug	45	33
Flywheel bellhousing to engine adaptor plate	90	66
Remote control bracket	25	18
Gear lever to selector rod bolt	25	18
Casing end plug:		
Large (countershaft access plug)	70	52
Small	28	21
Suspension arm balljoint nut	44	32
Left and right-hand mountings:		
Engine bolts	45	33
Bracket nuts	40	30
Through bolt	120	89
Rear mounting:		
Bracket to transmission bolts	90	66
Support plate to bracket bolts	75	55
Mounting to bracket bolts	60	44
Mounting to crossmember	60	44

Part A Five-speed transmission (1.3 models)

1 General description

The transmission is fitted transversely on the right-hand side in line with the engine at the front of the car.

The transmission casing incorporates the gear trains and the final drive/differential.

The 1st, 2nd, 3rd, 4th and reverse speed gears are integral with the mainshaft and cannot be detached from the shaft.

The 5th speed synchro unit is splined to the mainshaft while the 5th speed gear is free on the shaft.

The countershaft incorporates a final drive pinion and carries the 5th speed gear, 1st/2nd and 3rd/4th synchro units. The 1st, 2nd, 3rd and 4th speed gears are free on the shaft. The 1st/2nd synchro sleeve incorporates the reverse gear teeth.

Except for reverse gear, all gears are in constant mesh. The transmission operates by transmitting engine torque through the mainshaft and selected gear to the countershaft pinion then to the final drive (crownwheel), driveshafts and roadwheels.

2 Maintenance

1 Have the car standing on a level surface then at the intervals specified in Routine Maintenance wipe the oil filler/level plug clean and remove it using a ring spanner (photo).

2 If the oil level is correct, oil will just run out of the level plug. If it does not, top up with specified oil until it does (photo).

3 Refit the plug.

4 Draining and refilling the transmission is still specified by the manufacturers and in the interest of long life it is recommended that the oil is drained hot every 24 000 miles (40 000 km) or at two yearly intervals and the transmission then filled with fresh oil of the specified type.

5 The drain plug can be unscrewed with a 3/8 in square bar (photo).

Fig. 6.1 Cut-away view of transmission fitted to 1.3 models (Sec 1)

2.1 Transmission oil filler/level plug

2.2 Topping up the transmission

Fig. 6.2 Oil level/filler and drain plugs (Sec 2)

2.5 Unscrewing transmission drain plug

3.1 Gearchange lever connection to remote control rod

3 Gearchange lever – removal and refitting

1 Working under the car, remove the pivot bolt and disconnect the gear lever from the selector remote control rod (photo).
2 Remove the gear lever washers, bushes and the spacer collar and the O-rings.
3 Remove the gear lever knob and the centre console (Chapter 11) if fitted.
4 Remove the rubber gaiter, extract the circlip and withdraw the gear lever.
5 Remove the gear lever ball seat, stopper ring, O-rings and dust cover.
6 Renew any worn or deformed components.

7   Refitting is a reversal of removal. Apply grease to the spacer collar
and tighten the pivot bolt to the specified torque.

4   Gear selector shaft oil seal – renewal

1   Disconnect the torque rod from the transmission (photos).
2   Slide the selector shaft safety clip aside and drive out the roll pin
which secures the remote control rod to the selector shaft (photo).
3   Disconnect the remote control rod from the selector shaft. This
joint can rust. Soak it in penetrating fluid.
4   Pull back the gaiter from the selector shaft at the transmission
casing and prise out the shaft oil seal (photo).
5   Grease the lips of the new seal and drive it into position.
6   When refitting the gaiter, make sure that the drain hole is at the
bottom.
7   Reconnect the remote control rod, drive in the roll pin and fit the
clip. Smear the joint with grease to prevent corrosion (photo).
8   Reconnect the torque rod.

Fig. 6.3 Gear lever components (Sec 3)

1	Spacer collar	5	Dust cover
2	O-rings	6	Stopper ring
3	Bushes	7	O-rings
4	Sealing washer	8	Ball seat

4.1A Transmission torque rod

4.1B Removing transmission torque rod

4.2 Selector shaft roll pin safety clip

Fig. 6.4 Selector shaft connecting roll pin and safety clip
(Sec 4)

4.4 Selector shaft gaiter and oil seal

8 Apply grease to the lips of the new seal and drive it squarely into
9 Reconnect or refit the driveshaft according to side. Use a new
driveshaft circlip.
9 Reconnect or refit the driveshaft according to side.
10 Refill the transmission and connect the battery.

6 Transmission – removal and refitting

1 Disconnect and remove the battery.
2 Disconnect the transmission casing earth cable.
3 Disconnect the reverse lamp switch leads.
4 Disconnect the speedometer drive cable from the transmission. Do
this by pulling up the rubber cover and extracting the clip. *Do not
unbolt the retaining plate or the speedo pinion will drop into the
gearbox.*
5 Unbolt and move the starter motor aside.
6 Disconnect the clutch cable from the release lever at the
transmission (Chapter 5).
7 Raise the front of the car and support it securely on axle stands.
8 Remove the front right-hand roadwheel.
9 Drain the transmission oil.
10 Remove the right-hand and centre splash guard panels.
11 Disconnect the gear selector and torque rods from the transmission
(see Section 4).
12 Unscrew and remove the two lower bolts (Fig. 6.5) which hold the
rear mounting bracket to the transmission casing. Release but do not
remove, the bracket upper bolt as this is supporting the engine.
13 Support the right-hand lower suspension (track control) arm on a
jack, unscrew the taper pin nut and then using a suitable splitter tool,
disconnect the balljoint from the hub carrier. Have the car well
supported.
14 Using a suitable lever inserted between the driveshaft inboard
joints and the transmission casing, release both driveshafts from the
side gear securing clips.
15 Unscrew the right-hand driveshaft nut. This is very tight and the
hub will have to be held against rotation either by having an assistant
apply the brakes hard or by placing a long lever between two wheel
studs. If the latter method is used, screw on the nut first to protect the
threads.
16 Remove the right-hand driveshaft.
17 Support the engine using a hoist or by placing a block of wood and
jack under the sump pan.
18 Release the right-hand front mounting bracket from the body.
19 Unscrew the bolts which hold the exhaust support bracket to the
transmission.
20 Support the weight of the transmission on a trolley jack and
remove the transmission to engine flange connecting bolts.

4.7 Driving in selector shaft roll pin

5 Differential oil seals – renewal

1 These oil seals may be renewed without having to remove the
transmission from the car.
2 Disconnect the battery.
3 Drain the oil from the transmission
4 If the oil seal on the left-hand side is to be renewed then the
left-hand driveshaft must be removed as described in Chapter 8.
5 If the oil seal on the right-hand driveshaft is to be renewed then the
driveshaft need only be disconnected from the transmission while
remaining connected to the hub carrier.
6 The disconnection operations for the right-hand driveshaft are
covered in Chapter 1, Section 19.
7 Prise the oil seal from the transmission.

RM1625

Fig. 6.5 Rear mounting bracket bolts (Sec 6)

A   Lower bolts   *B   Upper bolt*

Fig. 6.6 Right-hand mounting bracket bolts (Sec 6)

21 Unscrew and remove the cover plate bolts from the face of the flywheel housing.
22 Withdraw the transmission and have an assistant catch the inboard end of the left-hand driveshaft and lower it to the floor. Fit new driveshaft spring clips.

Refitting
23 If the clutch has been disturbed, make sure that the driven plate has been centralised as described in Chapter 5.
24 Check that the engine to flywheel housing locating dowels are in position in the flange.
25 Apply a smear of grease to the splines of the input (clutch) shaft splines.
26 Offer the transmission to the engine. The input shaft splines should pass through those of the driven plate hub. If difficulty is experienced, have an assistant turn the crankshaft pulley bolt slightly to align the splines and grooves. As the transmission is being connected to the engine; have an assistant insert the left-hand driveshaft into the transmission.
27 Once the transmission is located on the dowels screw in and tighten the connecting bolts to the specified torque.
28 Bolt the right-hand mounting bracket to the body and the rear bracket to the transmission casing. Fit the exhaust support bracket.
29 Connect the torque rod and selector rod to the transmission as described in Section 4.
30 Fit the right-hand driveshaft and check that both driveshafts are locked positively in the transmission.
31 Connect the right-hand suspension arm balljoint to the hub carrier.
32 Fit the splash guards.
33 Tighten a new driveshaft nut to the specified torque again holding the hub against rotation using one of the methods described earlier in this Section.
34 Stake the nut into the shaft groove.
35 Fit the roadwheel and lower the car to the floor. Tighten the wheel nuts.
36 Fit the starter motor.
37 Connect the speedometer drive cable.
38 Connect and adjust the clutch cable, as described in Chapter 5.
39 Connect the reverse lamp switch leads.
40 Refit and reconnect the battery.
41 Reconnect the transmission casing earth cable.
42 Fill the transmission with oil of the specified type.

7 Transmission – dismantling into major components

1 Overhaul of the transmission is a viable proposition if minor items only require renewal such as a synchroniser assembly or worn bearings. Where the transmission is generally worn then an exchange unit is the best solution, as the purchase of gears and shafts is a very expensive and uneconomic way to renovate.
2 With the transmission removed from the car, clean away external dirt using paraffin and a stiff brush or a water soluble solvent.
3 Drain the oil completely and locate the unit on a clean bench or work area.
4 Unbolt and remove the 5th speed gear housing (40) (Fig. 6.7) from the end of the transmission casing (67). Retain the locating dowels (54).
5 Extract the circlip (56) and remove the dished spring washer (55) from the end of the mainshaft (72).
6 Draw off the mainshaft bearing (57).
7 Drive out 5th speed gear selector fork roll pin (85)
8 Push down the 5th gear synchro sleeve to lock the gears. Relieve the staking on the nut (1) on the end of the countershaft (23) and unscrew the nut. Obtain a new nut.
9 Pull off the selector fork (84) and 5th speed gear synchro sleeve (58) together as an assembly.
10 Remove 5th speed gear synchro hub (59) then the baulk ring (61) and spring (60).
11 Remove 5th speed gear (62).
12 Remove the needle roller bearing (63).
13 Remove the thrust washer (64).
14 Remove 5th speed gear (3) noting the boss is downwards. Remove the dished washer (2) noting its concave side is downwards. Use a puller if the gear is tight.
15 Unscrew the three selector detent plugs (93) and extract the coil springs (91) and balls (90) using a pencil magnet if necessary.
16 Unbolt the clutch cable bracket (42).
17 Unscrew the connecting bolts and separate the transmission casing from the flywheel housing (79). Do this by lifting the casing evenly from the housing.
18 Drive out the differential oil seal (43) and remove the circlip (27) from the transmission casing.
19 Expand the snap rings (4, 65) and tap the mainshaft and countershaft bearings from the transmission casing.
20 Withdraw the reverse idler gear shaft (71) and the gear (70).

Fig. 6.7 Exploded view of 1.3 model transmission (Sec 7)

1   Countershaft nut
2   Dished washer
3   5th speed countershaft gear
4   Circlip
5   Bearing
6   Flanged spacer collar
7   4th speed gear
8   Bearings
9   3rd/4th synchro baulk ring
10 Synchro spring
11 3rd/4th synchro sleeve
12 3rd/4th synchro hub
13 3rd speed gear
14 Spacer collar
15 Spacer washer
16 2nd speed gear
17 1st/2nd synchro baulk ring
18 Synchro spring
19 1st/2nd synchro sleeve
20 1st/2nd synchro hub
21 1st speed gear
22 Thrust washer
23 Countershaft
24 Differential side gear
25 Thrust washer
26 Differential pinion gear
27 Circlip
28 Bearing

29 Differential case
30 Pinion shaft
31 Roll pin
32 Crownwheel
33 Speedo pinion retaining clip
34 Speedo cable retaining clip
35 O-ring
36 Dust cover
37 Pinion housing
38 Retaining plate
39 Speedo gear pinion
40 5th gear housing
41 Reverse lamp switch
42 Clutch cable bracket
43 Differential oil seal
44 Filler/level plug
45 Breather baffle plate
46 Bearing retainer plate
47 Countershaft bearing
48 Oil guide plate
49 Selector shaft
50 Selector shaft oil seal
51 Selector shaft gaiter
52 Detent ball
53 Detent spring
54 Locating dowel
55 Dished spring washer
56 Circlip

57 Mainshaft bearing
58 5th speed gear synchro sleeve
59 5th speed synchro hub
60 Synchro spring
61 Baulk ring
62 Mainshaft 5th speed gear
63 Needle roller bearing
64 Thrust washer
65 Circlip
66 Mainshaft bearing
67 Transmission casing
68 Locating dowel
69 Drain plug
70 Reverse idler gear
71 Reverse idler shaft
72 Mainshaft
73 Mainshaft bearing
74 Oil seal
75 Magnet holder
76 Magnet
77 Clutch release arm and shaft
78 Dust seal
79 Flywheel housing
80 Locating dowel
81 Clutch release fork
82 Spring
83 Clutch release bearing

84 5th speed gear selector fork
85 Roll pin
86 3rd/4th selector fork
87 5th/reverse selector shaft
88 3rd/4th selector shaft
89 1st/2nd selector shaft
90 Detent ball
91 Detent spring
92 Washer
93 Detent plug
94 Roll pin
95 Reverse selector dog
96 3rd/4th selector dog
97 1st/2nd selector fork
98 Spring retainer
99 Spring
100 Selector arm shaft
101 Selector arm
102 Interlock shaft
103 Spring retainer
104 Spring
105 Reverse gear selector arm
106 Detent ball
107 Detent spring
108 Retainer plate
109 Selector arm holder
110 Selector shaft arm

21 Unscrew the reverse gear selector arm nut, take off the special washer and then remove the selector arm (105) the detent ball (106) and detent spring (107). Note that the ball is of larger diameter than the other three detent balls.

22 Bend up the lock tabs on the three selector fork lock bolts, unscrew and remove the bolts.

23 Remove the 5th/reverse selector shaft (87) and dog (95). The shaft chamfer should be at the top.

24 Remove 1st/2nd selector shaft (89) and then the 3rd/4th selector shaft (88) and dog (96).

25 Move the sleeve of the 1st/2nd synchro sleeve upwards into 2nd gear position and withdraw the 1st/2nd gear selector fork.

26 Lift the mainshaft and countershaft from the flywheel housing as an assembly meshed together.

27 Slide the selector arm (101) from side to side to obtain access to the selector arm holder bolts. Unscrew the bolts and remove the holder (109). Remove the selector shaft (49), detent ball (52) and spring (53).

28 Lift the differential/final drive from the flywheel housing.

29 Remove the differential oil seals (43).

30 Remove the selector shaft gaiter (51) and oil seal (50).

31 Unbolt the retaining plate (38) and withdraw the speedometer drivegear pinion assembly (37, 39).

32 Extract the countershaft bearing retainer plate (46) screws. An impact screwdriver will be required for this.

33 Remove the countershaft bearings (47) from the flywheel housing.

34 Lift out the oil guide plate (48).

35 Remove the breather baffle plate (45) from the flywheel housing.

36 Remove the mainshaft bearing (73) and oil seal (74) from the flywheel housing.

37 With the transmission dismantled into major components, all parts may be examined for wear.

8 Examination of components

1 Check the transmission casing and flywheel housing for cracks, especially around the bolt holes. Clean and refit the magnet.

2 Inspect all shafts for grooving or scoring and the gear teeth for chipping or wear.

3 Test the shaft bearings. If they are obviously shaky or rattle when spun, renew them. Always renew the bearings in the flywheel housing once they have been removed.

4 Check the clearance of the selector forks in their respective synchro sleeve grooves. If the clearance exceeds that specified, renew the fork.

5 Press each synchro-baulk ring onto its gear cone at the same time applying a twisting motion. If the ring sticks firmly and has a minimum ring to gear clearance of 0.40 mm (0.016 in) then the parts are in good condition. If not, renew the baulk ring.

6 Wear in a synchroniser assembly will already be evident from noisy gear changing and by the fact that the synchro could be easily beaten when changing gear. In this case, renew the synchro unit complete.

7 If a synchroniser unit is dismantled, note the hub can only be fitted into the sleeve in one of three positions as there are master splines. Always mark which way round the hub is located in its sleeve before separating the components. No sliding keys are used with this type of synchromesh.

8 To dismantle the countershaft refer to the next Section. The mainshaft cannot be dismantled as the gears are integral with the shaft. Any wear will therefore mean renewal of the mainshaft complete (photo).

9 Renew all oil seals and O-rings as a matter of routine. Buy a new nut for the countershaft.

9 Countershaft – dismantling and reassembly

1 Refer to Fig. 6.7 and remove the flanged spacer collar (6).

2 Remove the 4th speed gear (7).

3 Remove the baulk ring (9) and synchro spring (10).

4 Remove the 4th gear needle bearing (8).

5 Remove 3rd/4th synchro unit (11, 12).

6 Remove 3rd speed gear baulk ring (9) and spring (10).

7 Take off 3rd speed gear (13).

8 Remove the needle bearing (8) and spacer collar (14).

9 Remove the spacer washer (15) and 2nd speed gear (16).

10 Remove 1st/2nd synchro baulk ring (17) and spring (18).

11 Remove the needle bearing (8) and spacer collar (14).

12 Remove 1st/2nd synchro unit (19, 20). The synchro sleeve incorporates reverse gear.

13 Take off 1st speed gear (21) complete with baulk ring and spring.

14 Remove the needle bearing and thrust washer.

15 Clean and renew components as necessary, lightly oil and reassemble them as described in the following paragraphs (photo).

16 Fit the thrust washer and needle bearing (photos).

17 Fit 1st speed gear complete with baulk ring and spring (photos).

18 Fit 1st/2nd synchro unit with reverse followed by the baulk ring, spacer collar and needle bearing (photos).

8.8 Mainshaft

9.15 Countershaft stripped

9.16A Fitting thrust washer to countershaft

9.16B Fitting needle roller bearing to countershaft

9.17A Fitting 1st speed gear to countershaft

9.17B Fitting 1st speed gear baulk ring

9.18A 1st/2nd synchro with reverse gear and baulk ring on countershaft

9.18B 2nd speed gear spacer collar

19 Fit 2nd speed gear (photo).
20 Fit the spacer washer (photo).
21 Fit the spacer collar and needle bearing (photos).
22 Fit 3rd speed gear (photo).
23 Fit the baulk ring and spring (photo).
24 Fit 3rd/4th speed synchro unit (photo).
25 Fit the needle bearing (photo).
26 Fit the baulk ring and spring.
27 Fit 4th speed gear (photo).
28 Fit the flanged spacer collar (photo).
29 Apply light pressure to the flanged spacer collar, measure and record the endfloat of all gears. Check against the specified tolerances and if outside the limit, change 1st speed gear thrust washer, 2nd or 3rd speed gear spacer collars or 4th speed gear flanged spacer collar as necessary to rectify matters.
30 Spacer thickness availability is given in the Specifications Section at the beginning of this Chapter.
31 Place the 5th speed gear thrust washer on the mainshaft, followed by 5th speed gear, needle roller bearing and synchro. Apply light pressure to the synchro hub and check 5th speed gear endfloat. If not as specified renew the thrust washer.

9.18C 2nd speed gear needle roller bearing

9.19 Needle roller bearing and 2nd speed gear

9.20 Spacer washer

9.21A 3rd speed gear spacer sleeve

9.21B Needle bearing

9.22 Fitting 3rd speed gear to countershaft

9.23 3rd speed gear baulk ring and spring

9.24 Fitting 3rd/4th speed synchro unit

9.25 Needle bearing

9.27 4th speed gear, baulk ring and spring

9.28 Spacer collar

Fig. 6.8 Gear endfloat check points (Sec 9)

1 1st speed gear
2 2nd speed gear
3 3rd speed gear
4 4th speed gear

10 Differential/final drive – overhaul

1 Access to the differential is obtained by dismantling the transmission as described in Section 7.
2 It is rare for wear to occur in the differential or final drive components, but check visually for damaged teeth on the crownwheel, pinion and side gear teeth.
3 To dismantle, first mark the relationship of the crownwheel to the differential case and then unscrew the crownwheel bolts. *These bolts have a left-hand thread.*
4 Drive out the differential pinion shaft roll pin.
5 Tap the pinion shaft from the carrier.
6 Remove the pinion gears, thrust washers and side gears.
7 Using a suitable puller, draw off the differential case bearings.
8 Reassembly is a reversal of dismantling. Apply pressure only to the bearing inner tracks.
9 When refitting the crownwheel the chamfer on the flange should be towards the differential case and the positioning marks aligned. Use pinion thrust washers of identical thickness.
10 To check the backlash of both pinion gears the differential carrier should be supported on Vee blocks located under the bearings.
11 Temporarily connect the driveshafts and then check the pinion gear backlash with a dial gauge. If outside the specified limit, change the thrust washers. Thickness availability of these washers is given in the Specifications Section.

11 Transmission – reassembly

1 Fit the mainshaft bearing and the new oil seal into the flywheel housing.

Fig. 6.9 Differential/final drive components (Sec 10)

1 Differential side gears
2 Thrust washers
3 Pinion gears
4 Roll pin
5 Pinion shaft
6 Circlip
7 Differential case bearing
8 Differential case
9 Crownwheel
10 Pinion gear on countershaft

Fig. 6.10 Checking differential pinion gear backlash (Sec 10)

2 Fit the breather baffle into the flywheel housing.
3 Fit the oil guide plate.
4 Fit the countershaft bearing, its retainer plate and tighten the screws securely to the flywheel housing. Stake the screw heads (photos).
5 Fit the speedometer drivegear pinion assembly and secure it with the plate and screw (photo).
6 Fit the selector shaft seal and gaiter.
7 If the differential bearings are being renewed, lightly drive the new bearing into the transmission casing to seat the circlip. Then drive the differential into the flywheel housing until it is seated.
8 Mate the flywheel housing and transmission casing and check the side clearance between the circlip and the differential bearing outer track. If this is not as specified, change the circlip for one of different thickness from the selection available (see Specifications) (photo).
9 Remove the transmission casing and have the differential located in the flywheel housing (photo).
10 Insert the larger spring and ball in the hole in the flywheel housing, depress the ball and insert the selector shaft. Fit the selector arm to the shaft, tighten the lock bolt and bend up the lockplate tab (photos).

11.4A Flywheel housing components
1 Breather baffle plate   3 Mainshaft bearing
2 Bearing retaining plate   4 Countershaft bearing

11.4B Tightening bearing retainer plate screw with impact driver

11.5A Fitting speedometer driven gear pinion

11.5B Speedometer driven gear retaining plate

Fig. 6.11 Checking differential bearing to circlip clearance
(Sec 11)

11.8 Differential bearing circlip

11.9 Differential in flywheel housing

11.10A Selector shaft detent spring

11.10B Selector shaft detent ball

11.10C Inserting selector shaft into flywheel housing

11.10D Depressing selector shaft detent ball

11.10E Fitting selector arm to the shaft

11.10F Selector arm bolt and lockplate

11 Fit the selector arm holder with the selector shaft arm correctly located. Tighten the holder bolts to the specified torque.
12 Fit the mainshaft and countershaft simultaneously with their gears meshed together, into the flywheel housing (photos).
13 Move the 1st/2nd synchro sliding sleeve into 2nd gear position and locate the 1st/2nd selector fork in the sleeve groove (photo).
14 Fit 3rd/4th selector shaft and fork (photo).
15 Fit the 1st/2nd gear selector shaft (photo).
16 Locate the 5th/reverse selector dog and insert the selector shaft through it (photo).
17 Check that the detent grooves on the selector shafts are furthest from the flywheel housing and are also facing towards the outside of the transmission casing.
18 Tighten the three selector shaft fork lock bolts using new lockplates and bend up their tabs (photos).
19 Fit the reverse detent spring and ball followed by reverse selector arm, special washer and the nut (photos).
20 Fit reverse idler gear and shaft (photo).

11.12A Fitting geartrains to flywheel housing

11.12B Geartrains installed

11.13 Selector arm holder and 1st/2nd selector fork

11.14 3rd/4th selector shaft and fork

11.15 Fitting 1st/2nd selector shaft

11.16 Fitting 5th/reverse selector shaft

11.18A Tightening a selector fork lockbolt

11.18B Method of bending lockplate tabs

11.19A Reverse selector arm detent spring

11.19B Reverse selector arm detent ball

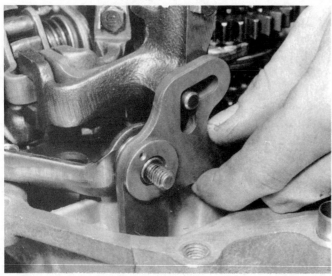

11.19C Fitting reverse selector arm

11.19D Reverse selector arm detent ball (arrowed)

11.19E Reverse selector arm special washer

11.19F Tightening reverse selector arm nut

11.20 Reverse idler gear and shaft

11.21 Transmission casing bearing circlips

21 Expand the mainshaft and countershaft bearing circlips using strong circlip pliers and fit the bearings into the transmission casing (photo).
22 Check that the positioning dowels are in place in the transmission casing flange and apply a thin bead of RTV sealant to the joint face. Fit the magnet (photos).
23 Lightly oil the shaft ends and differential bearing to facilitate the connection of the transmission casing and the flywheel housing.

24 Fit the casing to the housing and insert and tighten the connecting bolts to the specified torque and in the sequence shown (Fig. 6.12) (photos).
25 Fit the clutch cable bracket (photo).
26 Fit the detent balls, springs and plugs (photos).
27 Fit 5th speed gear to the countershaft so that its boss is towards the bearing (photo).
28 Fit the dished washer (concave side to the gear) (photo).

11.22A Applying transmission casing sealant

11.22B Fitting the magnet

11.24A Fitting transmission casing to flywheel housing

11.24B Tightening the casing bolts

11.25 Clutch cable bracket and breather hose

Fig. 6.12 Transmission casing to housing bolt tightening
sequence (Sec 11)

11.26A Inserting detent ball

11.26B Inserting detent spring

11.26C Screwing in a detent plug

11.27 Fitting 5th speed gear to the countershaft

11.28 Fitting dished washer to countershaft

Fig. 6.14 Measuring 5th speed gear housing internal depth (Sec 11)

2 Depth gauge   4 5th speed gear housing
3 Straight-edge   B Flange face to circlip seat

Fig. 6.13 Measuring 5th speed gear bearing height (Sec 11)

1 Mainshaft   A Casing to bearing outer track
2 Depth gauge

29 Fit 5th speed gear synchro hub and bearing onto the mainshaft. Using a depth gauge, measure the height A (Fig. 6.13). Take the average of three measurements around the bearing.
30 Remove the bearing and synchro hub from the shaft. Extract the circlip and the dished washer from 5th gear housing.
31 Place a straight-edge across the mounting flange of the 5th speed gear housing and again using the depth gauge measure the dimension B (fig. 6.14). Take the average of three measurements into the circlip seat at equidistant points.
32 To calculate the thickness of the 5th speed gear circlip, use the following formula: B–A–0.85 mm (thickness of dished washer) = thickness of circlip required. Fit the selected circlip and dished washer into 5th gear housing (photo).
33 Fit 5th speed gear thrust washer, 5th speed gear and needle roller bearing to the mainshaft (photos).
34 Fit the synchro baulk ring and spring.
35 Fit the synchro hub with its recessed side towards 5th speed gear (photo).
36 Engage the selector fork in the groove of the 5th speed gear

11.32 5th gear housing circlip

synchro sleeve (chamfered side of sleeve furthest from gear) and fit the sleeve and fork to the shaft as an assembly. Remember that the sleeve will only slide onto the hub on one of three positions due to the location of the master splines. Lock up the geartrains by pushing 5th speed gear synchro sleeve downwards (photo).

11.33A Thrust washer on mainshaft

11.33B Needle roller bearing on mainshaft

11.33C Fitting 5th speed gear to mainshaft

11.35 Fitting 5th speed synchro hub

11.36 5th speed gear selector fork

11.37A Tightening countershaft nut

11.37B Staking countershaft nut

11.38 Fitting 5th speed selector fork roll pin

11.39 Mainshaft ball bearing

11.40A Fitting 5th speed gear housing

11.40B Harness clip on 5th speed gear housing

11.41 Tightening reverse lamp switch

37 Tighten the new countershaft locknut to the specified torque. Slacken the nut and then tighten to the specified torque for the second time. Stake the nut into the shaft groove (photos).
38 Drive in 5th gear selector fork roll pin (photo).
39 Fit the mainshaft ball bearing so that the engraved numbers are visible when fitted (photo).
40 Apply RTV sealant to the flange joint check that the positioning dowels are in place and bolt on the 5th speed gear housing complete with selected circlip and dished washer (photos).
41 Screw in the reverse lamp switch (photo).
42 Check the selection of all gears by moving the selector shaft.
43 Fit the clutch release shaft and bearing.
44 Fill the transmission with oil after it has been fitted to the car (Section 6).

Part B Five-speed transmission (1.6 models)

12 General description

The gearbox is of Honda manufacture and is equipped with five forward and one reverse gear. Synchromesh gear engagement is used on all forward gears.

The mainshaft and countershaft carry the constant mesh gear cluster assemblies and are supported on ball and roller bearings. The short input end of the mainshaft eliminates the need for additional support from a crankshaft spigot bearing. The synchromesh gear engagement is by spring rings which act against baulk rings under the movement of the synchroniser sleeves. Gear selection is by means of a

Fig. 6.15 Cut-away view of the transmission fitted to 1.6 models (Sec 12)

1 Oil guide plate	5 Reverse idler gear
2 Mainshaft assembly	6 Gearbox breather and
3 Gearcase	bracket
4 Reverse idler shaft retaining	7 Bellhousing
bolt	8 Countershaft access plug
	9 Countershaft assembly

10 Gearchange holder and	12 Final drive differential
interlock assembly	13 Speedometer pinion
11 Differential endfloat circlip	14 Gearchange shaft
shim	

floor mounted transmitter to the selector forks via the gear change holder and interlock assembly.

The final drive (differential) unit is integral with the main gearbox and is located between the bellhousing and gearcase. The gearbox and final drive components both share the same lubricating oil.

13 Maintenance

1 Refer to Part A, Section 2.
2 Note the locations of the filler/level plug and the drain plug (photos).

14 Gearchange lever – removal and refitting

Refer to Part A, Section 3.

15 Differential oil seals – renewal

1 Leakage of oil from these seals may be rectified by renewing the seals without removing the transmission from the car.
2 Raise the front of the car and remove the roadwheel from the side on which the oil seal is to be renewed. Support the body members securely on stands.
3 Drain the transmission oil, retaining it for further use if required.
4 Place a jack under the lower suspension (track control) arm. Unscrew the balljoint taper pin nut and using a suitable splitter tool disconnect the balljoint from the hub carrier.
5 Using the same tool, disconnect the tie-rod end balljoint from the steering arm.
6 Disconnect the driveshaft from the transmission by inserting a lever between the driveshaft inboard joint and the transmission casing, and prising against the resistance of the driveshaft securing clip.
7 Prise out the oil seal, apply grease to the lips of the new one and drive it squarely into position.

13.2A Transmission filler/level plug

13.2B Transmission drain plug

16.11A Steady bar dished washer

8   Reconnect the driveshaft using a new securing clip, making sure that it engages positively in the differential side gear.
9   Reconnect the balljoints and tighten the nuts to the specified torque.
10 Fit the roadwheel.
11 Refill the transmission with oil.

16 Transmission – removal and refitting

1   Disconnect and remove the battery.
2   Remove the air cleaner.
3   Unbolt and move the starter motor aside.
4   Disconnect the speedometer cable from the transmission by pulling out the cable retaining clip.
5   Disconnect the reverse lamp switch leads.
6   Remove the clutch adjuster spring clip and then slip the clutch cable from the release arm and out of the support bracket.
7   Raise the front of the car and support it securely on stands. Remove the front left-hand roadwheel.
8   Drain the transmission oil.
9   Support the left-hand lower suspension (track control) arm on a jack. Unscrew the balljoint taper pin nut and using a suitable splitter tool, disconnect the balljoint from the hub carrier.
10 Insert a lever between the left-hand driveshaft joint and the transmission casing and prise the shaft out of the transmission.
11 Unscrew the bolt with washer which holds the steady bar to the transmission. Remove the bar and inner washer. Note that the lip on the inner washer is towards the flexible bush (photos).
12 Push the safety clip on the remote control selector rod aside and drive out the selector rod to shaft roll pin (photo).
13 Unscrew and remove the engine rear mounting bolts from the transmission and retrieve the spacer washers.
14 Support the engine under the sump pan using a jack and a block of wood as an insulator.
15 Unscrew the left-hand mounting through-bolt and detach the mounting bracket from the transmission.
16 Remove the battery tray.
17 Remove the clutch cable support bracket. Note that the earth straps will be disconnected as the battery tray and clutch cable bracket bolts are removed.
18 Attach a hoist to the transmission and take its weight.
19 Unscrew the transmission to engine adaptor plate bolts and withdraw the transmission from the engine about 25.4 mm (1.0 in). At

16.11B Steady bar flat washer

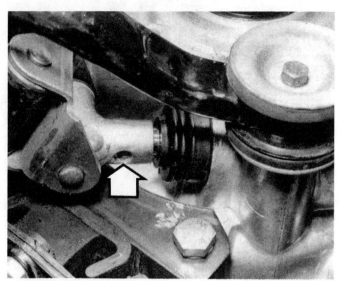

16.12 Gearchange rod roll pin

17.2 Removing the reverse lamp switch

this point, have an assistant prise the driveshaft inboard joint free from the transmission using a lever as previously described.
20 Withdraw the transmission completely from the engine and have the assistant catch the driveshaft as it drops out of the transmission.
21 Lower the transmission to the floor and withdraw it from under the car.
22 Refitting is a reversal of removal, but observe the following points.
23 Use new driveshaft retaining clips.
24 Tighten all nuts and bolts to the specified torque.
25 Set the clutch cable automatic adjuster as described in Chapter 5.
26 Fill the transmission with oil.

17 Transmission – dismantling into major assemblies

1   Refer to Part A, Section 7, paragraphs 1 to 3.
2   Stand the gearbox on its bellhousing face on the bench, and begin dismantling by removing the reversing lamp switch (photo).
3   Undo the retaining bolt and plate and lift out the speedometer pinion assembly.
4   Undo all the gearcase to bellhousing retaining bolts, noting the location of the breather pipe and bracket, which are also retained by one of the case bolts. Remove the breather pipe and bracket (photo).
5   Undo the reverse idler shaft retaining bolt located on the side of the gearcase (photo).
6   Using a large Allen key, hexagonal bar, or suitable bolt with two nuts locked together, undo the countershaft access plug on the end of the gearcase (photo).
7   Using circlip pliers inserted through the access plug aperture, spread the countershaft retaining circlip while at the same time lifting upwards on the gearcase. Tap the case with a soft mallet if necessary. When the circlip is clear of the groove, lift the case up and off the bellhousing and gear clusters (photos).
8   Undo the two retaining bolts and remove the reverse gear fork and bracket.
9   Lift out the reverse gear idler shaft with reverse gear.
10 Undo the three bolts and remove the gearchange holder and interlock assembly. Note that the holder locates in a slot in the 1st/2nd selector shaft.
11 With the help of an assistant lift up the mainshaft and countershaft as an assembly approximately 0.5 in (12.0 mm) and withdraw the selector shafts and forks from the bellhousing and gear clusters (photo).
12 Lift the mainshaft and countershaft out of their respective bearings in the bellhousing (photo).
13 Finally, remove the differential from the bellhousing (photo).

17.4 Breather pipe and bracket

17.5 Reverse idler shaft retaining bolt

17.6 Countershaft access plug

17.7A Releasing countershaft bearing circlip

17.7B Withdrawing transmission casing from flywheel housing

17.11 Supporting geartrains in order to remove selector forks and shafts

17.12 Removing mainshaft and countershaft together

17.13 Removing differential/final drive

Fig. 6.16 Exploded view of the 1.6 model transmission (Sec 17)

1 Clutch release bearing, fork and retaining spring wire
2 Clutch operating lever
3 Clutch operating lever oil seal
4 Differential oil seal
5 Bellhousing (flywheel housing)
6 Speedometer pinion assembly
7 Locating dowel
8 Gearchange shaft oil seal
9 Rubber boot
10 Gearchange shaft
11 Final drive case bearing
12 Final drive crownwheel
13 Roll pin
14 Final drive case
15 Differential sun and planet gear components
16 Final drive case bearing
17 Differential endfloat circlip shim
18 Differential oil seal
19 Oil guide plate
20 Countershaft roller bearing
21 Countershaft

22 Thrustwasher
23 Needle roller bearing
24 1st gear
25 Baulk ring
26 Spring ring
27 1st/2nd synchro hub
28 1st/2nd synchro sleeve
29 Spring ring
30 Baulk ring
31 Distance collar
32 Needle roller bearing
33 2nd gear
34 3rd gear
35 4th gear
36 5th gear
37 Countershaft ball bearing
38 Tongued washer
39 Retaining nut
40 Circlip
41 Mainshaft oil seal
42 Mainshaft ball bearing
43 Mainshaft
44 Needle roller bearing

45 3rd gear
46 Baulk ring
47 Spring ring
48 3rd/4th synchro hub
49 3rd/4th synchro sleeve
50 Spring ring
51 Baulk ring
52 4th gear
53 Needle roller bearing
54 Distance collar
55 Needle roller bearing
56 5th gear
57 Baulk ring
58 Spring ring
59 5th gear synchro hub
60 5th gear synchro sleeve
61 Mainshaft ball bearing
62 Selective circlips
63 Belleville washer
64 Oil guide plate
65 Reversing lamp switch
66 Transmission casing

67 Gearbox breather
68 Reverse idler shaft retaining bolt
69 Gearbox breather bracket
70 Roll pin
71 Reverse idler shaft
72 Reverse idler gear
73 Gearchange arm
74 Magnet
75 Detent ball
76 Detent spring
77 Detent plug
78 Reverse gear fork and bracket
79 Gearchange holder and interlock assembly
80 1st/2nd gear selector fork
81 1st/2nd gear selector shaft
82 Roll pin
83 5th/reverse gear selector
84 5th/reverse gear selector shaft
85 3rd/4th gear selector fork
86 5th gear selector fork
87 Circlip

Fig. 6.17 Transmission with casing removed (Sec 17)

1 Bellhousing
2 Reverse gear fork and
   bracket
3 3rd/4th gear selector fork
4 Mainshaft assembly
5 5th gear selector fork
6 Countershaft assembly
7 1st/2nd gear selector fork
8 Final drive differential
9 Gearchange holder and
   interlock assembly

18 Mainshaft – dismantling and reassembly

1 Remove the mainshaft bearing, using a two or three-legged puller if necessary, unless the bearing remained in the gearcase during removal.
2 Withdraw the 5th gear synchroniser hub and sleeve assembly from the mainshaft using a two or three-legged puller if it is tight. Recover the 5th gear baulk ring from the cone face of 5th gear and place it, together with the spring ring, on the synchroniser unit.
3 Slide off 5th gear followed by the 5th gear needle roller bearing.
4 Withdraw the distance collar followed by 4th gear and the needle roller bearing.
5 Remove the 3rd/4th synchro hub and sleeve assembly complete with baulk rings and spring rings.
6 Remove 3rd gear and its needle roller bearing.
7 Carry out a careful inspection of the mainshaft components as described in the following paragraphs.
8 Examine the shafts and gears for pitting, scoring ridges or chipped teeth. Check the fit of the gears on the mainshaft and countershaft splines and ensure that there is no lateral free play.
9 Check the smoothness of the bearings and check for any signs of scoring on the needle roller bearing tracks and distance collars.
10 Check the mainshaft for straightness, check for damaged threads or splines and ensure that the lubrication holes are clear (photo).
11 Mark one side of each synchro hub and sleeve before separating the two parts, so that they may be refitted in the same position.
12 Withdraw the hub from the sleeve and examine the internal gear teeth for wear or ridges. Ensure that the hub and sleeve are a snug sliding fit with the minimum of lateral movement.

13 Check the fit of the selector forks in their respective synchro sleeve grooves. If the clearance exceeds the figure given in the Specifications, check for wear ridges to give an indication of whether it is the fork or the sleeve groove that has worn. As a general rule the selector fork usually wears first, but not always. If in doubt compare with new parts.
14 Place each baulk ring on the cone face of its respective gear and measure the distance between the baulk ring and the gear face. If the clearance is less than specified renew the baulk ring. Renew them also if there is excessive wear or rounding off of the dog teeth around their periphery, if they are cracked, or if they are in any way damaged. If the gearbox is in reasonable condition and is to be rebuilt it is advisable to renew all the baulk rings as a matter of course. The improvement in the synchromesh action when changing gear will justify the expense.
15 When reassembling the synchro units make sure that the two master teeth in the synchro sleeve engage with the two master grooves in the hub (photo).
16 If any of the gears on the mainshaft are to be renewed then the corresponding gear on the countershaft must also be renewed and vice versa. This applies to the countershaft and differential final drivegear as well.
17 During reassembly, lightly lubricate all the parts with the specified grade of gear oil as the work proceeds.
18 Slide the 3rd gear needle roller bearing onto the mainshaft followed by 3rd gear with its flat face towards the other gears on the shaft (photo).
19 Place the 3rd gear baulk ring and spring ring on the cone face of 3rd gear, then fit the 3rd/4th synchro hub and sleeve assembly. Ensure that the lugs on the baulk ring engage with the slots in the synchro hub (photos).
20 Locate the 4th gear spring ring and baulk ring in the synchro unit, then slide on 4th gear with its needle roller bearing (photos).
21 Fit the distance collar with its shoulder towards 4th gear (photo).
22 Place the 5th gear needle roller bearing over the collar then slide 5th gear onto the bearing (photo).
23 Locate the 5th gear baulk ring and spring ring in the 5th gear synchro unit then fit this assembly to the mainshaft (photo).
24 If the mainshaft or any of its components, the gearcase or bellhousing have been renewed, then the mainshaft endfloat must be checked, and if necessary adjusted as follows. To do this it will be necessary to remove the mainshaft ball bearing in the gearcase, remove the selective circlips, Belleville washer and oil guide, then refit the bearing.
25 Position the assembled mainshaft in the bellhousing, fit the gearcase and temporarily secure it with several evenly spaced bolts. Tighten the bolts securely.
26 Support the bellhousing face of the gearbox on blocks, so as to provide access to the protruding mainshaft.
27 Place a straightedge across the bellhousing face, in line with the mainshaft, then accurately measure and record the distance from straightedge to mainshaft.

18.10 Mainshaft stripped. Oil holes arrowed

18.15 Synchro hub/sleeve master splines

18.18A Fitting 3rd speed gear needle roller bearing onto mainshaft

18.18B Fitting 3rd speed gear to mainshaft

18.19A 3rd speed gear baulk ring and spring

18.19B 3rd/4th synchro unit on mainshaft

18.20A 4th speed baulk ring and spring

18.20B 4th speed gear and needle roller bearing on mainshaft

18.21 Fitting distance collar with shoulder towards 4th speed gear

18.22A Sliding 5th speed gear needle roller bearing over distance collar

18.22B Fitting 5th speed gear to mainshaft

18.23 5th speed gear synchro unit

28 Turn the gearbox over so that the bellhousing is uppermost and gently tap the mainshaft back into the gearcase using a soft-faced mallet. Take a second measurement of the mainshaft to straightedge distance.
29 Subtract the first measurement from the second measurement and identify this as dimension A:
30 Measure the thickness of the Belleville washer and add an allowance of 0.007 in (0.17 mm) which is the nominal mainshaft endfloat. Identify this as dimension B:
31 Subtract dimension B from dimension A and the value obtained is the thickness of selected circlip(s) required to give the specified mainshaft endfloat.
32 Remove the gearcase and the mainshaft. Remove the bearing from the gearcase, refit the oil guide, Belleville washer and circlips of the required thickness, then refit the bearing.

19 Countershaft – dismantling and reassembly

1 Support the pinion gear on the countershaft in a vice between two blocks of wood. Tighten the vice just sufficiently to prevent the countershaft turning as the nut is undone.

2 Using a small punch release the staking on the countershaft nut then undo and remove the nut. Note that the nut has a left-hand thread and must be turned clockwise to unscrew it.
3 Remove the tongued washer then draw off the countershaft bearing using a two or three-legged puller.
4 Slide 5th, 4th, 3rd and 2nd gears off the countershaft noting their fitted directions.
5 Remove the 2nd gear baulk ring and spring ring.
6 Slide off the 2nd gear needle roller bearing followed by the distance collar. Use two screwdrivers to lever off the collar if it is tight.
7 Remove the 1st/2nd synchro hub and sleeve assembly followed by the 1st gear baulk ring and spring ring.
8 Slide off 1st gear followed by the needle roller bearing and thrust washer.
9 Carry out a careful inspection of the countershaft components as described in paragraphs 8 to 16 of Section 18, and obtain any new parts as necessary.
10 During reassembly, lightly lubricate all the parts with the specified grade of gear oil as the work proceeds.
11 Fit the thrustwasher to the countershaft followed by the needle roller bearing and 1st gear (photos).
12 Fit the baulk ring and spring ring to the cone face of 1st gear then slide on the 1st/2nd synchro unit. The synchro unit must be fitted with

19.11A Countershaft thrust washer

19.11B Fitting needle roller bearing to countershaft

19.11C 1st speed gear on countershaft

19.12A Baulk ring and spring against 1st speed gear

19.12B 1st/2nd synchro unit on countershaft

the selector fork groove in the synchro sleeve away from 1st gear. As the unit is fitted ensure that the lugs on the baulk ring engage with the slots in the synchro hub (photos).

13 Warm the distance collar in boiling water then slide it onto the countershaft with the oil hole offset towards 1st gear (photo).

14 Fit the 2nd gear needle roller bearing to the distance collar (photo).

15 Locate the 2nd gear baulk ring and spring ring on the synchro unit then slide 2nd gear into place over the needle roller bearing (photos).

16 Fit 3rd gear to the countershaft with its longer boss away from 2nd gear (photo).

17 Fit 4th gear with its boss towards the 3rd gear boss (photo).

18 Fit 5th gear with its flat face towards 4th gear then tap the countershaft bearing into position using a hammer and suitable tube (photos).

19 Fit the tongued washer followed by a new countershaft nut. Hold the pinion between blocks of wood in the vice as before and tighten the nut to the specified torque (photos).

20 Using feeler gauges, measure the clearance between the rear face of the pinion and 1st gear, and between the 2nd and 3rd gear faces. Compare the measurements with the endfloat dimension given in the Specifications. If the recorded endfloat is outside the tolerance range, dismantle the countershaft again and fit an alternative thrustwasher or distance collar (photos).

19.13 Countershaft distance collar. Oil hole (arrowed) nearer 1st speed gear

19.14 Sliding 2nd speed needle roller bearing over distance collar

19.15A 2nd speed baulk ring and spring

19.15B 2nd speed gear on countershaft

19.16 3rd speed gear with boss away from 2nd speed gear

19.17 4th speed gear with boss towards 3rd speed gear

19.18A 5th speed gear on countershaft

19.18B Countershaft bearing

19.18C Seating countershaft bearing

19.19A Tongued washer engaged in countershaft groove

19.19B Screwing on a new countershaft nut

19.20A Checking pinion to 1st speed gear clearance

21 With the countershaft assembled and the endfloat correctly set recheck the torque of the countershaft nut then stake it into the countershaft groove using a small punch.

20 Transmission casing and flywheel housing – examination and renovation

Transmission casing

1 Check the gearcase for cracks or any damage to its bellhousing mating face. Renew the case if damaged.
2 Check the condition of the mainshaft bearing in the gearcase and ensure that it spins smoothly with no trace of roughness or harshness. The bearing must be removed if it is worn, if the gearcase is to be renewed, or if it is necessary to gain access to the mainshaft endfloat selective circlips located behind it.
3 Removal of the bearing entails the use of a slide hammer with adaptor consisting of internally expanding flange or legs, to locate behind the inner race. A special tool is available for this purpose from Austin Rover but it may be possible to make up a suitable alternative with readily available tools. Whichever option is chosen it is quite likely that the oil guide plate will be damaged or broken in the process. If so a new one must be obtained.
4 If any of the mainshaft components are being renewed during the course of overhaul, do not refit the bearing, circlips, Belleville washer or oil guide plate until after the mainshaft endfloat has been checked and adjusted.
5 When the bearing is fitted this can be done by tapping it squarely into place using a hammer and tube of suitable diameter in contact with the bearing outer race.
6 If there is any sign of leakage, the differential oil seal in the gearcase should be renewed. Drive or hook out the old seal and install the new one with its open side facing inward ie towards the differential. Tap the seal squarely into place using a suitable tube or the old seal. Smear a little grease around the sealing lip to aid refitting of the driveshaft. **Note:** *If the differential or differential bearings have been renewed or disturbed from their original position, do not fit the oil seal until the gearbox has been completely reassembled.* The differential bearing clearances are checked through the oil seal aperture, and cannot be done with the seal in place (photo).

Flywheel housing

7 Remove the magnet and clean it (photo).
8 Remove the release bearing as described in Chapter 5.
9 Undo the retaining peg bolt securing the release fork to the clutch operating lever (photo).
10 Withdraw the lever from the fork and lift out the fork noting the fitted position of the release bearing retaining spring wire.

19.20B Checking 2nd to 3rd speed gear clearance

20.6 Differential oil seal

20.7 Swarf collecting magnet

20.9 Clutch release fork peg bolt

20.11A Gearchange shaft detent plug

11 Undo the gearchange shaft detent plug and lift out the detent spring and ball (photo).
12 Undo the bolt securing the gearchange arm to the shaft and slide the arm off the shaft (photo).
13 Withdraw the gearchange shaft from the bellhousing and recover the rubber boot.
14 Examine the bellhousing for cracks or any damage to its gearcase mating face. Renew the case if damaged.
15 Check the condition of the ball and roller bearings in the bellhousing ensuring that they spin smoothly with no trace of roughness or harshness.
16 Renewal of the bearings entails the use of a slide hammer with adaptor consisting of an internally expanding flange or legs, to locate through the centre of the bearing. A special tool is available from Austin Rover for this purpose, but it may be possible to make up a suitable substitute with readily available tools. Another alternative would be to take the bellhousing along to your dealer and have him renew the bearings for you. Whichever option is chosen it is quite likely that the oil guide plate behind the countershaft roller bearing will be damaged or broken in the process (assuming this bearing is to be renewed) and if so a new guide plate must be obtained (photo).

20.11B Gearchange shaft detent spring

20.11C Gearchange shaft detent ball

20.12 Gearchange arm retaining bolt

20.16 Flywheel housing bearings
A   Mainshaft ball bearing   C   Oil guide plate
B   Countershaft roller bearing   D   Bearing oil holes

17 Refit the bearings by tapping them squarely into place using a hammer and tube of suitable diameter. Ensure that the oil hole in the countershaft bearing faces the gearbox interior.
18 Carefully inspect all the oil seals in the bellhousing and renew any that show signs of leakage. The old oil seals can be driven out with a tube or punch and the new seals tapped squarely into place using a block of wood or the old seal. Ensure that in all cases the open side of the seal faces inward. In the case of the mainshaft oil seal it will be necessary to remove the mainshaft bearing to enable a new seal to be fitted.
19 Inspect the gearchange shaft for distortion or wear across the detent grooves and check the gearchange arm for wear of the forks. Renew these components if wear is evident.
20 With the new bearings and seals in position and any other new parts obtained as necessary, refit the gearchange shaft and rubber boot with the detent grooves facing outward, ie towards the gear clusters.
21 Slide on the gearchange arm so that its forked side is facing away from the bellhousing starter motor aperture. Refit the retaining bolt and washer and tighten the bolt.
22 Refit the detent ball followed by the spring and plug bolt. Tighten the bolt to the specified torque.
23 Slide the clutch operating lever into the bellhousing and engage the release fork. Ensure that the joined end of the bearing retaining spring wire is positioned behind the release fork arms. Refit and tighten the retaining bolt.
24 Refit the magnet with its forked end down, then refit the clutch release bearing as described in Chapter 5.

21 Selector forks and shafts – examination and renovation

1   Visually inspect the selector forks for obvious signs of wear ridges, cracks or deformation.
2   Slide the selector forks off the shafts, noting their fitted position and check the detent action as the fork is removed. Note that the detent balls and springs are located in the selector forks and cannot be removed. If the detent action is weak or if there is evidence of a broken spring or damaged ball, the fork must be renewed.
3   Check the fit of the selector forks in their respective synchro sleeves. If the clearance exceeds the figure given in the Specifications check for wear ridges to give an indication of whether it is the fork or the sleeve groove that is worn. If in doubt compare them with new parts and renew any that are worn.

4   Examine the selector shafts for wear ridges around the detent grooves and for any obvious signs of distortion. Renew any suspect shafts.

22 Differential/final drive – overhaul

1   The operations are similar to those described in Part A, Section 10, but the crownwheel bolts have a conventional (right-hand) thread.
2   If the crownwheel is to be renewed, the countershaft and drive pinion must be renewed also.

23 Transmission – reassembly

1   Poisition the differential in its location in the bellhousing and tap it down gently, using a soft-faced mallet to ensure that the bearing is fully seated.
2   Fit the gearcase to the bellhousing and secure it temporarily with several bolts tightened to the specified torque.
3   Using feeler gauges inserted through the oil seal aperture in the gearcase, measure the clearance between the bearing and the circlip type shim in the bearing recess. If the clearance is not equal to the side clearance dimension given in the Specifications, slacken the case retaining bolts, extract the circlip through the oil seal aperture and substitute a thicker or thinner circlip as required from the range available. Repeat this procedure until the correct clearance is obtained then remove the gearcase. Gearbox reassembly can now proceed as follows.
4   Insert the magnet into its location in the edge of the bellhousing, forked end first.
5   Refit the gearchange shaft and arm as described in Section 20 if this has not already been done.
6   With the bearings in place in the bellhousing, hold the assembled mainshaft and countershaft together and insert them into their locations.
7   With the help of an assistant, lift up the mainshaft and countershaft assemblies together approximately 0.5 in (12.0 mm). Engage the selector forks with their respective synchro sleeves and locate the selector shafts in the bellhousing. Return the mainshaft and countershaft to their original positions ensuring that the selector shafts

Fig. 6.18 Differential/final drive components (Sec 22)

1	Countershaft with drive pinion	3	Crownwheel	6	Differential case bearing	9	Thrust washer
2	Bearing	4	Roll pin	7	Shimming circlip	10	Planet gear pinion
		5	Differential case	8	Sun gear pinion	11	Pinion shaft

engage fully with their holes in the bellhousing.

8   Refit the gearchange holder and interlock assembly, noting that the holder locates in a slot in the 1st/2nd selector shaft (photo).

9   Refit the three gearchange holder and interlock retaining bolts and tighten them to the specified torque (photo).

10 Refit the reverse gear idler shaft with reverse gear, noting that the long boss on the gear must face the bellhousing, and the hole in the top of the shaft faces away from the gear clusters (photo).

11 Engage the reverse gear fork over the reverse gear teeth and over the peg on the 5th/reverse selector. Secure the reverse gear fork

bracket with the two retaining bolts tightened to the specified torque (photo).

12 Apply a continuous bead of RTV sealant to the gearcase mating face. Lower the gearcase over the gear clusters and engage the shafts and bearings in their locations. Using circlip pliers inserted through the countershaft access plug aperture, spread the circlip and tap the gearcase fully into position using a soft-faced mallet. Release the circlip ensuring that it enters the groove on the countershaft bearing.

13 Refit the gearcase retaining bolts and breather bracket then tighen the bolts progressively to the specified torque.

23.8 Gearchange holder and interlock

23.9 Gearchange holder fixing bolts (arrowed)

23.10 Reverse idler shaft and gear

23.11 Reverse selector fork engaged with reverse gear. Reverse selector peg arrowed

14 Refit the reverse idler shaft retaining bolt and tighten it to the specified torque.
15 Apply RTV sealant to the threads of the countershaft access plug, refit the plug and tighten it to the specified torque.
16 Refit the speedometer drive pinion, and the reversing light switch.

17 Finally refit the final drive differential oil seal to the gearcase if not already done.
18 Check the operation of the gearchange mechanism ensuring that all gears can be engaged, then refit the gearbox to the car as described in Section 16.

Part C All models

24 Fault diagnosis – manual transmission

Note: *Before diagnosing faults from the table below, check that the gearbox oil level is correct and that the correct grade of oil is in use.*
A noisy gearbox, or one on which synchro action is weak, may continue to function for a long time in such a state. It is up to the owner to decide the degree of noise or malfunction which justifies an overhaul.

Symptom	Reason(s)
Gearbox noisy in neutral	Mainshaft bearings worn
Gearbox noisy only when moving (in all gears)	Countershaft bearings worn Differential bearings worn Differential final drive gear or countershaft pinion chipped or worn
Gearbox noisy in only one gear	Worn, damaged or chipped gear teeth Worn needle roller bearings
Gearbox jumps out of gear	Worn synchro hubs or synchro sleeves Weak or broken selector shaft detent spring Weak or broken gearchange shaft detent spring Worn shaft detent grooves Worn selector forks
Ineffective synchromesh	Worn baulk rings or synchro hubs
Difficulty in engaging gears	Clutch fault Ineffective synchromesh Worn gear lever bushes and linkage

Chapter 7 Automatic transmission

For modifications, and information applicable to later models, see Supplement at end of manual

Contents

Specifications

Part A Three-speed (1.3 models)
Type .... Three forward speeds and reverse, torque converter and constant mesh geartrain

Gear ratios
1st .... 2.421 : 1
2nd .... 1.500 : 1
3rd .... 0.911 : 1
Reverse .... 1.954 : 1
Final drive .... 3.933 : 1

Fluid capacity
From dry .... 5.0 litres (8.75 pints)
Service fluid change .... 2.4 litres (4.25 pints)

Fluid type
For topping up .... Dexron IID type ATF (Duckhams D-Matic)
Complete refill .... Hondamatic fluid

Part B Four-speed (1.6 models)
Type .... Four forward speeds and reverse, torque converter

Gear ratios
1st .... 2.41 : 1
2nd .... 1.37 : 1
3rd .... 1.00 : 1
4th .... 0.74 : 1
Reverse .... 2.83 : 1
Final drive .... 3.28 : 1

Fluid capacity
From dry .... 5.75 litres (10.0 pints)
Service fluid change .... 2.0 litres (3.5 pints)

Fluid type .... Dexron IID type ATF (Duckhams D-Matic)

Torque wrench settings
Part A 1.3 models

	Nm	lbf ft
Drain plug	40	30
Cooler hose banjo bolts	29	21
Driveplate to crankshaft bolts	75	55
Driveplate to torque converter bolts	12	9
Torque converter housing to engine connecting bolts	45	33
Track control (lower suspension) arm balljoint nuts	44	32
Tie-rod end balljoint nuts	44	32
Mounting bracket to transmission	65	48
Mounting bracket to body	39	29

Part B 1.6 models

	Nm	lbf ft
Torque converter to adaptor plate:		
M10 bolts	45	33
M12 bolts	90	60
Driveplate to crankshaft screws	110	81
Driveplate to torque converter screws	32	24
Starter inhibitor switch	40	30
Fluid cooler centre screw	50	37
Sump pan screws	10	7
Drain plug	15	11
Transmission mounting bracket to casing bolts	45	33
Mounting to body bolts	40	30
Through-bolt	120	89
Track control (lower suspension) arm balljoint nuts	44	32
Tie-rod end balljoint nuts	44	32

Part A Three-speed (1.3 models)

1 General description

The transmission is of Honda manufacture and has a mechanical constant mesh geartrain driven through a torque converter.

Three forward speeds and reverse are provided, selection being made by a floor-mounted selector lever.

The transmission incorporates the final drive and is mounted transversely with the engine, at the front of the car.

A transmission fluid cooler is incorporated in the cooling system radiator.

2 Maintenance

1   Keep the fluid level correctly maintained as described in the following Section.

2   Keep the transmission casing clean by periodically removing grease and dirt.

3   Regularly check the condition of the fluid cooler hoses.

4   Maintain the adjustments described in the following Sections of this Chapter.

3 Transmission fluid – level checking and renewal

1   At the specified intervals, or at the first sign of any malfunction, check the transmission fluid level as follows.

2   Park the vehicle on a level surface, fully apply the handbrake and select 'P'. Start the engine and allow it to idle for a few minutes.

3   Open the bonnet and locate the dipstick (under the battery). Stop the engine. The level check must be completed within one minute of stopping the engine.

4   Unscrew the dipstick and withdraw it. Wipe it on a clean non-fluffy rag, re-insert it fully *without screwing it in*, withdraw it again and read the fluid level. The level should be between the MIN and MAX marks.

5   Top up if necessary to the midway point between the two marks with fluid of specified type, through the dipstick hole.

6   Refit the dipstick and screw it home.

7   At the intervals recommended in Routine Maintenance, the transmission fluid should be drained hot after coming in from a run. **Warning:** *Take precautions against scalding. The fluid may be very hot.*

8   Remove the dipstick and then the drain plug and catch the fluid in a suitably large container of 3.0 litres (5.3 pints). The torque converter will not drain.

9   Refit the drain plug.

10 Fill slowly through the dipstick hole using recommended fluid and check the level as previously described.

4 Kickdown cable – adjustment

1   Check that the throttle cable has some slackness at the carburettor. Under light finger pressure, the cable should deflect between 10.0 and 12.0 mm (0.39 and 0.47 in).

2   Check that the throttle lever is up against its stop (full throttle) when the accelerator pedal is fully depressed.

3   The engine should be at normal operating temperature with the idling speed correctly set (see Chapter 3). Switch off the engine.

4   Release the kickdown inner cable from the lever on the transmission and then release the outer cable (conduit) from its support bracket.

5   Measure the distance between the kickdown lever and the throttle cable bracket. This should be 83.5 mm (3.287 in). If it is incorrect, release the bracket bolts and move the bracket.

6   Depress the accelerator pedal using a 1.3 kg (2.9 lb) weight.

7   Set the kickdown cable conduit locknut (B) so that dimension (A) (Fig. 7.1) is 84.0 mm (3.306 in).

8   Connect the inner cable to the lever on the transmission and engage the conduit with its bracket. Tighten the locknut (C) without disturbing the set position of locknut (B).

9   Remove the weight from the accelerator pedal.

5 Selector cable – adjustment

1   Start the engine, apply the footbrake and engage reverse gear, then stop the engine.

2   Remove the centre console (Chapter 11), then select D.

3   Release the locknut (2) (Fig. 7.2). Remove the retaining pin (1).

4   Turn the adjuster (3) until its hole is in alignment with the one in the selector cable.

5   Tighten the locknut and refit the pin.

6   Check that the starter only operates in N and P and then road test the car to check the selection of all speeds.

7   Refit the centre console.

Fig. 7.1 Three-speed transmission kickdown cable (Sec 4)

A = 84.0 mm (3.306 in)   B and C Locknuts

Fig. 7.2 Three-speed transmission selector cable (Sec 5)

1   Retaining pin   3   Adjuster
2   Locknut

6   Selector cable – removal and refitting

1   Remove the engine compartment under shield.
2   Disconnect the exhaust downpipe from the manifold and then separate and remove the downpipe from the rest of the exhaust system.
3   Remove the exhaust retaining brackets from the transmission.

4   Unbolt and remove the semi-circular cover plate from the torque converter housing.
5   Select N, remove the selector cable clevis pin and disconnect the cable from the transmission.
6   Remove the centre console (see Chapter 11) and disconnect the cable from the selector lever.
7   Refitting is a reversal of removal. Adjust as described in Section 5.

7   Speed selector control lever – removal, overhaul and refitting

1   Remove the centre console as described in Chapter 11.
2   Disconnect the starter inhibitor/reverse lamp switch connector plug also the selector index illumination lead.
3   Extract the screws which retain the index plate.
4   Select R and remove the selector cable retaining pin.
5   Unscrew the selector lever retaining nuts and remove the lever assembly.
6   To dismantle the assembly, extract the securing screws and withdraw the handle from the lever. Remove the push-button and spring.
7   Select N and remove the starter inhibitor/reverse lamp switch.
8   Remove the index panel and twist the lamp through 90° to remove it.
9   Release the spring and remove the detent lever. Withdraw the pivot bolt and withdraw the selector lever.
10 Reassembly and refitting are reversals of removal and dismantling. Smear the pivots and rubbing surfaces with grease and check operation after installation.

8   Automatic transmission – removal and refitting

In the event of a fault occurring on the transmission, it is first necessary to determine whether it is of a mechanical or hydraulic nature and to do this the transmission must be in the car. Special test equipment is necessary for this purpose, together with a systematic test procedure, and the work should be entrusted to a suitably equipped BL dealer or automatic transmission specialist.

Do not remove the transmission from the car for repair or overhaul until professional fault diagnosis has been carried out.
1   Disconnect and remove the battery and remove its tray.
2   Disconnect the speedometer cable from the transmission by pulling up the rubber cover and extracting the retaining clip.
3   Disconnect the transmission earth cable.
4   Disconnect the leads from the starter motor. Then unbolt and remove the starter motor.
5   Disconnect the transmission fluid cooler hoses and plug them.
6   Drain the transmission fluid.
7   Raise the front of the car and support it securely then remove the front roadwheels.
8   Remove the engine compartment undershield.
9   Support the lower suspension arms on jacks and unscrew the nuts from their balljoints.
10 Using a suitable splitter tool, disconnect the balljoints from the hub carriers. Make sure that the car is well supported when the balljoint is released as the torque at the suspension arm is considerable.
11 Disconnect both steering rod balljoints using the same tool as for the hub carrier balljoint.
12 Prise both driveshafts from the transmission and lower them to the floor. Do this by inserting a lever between the transmission casing and the driveshaft inboard joint and prising against the tension of the shaft locking clip. The front suspension struts can now be pulled outwards within the limit of flexibility of their upper mountings and the driveshafts disconnected from the transmission. The left-hand brake-pipe bracket may have to be released to prevent strain on the pipe.
13 Unbolt and remove the exhaust downpipe from the manifold and the rest of the exhaust system.
14 Unbolt and remove the torque converter cover plate.
15 Disconnect the selector cable and the kickdown cable from the transmission.
16 Working through the aperture left by removal of the torque converter cover plate, unscrew the bolts which hold the driveplate to the torque converter. The crankshaft will have to be turned by means of its pulley bolt to bring the bolts into view.

17 Support the weight of the engine either on a hoist or by locating a jack and block of wood as an insulator under the sump pan.

18 Disconnect and remove the rear and right-hand transmission mountings.

19 Using a second hoist or workshop jack, take the weight of the transmission and then unscrew the engine to transmission connecting bolts.

20 Withdraw the transmission until it comes off its positioning dowels. Then lower it to the floor and remove it from under the car. During the removal operations, have an assistant keep the torque converter pushed fully into the bellhousing and retain it afterwards using a plate bolted to the bellhousing flange. Failure to do this may damage the fluid seal and will cause loss of fluid.

21 If the transmission is being changed for a new or reconditioned unit, make sure that you take off any items which are not supplied with the new unit. Check with your supplier.

22 Refitting is a reversal of removal. Use new driveshaft circlips. Tighten all bolts and nuts to the specified torque, adjust the control cables as previously described. Refill the transmission with fluid.

9 Differential fluid seals – renewal

The operations are as described in Chapter 6, Section 5, but use petroleum jelly to fill the seal lips.

Part B Four-speed (1.6 models)

10 General description

The transmission is of ZF four-speed type and incorporates a torque converter.

The transmission is mounted in line with the engine on the left-hand side at the front of the car.

A kickdown facility is provided.

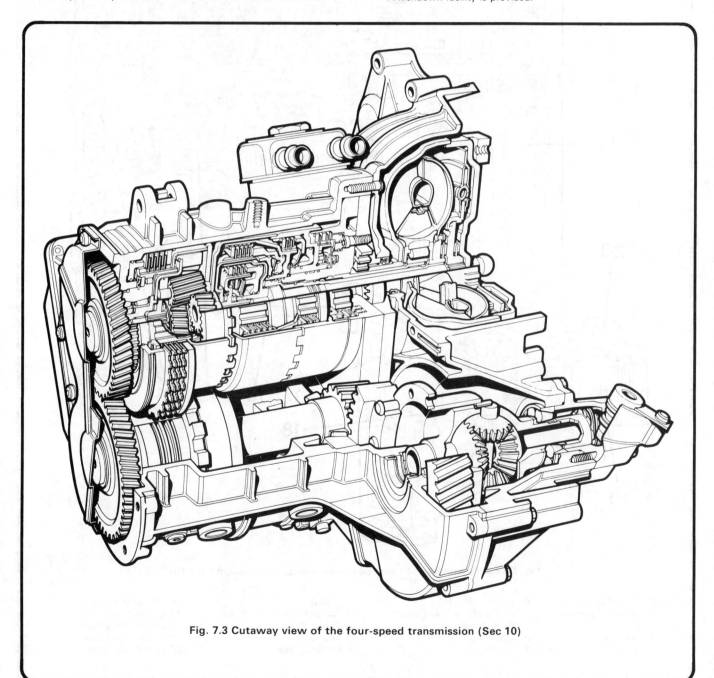

Fig. 7.3 Cutaway view of the four-speed transmission (Sec 10)

198

Fig. 7.4 Sectional view of four-speed automatic transmission (Sec 10)

1 Torque converter	6 Brake	11 Clutch	16 Countershaft
2 Torsional damper	7 2nd speed one-way clutch	12 1st speed one-way clutch	17 Crownwheel
3 Turbine	8 Brake band	13 Brake	18 Differential pinion gears
4 Impeller	9 Clutch	14 Spur gears	19 Speedo drive gear
5 Stator	10 Clutch	15 Planetary gear set	20 Speedo drive pinion

The final drive/differential is incorporated within the transmission casing.

The transmission fluid is cooled by an externally mounted cooler, through which engine coolant flows.

11 Maintenance

Refer to Section 2, Part A.

12 Transmission fluid – level checking and renewal

1   The fluid level should be checked when the car is standing on level ground with the transmission fluid hot, after at least 10 miles running. Check that the handbrake is fully applied.
2   With the engine idling in P (Park), withdraw the transmission dipstick and wipe it clean. Re-insert it and withdraw it again immediately. The fluid level should be between the MIN and MAX marks on the HOT side of the dipstick. 0.3 litre (0.5 pint) will raise the level from MIN to MAX.
3   Top up as necessary, but do not overfill.
4   At the intervals specified in Routine Maintenance, remove the drain plugs and the dipstick and drain the fluid. The torque converter cannot be drained. **Warning**: *Take precautions against scalding. The transmission fluid may be very hot.*
5   Refit the drain plugs and fill through the dipstick guide tube to the MAX mark on the cold side of the dipstick.
6   Start the engine and run it at idle speed. Move the speed selector lever slowly through all positions. With the engine still idling, withdraw the dipstick, wipe it clean, re-insert it and then withdraw it for the second time. The level should be between MIN and MAX on the COLD side of the dipstick.
7   Top up as necessary. 0.3 litre (0.5 pint) will raise the fluid level from the MIN to the MAX level marks.

13 Kickdown cable – adjustment

1   Slacken the locknuts at the kickdown and the throttle cable brackets in the engine compartment.
2   Adjust the nuts on the kickdown cable to give it some slackness.
3   Adjust the throttle cable nuts until all slack is removed from the cable, but it is not under tension.
4   Tighten the throttle cable locknuts.
5   Hold the throttle in the fully open position and pull the kickdown outer cable (conduit) until it is felt to pass the kickdown detent. Tighten the locknuts at the bracket.
6   Release the throttle and check that the gap between the crimped sleeve on the inner cable and the end of the outer cable threaded adjuster is between 0.2 and 0.5 mm (0.01 and 0.02 in). If it is not as specified then the crimped sleeve will have to be repositioned.

14 Selector cable – adjustment

1   Move the selector lever to P (Park).
2   Slacken the selector cable trunnion nut at the lever on the transmission and then rotate the lever fully anti-clockwise. Retighten the trunnion nut.
3   Check that the starter operates only when the selector lever is in N or P.

15 Selector cable – removal and refitting

1   Before removing the cable, make a sketch of its routing.
2   Remove the centre console (Chapter 11).
3   Extract the selector lever knob fixing screws and take off the knob, plunger and spring.
4   Extract the screws and remove the speed position indicator plate.
5   Unscrew the detent bracket bolts and move the bracket aside.
6   Extract the spring clip and withdraw the clevis pin.
7   Unscrew the cable locknut, take off the split washer and withdraw the cable from under the car.

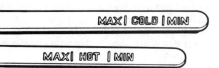

Fig. 7.5 Dipstick markings (Sec 12)

Fig. 7.6 Fluid drain plugs (Sec 12)

1   Gear case   *2   Final drive*

Fig. 7.7 Control cables (Sec 13)

1   Throttle cable
2   Locknuts
3   Kickdown cable
4   Locknuts

A   Crimped sleeve clearance on kickdown cable 0.2 to 0.5 mm (0.01 to 0.02 in)

8   Release the cable from the trunnion at the transmission and from its support bracket.
9   Refitting is a reversal of removal, but renew the nylon bush in the trunnion eye if it is worn. Wear in this bush could affect the operation of the starter inhibitor switch.
10 Adjust the cable as described in the preceding Section.

16 Selector lever – removal and refitting

1   Remove the centre console (Chapter 11).
2   Place the car over an inspection pit or raise the front end and support it securely on stands.
3   Carry out the operations described in Section 15, paragraphs 3 to 6.
4   Pull the selector lever into the car so that the lever pivot bolt can be unscrewed and the lever removed from the housing.
5   Extract the circlip and remove the lever plunger, spacers and dowel.
6   Unscrew the nut which retains the detent stud lever. Remove the lever and spring.
7   Refitting is a reversal of removal.

17 Brake band – adjustment

1   Place the car over an inspection pit, on ramps or raise the front end and support it securely.
2   Set the selector lever in N.
3   Slacken the brake band adjuster screw locknut and tighten the screw to 10.0 Nm (7.0 lbf ft). Unscrew the adjuster screw exactly two complete turns and tighten the locknut to 80.0 Nm (59.0 lbf ft).

18 Starter inhibitor/reverse lamp switch – removal and refitting

1   Open the bonnet, disconnect and remove the battery and its tray.
2   Remove the air cleaner.
3   Disconnect the electrical leads and unscrew and remove the switch.
4   Refitting is a reversal of removal. Tighten the switch to the specified torque.

19 Fluid cooler – removal and refitting

1   Disconnect the battery.
2   Drain the cooling system (Chapter 2).
3   Disconnect the coolant hoses from the fluid cooler.
4   Unscrew the fluid cooler centre mounting bolt and remove the cooler.
5   Discard all seals and renew them.
6   Refitting is a reversal of removal. Tighten the centre bolt to the specified torque.
7   Refill the cooling system.
8   Check the transmission fluid level and top up.

20 Automatic transmission – removal and refitting

1   Disconnect and remove the battery.
2   Drain the cooling system.
3   Drain the transmission fluid.
4   Raise the front end of the car, support it securely and remove the front roadwheels.
5   Remove the air cleaner and the battery tray.
6   Disconnect the selector cable from the transmission. Also disconnect the earth cable.
7   Disconnect the coolant hoses from the fluid cooler.
8   Disconnect the kickdown cable and the leads from the starter inhibitor/reverse lamp switch.
9   Unbolt and remove the starter motor.
10 Release the fuel filter mounting bracket from the transmission and move the filter assembly to one side (when applicable).

Fig. 7.8 Brake band adjuster screw (2) and locknut (1) (Sec 17)

11 Disconnect both driveshafts from the transmission as described in Section 8, paragraphs 8 to 12.
12 Working through the starter motor aperture, unscrew the bolts which hold the driveplate to the torque converter. The crankshaft will have to be turned by means of its pulley bolt to bring each of the three bolts into view.
13 Support the engine under the sump pan using a jack with a wooden block as an insulator.
14 Unscrew the bolts which hold the rear mounting to the transmission.
15 Unscrew the transmission to adaptor plate bolts noting that the bolts on either side of the sump plate can only be partially unscrewed at this stage.
16 Disconnect the speedometer drive cable from the transmission. Do this by pulling up the rubber cover and extracting the clip.
17 Release the hose from the side of the engine breather.
18 Release the transmission fluid filler tube bracket from the adaptor plate.
19 Disconnect the crankshaft sensor plug.
20 Unscrew any remaining transmission to adaptor plate bolts.
21 Take the weight of the transmission on a hoist or a trolley jack.
22 Remove the through-bolt from the left-hand mounting bracket.
23 Withdraw the transmission from the adaptor plate as far as the partially unscrewed bottom bolts on the torque converter housing will allow.
24 Remove the bottom bolts, lower the transmission and withdraw it from under the car. Have an assistant keep the torque converter pushed fully into the bellhousing during removal and retain it afterwards using a plate bolted to the bellhousing flange. Failure to do this may damage the oil seal and will cause loss of fluid.
25 If the transmission is being changed for a new or reconditioned unit, make sure that you take off any items which are not supplied with the new unit. Check with your supplier.
26 Refiting is a reversal of removal. Use new driveshaft circlips. Tighten all nuts and bolts to the specified torque. Check the adjustment of the selector and kickdown cables.
27 Check that the driveshafts are positively locked into the transmission with their circlips engaged.
28 Refill the transmission with specified fluid.
29 Refill the cooling system.

21 Differential fluid seals – renewal

The procedure is essentially the same as that described in Chapter 6, Section 15, but the lips of the new seals should be packed with petroleum jelly.

Part C All models

22 Fault diagnosis* – automatic transmission

Symptom	Reason(s)
Three-speed type	
No movement when a speed position selected	Low fluid level Selector cable out of adjustment
Poor acceleration	High fluid level Slack in throttle cable Selector cable out of adjustment
Engine vibrates at idle	Faulty fluid pump
Incorrect upshift or downshift, harsh shift or jumps between high and low speeds in D	Faulty internal shift valve
Car creeps in N	Faulty internal clutch
Four-speed type	
Transmission noisy and slips after a long journey	Blocked internal fluid strainer
Incorrect shifts up or down	Faulty valve block Low fluid level
With D selected car moves off in 2nd speed	Brake band requires adjustment
No drive in R	Adjustment required to selector cable
Engine will not start in N or P	Fault in starter inhibitor switch Selector cable requires adjustment
Kickdown point incorrect	Kickdown cable requires adjustment

*This is meant to be a guide only. For more comprehensive fault diagnosis, the car should be road tested by your dealer.

Chapter 8
Driveshafts, hubs, roadwheels and tyres

For modifications, and information applicable to later models, see Supplement at end of manual

Contents

Specifications

Type .... Open driveshaft with CV and tripode joints, sealed hub bearings, pressed steel or cast alloy roadwheels radial ply tyres

Driveshaft joint lubricant
Inboard (tripode) joint:
    Type .... Mobil 525 grease
    Quantity .... 185 cc (5.2 fl oz)
Outboard (CV) joint:
    Type .... Mobil 171-AM3 grease
    Quantity .... 90 cc (2.5 fl oz)

Roadwheels
Type:
    All models except Vitesse .... Pressed steel
    Vitesse .... Cast alloy
Size:
    1.3 models .... 4½ J x 13
    1.6 models (except Vitesse) .... 5J x 13
    Vitesse .... 5J x 14

Tyres
Size (depending upon model) .... 155 SR13, 165/70, SR 13, 165 SR 13, 165 R 1382S, 175/65R 1482T

Pressures, cold, in bar (lbf/in²)*:

	Front	Rear
All 213 models	1.7 (24)	1.7 (24)
216 models with 165/13 tyres	2.0 (28)	1.8 (26)
216 models with 175/65 14 tyres	2.0 (28)	2.0 (28)

These are the maker's recommended pressures at the time of writing. Pressures given in operator's handbook may vary slightly. If in doubt consult a Rover dealer or tyre specialist

Torque wrench settings

	Nm	lbf ft
Driveshaft to hub nut	185	137
Front suspension arm balljoint nut	44	32
Tie-rod end balljoint nut	44	32
Roadwheel nuts	81	60
Rear hub nut	185	137
Front brake caliper bolts	78	57

1 General description

The driveshafts are of unequal length, the right-hand one being solid while the left-hand one is of tubular construction.

The inboard joints are of tripode roller type while the outboard ones are of constant velocity type.

The outboard joint is renewable, but the inboard one is not and must be renewed complete with shaft.

The driveshafts are held in the differential by circlips.

The front hubs are supported on sealed type bearings which can be renewed independently of the hub carrier.

The rear hub bearings are integral with the hub and in the event of wear must be renewed as an assembly.

The roadwheels may be of pressed steel or cast alloy construction according to model while the tyres are of radial ply type.

2 Maintenance

1   This is largely visual and should be carried out at the intervals specified in Routine Maintenance.
2   Raise the front roadwheels and turn them slowly while examining the boots on the joints for splits or signs of leaking lubricant. Extend the boots with the fingers to ensure that there are no splits at the base of the pleats.
3   If the boot is found to be damaged then the joint must be dismantled as described in Section 4. All the old lubricant must be removed and the boot discarded. Fresh lubricant should be applied and a new boot fitted.
4   Also at the specified intervals, raise each roadwheel in turn (handbrake off), grip the top and bottom of the tyre and attempt to rock the wheel. Provided the hub nut has been correctly tightened any movement will be due to worn bearings. Noise when cornering will be due to the same reason.
5   Keep the tyres inflated to the specified pressure and examine them regularly for wear or damage.

3 Driveshaft – removal and refitting

1   Remove the centre cap from the roadwheel. Relieve the staking on the driveshaft/hub nut and remove the nut (photo). (If the roadwheel has no centre cap, the nut will have to be undone after removing the wheel, with an assistant applying the brakes.) Slacken the wheel nuts, raise and support the front of the vehicle and remove the wheel.
2   Support the front suspension lower suspension arm, unscrew the balljoint nut and then using a splitter tool, disconnect the balljoint from the hub carrier. Be prepared for reaction from the torsion bar on the suspension arm as the balljoint is released (photo).
3   On models equipped with automatic transmission, if the left-hand driveshaft is being removed, remove the brake pipe bracket bolt and disconnect the left-hand steering tie-rod end balljoint.
4   Insert a lever between the driveshaft inboard joint and the transmission casing and release the driveshaft (photo).
5   Pull the hub carrier outwards within the limit of the flexibility of the strut top mounting and disconnect the driveshaft from the transmission.
6   Push the driveshaft out of the hub carrier using a plastic-faced hammer (photo).
7   Refitting is a reversal of removal, use a new circlip and make sure that it engages in the differential side gear as the driveshaft is pushed into the transmission. Tighten all nuts and bolts to the specified torque. Use a new driveshaft/hub nut and stake it.

3.1 Releasing driveshaft/hub nut

3.2 Suspension lower arm balljoint nut

3.4 Driveshaft released from transmission

3.6 Driveshaft released from hub carrier

4.2 Driveshaft outboard joint

4.4 Removing outboard (CV) joint

4　Driveshaft boot – renewal

1　To renew a split or damaged boot, first remove the driveshaft as previously described.

2　Remove the clips from the outboard joint boot and peel it back to expose the joint (photo).

3　Hold the driveshaft vertically so that the outboard joint is at the bottom end.

4　Using a soft-faced mallet strike the edge of the lower (CV) joint to drive it from the shaft (photo).

5　Slide off the boot.

6　If it is the inboard joint boot which must be renewed, cut the clips and slide the boot from the shaft.

7　Clean away all original lubricant and repack the joints with the specified type and quantity of grease. Fit the new or original boot, if undamaged, and secure with new clips. Heavy quality ratchet type cable ties are suitable for this purpose.

8　Use a new circlip when refitting the outboard joint to the driveshaft. Compress the circlip with pliers to assist its entry into the joint.

5　Driveshaft outboard (CV) joint – renewal

1　This joint may be renewed by removing and refitting it as described in the preceding Section.

2　New joint and shaft circlips should be fitted whenever the driveshaft or joint is removed and refitted.

6　Front hub bearing – renewal

1　Refer to Section 3, paragraph 1.
2　Unscrew the brake caliper mounting bolts and tie the caliper up out of the way without straining the hydraulic hose.
3　Extract the fixing screws and remove the brake disc from the hub. If

Fig. 8.1 Driveshaft outboard (CV) joint (Sec 5)

1　Boot	3　Circlip
2　Driveshaft	4　CV joint

Fig. 8.2 Front hub components (Sec 6)

1 Hub carrier	4 Hub (drive flange)
2 Bearing	5 Brake disc
3 Circlip	6 Nut

6.7A Removing front hub from carrier

6.7B Removing bearing inner track from hub

necessary, two 8.0 mm diameter bolts may be screwed into the tapped holes provided to push the disc from the hub.

4 Disconnect the suspension arm and tie-rod end balljoints as described in Section 3.

5 Unscrew the pinch-bolt from the clamp at the base of the suspension strut and separate the hub carrier from the strut.

6 Pull the hub carrier from the driveshaft. If it is tight, use a three-legged puller so that its centre screw will push the driveshaft out of the hub.

7 Press the hub from the hub carrier. The bearing inner track may come out on the hub. Remove the track with an extractor. If a press is not available, drive the hub out with a piece of tubing (photos).

8 Extract the hub bearing circlip using circlip pliers and remove the bearing from the hub.

9 Fit the new bearing by reversing the removal operations.

10 Reassemble the other components, tighten all nuts and bolts to the specified torque.

11 Use a new hub nut and stake its collar into the groove in the driveshaft (photo).

6.11 Staking driveshaft/hub nut

Fig. 8.3 Rear hub components (Sec 7)

1   Brake drum
2   Cap
3   Nut
4   Thrust washer
5   Hub/bearing assembly

7   Rear hub bearing – renewal

1   As previously described, the rear hub and bearing are serviced as an assembly.
2   The bearing is a sealed unit and requires no lubrication.
3   Raise the rear of the car, support it securely and remove the roadwheel.
4   Remove the brake drum as described in Chapter 9, Section 6.
5   Remove the hub cap. Relieve the staking on the hub and unscrew the nut. Take off the thrust washer.
6   Using a suitable puller draw the hub from the stub axle.
7   Fit the new hub/bearing assembly, a new thrust washer and nut (photos).
8   Tighten the nut to the specified torque and then stake its collar into the groove in the stub axle (photo).
Caution: *The washer must be fitted on the stub axle shaft with the rounded edge facing the hub.*
9   Refit the brake drum, the hub cap and the roadwheel (photo).

7.7A Rear hub/bearing assembly

7.7B Fitting rear hub

7.7C Rear hub thrust washer

7.8 Staking rear hub nut

7.9 Fitting rear hub cap

8 Wheels and tyres

Wheels and tyres should give no real problems in use provided that a close eye is kept on them with regard to excessive wear or damage. To this end, the following points should be noted.

Ensure that tyre pressures are checked regularly and maintained correctly. Checking should be carried out with the tyres cold and not immediately after the vehicle has been in use. If the pressures are checked with the tyres hot, an apparently high reading will be obtained owing to heat expansion. Under no circumstances should an attempt be made to reduce the pressures to the quoted cold reading in this instance, or effective inderinflation will result.

Underinflation will cause overheating of the tyre owing to excessive flexing of the casing, and the tread will not sit correctly on the road surface. This will cause a consequent loss of adhesion and excessive wear, not to mention the danger of sudden tyre failure due to heat build-up.

Overinflation will cause rapid wear of the centre part of the tyre tread coupled with reduced adhesion, harsher ride, and the danger of shock damage occurring in the tyre casing.

Regularly check the tyres for damage in the form of cuts or bulges, especially in the sidewalls. Remove any nails or stones embedded in the tread before they penetrate the tyre to cause deflation. If removal of a nail *does* reveal that the tyre has been punctured, refit the nail so that its point of penetration is marked. Then immediately change the wheel and have the tyre repaired by a tyre dealer. Do *not* drive on a tyre in such a condition. In many cases a puncture can be simply repaired by the use of an inner tube of the correct size and type. If in any doubt as to the possible consequences of any damage found, consult your local tyre dealer for advice.

Periodically remove the wheels and clean any dirt or mud from the inside and outside surfaces. Examine the wheel rims for signs of rusting, corrosion or other damage. Light alloy wheels are easily damaged by 'kerbing' whilst parking, and similarly steel wheels may become dented or buckled. Renewal of the wheel is very often the only course of remedial action possible.

The balance of each wheel and tyre assembly should be maintained to avoid excessive wear, not only to the tyres but also to the steering and suspension components. Wheel imbalance is normally signified by vibration through the vehicle's bodyshell, although in many cases it is particularly noticeable through the steering wheel. Conversely, it should be noted that wear or damage in suspension or steering components may cause excessive tyre wear. Out-of-round or out-of-true tyres, damaged wheels and wheel bearing wear/maladjustment also fall into this category. Balancing will not usually cure vibration caused by such wear.

Wheel balancing may be carried out with the wheel either on or off

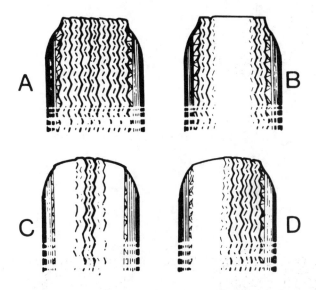

Fig. 8.4 Tyre tread wear patterns and causes (Sec 8)

A *Feathering due to incorrect toe-in*
B *Over inflation*
C *Under inflation*
D *Wear due to incorrect camber, worn wheel bearings and fast cornering*

the vehicle. If balanced on the vehicle, ensure that the wheel-to-hub relationship is marked in some way prior to subsequent wheel removal so that it may be refitted in its original position.

General tyre wear is influenced to a large degree by driving style – harsh braking and acceleration or fast cornering will all produce more rapid tyre wear. Interchanging of tyres may result in more even wear, but this should only be carried out where there is no mix of tyre types on the vehicle. However, it is worth bearing in mind that if this is completely effective, the added expense of replacing a complete set of tyres simultaneously is incurred, which may prove financially restrictive for many owners.

Front tyres may wear unevenly as a result of wheel misalignment.

The front wheels should always be correctly aligned according to the settings specified by the vehicle manufacturer.

Legal restrictions apply to the mixing of tyre types on a vehicle. Basically this means that a vehicle must not have tyres of differing construction on the same axle. Although it is not recommended to mix tyre types between front axle and rear axle, the only legally permissible combination is crossply at the front and radial at the rear. When mixing radial ply tyres, textile braced radials must always go on the front axle, with steel braced radials at the rear. An obvious disadvantage of such mixing is the necessity to carry two spare tyres to avoid contravening the law in the event of a puncture.

In the UK, the Motor Vehicles Construction and Use Regulations apply to many aspects of tyre fitting and usage. It is suggested that a copy of these regulations is obtained from your local police if in doubt as to the current legal requirements with regard to tyre condition, minimum tread depth, etc.

9 Fault diagnosis – driveshafts, hubs, roadwheels and tyres

Symptom	Reason(s)
Vibration	Driveshaft bent Worn universal joints Out-of-balance roadwheels
'Clonk' on taking up drive or on overrun	Worn universal joints Worn splines on shaft, hub carrier or differential side gears Loose driveshaft nut Loose roadwheel bolts
Noise or roar especially when cornering	Worn hub bearings Incorrectly tightened hub flange or driveshaft nuts

Chapter 9 Braking system

For modifications, and information applicable to later models, see Supplement at end of manual

Contents

Specifications

System type	Four wheel hydraulic dual circuit with vacuum servo assistance. Front discs, rear drums. Handbrake mechanical on rear wheels

Disc brakes
Disc diameter and type:
1.3 models	190.0 mm (7.1 in) solid
1.6 models	231.0 mm (9.0 in) ventilated

Thickness:
1.3 models	12.0 mm (0.47 in)
1.6 models	17.0 mm (0.67 in)

Regrind limit (minimum thickness):
1.3 models	10.0 mm (0.39 in)
1.6 models	15.0 mm (0.59 in)
Run-out (maximum)	0.10 mm (0.004 in)
Minimum disc pad friction material thickness	3.0 mm (0.12 in)

Drum brakes
Internal diameter	180.0 mm (7.09 in)
Regrind limit (maximum internal diameter)	181.0 mm (7.126 in)
Minimum shoe lining thickness	2.0 mm (0.08 in)

Pedal height from floor	174.0 mm (6.8 in)

Pedal free play	1.0 to 5.0 mm (0.04 to 0.20 in)

Brake fluid type/specification	Hydraulic fluid to FMVSS 116 DOT 4 (Duckhams Universal Brake and Clutch Fluid)

Torque wrench settings

	Nm	lbf ft
Hose banjo bolt caliper	35	26
Caliper guide pin bolts	18	13
Caliper mounting bolts	78	57
Brake pipe flare nuts	15	11
Bleed screws	9	7
Master cylinder stop bolt (1.3)	9	7
Rear brake backplate bolts	45	33
Rear hub nut	185	137
Roadwheel nuts	80	59

1 General description

The braking system is of dual-circuit hydraulic type.

The hydraulic circuit is split diagonally, front right-hand and rear left-hand brakes and front left-hand and rear right-hand brakes.

Vacuum servo assistance is provided.

The front disc calipers are of single piston sliding type and the rear drum brakes incorporate self-adjusting shoes.

A pressure regulating valve is incorporated in the hydraulic circuit to restrict pressure to the rear brakes during heavy braking and so prevent the rear wheels locking.

A low level warning sensor is fitted in the master cylinder fluid reservoir.

The handbrake is operated by cable to the rear wheels.

2 Maintenance and inspection

1   At the weekly service check, inspect the brake hydraulic fluid level in the translucent reservoir on the master cylinder. The level should be at, or just below the MAX MARK. If not, remove the cap and top up (photo).

2   The addition of fluid should only be necessary very infrequently, just a small quantity to compensate for the displaced fluid as the friction linings wear.

3   Where large quantities of fluid are needed, look for a leak in the pipelines or hydraulic cylinders. A leak can often be overlooked at the rear of the master cylinder pushrod inside the car. This is caused by failure of the master cylinder seals.

4   Regularly inspect the condition of the hoses and pipes as described in Section 13.

5   At the specified intervals, check the disc pads and brake linings for wear as described in the following Sections.

3 Disc pads – inspection and renewal

1   Raise the front end of the car and support it securely. Remove the front roadwheels.

2   Check the thickness of the disc pad friction material through the inspection hole in the caliper (photo).

3   If the pads have worn down to their specified minimum thickness, then they must be renewed. Unscrew the caliper lower guide pin bolt, release the upper bolt and pivot the caliper upwards (photo).

4   If the pads have worn unevenly then it is permissible to interchange them. In this case check that the caliper can slide freely on the guide pins.

5   Remove the pads, spring clips and note the shim on the back of the outboard pad (photo).

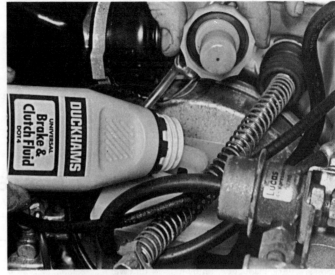

2.1 Topping up the brake fluid

Fig. 9.1 Master cylinder fluid reservoir (1.3 models) (Sec 2)

Fig. 9.2 Master cylinder fluid reservoir (1.6 models) (Sec 2)

3.2 Disc pad inspection hole. Note ventilated disc (1.6 models)

3.3 Pivoting caliper upwards

3.5 Removing a disc pad

6 Clean away dust and dirt from the caliper taking care not to inhale it as it is injurious to health.
7 The piston must now be pushed fully back into its cylinder in order to accommodate the new thicker pads. This will cause the fluid level to rise in the master cylinder reservoir. Anticipate this by syphoning out some of the fluid using a poultry baster or clean battery hydrometer.
8 Lightly smear the backs of the pads with silicone grease and clean both sides of the anti-squeal shim.
9 Fit the pads, shim and springs.
10 Pivot the caliper downwards and tighten the guide pin bolts to the specified torque.
11 Repeat the operations on the opposite wheel as new pads must be fitted as axle sets.
12 Refit the roadwheels, lower the car and apply the brake pedal several times to position the pads against the discs. Tighten the wheel nuts.
13 Check the fluid level in the reservoir and top up if necessary.
14 Avoid harsh braking if possible for the first few hundred miles to allow the new pads to bed in.

4 Caliper – removal, overhaul and refitting

1 Raise the front of the car, support it securely and remove the roadwheel.
2 Disconnect the brake hose from the caliper by unscrewing the banjo union bolt. Prevent loss of fluid by pinching the hose with a special clamp available from most motor stores or self-locking grips, provided their jaws have been taped to prevent damage. Alternatively, place a rubber disc on each side of the union and retain them with self-locking grips.

3 Unscrew the guide pin bolts and remove the caliper.
4 Remove the disc pads, shim and springs.
5 Clean away dust and dirt, taking care not to inhale it as it is injurious to health.
6 Remove the dust excluding boot.
7 Remove the piston. Do this by applying air pressure to the fluid union hole. Only a low air pressure is required such as is generated from a hand or foot-operated tyre pump.
8 Examine the surfaces of the piston and cylinder bore. If they are scored or there is any sign of rust or corrosion then a new caliper must be obtained. If the components are in good condition then extract the piston seal from its groove in the cylinder. Take great care not to scratch the bore surfaces when doing this. Discard the seal.
9 Obtain a repair kit which will contain all the necessary seals and other renewable items.
10 Clean the piston and cylinder in clean hydraulic fluid or methylated spirit – nothing else, and observe absolute cleanliness during the reassembly operations.
11 Fit the new piston seal, manipulating it into the cylinder groove using the fingers.
12 Smear the cylinder bore with clean hydraulic fluid and push the piston squarely into it. Do not push the piston fully home until the dust excluding boot has been engaged in its groove.
13 Refit the disc pads, springs and anti-squeal shim as described in Section 3.
14 Fit the caliper over the disc and screw in the guide pin bolts. Tighten them to the specified torque.
15 Use new sealing washers and reconnect the hydraulic hose to the caliper.
16 Refit the roadwheel and lower the car. Tighten the wheel nuts.
17 Bleed the brakes as described in Section 14.

Fig. 9.3 Front disc caliper (Sec 4)

1 Banjo union bolt	4 Anti-rattle springs	7 Guide pin	10 Piston
2 Guide pin bolts	5 Pad (inboard)	8 Dust excluder	11 Piston seal
3 Bleed screw	6 Pad (outboard)	9 Piston dust excluder	

5.2 Ventilated type disc (1.6 models)

Fig. 9.4 Point for checking disc run-out (Sec 5)

5 Brake disc – inspection, renovation or renewal

1   Raise the front of the car and remove the roadwheel.
2   Examine the disc for grooving or deep scoring, light scoring is normal (photo).
3   If severe scoring has occurred it may be possible to have the disc re-ground provided the finished thickness is not less than the specified minimum (see Specifications).
4   If as a result of reference to the Fault Diagnosis Section, the disc is suspected of being distorted, the run-out should be checked against the tolerance specified using a dial gauge or feeler blades inserted between the disc and a fixed point while the disc is being rotated.
5   It may be possible to correct disc run-out by moving the disc through 90° in relation to its location on the hub. If not then the disc must be renewed.
6   To remove the disc, first unbolt the caliper and tie it up out of the way. Extract the two disc fixing screws (photo).
7   Remove the disc from the hub, pushing it off if necessary using two 8.0 mm bolts screwed into the tapped holes provided.

8   Before fitting a new disc clean away any protective grease using a suitable solvent.
9   Fit the disc. Fit the caliper with pads and apply the brake pedal two or three times to locate the pads against the disc (see Section 4).
10 Refit the roadwheel and lower the car.

6 Rear brake shoes – inspection and renewal

1   At the intervals specfied in Routine Maintenance, raise the rear of the car and remove the roadwheels. Release the handbrake.
2   Remove the brake drums. If the drums will not come off, tap them carefully with a plastic-faced mallet or screw two 8.0 mm bolts into the tapped holes provided. If they still refuse to move, then the shoes are probably locked in wear grooves inside the drums. To release them, extract the rubber plug from the backplate, insert a screwdriver and turn the star wheel adjuster on the self-adjuster strut. Pivot the point of the screwdriver downwards (photo).

5.6 Disc retaining screws

6.2 Using bolts to draw off brake drum

6.3 Rear brake – right-hand side

Fig. 9.5 Rear brake assembly (Sec 6)

1 Adjuster star wheel
2 Adjuster strut
3 Handbrake lever
4 Shoe hold-down spring clip
5 Self-adjuster lever

3   With the drums removed, brush away dust, taking care not to inhale it as it is dangerous to health. Inspect the shoe linings. If they are worn down to their minimum thickness then the shoes must be renewed as an axle set (photo).
4   Do not attempt to re-line the shoes yourself, but fit new or factory re-lined ones. Shoes can be renewed without removing the hub, but the job will be easier if it is removed (see Chapter 8).
5   To remove the shoes, release the shoe hold-down spring pins by gripping them with a pair of pliers and then turn them through 90° (photo).
6   Pull the upper ends of the shoes outwards off the wheel cylinder tappets, pull the shoes slightly forward and gently release them taking care that the shoes do not damage the wheel cylinder rubber boots.
7   Prise the lower ends of the shoes apart and remove them from the anchor block.
8   Pull the shoes outwards against the tension of their return springs and remove them from around the hub drive flange.
9   Disconnect the handbrake cable from the shoe lever and withdraw the complete shoe assembly together with return springs, and adjuster mechanism (photos).
10 Lay the assembly on the bench noting the relative position of the leading and trailing shoes and the holes in the shoe webs in which the springs engage. Make a sketch if necessary (photo).
11 Transfer the handbrake lever from the old trailing shoe to the new one. This will require removal of the circlip and washer. When refitting, make sure that the head of the retaining pin will be towards the hub drive flange when the shoe is on the backplate.
12 Reassemble the shoes and return springs. Fit the adjuster strut having fully retracted it after having cleaned and lightly greased its threads. Engage the spring with the self-adjuster lever.
13 Apply a smear of high melting-point grease to the shoe rubbing high spots on the backplate and to the slots in the wheel cylinder tappets and anchor block. Be careful not to get grease onto the brake shoe linings.

6.5 Releasing brake shoe hold down pin

6.9A Disconnecting handbrake cable from shoe

6.9B Brake backplate (right-hand side) with shoes removed

6.10 Brake shoes (right-hand side) ready for fitting

14 Offer the shoe assembly to the backplate. Connect the handbrake cable to the shoe lever, then engage the shoe ends with the wheel cylinder and anchor block. Fit the hold-down clips and pins.
15 Centralise the shoes on the backplate, then rotate the star wheel adjuster until the brake drum will just slide over the shoes.
16 If the hub was removed, refit it as described in Chapter 8.
17 Refit the brake drum and the roadwheel.
18 Repeat the operations on the other rear wheel.
19 Lower the car and tighten the wheel nuts.
20 Apply the footbrake several times to operate the self-adjusting mechanism.
21 If the new shoes have been fitted, avoid harsh braking if possible for the first few hundred miles to allow the new shoes to bed in.

7 Rear wheel cylinder – removal, overhaul and refitting

1   Remove the brake shoes as described in the preceding Section.
2   Disconnect the brake pipe from the rear wheel cylinder and cap the pipe to prevent loss of fluid. A bleed nipple dust cap is useful for this purpose.
3   Unscrew the nuts and remove the wheel cylinder from the brake backplate.
4   Clean away external dirt, remove the dust excluding boots and take out the pistons and spring. The pistons may be ejected by shaking the cylinder or by applying low air pressure to the fluid entry port on the cylinder body (photo).
5   Inspect the surfaces of the cylinder bore and pistons. If there is any sign of scoring, rust or corrosion then the cylinder must be renewed complete.
6   If the components are in good condition, clean away external dirt, discard the seals and obtain a repair kit which will contain all the necessary seals and other renewable components.
7   Observe strict cleanliness during reassembly and manipulate the new seals into position using the fingers only, using clean hydraulic fluid as a lubricant. Make sure the seals are fitted the right way round (sealing lips facing the spring ends of the pistons).
8   Dip the pistons in clean hydraulic fluid and insert them into the cylinder with the spring between them. Fit the dust excluding boots.
9   Fit the cylinder to the backplate, tighten the retaining nuts and reconnect the brake pipe.
10 Refit the shoes and drum.
11 Refit the roadwheel, lower the car to the floor.
12 Bleed the hydraulic system as described in Section 14.

8 Brake drum – inspection, renovation or renewal

1   Whenever the brake drum is removed, take the opportunity to clean

7.4 Wheel cylinder components

out all dust and dirt and inspect it for scoring, grooving or cracks.
2   If any of these problems is evident or as a result of reference to the Fault Diagnosis Section the drum is suspected of being out of round, it may be possible to refinish it provided the finished internal diameter does not exceed the maximum specified.
3   If it does, then a new drum must be fitted.

9 Master cylinder – removal and refitting

1   Drain the master cylinder fluid reservoir. Do this either by syphoning or by opening the caliper bleed screws and pumping the brake pedal. Discard the ejected fluid.
2   Disconnect the fluid level sensor wiring plug and remove the reservoir cap.
3   Disconnect the brake pipes from the master cylinder and cap their open ends (photo).
4   Unscrew the retaining nuts and remove the master cylinder from the vacuum servo unit (photo).
5   Clean away external dirt.

9.3 Master cylinder

9.4 Removing master cylinder from servo

6   Refitting is a reversal of removal. On 1.3 models the servo pushrod clearance should be checked if a new or overhauled unit is being fitted. With the servo pushrod flush with the face of the servo shell, the depth of the master cylinder pushrod recess should be 45.5 mm (1.79 in) when measured with a depth gauge. The distance between the end-face of the master cylinder pushrod and the face of the master cylinder mounting flange should be 43.7 mm (1.72 in). If the actual measurements taken are shorter than those specified, reduce the length of the servo pushrod by the difference. If the measurements taken are longer than those specified, extend the length of the servo pushrod. To alter the length of the servo pushrod, release the locknut (not the pedal clevis fork locknut) and turn the adjuster nut. These nuts are very inaccessible under the facia and it may be easier to remove the servo completely as described in Section 17 (photos).
7   When correctly carried out, the adjustment will provide a clearance at the contact point of the servo and master cylinder pushrods of between 0 and 0.4 mm (0.016 in) when the servo and master cylinder are bolted together.
8   Check and adjust the pedal height as described in Section 20.
9   Bleed the complete hydraulic system as described in Section 14.

9.6A Checking servo pushrod is flush with face of servo shell

9.6B Checking depth of master cylinder pushrod recess

9.6C Checking flange to pushrod end face dimension on master cylinder

9.6D Vacuum servo pushrod
1   Clevis fork locknut   3   Pushrod locknut
2   Pushrod adjuster

10 Master cylinder (1.3 models) – overhaul

1   With the master cylinder removed from the car, clean away external dirt.
2   Refer to Fig. 9.6 and extract the primary piston end circlip.
3   Shake the primary piston from the cylinder.
4   Insert a rod and depress the secondary piston and then unscrew and remove the stop bolt.
5   Shake out the secondary piston assembly. If it is difficult to remove, apply low air pressure to the secondary fluid entry port.
6   Examine the surface of the cylinder bore. If it is corroded or scored, renew the master cylinder complete.
7   If the components are in good order, discard the primary piston and all other seals. Clean everything, including the reservoir and filter in clean hydraulic fluid or methylated spirit – nothing else.
8   Obtain a repair kit which will contain a new primary piston assembly complete with seals and all other renewable components.
9   Manipulate the new seals into position using the fingers only, dip the components in clean hydraulic fluid before assembly. Make sure that the seals are fitted the right way round.
10 Insert the secondary piston using a twisting motion to prevent trapping of the seal lips. Depress the piston using a rod and screw in the stop bolt.
11 Fit the primary piston and the circlip.
12 Fit the new mounting flange seal.

Fig. 9.6 Master cylinder (1.3 models) (Sec 10)

1   Fluid level sensor   5   Master cylinder   9   Primary piston
2   Sealing ring   6   Piston stop bolt and seal 10 Circlip
3   Filter   7   Sealing ring   11 Piston seals and spacers
4   Reservoir   8   Secondary piston   12 Circlip

11 Master cylinder (1.6 models) – overhaul

1 With the master cylinder removed from the car and cleaned externally, remove the fluid reservoir. Do this by rocking it from side to side and at the same time pulling it away from the cylinder body.

2 Refer to Fig. 9.7 and remove the sealing washers and the baffle plates.

3 Using a rod, compress the piston springs so that the secondary piston stop pin can be removed from the reservoir fluid inlet port.

4 Depress the primary piston slightly and extract the circlip.

5 Shake out the primary piston assembly.

6 Remove the secondary piston by tapping the end of the cylinder on a piece of hardwood or by applying low air pressure to the secondary fluid outlet port.

7 Inspect the surface of the cylinder bore. If it is scored or corroded, renew the master cylinder complete.

8 If the cylinder is in good condition, clean it in clean hydraulic fluid or methylated spirit – nothing else. Obtain a repair kit which will contain all the new seals and other renewable items.

Fig. 9.7 Master cylinder (1.6 models) (Sec 11)

1	Fluid reservoir	5	Secondary piston and spring	9	Spring retainer
2	Sealing washers	6	Primary piston and spring	10	Circlip
3	Baffle plates	7	Secondary piston	11	Spring seat
4	Secondary piston stop pin	8	Secondary piston seal	12	Primary piston seal

13	Primary piston seals and spacers
14	Spacer
15	Circlip
16	O-ring

9   Manipulate the new seals into place with the fingers, using clean hydraulic fluid as a lubricant. Make sure that the seals are fitted the right way round. Dip the secondary piston into clean hydraulic fluid and fit it into the cylinder using a twisting motion to avoid trapping the seal lips.
10 Depress the secondary piston with a rod and fit the stop pin.
11 Fit the primary piston in a similar way.
12 Secure it with the circlip.
13 Fit the reservoir with baffle plates and seals.

12 Pressure regulating valve – removal and refitting

1   The valve cannot be overhauled or repaired and in the event of a fault, it must be renewed.
2   Disconnect the brake pipes from the valve and quickly cap them to prevent loss of fluid. Catch fluid leaking from the valve to prevent damage to the engine compartment paintwork.
3   Refitting is a reversal of removal, make sure that the valve is mounted vertically.
4   Bleed the hydraulic system as described in Section 14.

Fig. 9.8 Pressure regulating valve (Sec 12)

1A From master cylinder   2A From master cylinder
1B To left-hand front brake   2B To right-hand front brake
1C To right-hand rear brake   2C To left-hand rear brake

13 Hydraulic pipes and hoses – inspection, removal and refitting

1   At intervals given in Routine Maintenance carefully examine all brake pipes, hoses, hose connections and pipe unions.
2   First check for signs of leakage at the pipe unions. Then examine the flexible hoses for signs of cracking, chafing and fraying.
3   The brake pipes must be examined carefully and methodically. They must be cleaned off and checked for signs of dents, corrosion or other damage. Corrosion should be scraped off and, if the depth of pitting is significant, the pipes renewed. This is particularly likely in those areas

underneath the vehicle body where the pipes are exposed and unprotected.
4   If any section of pipe or hose is to be removed, first unscrew the master cylinder reservoir filler cap and place a piece of polythene over the filter neck. Secure the polythene with an elastic band ensuring that an airtight seal is obtained. This will minimise brake fluid loss when the pipe or hose is removed.
5   Brake pipe removal is usually quite straightforward. The union nuts at each end are undone, the pipe and union pulled out and the centre section of the pipe removed from the body clips. Where the unions nuts are exposed to the full force of the weather they can sometimes be quite tight. As only an open ended spanner can be used, burring of the flats on the nuts is not uncommon when attempting to undo them. For this reason a self-locking wrench is often the only way to separate a stubborn union.
6   To remove a flexible hose, wipe the unions and brackets free of dirt and undo the union nut from the brake pipe end(s).
7   Next extract the hose retaining clip, or unscrew the nut, and lift the end of the hose out of its bracket. If a front hose is being removed, it can now be unscrewed from the brake caliper.
8   Brake pipes can be obtained individually, or in sets, from most accessory shops or garages with the end flares and union nuts in place. The pipe is then bent to shape, using the old pipe as a guide, and is ready for fitting to the car.
9   Refitting the pipes and hoses is a reverse of the removal procedure. Make sure that the hoses are not kinked when in position and also make sure that the brake pipes are securely supported in their clips. After refitting, remove the polythene from the reservoir and bleed the brake hydraulic system, as described in Section 14.

14 Hydraulic system – bleeding

1   The correct functioning of the brake hydraulic system is only possible after removal of all air from the components and circuit; this is achieved by bleeding the system. Note that only clean unused brake fluid, which has remained unshaken for at least 24 hours, must be used.
2   If there is any possibility of incorrect fluid being used in the system, the brake lines and components must be completely flushed with uncontaminated fluid and new seals fitted to the components.
3   *Never reuse* brake fluid which has been bled from the system.
4   During the procedure, do not allow the level of brake fluid to drop more than halfway down the reservoir.
5   Before starting work, check that all pipes and hoses are secure, unions tight and bleed screws closed. Take great care not to allow brake fluid to come into contact with the car paintwork, otherwise the finish will be seriously damaged. Wash off any spilled fluid immediately with cold water.
6   There is a number of one-man, do-it-yourself, brake bleeding kits currently available from motor accessory shops. Always follow the instructions supplied with the kit. It is recommended that one of these kits is used wherever possible, as they greatly simplify the bleeding operation and also reduce the risk of expelled air and fluid being drawn back into the system.
7   If brake fluid has been lost from the master cylinder due to a leak in the system, ensure that the cause is traced and rectified before proceeding further.
8   If the hydraulic system has only been partially disconnected and suitable precautions were taken to prevent further loss of fluid it should only be necessary to bleed the part of the system being worked on (i.e. at the brake caliper or wheel cylinder nearest to the disconnected pipe or hose).
9   If the complete system is to be bled then it should be done in the following sequence:

   Secondary circuit: Left-hand front then right-hand rear
   Primary circuit: Right-hand front then left-hand rear

10 To bleed the system, first clean the area around the bleed screw and fit the bleed tube. If necessary top up the master cylinder reservoir with brake fluid.
11 The system incorporates a vacuum servo, destroy the vacuum by giving several applications of the brake pedal in quick succession.

14.14 Unscrewing caliper bleed screw fitted with bleed tube

Fig. 9.9 Brake hydraulic circuits (Sec 14)

Secondary circuit

1   *Master cylinder to pressure regulating valve*
2   *Pressure regulating valve to LH front brake*
3   *Pressure regulating valve to RH rear brake*

Primary circuit

4   *Master cylinder to pressure regulating valve*
5   *Pressure regulating valve to RH front brake*
6   *Pressure regulating valve to LH rear brake*

Bleeding – two man method

12 Gather together a clean jar and a length of rubber or plastic tubing which will be a tight fit on the brake bleed screws.
13 Engage the help of an assistant.
14 Push one end of the bleed tube onto the first bleed screw and immerse the other end in the jar which should contain enough hydraulic fluid to cover the end of the tube (photo).
15 Open the bleed screw one half a turn and have your assistant depress the brake pedal fully then slowly release it. Tighten the bleed screw at the end of each pedal downstroke to obviate any chance of air or fluid being drawn back into the system.
16 Repeat this operation until clean brake fluid, free from air bubbles, can be seen coming through into the jar.
17 Tighten the bleed screw at the end of a pedal downstroke and remove the bleed tube. Bleed the remaining screws in a similar way.

Bleeding – using one-way valve kit

18 It is recommended that one of these kits is used wherever possible as it will greatly simplify the bleeding operation and also reduce the risk of air or fluid being drawn back into the system, quite apart from being able to do the work without the help of an assistant.

19 To use the kit, connect the tube to the bleed screw and open the screw one half turn.
20 Depress the brake pedal fully then slowly release it. The one-way valve in the kit will prevent expelled air from returning at the end of each pedal downstroke. Repeat this operation several times to be sure of ejecting all air from the system. Some kits include a translucent container which can be positioned so that the air bubbles can actually be seen being ejected from the system.
21 Tighten the bleed screw, remove the tube and repeat the operations on the remaining brakes.
22 On completion, depress the brake pedal. If it still feels spongy, repeat the bleeding operations, as air must still be trapped in the system.

Bleeding – using a pressure bleeding kit

23 These kits are available from motor accessory shops and are usually operated by air pressure from the spare tyre.
24 By connecting a pressurised container to the master cylinder fluid reservoir, bleeding is then carried out simply by opening each bleed screw in turn and allowing the fluid to run out, rather like turning on a tap, until no air is visible in the expelled fluid.
25 By using this method, the large reserve of brake fluid provides a safeguard against air being drawn into the master cylinder during bleeding which may occur if the fluid level in the reservoir is not maintained.
26 Pressure bleeding is particularly effective when bleeding 'difficult' systems or when bleeding the complete system at the time of routine fluid renewal.

All methods

27 When bleeding is completed, check and top up the fluid level in the master cylinder reservoir.
28 Check the feel of the brake pedal. If it feels at all spongy, air must still be present in the system and the need for further bleeding is indicated. Failure to bleed satisfactorily after a reasonable repetition of the bleeding operations may be due to worn master cylinder seals.
29 Discard brake fluid which has been expelled. It is almost certain to be contaminated with moisture, air and dirt, making it unsuitable for further use. Clean fluid should always be stored in an airtight container as it is hygroscopic (absorbs moisture readily) which lowers its boiling point and could affect braking performance under severe conditions.

15 Vacuum servo unit – description

1   A vacuum servo unit is fitted into the brake hydraulic circuit in series with the master cylinder, to provide assistance to the driver when

the brake pedal is depressed. This reduces the effort required by the driver to operate the brakes under all braking conditions.
2   The unit operates by vacuum obtained from the inlet manifold and comprises basically a booster diaphragm, control valve, and a non-return valve.
3   The servo unit and hydraulic master cylinder are connected together so that the servo unit piston rod acts as the master cylinder pushrod. The driver's braking effort is transmitted through another pushrod to the servo unit piston and its built-in control system. The servo unit piston does not fit tightly into the cylinder, but has a strong diaphragm to keep its edges in constant contact with the cylinder wall, so ensuring an airtight seal between the two parts. The forward chamber is held under vacuum conditions created in the inlet manifold of the engine and, during periods when the brake pedal is not in use, the controls open a passage to the rear chamber so placing it under vacuum conditions as well. When the brake pedal is depressed, the vacuum passage to the rear chamber is cut off and the chamber opened to atmospheric pressure. The consequent rush of air pushes the servo piston forward in the vacuum chamber and operates the main pushrod to the master cylinder.
4   In the event of failure of the servo unit, the hydraulic circuit remains unaffected except that increased pedal pressure will be required.
5   If a servo unit is suspected of being faulty, carry out the following test.
6   With the engine switched off, depress the brake pedal several times, finally press hard and hold for 15 seconds. If the pedal sinks then there is a leak in the hydraulic system and the servo is not necessarily faulty.
7   Hold the brake pedal depressed and start the engine. The pedal should sink slightly. If it does not, check the non-return valve and manifold adaptor; if these are satisfactory, then the servo is faulty.

16 Vacuum servo unit – maintenance

1   The following operations should be considered the limit of work carried out to the servo unit. A unit in need of repair should be changed for a new or factory reconditioned unit.
2   Keep the hoses in good condition and with their clips tight.
3   At the intervals specified in Routine Maintenance disconnect the non-return valve from the vacuum hose and blow through it. Air should pass in one direction only, otherwise renew it.

17 Vacuum servo unit – removal and refitting

1   Disconnect the hydraulic pipes from the master cylinder. Cap the ends of the pipes.
2   Disconnect the servo vacuum hose.
3   Remove the steering joint cover and disconnect the pushrod from the brake pedal.
4   Unscrew the fixing nuts and withdraw the servo from the engine compartment rear bulkhead. Retrieve the seal.
5   Unscrew the nuts and remove the master cylinder from the front face of the servo unit.
6   Refitting is a reversal of removal. On 1.3 models, check the pushrod clearance (Section 9) and the pedal height (Section 20).
7   Bleed the hydraulic system as described in Section 14.

18 Handbrake – adjustment

1   The handbrake is normally kept in constant adjustment by the action of the shoe automatic adjusters. However, if the handbrake lever has to be pulled through more than eight notches (clicks) of the ratchet quadrant to fully apply the brake, this will be due to cable stretch and must be rectified in the following way.
2   Raise the rear of the car so that the rear wheels are clear of the floor.
3   Pull the handbrake lever over one notch only.
4   Remove the cover from the rear of the centre console and turn the

18.4 Handbrake cable adjuster

cable adjuster nut until the rear wheels drag very slightly when the roadwheels are turned (photo).
5   Release the handbrake and check that the rear wheels rotate freely.
6   The handbrake should be fully applied when the lever has been pulled through between four and eight notches.
7   Lower the car to the floor.

19 Handbrake cable – renewal

1   Raise the rear of the car, support it securely and remove the roadwheel from the side on which the cable is to be renewed.
2   Remove the brake drum as described in Section 6.
3   Remove the brake shoes.
4   Fit a 12.0 mm ring spanner over the cable spigot to compress the retainer and release it from the backplate (photo).
5   Refer to Chapter 11 and remove the centre console.
6   Unscrew and remove the handbrake cable adjuster nut and disconnect the cable from the equaliser.
7   Remove the heatshield from the floor and disconnect the cable from its supporting guides and remove it.
8   Fit the new cable, apply grease to the cable guides.
9   Refit the brake shoes and drum as described in Section 6. Refit the roadwheel.

19.4 Compressing handbrake cable spigot in brake backplate

Fig. 9.10 Brake pedal height setting diagram (Sec 20)

1 *Pushrod locknut*   3 *174.0 mm (6.8 in)*
2 *Stop lamp switch*

10 Apply the footbrake several times to set the shoes and self-adjuster mechanism and then adjust the cable as described in Section 18.
11 Lower the car to the floor. Tighten the wheel nuts.

20 Brake pedal – setting

1 To check the brake pedal height, first remove the rubber cover from the pedal pad and peel back the floor carpet from under the pedal.
2 Refer to Fig. 9.10 and measure the height (3) from the underside of the pedal to the floor.
3 If it is not as specified, release the locknut on the stop lamp switch and unscrew the switch clear of the brake pedal.

4 Release the pushrod locknut and rotate the pushrod until the pedal height is correct. Tighten the locknut.
5 Screw in the stop lamp switch until its plunger is fully depressed then unscrew the switch exactly half a turn and tighten the locknut (photo).
6 Refit the pedal pad and the carpet.

21 Brake pedal – removal and refitting

1 Working inside the car remove the facia lower access panel (Chapter 11).
2 Disconnect the pedal return spring and the pushrod clevis fork from the pedal arm.
3 Unscrew the pivot cross-shaft nut and withdraw the shaft until the brake pedal can be removed. The clutch and brake pedals pivot on a common cross-shaft (see Chapter 5, Section 5).
4 On cars with automatic transmission, the brake pedal pivots on a shorter cross-shaft otherwise the arrangement is similar.

5 Refit by reversing the removal operations.

20.5 Brake stop lamp switch

22 Fault diagnosis – braking system

Before diagnosing faults from the following chart, check that any braking irregularities are not caused by:
Uneven and incorrect tyre pressures
Wear in the steering mechanism
Defects in the suspension and dampers
Misalignment of the body

Symptom	Reason(s)
Pedal travels a long way before the brakes operate	Incorrect pedal adjustment Brake shoes set too far from the drums (seized adjusters)
Stopping ability poor, even though pedal pressure is firm	Linings, discs or drums badly worn or scored One or more wheel hydraulic cylinders seized, resulting in some brake shoes not pressing against the drums (or pads against disc) Brake linings contaminated with oil Wrong type of linings fitted (too hard) Brake shoes wrongly assembled Servo unit not functioning
Car veers to one side when the brakes are applied	Brake pads or linings on one side are contaminated with oil Hydraulic wheel cylinder on one side partially or fully seized A mixture of lining materials fitted between sides Brake discs not matched Unequal wear between sides caused by partially seized wheel cylinders
Pedal feels spongy when the brakes are applied	Air is present in the hydraulic system
Pedal feels springy when the brakes are applied	Brake linings not bedded into the drums (after fitting new ones) Master cylinder or brake backplate mounting bolts loose Severe wear in brake drums causing distortion when brakes are applied Disc out of true
Pedal travels right down with little or no resistance and brakes are virtually non-operative	Leak in hydraulic system resulting in lack of pressure for operating wheel cylinders If no signs of leakage are apparent the master cylinder internal seals are failing to sustain pressure
Binding, juddering, overheating	One or a combination of reasons given above Shoes installed incorrectly with reference to leading and trailing ends Broken shoe return spring Drum out-of-round Disc distorted Incorrect pedal adjustment
Lack of servo assistance	Vacuum hose disconnected or leaking Non-return valve defective or incorrectly fitted Servo internal defect Master cylinder to servo flange seal ineffective

Chapter 10 Suspension and steering

For modifications, and information applicable to later models, see Supplement at end of manual

Contents

Specifications

Type

Front suspension	Independent, MacPherson strut with torsion bar springing and anti-roll bar
Rear suspension	Independent with trailing arms, telescopic shock absorbers and coil springs. Axle beam location by Panhard rod
Steering	Rack and pinion with rake adjustable safety steering column

Front suspension settings

Vehicle height – centre of roadwheel to wheel arch	372.0 to 392.0 mm (14.7 to 15.4 in)
Hub end play	0.05 mm (0.002 in)

Rear suspension settings

Vehicle height* – centre of roadwheel to wheelarch	353.8 to 373.8 mm (13.9 to 14.7 in)

*Non-adjustable, if not within the specified tolerance, suspect weak coil springs

Steering

Steering wheel diameter	377.0 mm (14.8 in)
Number of turns, lock to lock	4
Ratio	19 : 1
Turning circle (between kerbs)	10.0 m (33.0 ft)
Camber	1° negative to 1° positive
Castor	1° 25′ to 3° 25′ positive
Steering axis inclination	12° 15′ to 13° 15′
Toe	Parallel ± 0.7 mm (0.028 in)

Steering angles:
    Inner wheel .... 39° 35′ to 43° 35′
    Outer wheel .... 32° 23′ to 36° 23′
Lubricant .... Fluid grease (Duckhams Adgear 00)

Rear wheel alignment (non-adjustable) .... Parallel to 4.0 mm (0.16 in) toe-in

Torque wrench settings

	Nm	lbf ft
Front suspension		
Anti-roll bar clamp bolts	22	16
Anti-roll bar end nuts	22	16
Lower arm balljoint nut	44	32
Driveshaft nut	185	137
Strut pinch-bolt	65	48
Strut top mounting nuts	39	29
Strut spindle nut	44	32
Suspension arm to radius arm bolts	39	29
Radius arm to body	81	60
Front crossmember bolts	75	55
Torque tube retainer bolts	22	16
Rear suspension		
Panhard rod nut and bolt	55	41
Rear axle beam bolts	65	48
Shock absorber lower mounting bolt	55	41
Shock absorber upper mounting	22	16
Rear hub nut	185	137
Swing bearing nuts	55	41
Trailing arm pivot bolts	55	41
Stub axle to axle beam nuts	45	33
Steering		
Tie-rod end balljoint nuts	44	32
Tie-rod locknut	44	32
Steering shaft coupling pinch bolts	30	22
Steering column upper bracket bolts	22	16
Steering column upper bracket nuts	12	9
Steering rack adjuster screw locknut	25	18
Tie-rod to rack locknut	75	55
Steering gear mounting bolts	40	30
Steering wheel nut	50	37
Steering rake adjuster domed locknut	7.0	5.0
Roadwheel nuts	80	59

1 General description

The front suspension is of MacPherson strut independent type with torsion bar springing.

Each strut is located between the upper wing valance and the hub carrier.

An anti-roll bar is fitted.

The rear suspension is of trailing link beam type incorporating telescopic gas-filled shock absorbers and coil springs.

A tubular axle beam is fitted and this is positively located transversely by a Panhard rod.

The steering is of rack and pinion type with a collapsible safety column.

The steering wheel is adjustable for rake.

2 Maintenance

1 At the specified intervals, check all suspension flexible bushes for wear.

2 Occasionally check the condition and security of all steering and suspension nuts, bolts and components.

3 Inspect the struts and shock absorbers for signs of fluid leakage. If anything more than a slight weep from the top gland is evident, then the unit must be renewed.

4 If the car tends to roll on bends or dip under heavy braking, check the action of the struts and shock absorbers by pressing the corner of the car downwards and then releasing it. The up and down momentum of the car should be damped out immediately. If the car oscillates up and down several times, the condition of the particular unit should be checked after removal from the car as described in Sections 4 and 11.

5 Inspect the steering rack bellows for splits and loss of lubricant. Look particularly closely at the bottom of the bellows pleats when the steering is at full lock. Splits here can often pass unnoticed.

6 With the help of an assistant, check for wear in the steering tie-rod end balljoints. Move the steering wheel quickly a few degrees in each direction and observe the balljoints for shake or lost movement. If evident renew the tie-rod ends as described in Section 18.

7 Check the front suspension lower arm balljoint by inserting a lever carefully between the arm and the hub carrier and checking for vertical movement.

8 Renewal of the lower arm balljoint will mean the purchase of the complete radius arm with balljoint.

9 At the specified intervals, check the front wheel alignment (Sec 27).

3 Anti-roll bar – removal and refitting

Front

1 Remove the front crossmember as described in Section 7.

2 Unscrew the bolts which secure the anti-roll bar mounting bush clamps to the body.

3 Unscrew the end bolts and disconnect the anti-roll bar from the radius arms. Note the fitted sequence of the spacer cushions and cups.

4 Refitting is a reversal of removal, tighten nuts and bolts to the specified torque. See also Section 6, paragraph 8.

Rear (Vitesse and Sprint)

3 No information was available at the time of writing.

Fig. 10.1 Exploded view of one side of front suspension (Sec 1)

1	Cap
2	Circlip
3	Lower suspension arm
4	Bolt
5	Rubber cushion
6	Washer
7	Nut
8	Anti-roll bar
9	Bolt
10	Clamp
11	Flexible bush
12	Crossmember
13	Bolt
14	Washer
15	Cushion
16	Collar
17	Self-locking nut
18	Washer
19	Strut top mounting
20	Dust cover
21	Bump stop
22	Vehicle height adjusting bolt
23	Driveshaft
24	Strut
25	Radius arm
26	Radius arm bush
27	Self-locking nut
28	Vehicle height adjusting nut
29	Washer
30	Torsion bar
31	Seal
32	Torque tube
33	Circlip
34	Cap
35	Torque tube retainer
36	Bolt
37	Crossmember bolt
38	Caliper bolt
39	Guide bolt
40	Bleed screw cap
41	Bleed screw
42	Caliper bolt
43	Dust excluding boot
44	Caliper bracket
45	Brake pad clip
46	Brake pad
47	Shim
48	Piston seal
49	Piston
50	Dust excluding boot
51	Hub carrier
52	Disc shield
53	Screw
54	Hub bearing
55	Circlip
56	Wheel stud
57	Hub flange
58	Brake disc
59	Screw
60	Driveshaft nut

Fig. 10.2 Exploded view of one side of the rear suspension (Sec 1)

1 Cap	22 Wheel cylinder nut	42 Brake shoe
2 Self-locking nut	23 Brake backplate	43 Pin
3 Washer	24 Cap	44 Shoe steady spring clip
4 Mounting cushions	25 Bleed screw	45 Shoe return spring
5 Spring upper seat	26 Wheel cylinder	46 Hub
6 Pivot bolt	27 Spring	47 Brake drum
7 Stub axle (LH)	28 Piston seal	48 Thrust washer
8 Axle beam	29 Piston	49 Hub nut
9 Pivot bolt	30 Dust excluder	50 Stub axle (RH)
10 Sleeve	31 Blanking plug	51 Swing bearing
11 Bush	32 Self-adjuster lever	52* Swing bearing shield
12 Panhard rod	33 U-clip	53* Anti-roll bar (stabiliser) assembly
13 Coil spring	34 Washer	54* Bush retainer
14 Shock absorber	35 Shoe steady pin	55* Support bush
15 Mounting bolt	36 Self-adjuster strut	56* Bolt
16 Bush	37 Star wheel adjuster	57* Rear control link
17 Sleeve	38 Strut end fitting	58* Front control link
18 Washer	39 Shoe return spring	59* Link bushes
19 Self-locking nut	40 Self-adjuster spring	60* Nut
20 Shield	41 Shoe lever for handbrake	*Vitesse and Sprint only
21 Trailing arm		

4 Front suspension strut – removal and refitting

1 Raise the front of the car and remove the roadwheel.
2 Support the lower suspension arm on a jack and disconnect the brake hydraulic hose from the support bracket on the suspension strut (photo).
3 Working within the engine compartment, unscrew the strut top mounting nuts and then lower the jack under the lower suspension arm to separate the strut from the wing valance (photo).
4 Unscrew the clamp pinch-bolt from the base of the strut and slide the hub carrier off the strut. Be prepared for reaction from the torsion bar, so make sure that the car and the suspension is well supported. Withdraw the strut from the car. Alternatively, disconnect the driveshaft from the hub, remove the brake caliper and disconnect the lower arm and track rod end balljoints; the strut and hub carrier can then be removed together and separated on the bench (photo).
5 Unscrew the self-locking spindle nut and remove the top mounting, tubular shield and bump stop. The spindle can be held against rotation using an Allen key in its socket.
6 Fully extend and retract the strut piston rod. If it is jerky, noisy, or offers little or no resistance, the strut must be renewed. It is a sealed unit and cannot be dismantled.
7 To refit the strut, first assemble the top mounting, shield and bump

stop. Screw on the self-locking nut, again holding the spindle from turning using an Allen key.
8 Offer the strut up under the wing and tighten the nuts holding it to the valance.
9 Connect the lower end of the strut to the hub carrier making sure that the tab on the strut locates in the clamp slot. Tighten the pinch-bolt to the specified torque (photo).
10 If the hub carrier was removed with the strut, reconnect it as described in Chapter 8, Section 6.
11 Secure the brake hose to the strut bracket.
12 Refit the roadwheel and lower the vehicle. Tighten the wheel nuts.

5 Front hub carrier – removal and refitting

The operations are described in Chapter 8, Section 6.

6 Radius arm – removal and refitting

1 Raise the front of the car, support it securely and remove the roadwheel.

4.2 Disconnecting brake hose from strut

4.3 Front strut top mounting nuts. Allen key in spindle socket shown for information purposes only

4.4 Removing front strut and hub carrier

4.9 Strut to clamp alignment

6.2 Disconnecting suspension lower arm balljoint

6.4 Radius arm nut (arrowed)

6.8 Correct fitting of anti-roll bar securing bolt (with bolt head uppermost)

2   Support the lower suspension arm on a jack and disconnect the balljoint from the hub carrier using a balljoint splitter tool (photo).
3   Unbolt the radius arm from the lower suspension arm and then unscrew the bolt which holds the anti-roll bar to the radius arm. **Caution:** *Ensure that the jack supporting the lower suspension arm at the balljoint is securely positioned, otherwise the tension of the torsion bar may cause the lower suspension arm to jump suddenly away from the swivel hub as the balljoint is released.*
4   Unscrew the nut and withdraw the radius arm from its bushes (photo).
5   The bushes can be renewed, but wear in the radius arm balljoint can only be rectified by the purchase of a new arm complete.
6   Refit the radius arm into its bushes and screw on the nut finger tight.
7   Connect the radius arm to the lower suspension arm and tighten the bolts to the specified torque.
8   Reconnect the anti-roll bar, making sure that the end fitting components are in the correct sequence. **Caution:** *To ensure that there is adequate clearance between the driveshaft boot and the radius arm, the anti-roll bar securing bolt must be fitted with the bolt head uppermost (photo).*
9   Reconnect the lower suspension arm balljoint to the hub carrier and tighten the nut to the specified torque. Should the taper pin turn as the nut is being tightened locate a jack under the balljoint and force it upwards to press the taper pin into the conical seat of the eye.
10 Refit the roadwheel and lower the car to the floor.
11 With the weight of the car on the wheels, tighten the radius arm nut to the specified torque. Tighten the wheel nuts.

7   Front crossmember – removal and refitting

1   Raise the front of the car, support it securely and remove the front roadwheels.
2   Support both lower suspension arms and disconnect the balljoints from the hub carriers. Unscrew the nuts to do this and use a suitable balljoint splitter tool.
3   Unbolt the steering rack and move it to one side.
4   Remove the downpipe and front section of the exhaust pipe.
5   Release the engine rear mounting from the crossmember, at the same time supporting the engine under the sump pan.
6   Disconnect the gearchange rod and the steady rod from the transmission.
7   Unscrew the bolts from the torque tube end retainers. Remove the retainers and the rubber caps.
8   Unscrew the fixing bolts and release the anti-roll bar from the crossmember.
9   The crossmember may now be unbolted and removed (photo).
10 To strip the crossmember, unbolt and remove the engine mounting.
11 Unscrew and remove the vehicle height adjustment nuts and bolts.
12 Extract the torsion bar circlips and withdraw the bar complete with torque tube, see Section 9.

7.9 Crossmember bolt (arrowed)

13 Remove the radius arm and press out the lower suspension arms and bushes (Section 8).
14 Refitting is a reversal of removal, tighten all nuts and bolts to the specified torque and check the vehicle height on completion as described in Section 10. The method of setting the angle of the lower suspension arm is given in the next Section and fitting the torsion bar (Section 9).

8   Front suspension lower arm and bush – removal and refitting

1   Remove the front crossmember as described in the preceding Section.
2   Remove the vehicle height adjustment nut.
3   Extract the circlip from the rear end of the torsion bar and withdraw the torque tube.
4   Unbolt the lower suspension arm from the radius arm.
5   Remove the cap from the front end of the torsion bar, tap the bar slightly forward and extract the circlip.
6   Push the torsion bar through the crossmember and remove it.
7   Press the lower suspension arm from the crossmember.
8   Renew the lower suspension arm with bush as an assembly.
9   Refitting is a reversal of removal, but the new lower suspension arm bush should have its outer casing scribed to indicate the centre line of the arm. When pressing the arm and bush into the crossmember, align the mark on the bush with the one on the crossmember. If the crossmember mark is not visible, make one as shown in Fig. 10.4 and

set the lower suspension arm bush mark in alignment with it before pressing them into the crossmember.

10 The torsion bar should be fitted after reference to the next Section.

9 Torsion bar – removal and refitting

1 Raise the front end of the car, support it securely and remove the roadwheels.

2 Remove the vehicle height adjusting nut.

Fig. 10.3 Suspensión lower arm bush and crossmember alignment marks (Sec 8)

H16664

Fig. 10.4 Crossmember index mark scribing diagram (Sec 8)

A Crossmember front face
B Index mark
C Centre line of lower arm recess
D Suspension lower arm centre line at 5° to 9° in relation to centre line of bush recess

Fig. 10.5 Torsion bar components (Sec 9)

1 Sealing ring	4 Circlip	7 Vehicle height adjuster nut	9 Master spline alignment (RH bar)
2 Torque tube	5 Cap	8 Master spline alignment (LH bar)	
3 Torsion bar	6 Torque tube retainer		

3   Remove the rubber cap from the front end of the torsion bar (photo).

4   Unbolt and remove the torque tube retainer from the rear end of the tube. Remove the cap, extract the circlip (photos).

5   Tap the torsion bar forward just 12.5 mm (0.5 in) to expose the front circlip then extract it (photo).

6   Remove the torsion bar complete with torque tube towards the rear of the car.

7   Commence reassembly by greasing the torsion bar splines and the torque tube seals.

8   Insert the torsion bar into the torque tube so that the rear master spline is aligned (photos).

9   Fit the torsion bar/torque tube assembly making sure that the front master splines engage. It can be helpful if the end of the torsion bar and the rim of the lower arm splined hole are marked with white paint to indicate the relative positions of the master splines.

10 Tap the torsion bar towards the front of the car only enough to be able to fit the front circlip.

11 Tap the torsion bar towards the rear of the car and fit the rear circlip (photo).

12 Bolt on the torque tube retainer and replace the rubber cap.

13 Screw on the height adjuster nut and fit the torque tube front cap.

14 Fit the roadwheel and lower the car to the floor. Tighten the wheel nuts.

15 Check and adjust the vehicle ride height, see next Section.

9.3 Removing torsion bar front cap

9.4A Torque tube retainer

9.4B Removing torque tube retainer

9.5 Torsion bar front circlip

9.8A Torque tube splines

9.8B Torsion bar master spline

9.11 Torsion bar rear circlip

10 Vehicle ride height – adjustment

1   Have the car on a level surface with tyre pressures correct and the front roadwheels in the straight-ahead position.
2   The car should have a full fuel tank, but otherwise be unladen (kerb weight).
3   Bounce the car up and down two or three times to settle the suspension.
4   Measure between the centres of both front wheel hubs vertically to the wheel arch wing edge. If this is not as given in Specifications, raise the front wheels off the floor and turn the height adjusting nut clockwise to increase the height or anti-clockwise to reduce it (photo).
5   One complete turn of the nut will alter the vehicle height by 5.0 mm (0.197 in).
6   Lower the car and re-check the height.
7   The difference in vehicle ride height from side to side should not exceed 10.0 mm (0.39 in).

10.4 Vehicle height adjusting nut (arrowed)

11 Rear shock absorber and spring – removal and refitting

1   Raise the rear of the car, support it securely and remove the roadwheel.
2   Locate a jack under the rear axle beam and take its weight.
3   Open the luggage boot and take off the cap from the shock absorber top mounting.
4   Unscrew the self-locking nut from the spindle and take off the rubber cushion and retaining plate. Hold the spindle against rotation by inserting an Allen key in its socket (photo).
5   Gently lower the axle beam jack until all tension is relieved in the coil spring.
6   Unbolt the shock absorber lower mounting and then lower the jack again. Withdraw the shock absorber and spring from the car (photos).
7   Remove the spring and the shock absorber protective shield (photo).
8   Prise off the split collar and remove the sleeve upwards from the shock absorber.
9   Remove the bump stop.
10 Grip the shock absorber lower mounting in the jaws of a vice and holding the unit vertically, fully extend and retract it several times. If there is any jerkiness, seizure or lack of resistance, renew the shock absorber complete.
11 Refitting is a reversal of removal, but note the following.

11.4 Unscrewing rear shock absorber top mounting nut

11.6A Rear coil spring

11.6B Rear shock absorber lower mounting bolt

11.7 Rear shock absorber lower shield

12 The smaller diameter spring coils are at the lower end.
13 Tighten the upper mounting nut and lower mounting bolt to the specified torque only after the roadwheel has been fitted and the car lowered to the floor.

Fig. 10.6 Rear suspension trailing arm (RH) (Sec 12)

1   Swing bearing   3   Trailing arm
2   Brake backplate   4   Trailing arm front mounting

12 Rear suspension trailing arm – removal and refitting

1   Jack up the rear of the car, support it securely and remove the roadwheel.
2   Refer to Chapter 8 and remove the hub.
3   Refer to Chapter 9 and remove the brake shoes.
4   Disconnect the rear wheel cylinder hydraulic hose and cap the end of the hose to prevent loss of fluid.
5   If the right-hand side is being dismantled, unscrew the four nuts which hold the brake backplate and the trailing arm to the swing bearing. If the left-hand side is being dismantled, unbolt the components from the stub axle.
6   Unscrew and remove the mounting bolt from the front end of the trailing arm and withdraw the assembly.
7   Refitting is a reversal of removal, bleed the brakes on completion as described in Chapter 9.

13 Panhard rod – removal and refitting

1   Raise the rear of the car and support it securely.
2   Unscrew the Panhard rod nut from the axle beam (photo).
3   Unbolt the Panhard rod from the body bracket (photo).
4   Slide the Panhard rod from the stud on the axle beam and remove it.
5   Refitting is a reversal of removal. Tighten nuts and bolts to the specified torque.

13.2 Panhard rod at axle beam

13.3 Panhard rod connection to body bracket

14 Rear axle beam – removal and refitting

1 Raise the rear of the car and support it securely under the body jacking points.
2 Remove both rear roadwheels.
3 Disconnect both shock absorber lower mountings.
4 Disconnect the Panhard rod from the axle beam.
5 Support the axle beam on a trolley jack.
6 Remove the left-hand brake drum (Chapter 9, Section 6). Working through the holes in the hub, remove the four nuts which secure the axle beam to the left-hand stub axle.
7 On the right-hand side, remove the four nuts which secure the stub axle to the axle beam.
8 Free the axle beam from the stub axles, lower the trolley jack and remove the axle beam.
9 Refitting is a reversal of removal. Tighten all nuts and bolts to the specified torque.

15 Rear stub axle – removal and refitting

1 Raise and securely support the rear of the car.
2 Remove the roadwheel.
3 Remove the brake drum (Chapter 9) and the hub (Chapter 8).
4 Release the brake hose from its clip on the trailing arm.
5 Unscrew the nuts which hold the brake backplate and trailing arm to the stub axle (left-hand side) or to the swing bearing (right-hand side). On the right-hand side, also remove the four nuts which secure the stub axle to the axle beam.
6 Support the brake backplate and trailing arm. Free the stub axle (and swing bearing, when applicable) and remove it.
7 If the swing bearing needs to be renewed, consult a Rover dealer or other specialist. If the bearing is available separately, special press tools will be required for fitting it.
8 Refit by reversing the removal operation. Tighten all nuts and bolts to the specified torque.

16 Suspension arm flexible bushes – renewal

1 Worn or hardened flexible bushes can be renewed using a press or a long bolt with a nut, thick washers and suitable distance pieces. A wide-opening vice is also suitable for pressing out flexible bushes and pressing in the new ones using sockets of different diameters as removal tools.
2 Smearing the bushes with brake hydraulic fluid or soapy water will assist in the fitting of the bushes.

17 Steering rack bellows – renewal

1 Raise the front of the car, support it securely and remove the roadwheel from the appropriate side.

Fig. 10.7 Exploded view of the steering gear (Sec 17)

1 Steering column upper shroud
2 Steering column lower shroud
3 Intermediate shaft
4 Steering shaft
5 Cover
6 Lower bearing
7 Blanking plate
8 Nut
9 Circlip
10 Washer
11 Thrust ring
12 Horn push
13 Steering wheel
14 Contact plate
15 Upper bearing
16 Washer
17 Wave washer
18 Spacer
19 Bending plate guide rail
20 Bending plate guide
21 Retaining spring
22 Steering lock/ignition switch
23 Horn contact
24 Bracket
25 Bending plate
26 Rubber band
27 Column bracket
28 Bending plate base
29 Self-locking nut
30 Collar
31 Stopper
32 Spring
33 Tube
34 Steering column tube
35 Washer
36 Rake lever
37 Column pivot
38 Dust excluder clip
39 Dust excluder
40 Tie-rod and balljoint
41 Locknut
42 Bellows clip
43 Bellows
44 Clip
45 Tie-rod
46 Lockplate
47 Stop washer
48 Rack
49 Dust seal
50 Circlip
51 Circlip
52 Pinion bearing
53 Pinion shaft
54 Rack housing
55 Rack damper slipper
56 Spring
57 Adjuster screw
58 Locknut
59 Rack end bush
60 Mounting insulator
61 Mounting clamp
62 Mounting insulator
63 Mounting clamp

17.2 Tie-rod end castellated nut and split pin

17.3 Disconnecting tie-rod balljoint from steering arm

2   Release the tie-rod end locknut, but do not unscrew it more than one quarter of a turn. Extract the balljoint nut split pin (photo).
3   Unscrew the balljoint taper pin nut and then using a splitter tool, disconnect the balljoint from the eye of the steering arm (photo).
4   Unscrew the balljoint from the tie-rod.
5   Release the bellows clips and slide them from the rack housing.
6   If the bellows have been split for some time and dirt has entered or lubricant has been lost, clean away contaminated grease after extending the rack on the side affected. Apply fresh lubricant of the specified type to the rack teeth.
7   Slide on the new bellows with their retaining clips. Grease the tie-rod threads.
8   Screw on the tie-rod balljoint to its original position where the locknut will require only a quarter turn to lock it. Reconnect the balljoint to the steering arm, tighten the nut and insert a new split pin.
9   Refit the roadwheel and lower the car. Tighten the wheel nuts.
10 However carefully the refitted position of the tie-rod end balljoint was carried out, check the front wheel alignment as described in Section 27.

18 Tie-rod end balljoint – renewal

1   The operations are as described in the preceding Section.
2   When screwing on the balljoint taper pin nut, if it is found that the pin rotates preventing tightening of the nut, force the tie-rod end upwards using a jack. This will drive the taper pin further into the conical seat of the steering eye and prevent rotation.

19 Steering wheel – removal and refitting

1   Using a small screwdriver, prise out the blanking plate from the centre of the steering wheel hub (photo).
2   Check that the front roadwheels are in the straight-ahead position and mark the steering wheel hub to spindle relationship.
3   Unscrew the retaining nut and pull off the steering wheel. If the wheel is tight on the splines, jar it lightly with the hands, located at opposite sides at the rear of the wheel rim (photo).
4   The horn pad can be removed to expose the contact plate after extracting the screws from the rear face of the steering wheel hub.
5   Refitting is a reversal of removal. Tighten the retaining nut to the specified torque. It is important that, as the steering wheel is pushed onto its shaft, the direction indicator lugs engage in the cut-outs on the steering wheel hub boss (photo).

20 Steering intermediate shaft – removal and refitting

1   Remove the cover from the base of the steering column.
2   Unscrew the pinch-bolts from the intermediate shaft universally-jointed couplings.

19.1 Removing blanking plate from steering wheel

19.3 Unscrewing steering wheel nut

19.5 Steering wheel hub cut-outs

3 Centralise the steering with the front roadwheels in the straight-ahead position.
4 Remove the intermediate shaft from the pinion and steering shafts.
5 Refitting is a reversal of removal, but make sure that the pinch-bolt holes are aligned with the shaft groove and flat when pushing the couplings onto the splines.
6 Tighten the pinch-bolts to the specified torque.

21 Steering rack damper – adjustment

1 If free play exceeds 10.0 mm (0.40 in) when measured at the steering wheel rim or knocking is heard when traversing rough surfaces, adjust the rack damper in the following way.
2 Raise the front of the car, support it securely with the roadwheels hanging free.
3 Attach a spring balance to the outer end of a steering wheel spoke and check the pull required to turn the steering wheel. This should not exceed 1.5 kg (3.3 lb). A figure just below this is ideal.
4 To adjust, centralise the steering, slacken the rack damper locknut and tighten the adjuster screw until it is felt to contact the coil spring.

Fig. 10.8 Steering rack damper locknut (1) and adjuster screw (2) (Sec 21)

Check the steering wheel pull as previously described, adjusting the screw by a quarter turn at a time until the specified pull is obtained.
5 Tighten the locknut without altering the position of the adjuster screw.

22 Steering column – removal, overhaul and refitting

1 Remove the steering wheel as previously described.
2 Extract the screws, remove the steering column lower shroud and then unclip and remove the upper shroud (photos).
3 Disconnect the battery and the wiring plugs at the side of the steering column which serve the ignition and combination switches.
4 Remove the combination switch and indicator self-cancelling sleeve from the top of the steering column.
5 Remove the intermediate shaft cover and unscrew the pinch-bolt which secures the universal joint coupling to the steering shaft.
6 Unbolt the steering column lower bracket.
7 Unbolt the steering column upper bracket and bending plate.
8 Withdraw the column from the car.
9 To remove the column lower bush, remove the plastic collar and extract the bush.
10 Grease the new bush and push it into the column tube as far as it will go.
11 Align the nib on the plastic collar with the hole in the column tube and fit the collar.
12 To renew the top bush, extract the circlip and remove the washer.
13 Turn the ignition key to the 1 position. Remove the bottom bush as previously described and pull the shaft from the column tube.
14 From the top of the column, remove the thrust ring, top bush and horn contact.
15 Grease the new top bush and smear the shaft with grease to prevent rust.
16 Reassembly is a reversal of removal, but make sure that the concave side of the washer under the circlip is towards the circlip.
17 To refit the steering column, reverse the removal operations. Make sure that the bending and holder plates are not distorted. Renew if they are and fit them so that the arrow on the plate is uppermost and pointing towards the bottom of the column.
18 Tighten all nuts and bolts to the specified torque.

23 Steering column rake adjustment mechanism – overhaul

1 With the steering column removed from the car, take off the hanger springs and rubber bands which retain the bending and holder plates.
2 Release the screw and remove the stopper clip from the rake mechanism.

22.2A Unscrewing shroud screw

22.2B Shroud retaining clip

3   Unscrew and remove the domed locknut (29) (Fig. 10.7) collar (30) and stopper (31). *Note that the locknut has a left-hand thread.*
4   Remove the adjuster lever assembly (36).
5   Lubricate the sliding surfaces with grease, assemble the lever, stopper and collar without damaging the O-ring.
6   Fit the hanger springs and domed locknut, tightening to 7.0 Nm (5.0 lbf ft), with the collar pushed towards the locknut.
7   Check the force required to operate the adjustment lever. This should be between 5.9 and 9.0 kg (11.0 and 20.0 lb) when checked on a spring balance. If not as specified, slide the collar towards the stopper and slightly tighten or slacken the domed locknut.
8   Finally slide the collar towards the locknut and fit the stopper clip.
9   Fit the bending and holder plates with their spring and rubber bands.

24 Steering column lock – removal and refitting

1   Remove the steering column as described in Section 22.
2   Secure the column in the jaws of a vice and remove the lock fixing bolts. Do this by drilling them out or using a screw extractor. To remove the ignition switch from the lock, refer to Chapter 4.
3   Locate the new lock on the column and tighten the new shear head bolts finger tight. Check that the steering lock is correctly aligned with the hole in the column.
4   Insert the key into the lock and check for smooth operation of the lock tongue in the column cut-out.
5   Tighten the bolts until their heads shear off.

25 Steering rack – removal and refitting

1   Remove the cover from the base of the steering column and unscrew the pinch-bolt from the lower universal joint coupling.
2   Raise the front of the car, support it securely and remove the front roadwheels.
3   Disconnect the tie-rod end balljoints from their steering arms as described in Section 18.
4   Turn the steering to full left-hand lock.
5   Slide the safety clip off the roll pin which connects the gearchange remote control rod to the selector shaft of the transmission. Drive out the roll pin.
6   Disconnect the steady rod from the transmission.
7   Disconnect the front section of the exhaust pipe from the rest of the system.
8   Remove the retainers and pinion shaft dust seal from the car floor.
9   Unbolt the rack housing mounting clamps, lower the housing to clear the pinion shaft and then turn the housing through 180° (photo).

25.9 Steering rack mounting clamp bolts (arrowed)

10   Move the housing towards the left-hand side of the car until the right-hand tie-rod clears the exhaust pipe. Then lower the steering gear and withdraw it from the right-hand side of the car.
11   Refitting is a reversal of removal, but centralise the rack and steering wheel before connecting the intermediate shaft coupling.
12   Tighten all nuts and bolts to the specified torque. Check the front wheel alignment on completion.

26 Steering gear – overhaul

1   If the steering gear is well worn it is recommended that a new or factory reconditioned unit is fitted.
2   For those wishing to overhaul the original unit, proceed in the following way. Remove the gear (Section 25).
3   Clean away external dirt and clamp the rack housing in the jaws of a vice.
4   Release the bellows clips and pull them away from the rack housing.
5   Release the tie-rod lockwasher tabs (46) (Fig. 10.7). Hold the rack still by means of its flats and unscrew the tie-rods.
6   Unscrew the locknut and remove the rack damper components.
7   Extract the pinion dust seal and the circlip then withdraw the pinion shaft from the housing.
8   Slide the rack out of the pinion gear end of the rack housing.
9   Remove the mounting insulator followed by the rack end bush.
10   Clean and renew all components which appear worn.
11   Reassembly is a reversal of dismantling. Pack the pinion bearing with grease and smear grease onto the inner surface of the rack end bush. Do not fill the outer slots with grease or the air passages will be restricted.
12   The mounting insulator bush should be positioned between 1.0 and 3.0 mm from the end of the rack housing.
13   Apply specified grease to the teeth of the rack and then insert the rack from the pinion gear end of the housing.
14   Press 25 to 35 g of specified grease into the pinion shaft opening. Insert the pinion, fit the circlip and dust seal.
15   Reassemble the rack damper components having been smeared with grease.
16   Reconnect the tie-rods to the rack using a new lock washer and stop washer.
17   Partially fill the bellows with specified grease and fit them with their clips. Release one clip so that any air can be removed from the bellows by gently squeezing them.
18   After refitting the steering gear to the car, adjust the rack damper as described in Section 21.

27 Steering angles and front wheel alignment

1   Accurate front wheel alignment is essential to provide good steering and roadholding characteristics and to ensure slow and even tyre wear. Before considering the steering angles, check that the tyres are correctly inflated, that the front wheels are not buckled, the hub bearings are not worn or incorrectly adjusted and that the steering linkage is in good order, without slackness or wear at the joints.
2   Wheel alignment consists of four factors:
Camber, is the angle at which the road wheels are set from the vertical when viewed from the front or rear of the vehicle. Positive camber is the angle (in degrees) that the wheels are tilted outwards at the top from the vertical.
Castor, is the angle between the steering axis and a vertical when viewed from each side of the vehicle. Positive castor is indicated when the steering axis is inclined towards the rear of the vehicle at its upper end.
Steering axis inclination, is the angle when viewed from the front or rear of the vehicle between vertical and an imaginary line drawn between the top and bottom strut mountings.
Toe, is the amount by which the distance between the front inside edges of the roadwheel rims differs from that between the rear inside edges. If the distance between the front edges is less than that at the rear, the wheels are said to toe-in. If the distance between the front inside edges is greater than that at the rear, the wheels toe-out.
3   Owing to the need for precision gauges to measure the small angles of the steering and suspension settings, it is preferable that

Fig. 10.9 Camber angle diagram (Sec 27)

A   Vertical   B   Camber angle (positive)

Fig. 10.10 Castor angle diagram (LH) (Sec 27)

A   Vertical   B   Castor angle (positive)

Fig. 10.11 Front wheel alignment diagram (Sec 27) showing toe-in

$$Y - X = toe\text{-}in$$

measuring of camber and castor is left to a service station having the necessary equipment.

4   The camber, castor and steering axis inclination angles are set in production and cannot be adjusted. Where they differ from those specified, suspect collision damage or gross wear in the steering or suspension components.

5   To check the front wheel alignment, first make sure that the lengths of both tie-rods are equal when the steering is in the straight-ahead position. Adjust if necessary by releasing the tie-rod end locknuts and turning the tie-rods until the lengths of the exposed threads are equal on each side.

6   Obtain a tracking gauge. These are available in various forms from accessory stores or one can be fabricated from a length of steel tubing suitably cranked to clear the sump and bellhousing and having a setscrew and locknut at one end.

7   With the gauge, measure the distance between the two wheel inner rims (at hub height) at the rear of the wheel. Push the vehicle forward to rotate the wheel through 180° (half a turn) and measure the distance between the wheel inner rims, again at hub height, at the front of the wheel. This last measurement should differ from the first by the appropriate toe-in or toe-out according to specification (see Specifications Section).

8   Where the toe-in or toe-out is found to be incorrect, release the tie-rod balljoint locknuts and turn the tie-rods equally. Only turn them a quarter of a turn at a time before re-checking the alignment. Do not grip the threaded part of the tie-rod/balljoint during adjustment and make sure that the gaiter outboard clip is released otherwise the gaiter will twist as the tie-rod is rotated. Turn each tie-rod in the same direction when viewed from the centre line of the car otherwise the rods will become unequal in length. This would cause the steering wheel spoke position to alter and cause problems on turns with tyre scrubbing. On completion, tighten the tie-rod locknuts without

disturbing their setting, check that the balljoint is at the centre of its arc of travel and then retighten the bellows clip.

28 Rear wheel alignment

These angles are set in production of the car and any deviation from those specified must be due to collision damage or gross wear in the suspension components.

29 Fault diagnosis – suspension and steering

Symptom	Reason(s)
Front suspension	
Vehicle wanders	Incorrect wheel alignment
	Worn lower suspension arm balljoints
Heavy or stiff steering	Incorrect front wheel alignment
	Incorrect tyre pressures
Wheel wobble or vibration	Roadwheels out of balance
	Roadwheel buckled
	Incorrect front wheel alignment
	Faulty strut
	Weak torsion bar
Excessive pitching or rolling on corners or during braking	Faulty strut
	Weak or broken torsion bar
Tyre squeal when cornering	Incorrect front wheel alignment
	Incorrect tyre pressures
Abnormal tyre wear	Incorrect tyre pressures
	Incorrect front wheel alignment
	Worn hub bearing
Rear suspension	
Poor roadholding and wander	Faulty shock absorber
	Weak coil spring
	Worn hub bearing
	Worn trailing arm bush
Steering	
Car pulls to one side	Incorrect steering geometry
	Collision damage
Car wanders when driven straight-ahead	Play in steering gear
	Wear in steering balljoints
Heavy or stiff steering	Lack of lubricant in steering gear or balljoints
	Incorrect steering geometry
	Collision damage
Play at steering wheel	Wear in steering rack or balljoints
	Loose steering shaft coupling pinch-bolt or worn splines
	Worn steering column/shaft universal joints
Vibration at steering wheel	Roadwheels out of balance or loose
	Tyre damage
	Loose driveshaft-to-hub nuts
Rattles from steering when traversing rough surfaces	Steering damper defective or in need of adjustment
	Loose steering column mounting bolts
	Loose steering column/shaft coupling pinch-bolts
	Loose steering rack housing mounting bolts
	Worn steering column bearings
Excessive or uneven tyre wear	Incorrect steering geometry
	Worn steering components
	Collision damage

Note: *Before diagnosing steering faults, be sure that trouble is not due to incorrect or uneven tyre pressures, inappropriate tyre combinations, or braking system or suspension defects*

Chapter 11 Bodywork and fittings

For modifications, and information applicable to later models, see Supplement at end of manual

Contents

Specifications

Body dimensions are given in the introductory Section of this Manual.

Torque wrench settings

	Nm	lbf ft
Bumper bracket to body bolts	22	16
Door hinge bolts	22	16
Front seat track bolts	22	16
Rear seat back rest bolts	10	7
Seat belt anchor bolts	32	24

1 General description

The Rover 200 Series consists of six four-door Saloon models with either a 1342 cc or 1598 cc engine.

The body is of all-steel unitary construction with a level of trim and equipment dependent upon the model specified in the vehicle range.

2 Maintenance – bodywork and underframe

The general condition of a vehicle's bodywork is the one thing that significantly affects its value. Maintenance is easy but needs to be regular. Neglect, particularly after minor damage, can lead quickly to further deterioration and costly repair bills. It is important also to keep watch on those parts of the vehicle not immediately visible, for instance the underside, inside all the wheel arches and the lower part of the engine compartment.

The basic maintenance routine for the bodywork is washing – preferably with a lot of water, from a hose. This will remove all the loose solids which may have stuck to the vehicle. It is important to flush these off in such a way as to prevent grit from scratching the finish. The wheel arches and underframe need washing in the same way to remove any accumulated mud which will retain moisture and tend to encourage rust. Paradoxically enough, the best time to clean the underframe and wheel arches is in wet weather when the mud is thoroughly wet and soft. In very wet weather the underframe is usually cleaned of large accumulations automatically and this is a good time for inspection.

Periodically, except on vehicles with a wax-based underbody protective coating, it is a good idea to have the whole of the underframe of the vehicle steam cleaned, engine compartment included, so that a thorough inspection can be carried out to see what minor repairs and renovations are necessary. Steam cleaning is available at many garages and is necessary for removal of the accumulation of oily grime which sometimes is allowed to become thick in certain areas. If steam cleaning facilities are not available, there are one or two excellent grease solvents available such as Holts Engine Cleaner or Holts Foambrite which can be brush applied. The dirt can then be simply hosed off. Note that these methods should not be used on vehicles with wax-based underbody protective coating or the coating will be removed. Such vehicles should be inspected annually, preferably just prior to winter, when the underbody should be washed down and any damage to the wax coating repaired using Holts Undershield. Ideally, a completely fresh coat should be applied. It would also be worth considering the use of such wax-based protection for injection into door panels, sills, box sections, etc, as an additional safeguard against rust damage where such protection is not provided by the vehicle manufacturer.

After washing paintwork, wipe off with a chamois leather to give an unspotted clear finish. A coat of clear protective wax polish, like the many excellent Turtle Wax polishes, will give added protection against chemical pollutants in the air. If the paintwork sheen has dulled or oxidised, use a cleaner/polisher combination such as Turtle Extra to restore the brilliance of the shine. This requires a little effort, but such dulling is usually caused because regular washing has been neglected. Care needs to be taken with metallic paintwork, as special non-abrasive cleaner/polisher is required to avoid damage to the finish. Always check that the door and ventilator opening drain holes and pipes are completely clear so that water can be drained out (photos). Bright work should be treated in the same way as paint work. Windscreens and windows can be kept clear of the smeary film which often appears, by the use of a proprietary glass cleaner like Holts Mixra. Never use any form of wax or other body or chromium polish on glass.

Periodically oil all hinges and apply grease to the catches (photo).

2.4A Clearing door drain

2.4B Clearing sill drain

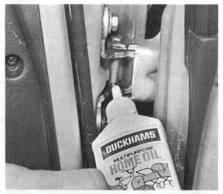

2.5A Oiling a door hinge

3 Maintenance – upholstery and carpets

Mats and carpets should be brushed or vacuum cleaned regularly to keep them free of grit. If they are badly stained remove them from the vehicle for scrubbing or sponging and make quite sure they are dry before refitting. Seats and interior trim panels can be kept clean by wiping with a damp cloth and Turtle Wax Carisma. If they do become stained (which can be more apparent on light coloured upholstery) use a little liquid detergent and a soft nail brush to scour the grime out of the grain of the material. Do not forget to keep the headlining clean in the same way as the upholstery. When using liquid cleaners inside the vehicle do not over-wet the surfaces being cleaned. Excessive damp could get into the seams and padded interior causing stains, offensive odours or even rot. If the inside of the vehicle gets wet accidentally it is worthwhile taking some trouble to dry it out properly, particularly where carpets are involved. *Do not leave oil or electric heaters inside the vehicle for this purpose.*

4 Minor body damage – repair

The colour bodywork repair photographic sequences between pages 32 and 33 illustrate the operations detailed in the following sub-sections.

Note: *For more detailed information about bodywork repair, the Haynes Publishing Group publish a book by Lindsay Porter called The Car Bodywork Repair Manual. This incorporates information on such aspects as rust treatment, painting and glass fibre repairs, as well as details on more ambitious repairs involving welding and panel beating.*

Repair of minor scratches in bodywork

If the scratch is very superficial, and does not penetrate to the metal of the bodywork, repair is very simple. Lightly rub the area of the scratch with a paintwork renovator like Turtle Wax New Color Back, or a very fine cutting paste like Holts Body + Plus Rubbing Compound, to remove loose paint from the scratch and to clear the surrounding bodywork of wax polish. Rinse the area with clean water.

Apply touch-up paint, such as Holts Dupli-Color Color Touch or a paint film like Holts Autofilm, to the scratch using a fine paint brush; continue to apply fine layers of paint until the surface of the paint in the scratch is level with the surrounding paintwork. Allow the new paint at least two weeks to harden: then blend it into the surrounding paintwork by rubbing the scratch area with a paintwork renovator or a very fine cutting paste, such as Holts Body + Plus Rubbing Compound or Turtle Wax New Color Back. Finally, apply wax polish from one of the Turtle Wax range of wax polishes.

Where the scratch has penetrated right through to the metal of the bodywork, causing the metal to rust, a different repair technique is required. Remove any loose rust from the bottom of the scratch with a penknife, then apply rust inhibiting paint, such as Turtle Wax Rust Master, to prevent the formation of rust in the future. Using a rubber or nylon applicator fill the scratch with bodystopper paste like Holts Body + Plus Knifing Putty. If required, this paste can be mixed with cellulose thinners, such as Holts Body + Plus Cellulose Thinners, to provide a very thin paste which is ideal for filling narrow scratches. Before the stopper-paste in the scratch hardens, wrap a piece of smooth cotton rag around the top of a finger. Dip the finger in cellulose

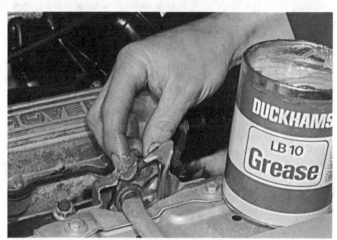

2.5B Applying grease to bonnet lock

thinners, such as Holts Body + Plus Cellulose Thinners, and then quickly sweep it across the surface of the stopper-paste in the scratch; this will ensure that the surface of the stopper-paste is slightly hollowed. The scratch can now be painted over as described earlier in this Section.

Repair of dents in bodywork

When deep denting of the vehicle's bodywork has taken place, the first task is to pull the dent out, until the affected bodywork almost attains its original shape. There is little point in trying to restore the original shape completely, as the metal in the damaged area will have stretched on impact and cannot be reshaped fully to its original contour. It is better to bring the level of the dent up to a point which is about ⅛ in (3 mm) below the level of the surrounding bodywork. In cases where the dent is very shallow anyway, it is not worth trying to pull it out at all. If the underside of the dent is accessible, it can be hammered out gently from behind, using a mallet with a wooden or plastic head. Whilst doing this, hold a suitable block of wood firmly against the outside of the panel to absorb the impact from the hammer blows and thus prevent a large area of the bodywork from being 'belled-out'.

Should the dent be in a section of the bodywork which has a double skin or some other factor making it inaccessible from behind, a different technique is called for. Drill several small holes through the metal inside the area – particularly in the deeper section. Then screw long self-tapping screws into the holes just sufficiently for them to gain a good purchase in the metal. Now the dent can be pulled out by pulling on the protruding heads of the screws with a pair of pliers.

The next stage of the repair is the removal of the paint from the damaged area, and from an inch or so of the surrounding 'sound' bodywork. This is accomplished most easily by using a wire brush or abrasive pad on a power drill, although it can be done just as effectively by hand using sheets of abrasive paper. To complete the preparation for filling, score the surface of the bare metal with a screwdriver or the tang of a file, or alternatively, drill small holes in the affected area. This will provide a really good 'key' for the filler paste.

To complete the repair see the Section on filling and re-spraying.

Repair of rust holes or gashes in bodywork

Remove all paint from the affected area and from an inch or so of the surrounding 'sound' bodywork, using an abrasive pad or a wire brush on a power drill. If these are not available a few sheets of abrasive paper will do the job just as effectively. With the paint removed you will be able to gauge the severity of the corrosion and therefore decide whether to renew the whole panel (if this is possible) or to repair the affected area. New body panels are not as expensive as most people think and it is often quicker and more satisfactory to fit a new panel than to attempt to repair large areas of corrosion.

Remove all fittings from the affected area except those which will act as a guide to the original shape of the damaged bodywork (eg headlamp shells etc). Then, using tin snips or a hacksaw blade, remove all loose metal and any other metal badly affected by corrosion. Hammer the edges of the hole inwards in order to create a slight depression for the filler paste.

Wire brush the affected area to remove the powdery rust from the surface of the remaining metal. Paint the affected area with rust inhibiting paint like Turtle Wax Rust Master; if the back of the rusted area is accessible treat this also.

Before filling can take place it will be necessary to block the hole in some way. This can be achieved by the use of aluminium or plastic mesh, or aluminium tape.

Aluminium or plastic mesh or glass fibre matting, such as the Holts Body+Plus Glass Fibre Matting, is probably the best material to use for a large hole. Cut a piece to the approximate size and shape of the hole to be filled, then position it in the hole so that its edges are below the level of the surrounding bodywork. It can be retained in position by several blobs of filler paste around its periphery.

Aluminium tape should be used for small or very narrow holes. Pull a piece off the roll and trim it to the approximate size and shape required, then pull off the backing paper (if used) and stick the tape over the hole; it can be overlapped if the thickness of one piece is insufficient. Burnish down the edges of the tape with the handle of a screwdriver or similar, to ensure that the tape is securely attached to the metal underneath.

Bodywork repairs – filling and re-spraying

Before using this Section, see the Sections on dent, deep scratch, rust holes and gash repairs.

Many types of bodyfiller are available, but generally speaking those proprietary kits which contain a tin of filler paste and a tube of resin hardener are best for this type of repair, like Holts Body+Plus or Holts No Mix which can be used directly from the tube. A wide, flexible plastic or nylon applicator will be found invaluable for imparting a smooth and well contoured finish to the surface of the filler.

Mix up a little filler on a clean piece of card or board – measure the hardener carefully (follow the maker's instructions on the pack) otherwise the filler will set too rapidly or too slowly. Alternatively, Holts No Mix can be used straight from the tube without mixing, but daylight is required to cure it. Using the applicator apply the filler paste to the prepared area; draw the applicator across the surface of the filler to achieve the correct contour and to level the filler surface. As soon as a contour that approximates to the correct one is achieved, stop working the paste – if you carry on too long the paste will become sticky and begin to 'pick up' on the applicator. Continue to add thin layers of filler paste at twenty-minute intervals until the level of the filler is just proud of the surrounding bodywork.

Once the filler has hardened, excess can be removed using a metal plane or file. From then on, progressively finer grades of abrasive paper should be used, starting with a 40 grade production paper and finishing with 400 grade wet-and-dry paper. Always wrap the abrasive paper around a flat rubber, cork, or wooden block – otherwise the surface of the filler will not be completely flat. During the smoothing of the filler surface the wet-and-dry paper should be periodically rinsed in water. This will ensure that a very smooth finish is imparted to the filler at the final stage.

At this stage the 'dent' should be surrounded by a ring of bare metal, which in turn should be encircled by the finely 'feathered' edge of the good paintwork. Rinse the repair area with clean water, until all of the dust produced by the rubbing-down operation has gone.

Spray the whole repair area with a light coat of primer, either Holts Body+Plus Grey or Red Oxide Primer – this will show up any

imperfections in the surface of the filler. Repair these imperfections with fresh filler paste or bodystopper, and once more smooth the surface with abrasive paper. If bodystopper is used, it can be mixed with cellulose thinners to form a really thin paste which is ideal for filling small holes. Repeat this spray and repair procedure until you are satisfied that the surface of the filler, and the feathered edge of the paintwork are perfect. Clean the repair area with clean water and allow to dry fully.

The repair area is now ready for final spraying. Paint spraying must be carried out in a warm, dry, windless and dust free atmosphere. This condition can be created artificially if you have access to a large indoor working area, but if you are forced to work in the open, you will have to pick your day very carefully. If you are working indoors, dousing the floor in the work area with water will help to settle the dust which would otherwise be in the atmosphere. If the repair area is confined to one body panel, mask off the surrounding panels; this will help to minimise the effects of a slight mis-match in paint colours. Bodywork fittings (eg chrome strips, door handles etc) will also need to be masked off. Use genuine masking tape and several thicknesses of newspaper for the masking operations.

Before commencing to spray, agitate the aerosol can thoroughly, then spray a test area (an old tin, or similar) until the technique is mastered. Cover the repair area with a thick coat of primer; the thickness should be built up using several thin layers of paint rather than one thick one. Using 400 grade wet-and-dry paper, rub down the surface of the primer until it is really smooth. While doing this, the work area should be thoroughly doused with water, and the wet-and-dry paper periodically rinsed in water. Allow to dry before spraying on more paint.

Spray on the top coat using Holts Dupli-Color Autospray, again building up the thickness by using several thin layers of paint. Start spraying in the centre of the repair area and then work outwards, with a side-to-side motion, until the whole repair area and about 2 inches of the surrounding original paintwork is covered. Remove all masking material 10 to 15 minutes after spraying on the final coat of paint.

Allow the new paint at least two weeks to harden, then, using a paintwork renovator or a very fine cutting paste such as Turtle Wax New Color Back or Holts Body+Plus Rubbing Compound, blend the edges of the paint into the existing paintwork. Finally, apply wax polish.

5 Major body damage – repair

1 This sort of work should be left to your Austin Rover dealer or specialist body repair works.
2 It is essential to have the body aligned on special jigs to ensure that the specified steering and suspension settings are maintained during repair.
3 This is of course beyond the scope of the home mechanic and if not carried out correctly will give rise to unroadworthy behaviour and severe tyre wear.

6 Front bumper – removal and refitting

1.3 models
1 On 1.3 models, unbolt and remove the splash panels from under the front end of the car.
2 Unscrew the two lower bumper mounting bolts.
3 Unscrew the two bolts which hold the bumper to the brackets.

1.6 models
4 Unscrew the two bolts which hold the bumper to the body crossmember.

All models
5 Working through the bumper grille, remove the bumper clamp bolts.
6 Support the bumper and ease it forward.
7 Disconnect the headlamp washer hose (where fitted) and remove the bumper from the car.
8 Refitting is a reversal of removal.

**Fig. 11.1 Front bumper locating clip (1) and bumper (2)
(Sec 6)**

7 Front spoiler – removal and refitting

1 Turn the steering to full lock and remove the two self-tapping screws from the flange of the front wheel arch.
2 Unscrew the three screws which hold the spoiler brackets to the lower edge of the bumper (photo).
3 Extract the three screws which hold the top edge of the spoiler to the bumper.
4 Lift the spoiler from the car.
5 Refitting is a reversal of removal.

8 Bonnet – removal and refitting

1 Open the bonnet and support it on its stay.

2 Mark the position of the hinges on the underside of the bonnet. Use a pencil or masking tape to prevent scoring the paint, as this could encourage rust (photo).
3 Release the washer hose from its clip and disconnect it. With the help of an assistant, unscrew the hinge bolts, disconnect the stay and lift the bonnet from the car (photo).
4 Refitting is a reversal of removal, but do not fully tighten the hinge bolts until the bonnet has been gently lowered and its alignment checked. There should be an equal gap at each side between wing and bonnet. Move the bonnet if necessary after releasing the hinge bolts.
5 It is acceptable to fit shims under the hinges to make the near end of the bonnet flush with the wing top surfaces.
6 Adjust the bonnet lock and bump stops to provide firm positive closure as described in the next Section (photo).

7.2 Front spoiler bracket

8.2 Bonnet hinge

8.3 Washer hose connector (arrowed)

8.6 Bonnet bump stop

9.1 Bonnet lock

9 Bonnet lock and cable

1   The bonnet lock may be moved within the limits of its elongated bolt holes so that the bonnet shuts smoothly and positively. This should be carried out in conjunction with adjusting the rubber bump stops. These should be screwed in or out so that the bonnet will be flush with the tops of the wings and not rattle when closed (photo).

2   The bonnet cable is not adjustable, but may be renewed after disconnecting it from the lock and release lever and withdrawing it through the bulkhead grommet into the engine compartment.

10 Radiator grille – removal and refitting

1   Extract the fixing screws from between the slots of the grille (photo).

2   Pull the grille sharply from the spring clips (photo).

3   Refitting is a reversal of removal.

11 Front wing – removal and refitting

1   Remove the front bumper (Section 6).

2   Remove the front direction indicator (Chapter 12).

10.1 Radiator grille screw (arrowed)

10.2 Withdrawing radiator grille

11.3 Underwing protective shield bolt (arrowed)

11.5 Front wing bolts (engine compartment) (arrowed)

3   Raise the front of the car and remove th roadwheel. Remove the underwing protective plastic shield (photo).
4   Open the bonnet.
5   Unscrew the row of bolts from the top edge of the wing (photo).
6   Open the front door and remove the wing upper fixing bolt which is accessible between the rear edge of the wing and the leading edge of the door (photo).
7   Extract the fixing screw from the front and rear lower edges of the wing (photo).
8   Remove the wing and recover the rubber buffer from halfway down the rear edge. If the wing is stuck tight, cut along the mastic joint using a sharp knife.
9   Before fitting the new wing, clean away all old jointing mastic and apply a bead of new material.
10 Once the wing has been fitted, apply protective coating to its underside and finish the outer surface to match the body colour.

12 Door interior trim panel – removal and refitting

1   Extract the screws and remove the armrest (photos).
2   Extract the screw and remove the escutcheon plate from the remote control handle (photos).
3   On cars without power-operated windows, extract the the spring clip and take off the window regulator handle. The clip can be removed using a piece of wire with a hook at its end or a strip of rag pulled in either direction under the handle boss (photo).
4   Extract the trim panel fixing screws (photo).
5   Insert the fingers or a broad blunt blade between the trim panel and the door and release the clips.
6   Remove the trim panel. On cars with electrically-powered windows, disconnect the multi-pin plug as the panel is withdrawn.
7   Peel away the waterproof sheet for access to the door interior.

11.6 Front wing bolt (pillar)

11.7 Front wing bolt (sill) (arrowed)

12.1A Extracting door armrest screw

12.1B Removing door armrest

12.2A Extracting door lock remote control escutcheon plate screw

12.2B Removing escutcheon plate

12.3 Door window regulator handle

12.4 Extracting door trim panel screw

12.8 Window regulator handle ready for fitting

Fig. 11.2 Front door window components (Sec 13)

8   Refitting is a reversal of removal. To fit the regulator handle, position the spring clip on the handle and fit it to the splined shaft of the regulator simply by striking it with the hand (photo).

1 Glass channel weatherseal	5 Glass regulator
2 Glass	6 Regulator handle escutcheon
3 Escutcheon plate	7 Clip
4 Glass channel	8 Regulator handle

13 Front door – dismantling and reassembly

Window glass
1   Remove the exterior rear view mirror, see Section 28.
2   Unclip and remove the door waist outer weather sealing strip.
3   Remove the door trim panel as described in the preceding Section and peel away the weatherproof sheet.
4   Remove the front speaker from the door (photo).
5   Temporarily refit the regulator handle and lower the glass until the glass bottom slide channel bolts are visible (photo).
6   If power-operated windows are fitted, use jump leads to energise the winding motors.
7   Extract the slide channel bolts and lift the glass upwards, turning it as necessary to remove it from the door waist slot.

Window winder regulator
8   With the door glass removed as previously described, unscrew the regulator mounting bolts and manoeuvre the regulator through the lower aperture in the door (photo).

Door lock
9   Unscrew the exterior handle bolts which are accessible from inside the door cavity.
10 Pull out the forked spring retainer and take out the lock cylinder at the same time disconnecting the link rod.
11 Extract the screws from the edge of the door and push the latch and

13.4 Front door with trim panel removed

13.5 Door glass regulator arms and glass bottom channel

13.8 Regulator mounting bolts (arrowed)

Fig. 11.3 Front door lock components (Sec 13)

1 Exterior door handle	8 Rod connector
2 Screw insert	9 Rod retainer
3 Key	10 Anti-rattle cushion
4 Lock cylinder	11 Link rod
5 Lock plunger	12 Latch
6 Remote control lever	13 Striker
7 Escutcheon plate	14 Lock cylinder retainer

13.11 Door latch screws

rod inside the door cavity. Measure the exposed threads on the latch rod and unscrew the exterior handle from it. Withdraw the latch from the door cavity (photo).
12 The lock remote control rod can be removed after extracting the fixing screws (photo).

Refitting
13 Refitting is a reversal of removal, but observe the following points.
14 When fitting the glass, set it centrally between the side guides before tightening the bottom slide channel bolts.
15 When screwing the exterior handle onto the latch rod, set it so that the original length of thread is exposed. Then check for full movement of the handle and unscrew or screw it further onto the rod to achieve this.

14 Rear door – dismantling and reassembly

Door glass
1   Remove the trim panel as described in Section 12.
2   Lower the glass fully.
3   Extract the sash screws, tilt the sash and remove the quarter-light (photo).
4   Adjust the position of the glass by temporarily fitting the regulator handle until the glass to regulator fixing screws are visible. Extract the screws and manoeuvre the glass up and out of the door waist slot.

Window regulator
5   With the door glass removed as previously described, unbolt the regulator and remove it through the lower aperture of the door.

13.12 Door lock remote control handle

14.3 Rear door sash top screw located under weatherseal

Fig. 11.4 Rear door window components (Sec 14)

1	Glass channel weatherstrip	5	Sash
2	Door glass	6	Regulator
3	Quarter glass channel	7	Escutcheon plate
	weatherstrip	8	Clip
4	Quarter glass	9	Regulator handle

Door lock

6 Working through the door cavity, unscrew the door exterior handle fixing bolts.

7 Remove the lock crank and disconnect the link rods.

8 Extract the latch screws from the door edge and push the latch and rods inside the door. Measure the length of exposed thread on the latch rod and then withdraw the exterior handle until it can be unscrewed from the latch rod.

9 Remove the latch and rods from the door.

Refitting

10 Refitting is a reversal of removal, but observe the following points.

11 When fitting the glass, centralise it between the side channels before tightening the bottom slide channel to regulator bolts.

12 When screwing the exterior handle onto the latch rod, set it so that the original length of thread is exposed then check for full operation of the handle and unscrew it or screw it further onto the rod to achieve this.

15 Door – removal and refitting

1 Remove the trim panel as described in Section 12.

2 Disconnect the wiring plugs from the speaker, window winder motor or door lock solenoid as appropriate.

3 Withdraw the wiring harness through the grommet (photo).

4 Drive the pin from the door check link (photo).

5 Open the door fully and support its lower edge on blocks or jacks covered with pads of rags.

6 Extract the circlips from the door hinge pins and drive out the pins. Lift the door from the car (photo).

Fig. 11.5 Rear door lock components (Sec 14)

1	Exterior door handle	8	Anti-rattle cushion
2	Screw insert	9	Remote control lever
3	Striker	10	Lock plunger
4	Latch	11	Link rod
5	Rod connector	12	Crank
6	Opener rod	13	Link rod
7	Rod retainer	14	Escutcheon plate

7 Refitting is a reversal of removal. Any adjustment of the door can be made by releasing the hinge bolts and moving the door within the limits of the pillar bolt holes (photo)..

8 Close the door gently and check that the striker is correctly located. If not, release the striker screws and move its position on the body pillar as necessary (photo).

15.3 Door wiring harness (arrowed)

15.4 Door check link

15.6 Door hinge

15.7 Door hinge bolts

15.8 Door striker

16 Luggage boot lid – removal and refitting

1   Open the lid fully and mark the position of the hinges on the underside of it (photo).

2   With the help of an assistant, support the weight of the lid, unscrew the hinge bolts and remove the lid from the car.

3   Refitting is a reversal of removal, but do not fully tighten the hinge bolts until the lid has been closed gently and checked for alignment. If an equal gap does not exist on both sides of the lid, move it as necessary within the limits of the elongated hinge bolt holes and then tighten the bolts.

4   As the lid is closed, the lock should engage smoothly and positively. If it does not, release the striker or lock bolts or both and adjust for alignment and closure (photo).

5   If for any reason the boot lid counterbalance torsion rod must be removed, then the end of the rod must be released from its anchorage slot. Do this using a large adjustable spanner or a long lever. *Exercise caution as the rod is under considerable torsion (photo).*

16.1 Luggage boot lid hinge

16.4A Removing luggage boot lock cover

16.4B Luggage boot lid lock

16.4C Luggage boot lid lock striker

16.5 Luggage boot lid lock hinge and torsion rod (arrowed)

17 Luggage boot lock and controls – removal and refitting

Lock
1 Open the boot lid and disconnect the remote control cable from it.
2 Unscrew the lock fixing screws, withdraw the lock until the link rod from the lock cylinder can be disconnected and the lock removed from the car.

Control cable and lever
3 Working inside the car, remove the boot control lever cover and housing from the side of the driver's seat (photo).
4 Unbolt the lever bracket and disconnect the control cable from the lever.
5 Remove the rear seat cushion (Section 25), and the sill mouldings from the front and rear right-hand door openings.
6 Peel back the floor carpet to expose the control cable.
7 Remove the fixing tape and pull the cable through into the luggage boot. Disconnect the cable from the lock and its locating clips.

Fig. 11.6 Luggage boot lid lock (Sec 17)

5 Lock control cable	8 Latch
6 Lock cylinder	9 Link rod
7 Striker	

Fig. 11.7 Boot and fuel filler flap remote control (Sec 17)

1 Release lever (fuel flap)	4 Cable (fuel flap)
2 Release lever (luggage boot)	5 Cable (luggage boot)
3 Lever mounting bracket	

Fig. 11.8 Fuel filler flap lock (Sec 18)

4 Control cable	12 Bezel
10 Latch	13 Cylinder retaining clip
11 Lock cylinder	

17.4 Fuel flap and boot lid control levers

Lock cylinder
8 Open the luggage boot, remove the nuts which hold the rear number plate panel and remove the panel.
9 Pull out the lock cylinder forked retaining clip, disconnect the cylinder link rod.
10 Unscrew the cylinder fixing bolt and then rotate the cylinder to disengage the retaining lugs. Remove the cylinder.

Refitting
11 The refitting of all components is a reversal of removal.

18 Fuel filler flap lock and controls – removal and refitting

1 The control cable for the fuel filler flap lock runs along the same route as the one for the luggage boot and removal and refitting procedures are as described in the preceding Section.
2 To remove the cable release lock tongue, open the flap, pull out the forked retaining clip and withdraw the assembly into the luggage boot (photo).
3 The lock cylinder can be removed after extracting the retaining clip.

18.2 Fuel filler flap lock

19 Rear spoiler – removal and refitting

1 Open the luggage boot lid, unscrew the five spoiler retaining nuts and lift the spoiler away.
2 Refitting is a reversal of removal.

20 Rear bumper – removal and refitting

1 Extract the three screws from each wheel arch which secure the bumper to the rear wing panel.
2 Unbolt the bumper brackets from the body.
3 Open the luggage boot lid and disconnect the bumper lamps wiring harness plug.
4 Release the grommet from the body panel and feed the wiring through the hole in the panel.
5 Remove the bumper.
6 Refitting is a reversal of removal.

21 Windscreen and heated rear screen – renewal

1 Removal and refitting of the front and rear screens should be left to a professional screen replacement specialist.
2 The glass is flush-mounted, and removal requires the use of a hot knife or wire to release the sealant.

22 Centre console – removal and refitting

1 On cars with manual transmission, unscrew and remove the gear lever knob.

2 Remove the rear flap and centre cover from (photos).
3 Extract the five fixing screws from the centre
4 If a radio speaker balance control is fitted withdraw the centre console only far enough to be able to disconnect the wiring multi-pin plug before lifting the console over the handbrake lever.
5 Refitting is a reversal of removal.

23 Facia panel – removal and refitting

1 Disconnect the battery.
2 Remove the steering wheel (Chapter 10).
3 Remove the facia under cover access panel from around the steering column by extracting the screws (photo).
4 Remove the glove box (two screws).
5 Remove the ashtray.
6 Remove the radio (Chapter 12).
7 Prise out the clock and then disconnect its multi-plug.
8 Refer to Chapter 12 and remove the instrument panel.
9 Extract the screw which secures the bonnet release lever to its bracket and move the lever to one side.
10 Remove the caps from both ends of the facia panel. Do this by prising them out sideways (photos).
11 Remove the two blanking caps from the lower centre of the facia panel to expose the facia lower mounting bolts (photos).
12 Remove the facia centre air vent. Do this by prising out with a thin blade inserted at the sides of the central switch (photos).
13 On 1.3 models, remove the choke knob and disconnect the cable from the facia as described in Chapter 3.
14 Pull off the heater control lever knobs and release the heater control escutcheon plate retainers. Withdraw the plate until the illumination bulb can be disconnected.
15 Extract the three screws which retain the heater control lever mounting base and separate it from the facia.

Fig. 11.9 Rear bumper (Sec 20)

| 1 End cover | 2 Locating clip | 3 Bumper |

22.2A Centre console rear flap

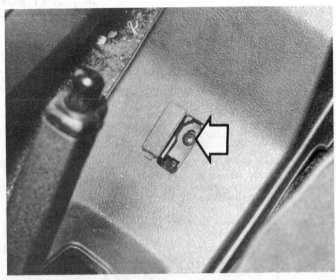

22.2B Centre console top screw (arrowed)

22.3 Centre console side screw (arrowed)

23.3 Facia under cover

23.10A Facia end cap

23.10B Facia end fixing bolt (arrowed)

23.11A Facia lower screw blanking cap

23.11B Facia lower fixing screw (arrowed)

23.12A Removing facia centre air vent

23.12B Facia air vent removed showing retaining lugs

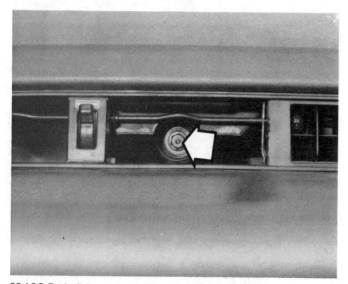
23.12C Facia fixing screw behind air vent (arrowed)

16 On 1.3 models, release the facia wiring harness multi-plugs at the fusebox.
17 On 1.6 models, unscrew the two nuts which hold the fusebox to its bracket.
18 Release the facia wiring harness multi-plug fom the fusebox and the main harness.
19 Disconnect the heater blower wiring harness.
20 Disconnect the steering column bracket earth leads. Set the steering column in its lowest rake position.
21 Unscrew all the facia fixing bolts and with the help of an assistant, remove the facia panel sideways from the car.
22 Refitting is a reversal of removal.

24 Front seat – removal and refitting

1 Push the seat fully forwards and unscrew the bolts which hold the rear end of the seat track to the floor (photo).
2 Push the seat fully back and unscrew the track front end bolts.
3 Lift the seat from the car.
4 Refitting is a reversal of removal.

24.1 Front seat slide bolt

25 Rear seat – removal and refitting

Seat cushion
1   Extract the screw from the centre of the joint between the cushion and the backrest (photo).
2   Pull the rear edge of the cushion upwards and then release the retaining hooks at the front lower edge of the cushion. Remove the cushion (photo).

Backrest
3   From each side of the lower edge of the backrest, unscrew the bolt which holds it to the wheel arch (photo).
4   If the backrest is fitted with an opening hatch to facilitate the carrying of long articles of luggage, then the backrest top rail will have to be removed.
5   Raise the backrest to disengage its locating tongues, and remove it from the car (photo).
6   Refitting is a reversal of removal.

25.1 Removing rear seat screw

25.2 Rear seat cushion retaining hook (arrowed)

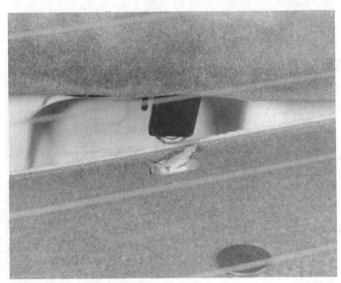

25.3 Rear seat back retaining bolt

25.5 Rear seat back locating tongues

26.1 Seat belt pillar clip

26.4 Seat belt anchor bolt cap

26.6 Seat belt floor stalk

26 Seat belts – maintenance, removal and refitting

1   Periodically inspect the seat belts for fraying or other damage. If evident, renew the belt (photo).
2   The belts may be cleaned using warm water and liquid detergent. Do not use solvents of any kind.
3   If the car is involved in a front end collision and the belts have restrained the front or rear seat occupants, renew the belts.
4   Before unbolting the seat belt anchor bolts, remove the centre pillar lower trim panel (photo).
5   When refitting, always maintain the original fitted sequence of washers and spacers.
6   Set the floor stalk at 45° to the floor before tightening its bolt (photo).

27 Interior grab handles – removal and refitting

1   Prise up the screw covers, remove the screws and the grab rails (photo).

Fig. 11.10 Front seat belt (Sec 26)

1 Belt	4 Retracting reel
2 Upper anchor plate	5 Floor stalk
3 Lower anchor plate	

28 Rear view mirrors – removal and refitting

Interior
1   The interior mirror is bonded directly to the windscreen glass. Removal will require the use of a hot air gun.
2   A new mirror is supplied complete with a self-bonding patch.

Exterior
3   Slide the mirror control knob from the operating rod (photo).
4   Prise out the triangular escutcheon plate, to expose the mirror fixing screws (photos).
5   Remove the screws and withdraw the mirror. Disconnect the wiring plug on electrically-operated mirrors.
6   Refitting is a reversal of removal.

Fig. 11.11 Rear seat belts (Sec 26)

1 *Left-hand belts*   2 *Centre belts*   3 *Right-hand belts*

27.1 Grab handle screw (arrowed)

28.3 Removing exterior mirror remote control handle

28.4A Removing mirror escutcheon plate

28.4B Exterior mirror fixing screws (arrowed)

29 Headlining – removal and refitting

1   The headlining is of moulded type and in consequence can be removed more easily than is the case with conventional linings.

2   Working inside the car, remove the sun visors, the front pillar trim, the interior lamp, the roof rear trim and the grab handles.
3   Remove the upper seat belt anchor bolts.
4   Release the body pillar upper trims and wedge them away from the pillars at the tops.
5   Remove the headlining side moulding strips.
6   Remove the headlining clips and then with the help of an assistant, remove the headlining from the car interior.
7   Fitting the headlining is a reversal of removal, but a new one will require cross-cuts to be made for the sun visor mounting.

Fig. 11.12 Headlining components (Sec 29)

1 Headlining	5 Front pillar trim
2 Clip	6 Sun visor
3 Side moulding	7 Sun visor clip
4 Grab handle	

Chapter 12 Electrical system

For modifications, and information applicable to later models, see Supplement at end of manual

Contents

Specifications

System type ....

12 volt negative earth, battery, alternator and pre-engaged starter motor

Battery ....

45Ah, maintenance-free

Alternator

Regulated voltage .... 13.9 to 15.1 volt
Output at 14 volt and 6000 rev/min 55A
Minimum brush length:
    Hitachi .... 5.0 mm (0.2 in)
    Lucas .... 10.0 mm (0.4 in)
Drivebelt deflection under load:
    1.3, new belt .... 4.0 to 6.5 mm (0.18 to 0.26 in) under load of 98 N (22 lbf)
    1.3, used belt .... 7 to 10 mm (0.28 to 0.39 in) under same load
    1.6, new or used belt .... 7 to 12 mm (0.28 to 0.47 in) under load of 44N (10 lbf)

Starter motor

Minimum brush length .... 10.0 mm (0.4 in) Lucas, 12 mm (0.5 in) Hitachi

Fuses

Number	Circuit protected	Rating (A)
1	Rear fog warning lamp	10
2	Wipers, washers	15
3	Direction indicators, reverse lamp	10
4	Alternator	10
5	LH headlamp (dipped beam)	10
6	RH headlamp (dipped beam)	10
7	LH headlamp (main beam)	10
8	RH headlamp (main beam)	10
9	Horn and stop lamps	15
10	Hazard warning lamps	10
11	Interior lamp, clock, cigar lighter	15
12	Tail, rear number plate and instrument illumination	15
13	Radiator cooling fan	15
14	Heater booster fan, heated rear window relay	20
15	Radio	10
16	Heated rear window	15
17	Central locking	15
18	Headlamp washer	15
19	Electric window (front right)	15
20	Electric window (front left)	15
21	Electric window (rear right)	15
22	Electric window (rear left)	15
23	Spare	

Continuous current fuses colour coding

Red	10A
Blue	15A
Yellow	20A

Fusible links

Main	55A
Link	45A

Bulbs

Lamp	Wattage	Number
Headlamp (Halogen)	60/55	GLB 472
Front parking lamp	4	GLB 233
Stop/tail lamp	25/5	GLB 380
Direction indicator and reverse lamps	21	GLB 382
Rear number plate lamp	5	GLB 501
Interior lamp	5	BNP4 195
Luggage boot lamp	3.4	GLB 758
Cigar lighter illumination	2.2	GLB 643
Instrument panel, warning lamps	1.4	GLB 286
Instruments	3	GLB 504
Switch warning lamp	1.4	GLB 748
Heater controls, ashtray illumination	1.4	GLB 286
Rear fog warning lamp	21	GLB 382

Wiper blades	Champion C-4501

Torque wrench settings

	Nm	lbf ft
Alternator mounting bolt	45	33
Alternator adjuster link bolt	24	18
Starter mounting bolts	45	33
Wiper arm domed nut	14	10

1 General description

The electrical system is of 12 volt negative earth type and consists of a battery, an alternator, pre-engaged starter motor and the usual lamps and accessories.

On certain models, central door locking and power-operated windows are fitted.

2 Battery – maintenance and charging

1 A maintenance-free type battery is fitted which requires no topping up of the electrolyte.

2 Keep the top of the battery clean and the terminals tight and smeared with petroleum jelly to reduce corrosion.

3 The battery will not normally require charging from the mains supply, but if only very short journeys are made with much use being made of the starter and electrical accessories then a regular charge from an outside source may be required.

4 Before charging the battery, remove it from the car as described in the next Section.

5 Connect the leads correctly and make sure that no sparks or naked flame are allowed near the battery during charging as the hydrogen being produced by the battery could cause an explosion.

3 Battery – removal and refitting

1 Open the bonnet and disconnect the battery negative (–) lead then the positive (+) lead in that order (photo).

3.1 Battery, showing close proximity of distributor cap on 1.3 models

4.8 Alternator adjuster link

4.9 Alternator drivebelt

2   Unscrew the nuts from the battery retaining bar and unhook the down rods and lift the components away.
3   Lift the battery carefully from its tray and mounting platform.
4   Refitting is a reversal of removal.

4   Alternator – precautions and maintenance

1   The alternator can be damaged if the following precautions are not observed.
2   Never connect the battery leads incorrectly.
3   Never run the engine with the alternator multi-plug disconnected.
4   Do not pull off a battery lead as a means of stopping the engine.
5   When charging the battery from the mains, disconnect it from the car's electrical system or remove it.
6   When using electric welding equipment on the car, always disconnect both battery leads and the alternator multi-plug.
7   Do not operate the starter motor if the engine earth lead is not connected.
8   Regularly inspect the condition of the alternator drivebelt and if frayed or cut, renew it. To do this, slacken the alternator mounting and adjuster link bolts and move the alternator as far as it will go towards the engine. Slip the belt off the pulleys. If it is tight, press the belt against the rim of a pulley while the crankshaft pulley bolt is turned. The belt will then ride up the pulley rim and come off (photo).
9   Fit the new belt using the same method (photo).
10 To tension the drivebelt, pull the alternator away from the engine as far as it will come and nip up the adjuster link bolt. At the mid-point of the longest run of the belt, it should deflect by the specified amount under finger pressure. If further tension is required, prise the alternator away from the engine using a piece of wood or the handle of a hammer. Keep the prising force applied while the adjuster link bolt is tightened.
11 Once the belt tension is correct, tighten the alternator mounting bolt.
12 Drivebelt tension should be checked and adjusted at the intervals specified in Routine Maintenance. If a new belt has been fitted, check its tension after the first few miles of operation.
13 Apart from keeping the outside of the casing clean and the connecting leads secure, no further maintenance is required to the alternator.
14 If an air conditioner is fitted, then the compressor drivebelt will have to be removed (see Chapter 2) before the alternator drivebelt can be removed.

5   Alternator – removal and refitting

1   Disconnect the battery.
2   Disconnect the leads from the rear of the alternator. On 1.6 models, release the dipstick guide tube from the camshaft cover.
3   Remove the drivebelt as described in the preceding Section.
4   Remove the alternator mounting and adjuster link bolts and remove the unit from the engine compartment (photo).
5   Refitting is a reversal of removal, tension the drivebelt as described in the preceding Section.

5.4 Alternator mounting bolt

6   Alternator – overhaul

1   Renewal of the brushes should be the limit of overhaul work to the alternator. If the unit has covered a high mileage, exchange it for a new or factory reconditioned assembly. Renewal of several internal components will prove more expensive than the price of a complete alternator.

Hitachi
2   To renew the brushes, unscrew the nuts and take off the rear cover (photos).
3   Remove the brush holder with brushes. If the brushes have worn down or nearly down to their limit (see Specifications) then the brush holder assembly must be renewed (photo).
4   While the brush holder is out, take the opportunity to clean the slip rings with a fuel-soaked rag or very fine glasspaper if they are severely discoloured.
5   Fit the brush holder and the rear cover.

Lucas
6   The brush holder/voltage regulator unit can be removed from the rear of the alternator after undoing its securing screws. Disconnect the lead as the unit is withdrawn.
7   Inspect the brushes and clean the slip rings as described in paragraphs 3 and 4.
8   If new brushes can be obtained separately, the old brushes can be unsoldered and the new ones soldered into place. Some skill with a soldering iron is required.
9   Reconnect the brush holder/voltage regulator unit and secure it with the screws.

Fig. 12.1 Exploded view of Hitachi alternator (Sec 6)

1 Terminal insulator	6 Rear housing	10 Spacer	15 Pulley
2 Rear end cover	7 Bearing housing and oil seal	11 Bearing	16 Stator
3 Brush holder	8 Insulator	12 Bearing retainer	17 Tie-bolt
4 Voltage regulator	9 Brushes	13 Bearing	18 Rotor
5 Diode assembly		14 Pulley nut	

6.2A Alternator rear cover

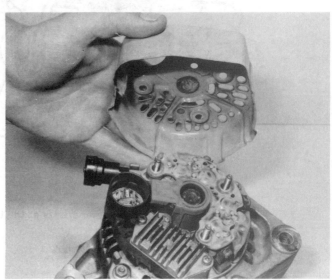

6.2B Removing alternator rear cover

6.3A Removing alternator brush holder

6.3B Alternator brush holder with brushes

Fig. 12.2 Components of the Lucas type alternator (Sec 6)

1	Suppressor	5	Rectifier	9	Rotor	13	Spacer
2	Regulator/brush box	6	Terminal parts (8.0 mm)	10	Stator	14	Bearing
3	Slip ring end bracket	7	Terminal parts (10.0 mm)	11	Tie-bolts	15	Pulley nut and spring
4	Bearing	8	Slip rings	12	Drive end bracket		washer

7.5 Starter motor solenoid terminals

7.7 Starter motor location

7 Starter motor – testing, removal and refitting

1   Failure of the starter motor to operate at all or to turn too slowly to start the engine may be due to a discharged battery or loose leads at the battery terminals.
2   Check the leads at the starter motor terminals for security.
3   Listen for the starter motor solenoid 'clicking' when the ignition key is turned to the start position. If this cannot be heard when the battery is known to be fully charged, suspect a faulty solenoid.
4   To remove the starter motor, disconnect the battery negative lead.
5   Disconnect the starter motor leads. On 1.6 automatic transmission models, disconnect the knock sensor multi-plug (photo).
6   On 1.6 manual transmission models, remove the air cleaner.
7   Unscrew the mounting bolts and withdraw the starter motor from the flywheel or torque converter (automatic transmission) housing (photo).
8   Refitting is a reversal of removal.

8 Starter motor (Hitachi) – overhaul

1   If the starter motor has given good service over a high mileage then overhaul work should be limited to the operations described in this Section. The renewal of other internal components, bearings etc. will not prove an economic proposition and it will be better to exchange the starter for a new or factory reconditioned unit.
2   Disconnect the link cable from the solenoid and then unscrew the nuts which hold the solenoid to the starter motor.
3   Prise off the dust cover from the centre of the starter motor rear cover. On some starters the dust cover is held by two screws (Fig. 12.3) (photo).
4   Remove the U-shaped lockplate, coil spring and washer. Some versions have an E-clip and washer (photos).
5   Unscrew the tie-bolts.
6   Withdraw the end cover and drivegear end bracket from the field coil housing (photo).
7   Inspect the brushes in the brush holder. If the brushes have worn down to or nearly down to their wear limit (see Specifications), then they must be renewed by unsoldering the old ones and soldering on the new. When using the soldering iron on the field coil brushes, use a pair of pliers as a heat sink as shown, to prevent damage to the field

coils. Do not allow solder to run down the brush leads or their flexibility will be ruined (photo).
8   Inspect the commutator, if discoloured clean it with a petrol moistened cloth or if very dirty use very fine glasspaper.
9   Check that the mica separators of the commutator are undercut to the correct depth. If not, use a thin hacksaw blade keeping the corners of the undercut square.
10 A worn or faulty pinion/clutch assembly may be renewed by tapping the stop collar up the armature shaft to expose the jump ring. Remove the ring and slide the pinion assembly off the shaft.
11 Use a new jump ring when refitting. The collar can be drawn down over the jump ring using a small two-legged puller.
12 Reassembly is a reversal of dismantling. Apply a smear of molybdenum disulphide grease to the bearings and friction surfaces.
13 Check that the brushes slide freely in their guides and use a hooked piece of wire to lift them onto the commutator as the holder is located (photo).
14 When the starter is fully reassembled, slide the drive pinion along the armature shaft and using a feeler gauge, check the clearance between the end of the pinion and its stop. This should be between 0.1 and 4.0 mm (0.004 and 0.157 in). If the clearance is outside this tolerance, change the stop for one of different thickness.

9 Starter motor (Lucas) – overhaul

1   Refer to paragraph 1 of the preceding Section.
2   With the starter motor removed from the car, clean away external dirt.
3   Disconnect the lead from the solenoid STA terminal.
4   Extract the two solenoid securing screws, withdraw the solenoid and disconnect the solenoid plunger from the engagement lever.
5   Refer to Fig. 12.4 and remove the end cap and spare washer. The latter will be destroyed and must be renewed.
6   Mark the relationship of the field coil yoke to the drive end bracket by scribing a line across the joint.
7   Unscrew the two tie-bolts and withdraw the end bracket to expose the brushes. Release the field brushes from the brush box and remove the end bracket.
8   Renew the brushes and the drive assembly if necessary as described in the preceding Section.
9   The face type commutator may be cleaned with very fine glasspaper, but do not attempt to undercut its mica segments.

8.3 Removing starter motor dust cover

8.4A Removing starter motor E-clip

8.4B Starter motor thrust washer

8.6 Removing starter motor end cover

8.7 Soldering a starter motor field brush

8.13 Releasing a brush spring

Fig. 12.3 Exploded view of Hitachi starter motor (Sec 8)

1 End cap	10 Nut	19 Screw
2 Bearing	11 Washer	20 End cap
3 Drivegear end bracket	12 Nut	21 U-shaped lockplate
4 Mounting nut	13 Spring washer	22 Coil spring
5 Jump ring	14 Solenoid	23 Washer
6 Stop collar	15 Cover	24 End cover
7 Pinion/clutch	16 Engagement lever	25 Bearing
8 Armature	17 Tie-bolt	26 Brush holder plate
9 Cover	18 Clip	27 Field coils and yoke

Fig. 12.4 Exploded view of Lucas starter motor (Sec 9)

1	Bracket screws	7	Thrust collar	12	Field coils and yoke	19	Drive end bracket (automatic transmission)
2	Drive end bracket (manual transmission)	8	Drive/clutch assembly (manual transmission)	13	Field brush	20	Drivegear/clutch (automatic transmission)
3	Bush	9	Engagement lever (manual transmission)	14	Commutator end bracket	21	Engagement lever (automatic transmission)
4	Cap	10	Armature	15	Tie-bolt	22	Bush
5	Solenoid	11	Thrust washer	16	Bush		
6	Jump ring			17	Spire washer		
				18	End cap		

Fig. 12.5 Lucas starter motor pinion setting diagram (Sec 9)

1 Solenoid pressed fully in
2 Adjuster screw
3 Pinion pressed fully in
A Pinion setting dimension

Manual transmission 44.1 to 44.6 mm (1.746 to 1.754 in)
Automatic transmission 21.0 to 21.2 mm (0.826 to 0.834 in)

10 Once the starter motor has been reassembled insert a spacer to set the pinion to dimension A Fig. 12.5 Press the solenoid plunger fully into the body and then use a spring balance to check the force being exerted on the temporary spacer by the drive pinion. This should be between 13 and 17 lb. Adjust the screw if necessary using an Allen key to obtain the specified force.
11 Lock the adjuster screw with a suitable sealant on completion.

10 Fuses and relays

1 Three main fusible links are located in the engine compartment. Should one of these blow at any time, do not renew it until the charging circuit has been checked and tested by your dealer or an auto electrical engineer (photo).
2 The fuses which protect all the other electrical circuits in the car are located in the fusebox under the facia panel (photos).
3 The fuse ratings and circuits protected are given in the Specifications Section at the beginning of this Chapter.
4 If a fuse blows, renew it with one of identical rating. Never substitute anything for the correct type of fuse. If the new fuse blows immediately, check and rectify the problem, usually shorting of a wire due to chafed insulation.

10.1 Fusible links

10.2A Fuse cover and diagram

10.2B Fuse block
1 Wiper intermittent relay
2 Direction indicator/hazard warning relay

5 Relays for the intermittent windscreen wiper and direction indicator/hazard warning systems are plugged into the fuse block. Other relays are located in the engine compartment or beside the front footwells and include those for the following circuits:

Heated rear window
Power-operated windows
Headlamp washers
Air conditioning
Inlet manifold heater and fuel pump (1.6 models)

6 A trailer flasher relay may be found suspended under the instrument panel to the right of the steering column (photo).
7 The location of most relays is indicated in the wiring harness layouts at the end of this Chapter.

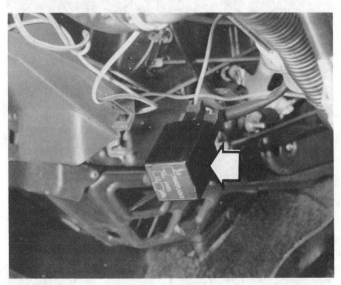

10.6 Trailer flasher relay

11 Switches – removal and refitting

Steering column switch

1 Disconnect the battery negative lead.
2 Remove the steering wheel and the steering column shrouds as described in Chapter 10.
3 Disconnect the switch wiring multi-plugs.
4 Pull the direction indicator cancelling sleeve from the steering shaft.
5 Extract the two screws which hold the switch to its bracket and remove the switch.
6 When refitting, make sure that the cancelling sleeve is pushed fully home.
7 When fitting the steering wheel, check that the lugs engage correctly with the cut-outs in the cancelling cam before tightening the securing nut to the specified torque.

Heated rear window switch

8 Disconnect the battery negative lead.
9 Carefully prise the switch from the facia panel. Disconnect the multi-plug from the switch.
10 Refitting is a reversal of removal.

Rear fog warning lamp switch

11 The operations are as described for the heated rear window switch.

Central door lock switch

12 Have the driver's door window fully raised and disconnect the battery.

13 Remove the door trim panel and waterproof sheet as described in Chapter 11.
14 Disconnect the switch wiring multi-plug.
15 Extract the fixing screws and remove the switch from the door.
16 Refitting is a reversal of removal, but make sure that the switch operating arm is correctly engaged with the peg on the door lock.

Power-operated window switch

17 Disconnect the battery and then remove the door trim panel as described in Chapter 11.
18 Disconnect the wiring plug and extract the screws which hold the switch to the trim panel.
19 Refitting is a reversal of removal.

Instrument panel lamp dimmer switch (rheostat)

20 Disconnect the battery and remove the facia panel access under cover.
21 Reach up behind the switch and disconnect the multi-plug.
22 Prise off the switch knob and remove the plain washer.
23 Unscrew the bezel nut and remove the switch from the facia panel.
24 Refitting is a reversal of removal.

Ignition switch

25 This is described in Chapter 4.

Heater blower switch

26 This is described in Chapter 2.

Courtesy lamp switch

27 These are of sliding type and control the interior lamp (photo).
28 Extract the screw which holds the switch to the body pillar, withdraw the switch and disconnect the leads.
29 Tape the leads to the body to prevent them from slipping into the pillar interior.
30 When refitting the switch, smear the contacts with petroleum jelly to prevent corrosion.

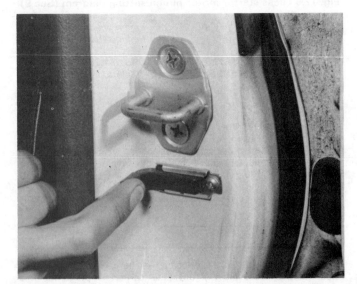

11.27 Courtesy lamp switch

Glovebox lamp switch

31 Access is obtained by removing the glovebox. Disconnect the wiring plugs and pull the switch from its mounting bracket while holding the retaining tags squeezed inwards (photo).

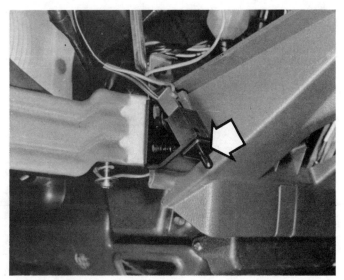

11.31 Glovebox lamp switch

12 Exterior bulbs – renewal

Headlamp

1 Open the bonnet.
2 Rotate the cover on the back of the headlamp in an anti-clockwise direction and withdraw it until the connector plug can be pulled from the bulb spade terminals (photos).
3 Prise back the spring clips and remove the bulb (photos).
4 Fit the new bulb, avoiding touching the glass with the fingers. If it is inadvertently touched, clean it with methylated spirit.
5 When fitting the rear cover, make sure that the drain hole is at the bottom.

Front parking lamp

6 This bulb is a push fit in the headlamp reflector. Access to it is as described for the headlamp bulb.

Front direction indicator lamp

7 Extract the lens fixing screws and pull the lens gently from the car (photo).
8 Twist the bulbholder to remove and then take out the bulb which is of bayonet fitting type (photo).

12.2A Headlamp rear cover

12.2B Headlamp rear cover removed

12.2C Headlamp wiring plug

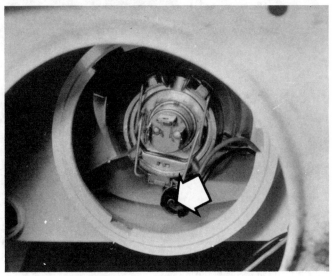

12.3A Front parking lamp bulb

12.3B Headlamp halogen type bulb

12.7 Removing front direction indicator lamp lens screw

12.8 Front indicator bulb and holder

Rear lamp bulbs

9   Working inside the luggage boot, turn the quick release retainers through half a turn and remove the cover plate (photo).
10   Remove the bayonet fitting type bulb noting that the twin filament stop/tail bulb has offset pins and it will only fit in its holder in one position (photo).

Rear number plate lamp

11   Press the lamp in the forward direction and remove it from the bumper.
12   Twist the bulbholder in an anti-clockwise direction to release it from the lamp body (photo).
13   The bulb is of wedge base type and is simply pulled from its holder.

Reverse and rear fog warning lamps

14   Access to the bulbs is obtained by extracting the screws and taking off the lens. The bulb is of bayonet fitting type (photos).

12.9 Rear lamp cluster cover plate

12.10 Rear lamp bulbs
1   *Direction indicator*   3   *Stop/tail*
2   *Stop/tail*

12.12 Rear number plate lamp and bulb

12.14A Rear fog guard lamp lens

12.14B Rear fog guard lamp bulb

13 Interior bulbs – renewal

Interior lamp

1 Prise the lens carefully from the lamp (photo).
2 Pull the festoon type bulb from its contacts and push the new one into place.
3 Refit the lens.

13.1 Interior lamp lens

Fig. 12.6 Push-button switch and bulb (Sec 13)

Fig. 12.7 Ashtray lamp bulb (Sec 13)

Switch illuminating lamps

4 Reach up behind the heated rear window or rear fog warning switch and push it from the facia panel.
5 Pull off the wiring plug and then turn the bulbholder in an anti-clockwise direction to remove it.
6 Renew the bulb, refit the holder and the switch.

Ashtray lamp

7 Remove the ashtray.
8 Extract the screws from the ashtray carrier and lower the carrier.
9 Twist the bulbholder in an anti-clockwise direction and renew the wedge type bulb.

Cigar lighter lamp

10 Withdraw the lighter element.
11 Remove the ashtray and lower the ashtray carrier.

12 Slacken the locking ring and rotate the lighter unit until the hood can be squeezed and released from the unit.
13 Remove the bulbholder from the hood.
14 Renew the bulb which is of bayonet fitting type.

Warning and instrument panel lamps

15 The instrument panel must be released and pulled forward for access to these lamps. Refer to Section 17. Some upper bulbs are accessible after removal of the hood from the instrument panel (see Section 17) (photos).

Fig. 12.8 Cigar lighter lamp bulb (Sec 13)

13.14A Instrument panel bulb renewable after instrument panel withdrawn

13.14B Instrument panel bulb renewable without removing instrument panel

13.14C Instrument panel bulb renewable without removing instrument panel

Glove compartment lamp
16 Open the glove compartment and prise out the lens (photo).

14 Headlamp lens – removal and refitting

1   In the event of damage to the headlamp lens, only a complete headlamp assembly is obtainable from Rover dealers or Lucas electrical factors. If a secondhand lens can be obtained, it can be fitted after releasing the spring clips, removing the old lens and clipping the new lens into place (photo).

15 Headlamp – removal and refitting

1   Refer to Chapter 11 and remove the radiator grille and the front bumper.
2   Remove the front parking lamp lens.
3   Disengage the wiring multi-plug.
4   Extract the two lower and two upper headlamp fixing screws. Remove the unit (photo).
5   Refitting is a reversal of removal. Check the headlamp beam alignment.

13.15 Luggage boot lamp

14.1 Headlamp lens clip

15.4 Extracting a headlamp upper fixing screw

16 Headlamp beam alignment

1   It is recommended that this is carried out by a service station having the necessary optical beam setting equipment.
2   In an emergency, the adjustment screws shown in the photograph may be turned to give an acceptable light pattern (photo).
3   Holts Amber Lamp is useful for temporarily changing the headlight colour to conform with the normal usage on Continental Europe.

17 Instrument panel – removal and refitting

1   Prise out the blanking plates which cover the hood securing screws. These are brittle so exercise care (photos).
2   Extract the screws now exposed and remove the hood.
3   Disconnect the battery.
4   Reach behind the instrument panel, press the arm of the speedometer cable retaining clip and disconnect the cable from the speedometer head.

Fig. 12.9 Headlamp unit (Sec 14)

1   Wiring connector plug
2   Headlamp lower fixing screws
3   Upper fixing screws
4   Beam alignment screw (vertical)
5   Beam alignment screw (horizontal)

16.2 Headlamp beam alignment screws (arrowed)

Fig. 12.10 Instrument panel hood (Sec 17)

1 Hood	4 Blanking plate
2 Blanking plate	5 Screw
3 Screw	

17.1A Instrument panel hood front screw blanking plate

17.1B Instrument panel hood screw

17.1C Instrument panel hood screw blanking plate

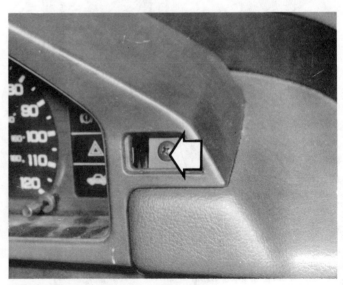

17.1D Instrument panel hood screw

Fig. 12.11 Components of the instrument panel (Sec 17)

1 Bulb	8 Speedometer	14 Lens and frame
2 Bulbholder	9 Blanking panel	15 Instrument illumination
3 Bulb	10 Grommet	lens
4 Bulbholder	11 Speedometer odometer reset	16 Illumination circuit board
5 Printed circuit	knob	17 Lens cover
6 Instrument panel	12 Tachometer	18 Fixing screw
7 Fuel gauge	13 Coolant temperature gauge	

5   Extract the instrument panel fixing screws (photo).
6   Raise the instrument panel until the wiring multi-plugs can be disconnected (photo).
7   Remove the panel (photos).
8   The instrument panel may be dismantled in the following way.
9   Prise the trip reset knob from its spindle.
10 Release the plastic clips and separate the panel and lens.
11 Unscrew the nuts or screws and remove the instruments as necessary. Handle the printed circuit with care using clean hands.
12 Refitting is a reversal of removal.

18 Speedometer drive cable – renewal

1   Disconnect the battery.
2   Remove the instrument panel hood as described in the preceding Section.
3   Reach behind the instrument panel and disconnect the cable from the speedometer head (photo).
4   Working under the facia panel, remove the access under cover panel and release the speedometer cable grommet and boot from the bulkhead.

17.5 Instrument panel fixing screw (hood removed)

17.6 Instrument panel multi-plug

17.7A Instrument panel removed

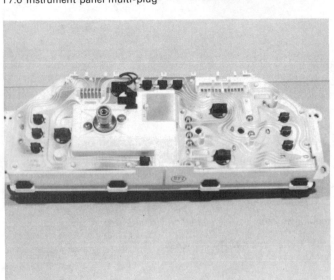

17.7B Rear view of instrument panel

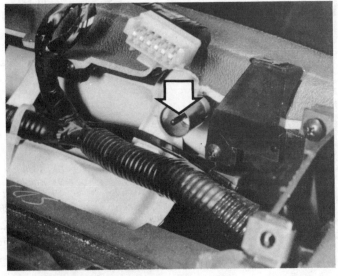

18.3 Speedometer cable connector at head

5 Feed the speedometer cable through the bulkhead into the engine compartment.
6 Working at the transmission, pull the boot up the cable and extract the spring clip which retains the cable. On no account remove the bolt or lockplate or the pinion might drop into the transmission (photo).
7 Fit the new cable by reversing the removal operations.

19 Clock – removal and refitting

1 Disconnect the battery.
2 Using a small screwdriver, carefully prise the clock from the facia panel until the wiring harness can be disconnected.
3 Refit the clock by reversing the removal operations.
4 The clock normally only displays when the ignition is on, but if the ignition is off, it will display if the button cover panel is pressed in (photo).
5 To set the clock depress the centre MIN button until the minutes are correct.
6 Depress the left-hand HOUR button until the hour is correct.
7 If it is wished to synchronise the clock with a radio time signal or another clock, set the car clock to within a few minutes before the hour. As the time signal is heard, depress the reset button on the car clock.

20 Windscreen wiper blades and arms – removal and refitting

1 The wiper blades should be renewed as soon as they cease to clean the glass without leaving streaks.
2 Lift the wiper arm from the screen until it locks.
3 Turn the blade through 90°, depress the retaining tab with the thumb nail and slide the blade down the arm until it can be withdrawn over the hook of the arm (photo).
4 Refit the new blade, pushing it fully into the hook until it locks.
5 To remove a wiper arm, have the arm in the parked position. Run some masking tape along the edge of the blades on the glass as a guide to refitting the arms.
6 Unscrew the domed nut and remove the wiper arm from the splined spindle (photo).
7 Refit by reversing the removal procedure.

21 Windscreen wiper motor and linkage – removal and refitting

1 Remove the wiper arms as described in the preceding Section.
2 Open the bonnet and pull off the rubber weatherstrip from the front

18.6 Speedometer cable connecting clip at transmission

19.4 Pressing clock setting button cover panel

20.3 Wiper blade to arm connection

20.6 Unscrewing wiper arm nut

Fig. 12.12 Windscreen wiper components (Sec 21)

1	Fixing screw	9	Shield	16	Link rod	23	Wiper motor
2	Air intake grille	10	Bolt	17	Dust seal	24	Motor mounting bolt
3	Cover	11	Spindle housing	18	Crank arm	25	Spring clip
4	Screw	12	Splined spindle	19	Nut	26	Cover
5	Weatherseal	13	Washer	20	Spring washer	27	Mounting cushion
6	Domed nut	14	Circlip	21	Spacer	28	Ferrule
7	Wiper arm	15	Connecting rod	22	Shield	29	Air scoop
8	Spindle seal						

Fig. 12.13 Wiper motor terminals (Sec 21)

1 Green/black
2 Blue/white
3 Black

4 Blue
5 Blue/yellow

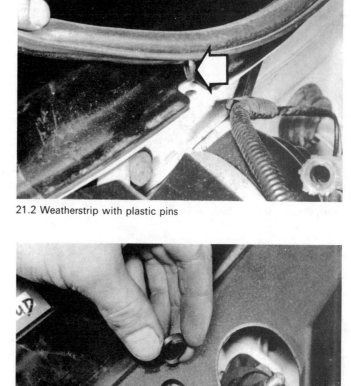

21.2 Weatherstrip with plastic pins

21.3 Scuttle plate screw cover plate

edge. The weatherstrip incorporates plastic pins which serve to hold the front edge of the scuttle plastic cover (air scoop) (photo).

3 Prise out the circular plastic blanking plates just below the windscreen and extract the exposed screws (photo).

4 Remove the scuttle plastic cover (air scoop) (photos).

5 Disconnect the wiper motor multi-plug (photos).

21.4A Scuttle grille

21.4B Removing scuttle air scoop

21.6A Wiper motor crankarm and link

21.6B Wiper motor cover

6   Prise the crank arm to link rod balljoint apart. Remove the wiper motor cover (photos).
7   Unbolt and remove the wiper motor.
8   Remove the wheelbox fixing bolts and withdraw the complete wiper linkage.
9   Refitting is a reversal of removal.

22 Washer system

1   Depending upon the car model, a windscreen washer system may be fitted only, or a combined windscreen and headlamp washer system.

Fig. 12.14 Combined windscreen and headlamp
washer fluid reservoir (Sec 22)

1	Reservoir	3	Headlamp washer pump
2	Fixing screw	4	Windscreen washer pump

2 The reservoir capacity differs between the two systems and two independent electric pumps are used where a windscreen and headlamp washer are fitted.

3 The pumps are detachable from the reservoirs after disconnecting the wiring plugs and tubes. When removing a tube from a pump or jet nozzle, warm the tube with a rag soaked in boiling water otherwise the nozzle may fracture.

4 The jets may be adjusted by inserting a pin into the nozzles.

5 Do not use household detergent or cooling system antifreeze in the washer reservoir or the pumps and car paintwork will be damaged.

6 In very cold weather, a little methylated spirit may be added to the reservoir in addition to the normal mixture of water and screen cleaning fluid.

23 Heated rear screen

1 To prevent damage to the elements of the heated rear window, observe the following precautions:

 (a) *Clean the interior surface of the glass with a damp cloth or chamois leather, rubbing in the direction that the elements run*

 (b) *Avoid scratching the elements with rings on the fingers or contact with articles in the luggage compartment*

 (c) *Do not stick adhesive labels over the elements*

2 Should the element be broken, it can be repaired using a conductive silver paint, without the need to remove the glass from the window.

3 The paint is available from many sources and should be applied with a soft brush to a really clean surface. Use two strips of masking tape as a guide to the thickness of the element to be repaired.

4 Allow the new paint to dry thoroughly before switching the heater on.

24 Radio/cassette player – removal and refitting

1 All models are supplied with a windscreen pillar aerial and either a radio or radio/cassette player depending upon the particular vehicle specifications.

2 The leads and connecting plugs at the back of the radio are accessible on certain models without having to remove the receiver if the facia panel under cover is removed and the hand inserted round behind the radio.

3 To remove the radio/cassette player, carry out the following operations.

Standard fitting

4 Disconnect the battery negative lead.

5 On 1.3 models, remove the choke control knob. Undo the retaining nut and release the choke control.

6 On all models, prise the knobs off the heater controls, then prise the heater control plate out of the facia. Move the plate aside without disconnecting the leads from it.

7 Carefully pull off the radio knobs and bezels. Remove the two nuts now exposed and lift off the finisher plate.

8 Open the glovebox to gain access to the rear of the radio. Push the front of the radio into the facia and remove the mounting plate, then pull it outwards and disconnect the aerial plug and multi-plug from it.

9 Refit by reversing the removal operations.

DIN fitting

10 Two DIN removal tools will be needed. These should have been supplied with the radio; if not, they can be obtained from car audio specialists.

11 Insert the removal tools into the holes in the radio face plate (photo).

12 Pull the tools away from each other and into the vehicle to release the radio from its mountings. Draw it from its recess and disconnect the wiring from it.

13 When refitting, connect the wiring, then push the radio home until it clicks into place. Recover the removal tools.

24.11 Using DIN tools to remove radio/cassette unit

25 Aerial – removal and refitting

1 Remove the facia undercover from the side on which the aerial is located.

2 Extract the screws from the aerial mounting base at the top of the windscreen pillar (photo).

3 Reach behind the radio and disconnect the aerial lead.

4 Withdraw the aerial and lead upwards out of the pillar. A length of cord should be securely taped to the end of the aerial lead so that it can be drawn through the pillar and used to guide the new aerial lead through the pillar cavity.

5 If a new aerial is fitted, always adjust the aerial trim. This is done by tuning in to a station with low signal strength on the medium wave band. Using a small screwdriver turn the trim screw provided in the radio in or our until the loudest volume is obtained.

25.2 Extracting aerial mounting base screw

26 Electrically-operated windows

1 The system is controlled by a master switch on the driver's door and individual switches on the other doors.

2 The electric motor and regulator mechanism are accessible once the door trim panel has been removed as described in Chapter 11.

**Fig. 12.15 Front door power-operated window mechanism
(Sec 26)**

1   *Glass lifting pads*   3   *Electric motor*
2   *Regulator unit*

3   Always disconnect the battery before working on the components.
A fault in the lift motor should be rectified by renewing the motor.

27 Central door locking

1   The master switch which operates all door locks is controlled from
the driver's door lock or lock plunger.
2   The lock plunger on the other doors, if lifted, will unlock only the
relevant door.
3   Always disconnect the battery before removing any part of the
system.
4   To remove the central locking control unit, slide the driver's seat

**Fig. 12.16 Rear door power-operated window mechanism
(Sec 26)**

1   *Regulator*   2   *Electric motor*

fully to the rear. Unbolt the control unit mounting plate, disconnect the
wiring multi-plug and unclip the control unit from the plate. Where
more than one control unit is fitted, the central locking unit is on the
left-hand side of the mounting plate.
5   Removal and refitting procedures for the door lock motors will be
found in the Supplement at the end of this manual.

28 Horns

1   The horns are located below the headlamps within the bumper.
2   Although the horns normally require no attention, if they must be
removed then the headlamps and front bumper must be removed
(Section 15). See also Chapter 11.
3   Apply silicone grease to the horn terminals when refitting to
prevent corrosion.

29 Fault diagnosis – electrical system

Symptom	Reason(s)
Alternator not charging*	Drivebelt loose and slipping, or broken Brushes worn, sticking, broken or dirty Brush springs weak or broken

If all appears to be well but the alternator is still not charging, take the car to an automobile electrician for checking of the alternator

Battery will not hold charge for more than a few days	Battery defective internally Electrolyte level too low or electrolyte too weak due to leakage Plate separators no longer fully effective Battery plates severely sulphated Drivebelt slipping Battery terminal connections loose or corroded Alternator not charging properly Short in lighting circuit causing continual battery drain
Ignition light fails to go out, battery runs flat in a few days	Drivebelt loose and slipping, or broken Alternator faulty

Symptom	Reason(s)

Failure of individual electrical equipment to function correctly is dealt with below

Symptom	Reason(s)
Fuel gauge gives no reading	Fuel tank empty! Electric cable between tank sender unit and gauge earthed or loose Fuel gauge case not earthed Fuel gauge supply cable interrupted Fuel gauge unit broken
Fuel gauge registers full all the time	Electric cable between tank unit and gauge broken or disconnected
Horn operates all the time	Horn push either earthed or stuck down Horn cable to horn push earthed
Horn fails to operate	Blown fuse Cable or cable connections loose, broken or disconnected Horn has an internal fault
Horn emits intermittent or unsatisfactory noise	Cable connections loose Horn incorrectly adjusted
Lights do not come on	If engine not running, battery discharged Light bulb filament burnt out or bulbs broken Wire connections loose, disconnected or broken Light switch shorting or otherwise faulty
Lights come on but fade out	If engine not running, battery discharged
Lights give very poor illumination	Lamp glasses dirty Reflector tarnished or dirty Lamps badly out of adjustment Incorrect bulb with too low wattage fitted Existing bulbs old and badly discoloured Electric wiring too thin not allowing full current to pass
Lights work erratically, flashing on and off, especially over bumps	Battery terminals or earth connections loose Lights not earthing properly Contacts in light switch faulty
Wiper motor fails to work	Blown fuse Wire connections loose, disconnected or broken Brushes badly worn Armature worn or faulty
Wiper motor works very slowly and takes excessive current	Commutator dirty, greasy or burnt Drive to spindles bent or unlubricated Drive spindle binding or damaged Armature bearings dry or unaligned Armature badly worn or faulty
Wiper motor works slowly and takes little current	Brushes badly worn Commutator dirty, greasy or burnt Armature badly worn or faulty
Wiper motor works but wiper blades remain static	Linkage disengaged or faulty Drive spindle damaged or worn Wiper motor gearbox parts badly worn

Key to Fig. 12.17

No.	Description	Grid reference
1	Alternator	A1
3	Battery	A1
4	Starter motor solenoid	A1
5	Starter motor	A1
6	Lighting switch	B2
7	Headlamp dip/flash switch	B2
8	Dip headlamp	B1
9	Main headlamp	B1
10	Main beam warning lamp	B1
11	RH parking lamp	C1
12	LH parking lamp	C1
14	Panel illumination lamps	C2
15	Number plate illumination lamps	C1
16	Stop lamps	C1
17	RH rear lamp	C1
18	Stop lamp switch	C2
19a	Fuse No. 1 – 10 amp	B2
19b	Fuse No. 2 – 15 amp	A3
19c	Fuse No. 3 – 10 amp	A3
19d	Fuse No. 4 – 10 amp	A2
19e	Fuse No. 5 – 10 amp	B2
19f	Fuse No. 6 – 10 amp	B2
19g	Fuse No. 7 – 10 amp	B2
19h	Fuse No. 8 – 10 amp	B2
19j	Fuse No. 9 – 15 amp	A3
19k	Fuse No. 10 – 10 amp	A3
19l	Fuse No. 11 – 10 amp	A3
19m	Fuse No. 12 – 15 amp	A2
19n	Fuse No. 13 – 15 amp	A2
19p	Fuse No. 14 – 20 amp	A2
19r	Fuse No. 15 – 10 amp	A3
19s	Fuse No. 16 – 15 amp	A2
19t	Fuse No. 17 – 20 amp	A3
19u	Fuse No. 18 – 15 amp	A2
20	Interior lamp	B3
21	Interior lamp switches	B4/C4
22	LH rear lamp	C1
23	Horn	B3
24	Horn switch	B2
26	Direction indicator switch	C3
27	Direction indicator warning lamps	C1
28	RH front direction indicator lamp	C1
29	LH front direction indicator lamp	C1
30	RH rear direction indicator lamp	C1
31	LH rear direction indicator lamp	C1
32	Heater/recirculation blower motor switch	B2
33	Heater/recirculation blower motor	A2
34	Fuel gauge	B4
35	Fuel tank gauge unit	B4
37	Windscreen wiper motor	A4
38	Ignition switch	A2
39	Ignition coil	A1
40	Distributor	A1
42	Oil pressure switch	B4
43	Oil pressure warning lamp	B4
44	Ignition/no charge warning lamp	A2
46	Coolant temperature gauge	B4
47	Coolant temperature sender unit	B4

No.	Description	Grid reference
49	Reversing lamp switch	C2
50	Reverse lamp	C1
56	Clock	C3
57	Cigar lighter	B4
65	Luggage compartment lamp switch	B4
66	Luggage compartment lamp	B4
75	Automatic gearbox inhibitor switch	A1
76	Automatic selector illumination	C2
77	Windscreen washer motor	A3
81	Ashtray illumination lamp	C2
95	Tachometer	B3
110	Direction indicator repeater lamps, if fitted	C1
115	Heated rear window switch	A3
116	Heated rear window	B3
152	Hazard warning lamp	C3
153	Hazard warning lamp switch	C3
165	Handbrake warning lamp switch	B4
178	Radiator cooling fan thermostat	B2
179	Radiator cooling fan motor	A2
182	Brake fluid level switch	B4
208	Cigar lighter illumination	C1
211	Heater control illumination	C2
212	Choke warning lamp switch	B4
213	Choke warning lamp	B4
240	Heated rear window relay	A3
243	Fuel cut-off solenoid	A1
246	Glovebox lamp	B4
247	Glovebox lamp switch	B4
267	Headlamp washer motor	B3
286	Rear fog guard lamp switch	B2
287	Rear fog guard warning lamp	B2
288	Rear fog guard warning lamp	B1
297	Brake warning lamp	B4
298	Windscreen wiper delay unit	A4
308	Direction indicator/hazard warning flasher unit	C3
313	Headlamp washer relay	A3
326	Brake pad wear sensor	B4
402	Windscreen washer/wiper switch	A4
413a	Fusible link – 55 amp	A1
413b	Fusible link – 45 amp	A1
417	Luggage compartment warning lamp	B4
418	Lighting switch alarm	C4

Connections to supplementary circuit diagrams

No.	Description	Grid reference
1	Radio cassette player	A3
2	Air conditioning	A2
3	Air conditioning	A2
4	Air conditioning	A1
5	Air conditioning	A2
6	Air conditioning	B2
7	Radio cassette player	B3
17	Electric windows	A3
18	Electric windows	A4
19	Central locking	A2
20	Panel illumination dimmer	C2
21	Automatic selector illumination	C2

Symbols used in wiring diagrams

1 Component earthed by its lead
2 Component earthed by its fixing
3 If fitted
4 Printed circuit
5 Line connector
6 Sealed joint

Cable colour code

B	=	Black	O	= Orange
BR	=	Brown	P	= Purple
G	=	Green	R	= Red
GR	=	Grey	SB	= Sky Blue
K	=	Pink	W	= White
L	=	Blue	Y	= Yellow
LG	=	Light Green		

When two colour code letters are shown on a wire the first denotes the main colour and the second denotes the tracer colour.

Fig. 12.17 Wiring diagram – 1.3 models

Fig. 12.17 Wiring diagram – 1.3 models (continued)

Fig. 12.18 Wiring diagram – 1.6 models

Fig. 12.18 Wiring diagram – 1.6 models (continued)

No.	Description	Grid reference	No.	Description	Grid reference
1	Alternator	A1	65	Luggage compartment lamp switch	B4
3	Battery	A1	66	Luggage compartment lamp	B4
4	Starter motor solenoid	A1	75	Automatic inhibitor switch	A1
5	Starter motor	A1	76	Automatic gearbox selection indicator lamp	C2
6	Lighting switch	B2	77	Windscreen washer motor	A3
7	Headlamp dip switch	B2	81	Ashtray illumination lamp	C2
8	Dip headlamp	B1	95	Tachometer	B3
9	Main headlamp	B1	115	Heated rear window switch	A3
10	Main beam warning lamp	B1	116	Heated rear window	B3
11	RH parking lamp	C1	118	Combined windscreen washer/wiper switch	A4
12	LH parking lamp	C1	150	Heated rear screen warning lamp	A3
14	Panel illumination lamps	C2	152	Hazard warning lamp	C3
15	Number plate illumination lamps	C1	153	Hazard warning lamp switch	C3
16	Stop lamps	C1	165	Handbrake warning lamp switch	B4
17	RH rear lamp	C1	174	Starter solenoid relay	A1
18	Stop lamp switch	C2	178	Radiator cooling fan thermostat	B2
19a	Fuse No. 1 – 10 amp	B2	179	Radiator cooling fan motor	A2
19b	Fuse No. 2 – 15 amp	A3	182	Brake fluid level switch	B4
19c	Fuse No. 3 – 10 amp	A3	208	Cigar lighter illumination	C1
19d	Fuse No. 4 – 10 amp	A2	211	Heater control illumination	C2
19e	Fuse No. 5 – 10 amp	B2	240	Heated rear window relay	A3
19f	Fuse No. 6 – 10 amp	B2	246	Glovebox lamp	B4
19g	Fuse No. 7 – 10 amp	B2	247	Glovebox lamp switch	B4
19h	Fuse No. 8 – 10 amp	B2	267	Headlamp washer pump motor	B3
19j	Fuse No. 9 – 15 amp	A3	286	Rear fog guard lamp switch	B2
19k	Fuse No. 10 – 10 amp	A3	287	Rear fog guard warning lamp	B2
19l	Fuse No. 11 – 15 amp	A3	288	Rear fog guard lamp	B1
19m	Fuse No. 12 – 15 amp	A2	297	Brake warning lamp	B4
19n	Fuse No. 13 – 15 amp	A2	298	Windscreen wiper delay unit	A4
19p	Fuse No. 14 – 20 amp	A2	308	Direction indicator/hazard warning flasher unit	C3
19r	Fuse No. 15 – 10 amp	A4	313	Headlamp washer control relay	A3
19s	Fuse No. 16 – 15 amp	A2	326	Brake pad wear sensor	B4
19t	Fuse No. 17 – 15 amp	A2	381	Knock sensor	A1
19u	Fuse No. 18 – 20 amp	A3	382	Crankshaft sensor	A1
20	Interior lamp	B3	393	Programmed ignition ECU	A1
21	Interior lamp switches	C4	413	Fusible links	A1
22	LH rear lamp	C1	417	Luggage compartment warning lamp	B4
23	Horn	B3	418	Lighting switch alarm	C4
24	Horn switch	B2			
26	Direction indicator switch	C3			
27	Direction indicator warning lamps	C1		**Connections to supplementary circuit**	
28	RH front direction indicator lamp	C1	1	Radio cassette player	A4
29	LH front direction indicator lamp	C1	2	Air conditioning	A2
30	RH rear direction indicator lamp	C1	3	Air conditioning	A2
31	LH rear direction indicator lamp	C1	4	Air conditioning, fuel injection or carburettor	A1
32	Heater/recirculation blower motor switch	B2	5	Air conditioning	A2
33	Heater/recirculation blower motor	A2	6	Air conditioning	B2
34	Fuel gauge	B4	7	Radio cassette player	B3
35	Fuel tank gauge unit	B4	8	Fuel injection or carburettor	B4
37	Windscreen wiper motor	A4	9	Fuel injection or carburettor	A2
38	Ignition switch	A2	10	Fuel injection	A1
39	Ignition coil	A2	11	Fuel injection or carburettor	A1
42	Oil pressure switch	B4	12	Fuel injection	A1
43	Oil pressure warning lamp	B4	13	Fuel injection or carburettor	A2
44	Ignition/no charge warning lamp	A2	14	Fuel injection	A1
45	Headlamp flash switch	B2	15	Carburettor	A2
46	Coolant temperature gauge	B4	17	Electric windows	A4
49	Reversing lamp switch	C2	18	Electric windows	A4
50	Reverse lamp	C1	19	Central locking	A1
56	Clock	C3	20	Panel illumination dimmer	C2
57	Cigar lighter	B4	21	Panel illumination dimmer	C2

Symbols used in wiring diagrams

1 Component earthed by its lead
2 Component earthed by its fixing
3 If fitted
4 Printed circuit
5 Line connector
6 Sealed joint

Cable colour code

B = Black   O = Orange
BR = Brown   P = Purple
G = Green   R = Red
GR = Grey   SB = Sky Blue
K = Pink   W = White
L = Blue   Y = Yellow
LG = Light Green

When two colour code letters are shown on a wire the first denotes the main colour and the second denotes the tracer colour.

Fig. 12.19 Wiring diagram – power operated windows

19v	Fuse No. 19 – 15 amp	215	Driver's door master control	219	LH rear window lift switch
19w	Fuse No. 20 – 15 amp		unit and switch	220	Window lift motors
19x	Fuse No. 21 – 15 amp	217	RH rear window lift switch	222	Window lift control unit
19y	Fuse No. 22 – 15 amp	218	LH front window lift switch	364	Window power wind relay

Connections to main wiring diagram – 17, 18

Symbols used in wiring diagrams

1 Component earthed by its lead
2 Component earthed by its fixing
3 If fitted
4 Printed circuit
5 Line connector
6 Sealed joint

Cable colour code

B	= Black	O	= Orange
BR	= Brown	P	= Purple
G	= Green	R	= Red
GR	= Grey	SB	= Sky Blue
K	= Pink	W	= White
L	= Blue	Y	= Yellow
LG	= Light Green		

When two colour code letters are shown on a wire the first denotes the main colour and the second denotes the tracer colour.

Fig. 12.20 Wiring diagram – air conditioner (typical)

178	Radiator cooling fan thermostat	371	Air conditioning fan relay	423	Air conditioning pressure switch
179	Radiator cooling fan motor	419	Air conditioning switch	424	Condenser fan motor
187	Air conditioning relay	420	Magnetic switch	425	Air conditioning solenoid valve
353	Air conditioning clutch relay	421	Air conditioning delay relay		
		422	Air conditioning thermostat		

Connections to main wiring diagram – 2, 3, 4, 5, 6
Connections to fuel injection circuit – 16

Symbols used in wiring diagrams

1 *Component earthed by its lead*
2 *Component earthed by its fixing*
3 *If fitted*
4 *Printed circuit*
5 *Line connector*
6 *Sealed joint*

Cable colour code

B	= Black	O	= Orange
BR	= Brown	P	= Purple
G	= Green	R	= Red
GR	= Grey	SB	= Sky Blue
K	= Pink	W	= White
L	= Blue	Y	= Yellow
LG	= Light Green		

When two colour code letters are shown on a wire the first denotes the main colour and the second denotes the tracer colour.

Fig. 12.21 Wiring diagram – carburettor

41	Fuel pump	294	Fuel cut-off valve	398	Inlet manifold heater relay
47	Coolant thermistor	347	Fuel ECU	399	Inlet manifold heater
164	Ballast in-line resistor	355	Accelerator pedal switch	400	Inlet manifold heater
250	Inertia switch	359	Carburettor stepper motor		switch

Connections to main wiring diagram – 4, 8, 9, 11, 13, 15

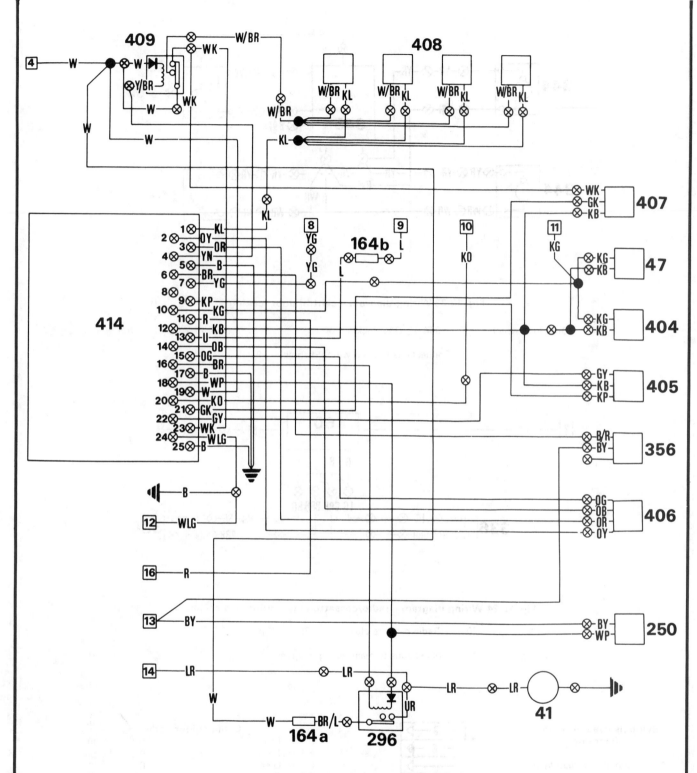

Fig. 12.22 Wiring diagram – fuel injection

41	Fuel pump	250	Fuel cut-off switch	406	Air valve stepper motor
47	Coolant thermistor	296	Fuel pump relay	407	Air flow meter
164	In-line resistor	356	Speed transducer	408	Injectors
a –	Fuel pump resistor (1 ohm)	404	Fuel temperature switch	409	Main relay
b –	Engine speed resistor (6.8 k ohm)	405	Throttle potentiometer	414	Fuel ECU

Connections to main wiring diagram – 4, 8, 9, 10, 11, 12, 13, 14
Connections to air conditioning circuit – 16

Fig. 12.23 Wiring diagram – central door locking

| 260 | Door lock switch | 344 | Door lock motor | 345 | Door lock motor control unit |

Connections to main wiring diagram – 19

Fig. 12.24 Wiring diagram – radio/cassette player with two speakers

| 60 | Radio cassette player | 336 | Speakers |

Connections to main wiring diagram – 1

Symbols used in wiring diagrams

1   Component earthed by its lead
2   Component earthed by its fixing
3   If fitted
4   Printed circuit
5   Line connector
6   Sealed joint

Cable colour code

B	= Black	O	= Orange
BR	= Brown	P	= Purple
G	= Green	R	= Red
GR	= Grey	SB	= Sky Blue
K	= Pink	W	= White
L	= Blue	Y	= Yellow
LG	= Light Green		

When two colour code letters are shown on a wire the first denotes the main colour and the second denotes the tracer colour.

Fig. 12.25 Wiring diagram – radio/cassette player with four speakers

| 60 | Radio cassette player | 335 | Balance control | 336 | Speakers |

Connections to main wiring diagram – 1, 7

Fig. 12.26 Wiring diagram – instrument panel rheostat

14	Panel illumination lamps	210	Panel illumination rheostat
76	Automatic quadrant		(dimmer) switch
	illumination lamp	211	Heater control illumination
81	Ashtray illumination lamp		lamp

Connections to main wiring diagram – 20, 21

Symbols used in wiring diagrams

1 Component earthed by its lead
2 Component earthed by its fixing
3 If fitted
4 Printed circuit
5 Line connector
6 Sealed joint

Cable colour code

B	= Black	O	= Orange
BR	= Brown	P	= Purple
G	= Green	R	= Red
GR	= Grey	SB	= Sky Blue
K	= Pink	W	= White
L	= Blue	Y	= Yellow
LG	= Light Green		

When two colour code letters are shown on a wire the first denotes the main colour and the second denotes the tracer colour.

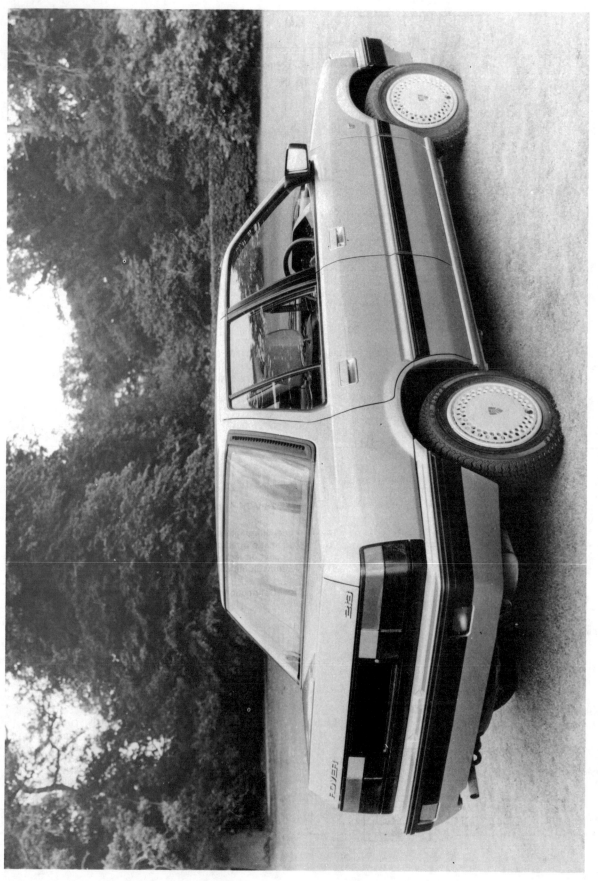

1987 model Rover 213

Chapter 13 Supplement:
Revisions and information on later models

Contents

1 Introduction

This Supplement contains information relating to models produced from August 1986 onwards and material which is additional to, or a revision of, that contained in the preceding Chapters.

The Sections in this Supplement follow the same order as the Chapters to which they relate, and it is recommended that before any particular operation is undertaken, reference be made to the appropriate Section(s) of the Supplement. In this way, any changes to procedures or components can be noted before referring to the main Chapters.

Project car

The vehicles used in the original preparation of this Supplement and appearing in many of the photographic sequences were a Rover 213 SE Automatic and a Rover 216 EFi Vanden Plas.

2 Specifications

Engine
1.3 engine
Oil pressure:

At 3000 rev/min	3.5 to 4.2 bar (50 to 60 lbf/in^2)
Minimum pressure at idle speed of 800 rev/min	0.7 bar (10 lbf/in^2)

1.6 engine
Oil pressure (with oil temperature above 40°C/104°F):
    At 2500 rev/min... 3.75 to 5.5 bar (55 to 80 lbf/in²)
    Minimum pressure at idle speed.. 0.7 bar (10 lbf/in²)

1.6 engine – unleaded with HIF carburettor from 1989
Details as per other 1.6 engine types, but with the following differences:
    Engine number prefix .... 16 HE 58
    Compression ratio.. 9.2:1

Torque wrench settings	Nm	lbf ft
1.6 engine (from 1987):		
Connecting rod big-end nuts	40	30
Engine/transmission mountings (1.6 engine):		
Right-hand mounting nuts	75	55
Right-hand mounting through-bolt	65	48
Left-hand mounting-to-body bolts	45	33

Cooling system
Antifreeze requirement
1.3 model up to VIN 800 000 (1985 model year) .... 2.3 litre (4 pints) (50% solution)
1.3 model from VIN 800 000 (1985 model year) .... 3.2 litre (5.5 pints) (50% solution)
1.6 model.. 2.1 litre (3.5 pints) (33% solution)

Fuel and exhaust systems
1.6 engine – unleaded with HIF carburettor from 1989 (Engine No. prefix 16 HE 58)
Carburettor specification number .... FZX 1478
Fast idle speed .... 1150 to 1250 rev/min
Fuel octane rating .... 95 RON (unleaded) or 97 RON (leaded)

Torque wrench setting (1.6 engine from 1987)	Nm	lbf ft
Exhaust manifold to cylinder head	28	21

Ignition system
1.6 engine – unleaded with HIF carburettor from 1989 (Engine No. prefix 16 HE 58)
Ignition timing:
    At 1100 rev/min – vacuum pipe disconnected........................... 11° BTDC
    At 1100 rev/min – vacuum pipe connected .... 28° ± 2° BTDC
Spark plugs:
    Type .... Unipart GSP 3526 or GSP 4526
    Electrode gap .... 0.85 mm (0.035 in)

Manual transmission
Ratios (Sprint) .... As for fuel injection models (see Chapter 6 Specifications)

Driveshafts, hubs, roadwheels and tyres
Roadwheels
Size:
    Sprint, 216 SE and Vanden Plas:
        Standard .... 5J x 13 steel
        Optional .... 5.5J x 14 alloy
    Vitesse (later models)... 5.5J x 14 alloy

Tyres
Sprint with steel wheel .... 175/70 SR 13
Sprint with alloy wheel .... 175/65 TR 14
Vitesse.. 175/65 TR 14

Tyre pressures in bar (lbf/in²):	Front	Rear
1.3 models	1.8 (26)	1.8 (26)
1.6 models	2.0 (28)	1.8 (26)

Braking system
Disc brakes
Disc diameter – later 1.3 models .... 231.0 mm (9.0 in)

Torque wrench setting (from 1987)

	Nm	lbf ft
Caliper mounting bolts	75	55

Suspension and steering
Torque wrench settings (from 1987)

	Nm	lbf ft
Rear suspension:		
Panhard rod nut/bolt	75	55
Trailing arm pivot bolts	61	45
Steering:		
Tie-rod-to-rack locknut	55	40
Tie-rod end balljoint nut	60	44
Steering column coupling bolts	25	18

Bodywork and fittings
Torque wrench setting (from 1987)

	Nm	lbf ft
Seat belt anchorage point bolts	40	30

Electrical system
Starter motor (Lucas)

Type	Lucas 9M90 (pre-engaged) or Lucas M79 (pre-engaged)
Minimum brush length:	
9M90	10.0 mm (0.4 in)
M79	3.5 mm (0.15 in)
Commutator minimum thickness:	
9M90	2.0 mm (0.8 in)
Commutator minimum diameter:	
M79	28.8 mm (1.134 in)

Starter motor (Nippondenso)

Minimum brush length	10.0 mm (0.4 in)

Fuses (August 1986 onwards)

Number	Circuit protected	Rating (amps)
1	Rear fog guard lamps	10
2	Wipers, washers, power window relay	15
3	Direction indicators, reversing lamps	10
4	Alternator, solenoid valve	10
5	LH headlamp (dipped beam)	10
6	RH headlamp (dipped beam)	10
7	LH headlamp (main beam)	10
8	RH headlamp (main beam)	10
9	Horn, stop lamps	15
10	Hazard warning lamps	15
11	Ignition auxiliaries	15
12	Tail, number plate and instrument illumination	15
13	Radiator cooling fan	15
14	Heater fan, heated rear window relay	20
15	Radio	10
16	Heated rear window	20
17	Central locking	15
18	Headlamp washer	20
19	Electric window (front right)	15
20	Electric window (front left)	15
21	Electric window (rear right)	15
22	Electric window (rear left)	15
23	Electric door mirrors	10
24	Electric sunroof	15
25	Spare fuses	15

Capacities
Washer system reservoir – 1.3

Windscreen washer only	2.2 litres (4.0 pints)
Windscreen/headlamp washer	5.5 litres (9.5 pints)
Washer system reservoir – 1.6	
Windscreen washer only	2.0 litres (3.5 pints)
Windscreen/headlamp washer	5.8 litres (10.0 pints)

3   Engine (1.3 litre)

Camshaft sprocket and timing belt – refitting

1   The camshaft sprocket used will either be a cast type or a pressed steel type. Although the fitting procedure for both is the same, it should be noted that the steel type does not have an 'UP' timing mark. When refitting the timing belt to this type, it is therefore necessary to align the sprocket timing marks so that they are level with the top surface of the cylinder head, then check that the camshaft is set so that the number 1 cylinder valves are fully closed and the valve rockers are free.

Rocker shafts, camshaft and cylinder head – removal and refitting

2   Proceed as described in Sections 11, 12 and or 13 of Chapter 1 (as applicable), but if a pressed steel type camshaft sprocket is fitted, check it for correct positioning as described in paragraph 1 above before locating the timing belt onto the sprocket.

4   Engine (1.6 litre)

Engine/transmission mountings

When reconnecting the engine/transmission mountings on later models it should be noted that some of the retaining bolt/nut torque wrench settings have been revised. Refer to Section 2 in this Chapter for details.

5   Fuel and exhaust systems

Unleaded fuel – general

1   Unleaded fuel is becoming more widely available in the UK, and in EC countries generally. It is sometimes cheaper than leaded fuel. Its use is desirable on environmental grounds.
2   All 1.3-engined models covered by this manual may be run on

unleaded fuel if wished. No modifications are necessary. No harm will result from reverting to leaded fuel if unleaded is not available.
3   Some 1.6 models are capable of running on unleaded fuel, but only if the cylinder head is fitted with suitable valve seat inserts. A fuel advice label is located on the bonnet lock platform.
4   If in any doubt as to which type of fuel to use, consult your Rover dealer for further information.

Tamperproof adjustment screws – caution

5   Certain adjustment points in the fuel system (and elsewhere) are protected by 'tamperproof' caps, plugs or seals. The purpose of such tamperproofing is to discourage, and to detect, adjustment by unqualified operators.
6   In some EC countries (though not yet in the UK) it is an offence to drive a vehicle with missing or broken tamperproof seals.
7   Before disturbing a tamperproof seal, satisfy yourself that you will not be breaking local or national anti-pollution regulations by doing so. Fit a new seal when adjustment is complete when this is required by law.
8   Do not break tamperproof seals on a vehicle which is still under warranty.

Carburettor (1.6 models, later versions) – adjustment

9   When adjusting the throttle lever lost motion gap on later versions of the SU HIF carburettor, adjustment is made on the throttle lever lost motion lugs, and not by a screw as on earlier versions. See Fig. 13.1.

Idle speed and mixture adjustment (fuel injection systems)

10   The procedure in Chapter 3, Section 36 provides basic settings only. If satisfactory running cannot be obtained the vehicle should be professionally adjusted by a Rover dealer or other specialist with the necessary dedicated test equipment.

Fuel cut-off solenoid (fuel injection systems) – general description

11   On later fuel injection systems a fuel cut-off solenoid is mounted in the spill return line. It is wired in series with the fuel temperature switch

Fig. 13.1 Carburettor (SU HIF) later versions (Sec 5)

1 Piston damper oil level	5 Fast idle adjustment screw	A Clearance (lost motion gap) 3.65 to 4.15 mm (0.143 to 0.163 in)	B Clearance (fast idle pushrod) 0.13 mm (0.005 in) minimum
2 Idle speed adjustment screw	6 Fast idle pushrod		
3 Progressive throttle cam	7 Mixture adjustment screw		C Linkage with throttle lever
4 Throttle lever adjustment screw	8 Lost motion adjustment lugs		

Fig. 13.2 Exhaust vibration counter-measure (1.3 models) (Sec 5)

A Plate (65 x 16   B Bracket   C U-Bolt   D Nut
   x 5 mm approx)

and, when the fuel temperature switches closes, the cut-off solenoid is energised, closing the spill return line. Fuel pressure in the fuel rail is raised to pump pressure, creating additional fuel availability during hot start conditions, and overcoming vaporisation.

Fuei cut-off solenoid – removal and refitting
Warning: *Take adequate fire precautions during this procedure*
12   Disconnect the battery negative terminal.
13   Disconnect the fuel cut-off solenoid.
14   Remove the screw from the solenoid support bracket on the air cleaner bracket.
15   Remove the fuel hose clips, pull the hoses off the solenoid and lift out the solenoid. Be prepared for fuel spillage.
16   Refit in the reverse sequence, ensuring the connector end of the solenoid forces away from the pressure regulator, and the bracket is uppermost.

Exhaust downpipe vibration (1.3 models)
17   Vibration or resonance in the downpipe spring-loaded balljoint can be cured by attaching a metal plate just in front of the joint, using a standard U-bolt and exhaust bracket. See Fig. 13.2.

6   Clutch

Clutch release arm – 1.6 models
1   The clutch release arm on later models is now fitted with a damper block (see Fig. 13.3). The damper is attached to the arm by two bolts. This fitting does not affect the removal or refitting procedures of any of the clutch system components.

Fig. 13.3 Clutch release arm (1) and damper block (2) – later 1.6 models (Sec 6)

7   Manual transmission

Identification and interchangeability (1.6 models)
1   Later type manual transmission units differ from early types in respect of certain internal components, and the components are not interchangeable.
2   It is important, therefore, to correctly identify the transmission unit when ordering components for repair purposes.
3   Early transmission units have a gold coloured label and the serial number begins with the figure one. Later types have a white label and the serial number begins with the figure two.

8   Automatic transmission

Transmission fluid (three-speed transmission) – level checking and renewal
1   When checking the automatic transmission fluid level using the procedure described in Chapter 7, Section 3, it should be emphasised that the engine and transmission must be at normal operating temperature, preferably after a short journey.
2   When refilling the transmission after draining, carry out the procedure described in Chapter 7, Section 3, but make a final check of the level with the engine and transmission at normal operating temperature. For clarity the transmission drain plug location is shown in the accompanying photo.

Selector cable (three-speed transmission) – removal and refitting
3   When removing and refitting the selector cable as described in Chapter 7, Section 6, the accompanying photos detail the cable attachment points at the transmission and on the underbody.

Kickdown cable (four-speed transmission) – adjustment
4   The kickdown cable adjustment on later models differs to that described in Chapter 7 as follows, but note that the VIN reference is not available and reference to your Rover dealer will be necessary to decide which adjustment is applicable where this is uncertain.

Fig. 13.4 Kickdown cable arrangement/adjustment on later four-speed automatic transmission model (Sec 8)

1 Throttle cable	A Crimped sleeve clearance
2 Kickdown cable	0.5 to 1.5 mm (0.02 to 0.04 in)
3 Adjuster/locknuts	

5   Ensure that the handbrake is fully applied, move the selector lever to the P position, then start the engine and allow it to warm up to its normal operating temperature.
6   With the engine running at its normal idle speed, loosen off the kickdown cable locknuts at the location bracket to release the cable tension (see Fig. 13.4). Measure the clearance between the inner cable crimped sleeve-to-adjuster clearance. This must be between 0.5 to 1.5 mm (0.02 to 0.04 in). If necessary adjust the sleeve to provide this clearance, then retighten the locknuts against the location bracket.

Selector cable (four-speed transmission) – adjustment

7   The information given in paragraph 4 (for the kickdown cable) also applies for the selector cable.
8   Remove the cassette holder by opening it and undoing the two retaining screws.
9   Detach the gear selector knob and remove it together with the spring.
10   Unscrew and remove the upper to lower console retaining screws, release the console, then detach the gear selector plate illumination bulbholder and withdraw the upper console.
11   Loosen the gear selector lever locknut (see Fig. 13.5), move the lever to the '1' position, then rotate the selector lever on the transmission fully anti-clockwise and retighten the cable locknut.
12   Check that the starter motor will only operate when the lever is in the 'P' or 'N' position, then refit the console, gear lever knob (and spring) and the cassette holder.

Selector cable (four-speed transmission) – removal and refitting

13   Before removing the cable, make a sketch of its routing to ensure correct refitting. Remove the centre console.

Fig. 13.5 Selector lever and cable on the four-speed automatic transmission (Sec 8)

1 Clevis pin	7 Retaining pin
2 Locknut	8 Gaiter
3 Split pin	9 Cable nut
4 'R' clip	10 Mounting rubbers
5 Flat washers	11 Bracket
6 Sleeve	12 Cable

Fig. 13.6 Selector lever components – four-speed automatic transmission (Sec 8)

1 Mounting plate	5 Detent bush	9 Spring	13 Locknut
2 Pivot bolt	6 Selector lever	10 Bush	14 Rubber seal
3 Bracket	7 Lock pin	11 Detent plate spring	15 Console support bracket
4 Detent plate	8 Plunger	12 Olive	

8.2 Automatic transmission fluid drain plug location (arrowed)

8.3A Selector cable lever attachment at transmission (arrowed)

8.3B Selector cable guide on underbody

8.3C Selector cable attachment at selector lever

8.3D Selector cable adjuster (viewed with centre console removed)

14   Extract the split pin from the cable clevis pin, then withdraw the clevis pin. Unscrew the cable locknut and withdraw the split olive.
15   In the engine compartment, loosen off the retaining clip and detach the air intake hose from the air cleaner. Detach the air intake hose adaptor from the body crossmember and remove the intake hose.
16   Extract the 'R' clip from the selector cable pin at the lever and collect the two flat washers and the central sleeve.
17   Detach the gaiter from the cable nut, unscrew the nut and release the cable.
18   If a new cable is being fitted, pull back the gaiter from the nut and remove it.
19   Refit in the reverse order of removal. Ensure that the cable is correctly re-routed (as noted during removal). Apply a small amount of grease to the cable pin and lever pivot bush. When reconnecting the cable at the lever end, ensure that the split olive is aligned before tightening the locknut. Lubricate the clevis pin and when fitted, secure it with a new split pin.
20   Check and adjust the cable as described previously in this Section to complete.

Selector lever (four-speed transmission) – removal and refitting

21   Remove the centre console as described in Chapter 11.
22   Position the car over an inspection pit or raise it at the front end and support it on stands.
23   Disconnect the selector cable from the lever as described previously. Recover the split olive.
24   Working underneath the car, disconnect the two selector lever front to floor pan retaining bolts and the four nuts/bolts securing the mounting plate to the floorpan.
25   Pull the lever mounting plate unit up into the car and then remove the console support and rubber seal.
26   Detach the spring from the detent plate. Remove the spring, selector bracket detent plate and bush.
27   Undo the lockpin to detach the plunger and spring from the lever.
28   Unscrew and remove the lever pivot bolt, then lift the lever clear of the mounting plate. Remove the lever pivot bush.
29   Refit in the reverse order of removal. Lubricate the pivot bush and the lever end lightly with grease prior to reassembly. Reconnect and adjust the cable as described previously in this Section.

Starter inhibitor/reverse lamp switch (three-speed transmission) – removal and refitting

30   Detach the centre console and move it rearwards and over the selector lever.
31   Detach and withdraw the selector quadrant indicator plate.
32   Detach the wiring connector from the inhibitor switch and the switch from the mounting bracket.
33   When refitting the switch, align the slider with the selector pin and ensure that the earth lead is positioned above the switch. Refit the quadrant indicator plate then check that the starter operates only when the selector lever is in the 'P' or 'N' position. Also check that the reversing light operates when the lever is moved to the 'R' position. Refit the console.

9   Braking system

Brake linings

1   When renewing the brake linings, not only is it important that the linings are renewed on each side of the same axle, but also with the same lining type fitted on each side. Never intermix asbestos and asbestos-free linings of the same axle.

Brake fluid

2   Later models have DOT 4 specification brake fluid and the manufacturers recommend that this fluid is now used when topping-up or renewing the brake fluid on earlier models (which previously used DOT 3 specification fluid).
3   The advantage of the DOT 4 fluid is that it has a higher boiling point than the DOT 3 type, but is compatible to be mixed with the earlier type when topping-up is required.

10   Bodywork and fittings

Front door interior trim panel (August 1986 onwards) – removal and refitting

1   On cars without power-operated windows, extract the spring clip and take off the window regulator handle. The clip can be removed using a piece of wire with a hook at its end or a strip of rag pulled in either direction under the handle boss.
2   Carefully prise out the speaker grille, then undo the four screws and withdraw the speaker. Disconnect the wiring and remove the speaker (photos).
3   Prise out the escutcheon plate from the remote control lock handle, rotate the plate as necessary and slide it off the handle (photos).
4   Prise out the tweeter from the top of the trim panel, disconnect the wiring and remove the tweeter (photo).
5   Release the clips securing the centre trim pad to the panel by pulling the pad outwards, then remove it from the door (photo).
6   Undo the two screws on the rear edge of the trim panel, three screws at the upper front, two screws in the speaker aperture, and four screws in the centre (photos).
7   Insert the fingers or a broad blunt blade between the trim panel and the door and release the clips.
8   Where fitted, disconnect the door lock/power-operated window control multi-plug, then lift the trim panel upwards and off the door (photo).
9   Carefully peel back the waterproof sheet as necessary for access to the door internal components (photo).
10   Refitting is the reversal of removal. To fit the regulator handle (where applicable), position the spring clip on the handle and fit it to the splined shaft of the regulator simply by striking it with the hand.

Rear door interior trim panel (August 1986 onwards) – removal and refitting

11   The procedure is the same as for the front door described pre-

10.2A Remove the speaker grille from the interior trim panel ...

10.2B ... undo the speaker retaining screws ...

10.2C ... withdraw the speaker and disconnect the wiring

10.3A Prise out the escutcheon plate from the remote control handle ...

10.3B ... then rotate the plate to remove

10.4 Prise out the tweeter from the top of the trim panel

10.5 Remove the centre trim panel

10.6A Undo the upper screw on the trim panel rear edge (arrowed)

10.6B ... and the lower screw behind the storage bin (arrowed)

10.6C Undo the three screws at the upper front (arrowed) ...

10.6D ... and the fan screws at the centre (arrowed)

10.8 Release the clips and lift the panel upwards to remove

viously except for fewer panel retaining screws and the absence of door speakers.

Centre console (August 1986 onwards) – removal and refitting

12   Refer to Section 11 of this Supplement and remove the radio/cassette player.

13   On manual transmission models unscrew the gear lever knob. On automatic transmission models undo the screw on the front face of the selector lever (photo). Lift off the selector and remove the spring (photo).

14   Remove the ash tray from the rear console, unclip the access panel and undo the screw securing the rear console upper cover (photos).

15   Where fitted, disconnect the sunroof switch multi-plug, apply the handbrake fully and withdraw the rear console upper cover over the handbrake lever.

16   Undo the two screws at the rear of the front console upper cover (photo).

17   Open the cassette holder lid and undo the two screws from inside the cassette holder (photo). Withdraw the cassette holder from the front console.

18   Undo the two front console upper cover screws from within the cassette holder aperture and lift off the upper cover (photos). Disconnect the panel illumination bulb wiring connectors (where fitted) and remove the upper cover.

19   Undo the two screws at the rear, the centre clamp plate screw, and the three screws on each side at the front securing the front and rear consoles (photos).

20   Lift out the rear console, disconnect the window lift switch wiring (where fitted), and lift out the front console.

21   Refitting is a reversal of removal.

Facia panel (August 1986 onwards) – removal and refitting

22   The procedure for later models is the same as described in Chapter 11, Section 23, but it is first necessary to remove the centre console as described previously in this Section.

10.9 Peel back the waterproof sheet for access to the door components

10.13A On automatic transmission models undo the selector lever retaining screw (arrowed) ...

10.13B ... lift off the lever and remove the spring (arrowed)

10.14A Remove the ashtray from the rear console ...

10.14B ... followed by the upper cover and retaining screw (arrowed)

10.16 Undo the screws at the rear of the front console upper cover

10.17 Undo the screws from the inside of the cassette holder and remove the holder

10.18A Undo the two front console upper cover screws (arrowed) ...

10.18B ... and lift off the upper cover

10.19A Undo the two screws at the rear (arrowed) ...

10.19B ... the centre clamp plate ...

10.19C ... and the three screws each side at the front (arrowed)

Fig. 13.7 Manually-operated exterior rear view mirror glass details (Sec 10)

1 Mirror arm	4 Mirror glass
2 Ball	5 Retaining spring
3 Socket	

Fig. 13.8 Electrically-operated rear view mirror glass details (Sec 10)

1 Mirror retaining clips	3 Mirror glass
2 Glass retaining ring	4 Wiring connectors

Exterior rear view mirror glass – renewal

Note: *It is assumed that the mirror glass is being removed because it is already broken. This will be the likely result in any case when attempting to remove an unbroken mirror.*

Manually-operated mirror

23 Push the mirror glass forward to give access to the mirror ball and socket (Fig. 13.7).

24 Disconnect the ball from the socket, disconnect the retaining spring and withdraw the glass from the mirror arm.

25 Refitting is the reversal of removal.

Electrically-operated mirror

26 Push the mirror glass forward to give access to the mirror glass retaining clips (Fig. 13.8).

27 Release the clips from the retaining ring, disconnect the wiring and remove the glass from the retaining ring.

28 Refitting is the reversal of removal.

Luggage boot lock and controls (August 1986 onwards) – general

29 With the provision of the low loading sill and modified boot lid arrangement on later models the layout of the boot lid and controls has also been changed.

30 The lock and lock cylinder have been repositioned from the rear panel to the boot lid itself, and the striker moved from the boot lid to the rear panel (photos).

31 Apart from these location changes the components are unaltered and the procedures contained in Chapter 11 are still applicable.

Headlining – general

32 Should it be necessary to remove the headlining on cars equipped with a sunroof it is recommended that the work be entrusted to a Rover dealer due to the complications involved (see next sub-section).

Sunroof – general

33 A mechanical or electrically-operated sunroof is available as standard or optional equipment on certain models in the range.

34 The sunroof operating mechanism is quite complex and the components removal, refitting and adjustment procedures are equally involved, reflecting this complexity. For the roof to operate smoothly, without water leaks and without excessive wind noise, adjustment is critical, and in some instances special tools are necessary. For these reasons it is recommended that work on the sunroof be entrusted to a suitably equipped dealer, and is considered beyond the scope of the DIY mechanic.

Plastic components

35 With the use of more and more plastic body components by the vehicle manufacturers (eg bumpers, spoilers, and in some cases major body panels), rectification of more serious damage to such items has become a matter of either entrusting repair work to a specialist in this field, or renewing complete components. Repair of such damage by the DIY owner is not really feasible owing to the cost of the equipment and materials required for effecting such repairs. The basic technique involves making a groove along the line of the crack in the plastic using a rotary burr in a power drill. The damaged part is then welded back

10.30A Boot lid lock ...

10.30B ... lock cylinder ...

10.30C ... and striker plate locations ...

Fig. 13.9 Exploded view of the Lucas M79 starter motor (Sec 11)

1 Solenoid and plunger	5 Pivot and packing piece	10 Bush – drive end bracket	13 Insulation plate
2 Commutator end bracket assembly	6 Armature	11 Bush – commutator end bracket	14 Commutator end bracket
3 Brushes	7 Jump ring and thrust collar	12 Drive end bracket – manual	15 Circlip and washers
4 Brush springs	8 Drive assembly		16 Sealing cup and gasket
	9 Field coils and yoke		

together by using a hot air gun to heat up and fuse a plastic filler rod into the groove. Any excess plastic is then removed and the area rubbed down to a smooth finish. It is important that a filler rod of the correct plastic is used, as body components can be made of a variety of different types (eg polycarbonate, ABS, polypropylene).

36 Damage of a less serious nature (abrasions, minor cracks etc) can be repaired by the DIY owner using a two-part epoxy filler repair material, like Holts Body + Plus or Holts No Mix which can be used directly from the tube. Once mixed in equal proportions (or applied direct from the tube in the case of Holts No Mix), this is used in similar fashion to the bodywork filler used on metal panels. The filler is usually cured in twenty to thirty minutes, ready for sanding and painting.

37 If the owner is renewing a complete component himself, or if he has repaired it with epoxy filler, he will be left with the problem of finding a suitable paint for finishing which is compatible with the type of plastic used. At one time the use of a universal paint was not possible owing to the complex range of plastics encountered in body component applications. Standard paints, generally speaking, will not bond to plastic or rubber satisfactorily, but Holts Professional Spraymatch paints to match any plastic or rubber finish can be obtained from dealers. However, it is now possible to obtain a plastic body parts finishing kit which consists of a pre-primer treatment, a primer and coloured top coat. Full instructions are normally supplied with a kit, but basically the method of use is to first apply the pre-primer to the component concerned and allow it to dry for up to 30 minutes. Then the primer is applied and left to dry for about an hour before finally applying the special coloured top coat. The result is a

correctly coloured component where the paint will flex with the plastic or rubber, a property that standard paint does not normally possess.

---

11 Electrical system

Alternator drivebelt tensioner – 1.3 models (1987 onwards)

1 A positive tensioning device is fitted to these models. Adjust the drivebelt tension as follows.

2 Disconnect the battery negative lead.

3 Slacken the alternator pivot and adjusting link bolts.

4 Turn the tensioning bolt until the belt tension is correct (see Chapter 12 Specifications). Be careful not to over-tension.

5 Tighten the link and pivot bolts. Recheck the belt tension, then reconnect the battery.

Starter motor (later models)

6 A Lucas M79 starter motor is fitted to some 1988-on models. Overhaul and repair procedures are similar to those described for earlier type starter motors in Chapter 12, using the Specifications given in this Supplement and Figs. 13.9 and 13.10.

7 A Nippondenso (ND) starter motor may be found on some 1.3 models. This is similar to the Hitachi motor shown in Chapter 12.

Relays and control units (1987 onwards) – location

8 The location of the various relays in the fusebox is as shown in Fig. 13.11.

Fig. 13.10 Starter solenoid details – Lucas M79 starter motor (Sec 11)

1	*Battery terminal BAT*	*4*	*Retaining screws*
2	*Starter terminal STA*	*5*	*Solenoid*
3	*Solenoid terminal 50*	*6*	*Solenoid plunger*

9 The location of other relays/control units is as follows:

Passenger compartment

Inertia switch (1.6 models) – behind panel above fusebox
Fuel system ECU (1.6 models) – below left-hand front seat
Door lock control unit (where fitted) – below right-hand front seat
'One touch' window lift control (where fitted) – below right-hand front seat
Sunroof changeover relay – behind sunroof motor access panel

Engine compartment

Ignition ECU (1.6 models) – left-hand front suspension tower
Manifold heater relay 1.6 carburettor models – left-hand suspension tower
Fuel pump relay (1.6 carburettor models) – right-hand suspension tower
Starter solenoid relay (1.6 EFi automatic) – left-hand suspension tower

Power-operated window switch (August 1986 onwards) – removal and refitting

10 Open the cassette holder lid, undo the two screws from inside the cassette holder and remove it from the centre console.
11 Working through the cassette holder aperture, reach behind the window switch and push it out of the console.
12 Disconnect the switch wiring and remove the switch.
13 Refitting is a reversal of removal.

Power-operated window motor and regulator – removal and refitting

Front door

14 Remove the door interior trim panel as described in Chapter 11, or in Section 10 of this supplement for August 1986 models onwards.
15 On early models remove the door speaker if fitted.
16 Lower the window until the bolts securing the lifting channel to the

Fig. 13.11 Relay location in fusebox (1987 onwards) (Sec 11)

1	*Headlamp washer timer unit*	*4*	*Courtesy light delay unit*	*7*	*Window lift relay – front*	*10*	*Intermittent wiper control*
2	*Auxiliary circuits relay*	*5*	*Instrument illumination relay*	*8*	*Window lift relay – rear*	*11*	*Hazard warning/indicator flasher*
3	*Heated rear screen relay*	*6*	*Sidelight warning alarm*	*9*	*Headlamp dim-dip unit*		

11.19 Front door window regulator mechanism retaining bolts (A) and regulator channel bolts (B)

11.25 Rear door lifting plate-to-glass retaining bolts (arrowed)

11.29A Regulator channel lower retaining bolts (arrowed) ...

11.29B ... and upper retaining nuts (arrowed)

11.43 Central locking rear door lock motor retaining screws (arrowed) – motor lock assembly shown removed for clarity

11.48 Reversing lamp bulb and holder location in the boot lid

glass are accessible through the aperture in the door.
17   Slacken, but do not remove, the bolts securing the lifting channel to the glass. Move the channel forwards until the bolts are released from the slots.
18   Disconnect the battery negative lead.
19   Undo the bolts securing the regulator channel and mechanism to the door (photo).
20   Lower the regulator assembly to the bottom of the door while holding the glass. Now raise the glass by hand and hold it in the raised position with adhesive tape.
21   Remove the motor and regulator assembly through the rearmost aperture in the door and disconnect the motor wiring.
22   The motor can be removed if necessary after undoing the retaining bolts and releasing the drain tube.
23   Refitting is a reversal of removal.
Rear door
24   Remove the door interior trim panel as described in Chapter 11, or in Section 10 of this Supplement for August 1986 models onwards.
25   Lower the window until the bolts securing the lifting plate to the glass are accessible through apertures in the door (photo).
26   Using a suitable socket undo the two bolts.
27   Raise the window glass by hand and hold it in the raised position with adhesive tape.
28   Disconnect the battery negative lead.
29   Undo the two lower bolts and two upper nuts securing the regulator channel to the door (photos).
30   Note the location of the motor wiring connectors and disconnect them.
31   Undo the bolts securing the motor and regulator and remove the assembly from the door.
32   Refitting is the reversal of removal.

Power-operated window control unit – removal and refitting
33   Disconnect the battery negative lead.
34   Move the driver's seat fully rearward.
35   Undo the bolt and withdraw the control unit mounting plate from under the seat.
36   Disconnect the multi-plug connectors, depress the spring clip and

remove the control unit from the mounting plate. Where more than one control unit is fitted, the power-operated window unit is the one on the right-hand side of the plate.
37   Refitting is a reversal of removal.

Central locking door lock motor – removal and refitting
38   On cars equipped with central locking, the passenger's side front door and both rear door locks are operated by the electric motors attached to the lock mechanism. These are activated by a switch unit attached to the driver's side door lock. Removal and refitting of the switch unit and the system control unit are described in Chapter 12. Removal and refitting of the door lock motors is as follows.
39   Raise the window fully, then disconnect the battery negative lead.
40   Remove the door interior trim panel as described in Chapter 11, or in Section 10 of this Supplement for August 1986 models onwards.
41   Disconnect the motor wiring at the multi-plug connector.
42   If working on the front door, undo the three screws securing the door latch to the door, depress the interior lock button, and move the latch until the motor retaining screws are accessible. Undo the screws and remove the motor.
43   If working on the rear door, depress the interior lock button and, working through the door aperture, undo the motor retaining screws (photo). Remove the motor.
44   Refitting is a reversal of removal.

Dim-dip lighting system (1987 onwards) – general
45   A dim-dip headlamp lighting system is fitted to later models. The system causes the headlamps to light at reduced intensity when both the ignition and the sidelights are switched on.
46   The dim-dip relay is located in the central fusebox, and a resistor is located behind the right-hand headlamp unit, low down in the engine compartment.
47   Where a dim-dip system is fitted, only headlamp bulbs of the recommended wattage should be fitted, or damage to the circuit components may result.

Reversing lamp bulb (August 1986 onwards) – renewal
48   From within the luggage compartment turn the bulbholder anti-

clockwise to remove it from the boot lid (photo).
49   Push and turn the bayonet fitting bulb to remove.
50   Refitting is a reversal of removal.

Automatic transmission selector quadrant bulb (August 1986 onwards) – renewal

51   Refer to Section 10 of this Supplement and remove the front centre console upper cover.
52   Withdraw the bulbholder from the rear of the cover and remove the push fit bulb from the bulbholder (photos).
53   Refitting is a reversal of removal.

Clock (later models) – removal and refitting

54   Disconnect the battery earth lead.
55   Using a small screwdriver, carefully prise free the trinket tray from the facia and the electric mirror switch, if fitted.
56   Reaching to the rear of the clock, carefully push it out of its aperture and detach the wiring connector from its rear face.
57   Refit in the reverse order of removal and reset the clock.

Instrument panel light dimmer switch – removal and refitting

58   Disconnect the battery earth lead.
59   Remove the instrument panel lower access facia, then reach through to the rear of the switch and detach the wiring connector.
60   Pull free the knob from the switch, withdraw the plain washer, unscrew and remove the retaining nut. Withdraw the switch.

61   Refit in the reverse order of removal, then check for satisfactory operation on completion.

Radio/cassette player

62   The radio/cassette player fitted to later models has an integral anti-theft security code system. With this unit type, whenever the battery is to be disconnected or the radio/cassette is to be removed, the code must be deactivated. Only the car owner and the original dealer will know the four digit code. The code is pre-set by the owner and the dealer is then advised of the code number. To deactivate the security system code, depress the UP tuning button and switch the radio on. Continue to depress the UP button and correctly enter the security code as follows:

(a)   Depress the number 1 preset button and press one of the arrowed tuner buttons to select the 1st digit of the code. When selected, the digit will show in the display panel. Press the pre-set button to store the number.

(b)   Now depress one of the arrowed tuner buttons to select the 2nd digit of the code, then when this is registered as entered by the display panel, press the pre-set button to store this number.

(c)   Repeat the procedure to select the 3rd and 4th digits of the code. When the 4th digit is entered, a twin tone beep will be heard, and this signified that the code is deactivated.

63   If removing the radio/cassette unit, proceed as described in Section 24 in Chapter 12 (paragraph 10 on). In some instances it may be necessary to remove the end covers to gain access to the release holes. When refitting the unit ensure that any foam padding withdrawn during removal is correctly repositioned.

11.52A Selector quadrant bulb holder locations ...

11.52B ... and removing the selector quadrant bulbs

Fig. 13.12 Wiring diagram: 1.3 models (August 1986 to 1987)

Fig. 13.12 Wiring diagram: 1.3 models (August 1986 to 1987) (cont)

Key to Fig 13.12

No	Description	Grid reference
1	Alternator	A1
3	Battery	A1
4	Starter motor solenoid	A1
5	Starter motor	A1
6	Lighting switch	B2
7	Headlamp dip/flash switch	B2
8	Dip headlamp	B1
9	Main headlamp	B1
10	Main beam warning lamp	B1
11	RH side lamp	C1
12	LH side lamp	C1
14	Panel illumination lamps	C1
15	Number plate illumination lamps	C1
16	Stop lamps	C1
17	RH rear lamp	C1
18	Stop lamp switch	C2
19	Fuses	A2/A3/A4/B1/B2
20	Interior lamp	B3
21	Interior lamp switches	B4/C4
22	LH rear lamp	C1
23	Horn	B2
24	Horn switch	B2
26	Direction indicator switch	C2
27	Direction indicator warning lamps	C1
28	RH front direction indicator lamp	C1
29	LH front direction indicator lamp	C1
30	RH rear direction indicator lamp	C1
31	LH rear direction indicator lamp	C1
32	Heater/recirculation blower motor switch	B2
33	Heater/recirculation blower motor	A2
34	Fuel gauge	B4
35	Fuel tank gauge unit	B4
37	Windscreen wiper motor	A3
38	Ignition switch	A1
39	Ignition coil	A1
40	Distributor	A1
42	Oil pressure switch	B4
43	Oil pressure warning lamp	B4
44	Ignition/no charge warning lamp	A1
45	Headlamp flasher switch	B2
46	Coolant temperature gauge	B4
47	Coolant temperature sender unit	B4
49	Reversing lamp switch	C2
50	Reverse lamp	C1
56	Clock	C3
57	Cigar lighter	A4
65	Luggage compartment lamp switch	B4
66	Luggage compartment lamp	B4
75	Automatic gearbox inhibitor switch	A1
76	Automatic selector illumination	C3
77	Windscreen washer motor	A3
81	Ashtray illumination lamp	C1
95	Tachometer	B3
110	Direction indicator repeater lamps, if fitted	C1
115	Heated rear window switch	A2
116	Heated rear window	B2
118	Windscreen washer/wiper switch	A4
145	Dim-dip relay	B2
150	Heated rear window warning lamp	B2
152	Hazard warning lamp	C2
153	Hazard warning lamp switch	C2
165	Handbrake warning lamp switch	B4
178	Radiator cooling fan thermostat	B2
179	Radiator cooling fan motor	A2
182	Brake fluid level switch	B4
208	Cigar lighter illumination	C1
211	Heater control illumination	C1
212	Choke warning lamp switch	B4
213	Choke warning lamp	B4
240	Heated rear window relay	A2
243	Fuel cut-off solenoid	A1
246	Glove box lamp	B4
247	Glove box lamp switch	B4
286	Rear fog guard lamp switch	B2
287	Rear fog guard warning lamp	B2
288	Rear fog guard warning lamp	B1
297	Brake warning lamp	B4
298	Windscreen wiper delay unit	A4
305	Auxiliary relay	A3
308	Direction indicator/hazard warning flasher unit	C2
326	Brake pad wear sensor	B4
413	Fusible links	A1
417	Luggage compartment warning lamp	B4
418	Lighting switch alarm	C4
493	Dim-dip resistor	B2
495	Instrument panel illumination diameter	B2

Connections to supplementary circuit diagrams

No	Description	Grid reference
1	Radio cassette player	A4
2	Air conditioning	A2
3	Air conditioning	A2
4	Air conditioning	A1
5	Air conditioning	A2
6	Air conditioning	B2
7	Radio cassette player	B3
8	Central locking	B1
10	Door mirrors	C3
19	Electric mirrors	A4
22	Electric windows	A4
24	Electric sunroof	A4
30	Electric windows	C1

Symbols used in wiring diagrams

1 Component earthed by its lead
2 Component earthed by its fixing
3 If fitted
4 Printed circuit
5 Line connector
6 Sealed joint

Cable colour code

B =	Black	O =	Orange
BR =	Brown	P =	Purple
G =	Green	R =	Red
GR =	Grey	SB =	Sky Blue
K =	Pink	W =	White
L =	Blue	Y =	Yellow
LG =	Light Green		

When two colour code letters are shown on a wire the first denotes the main colour and the second denotes the tracer colour.

Fig. 13.13 Main wiring diagram – 1.6 models (August 1986 to 1987)

Fig. 13.13 Main wiring diagram – 1.6 models (August 1986 to 1987) (cont)

Key to Fig. 13.13

No	Description	Grid reference	No	Description	Grid reference
1	Alternator	A1	65	Luggage compartment lamp switch	B4
3	Battery	A1	66	Luggage compartment lamp	B4
4	Starter motor solenoid	A1	75	Automatic inhibitor switch	A1
5	Starter motor	A1	76	Automatic gearbox selection indicator lamp	C3
6	Lighting switch	B2	77	Windscreen washer motor	A3
7	Headlamp dip switch	B2	81	Ashtray illumination lamp	C1
8	Dip headlamp	B1	95	Tachometer	B3
9	Main headlamp	B1	110	Direction indicator repeater lamps	C1
10	Main beam warning lamp	B1	115	Heated rear window switch	A2
11	RH side lamp	C1	116	Heated rear window	A2
12	LH side lamp	C1	118	Combined windscreen washer/wiper switch	A4
14	Panel illumination lamps	C1	150	Heated rear screen warning lamp	A2
15	Number plate illumination lamps	C1	152	Hazard warning lamp	C2
16	Stop lamps	C1	153	Hazard warning lamp switch	C2
17	RH rear lamp	C1	165	Handbrake warning lamp switch	B4
18	Stop lamp switch	C2	174	Starter solenoid relay	A1
19	Fuses	A2/A3/A4/B2	178	Radiator cooling fan thermostat	A2
20	Interior lamp	B3	179	Radiator cooling fan motor	A2
21	Interior lamp switches	B4	182	Brake fluid level switch	B4
22	LH rear lamp	C1	208	Cigar lighter illumination	C1
23	Horn	B2	211	Heater control illumination	C1
24	Horn switch	B2	240	Heated rear window relay	A2
26	Direction indicator switch	C2	246	Glove box lamp	B4
27	Direction indicator warning lamps	C1	247	Glove box lamp switch	B4
28	RH front direction indicator lamp	C1	267	Headlamp washer pump motor	A3
29	LH front direction indicator lamp	C1	286	Rear fog guard lamp switch	B2
30	RH rear direction indicator lamp	C1	287	Rear fog guard warning lamp	B2
31	LH rear direction indicator lamp	C1	288	Rear fog guard warning lamp	B1
32	Heater/recirculation blower motor switch	B2	297	Brake warning lamp	B4
33	Heater/recirculation blower motor	A2	298	Windscreen wiper delay unit	A4
34	Fuel gauge	B4	305	Auxiliary relay	A3
35	Fuel tank gauge unit	B4	308	Direction indicator/hazard warning flasher unit	C2
37	Windscreen wiper motor	A3	313	Headlamp washer control relay	A3
38	Ignition switch	A1	326	Brake pad wear sensor	B4
39	Ignition coil	A2	381	Knock sensor	A1
42	Oil pressure switch	B4	382	Crankshaft sensor	A1
43	Oil pressure warning lamp	B4	393	Programmed ignition E.C.U.	A1
44	Ignition/no-charge warning lamp	A2	401	Courtesy light delay unit	C4
45	Headlamp flash switch	B2	413	Fusible links	A1
46	Coolant temperature gauge	B4	417	Luggage compartment warning lamp	B4
49	Reversing lamp switch	C2	418	Lighting switch alarm	C4
50	Reverse lamp	C1	493	Dim-dip resistor	B2
56	Clock	C3	494	Dim-dip relay	B2
57	Cigar lighter	A4	495	Instrument panel illumination relay	B2

Connections to supplementary circuits

No	Description	Grid reference	No	Description	Grid reference
1	Radio cassette player	A4	12	Fuel injection	A1
2	Air conditioning	A2	13	Fuel injection or Carburettor	A2
3	Air conditioning	A2	14	Fuel injection	A1
4	Air conditioning, Fuel injection or Carburettor	A1	15	Carburettor	A2
5	Air conditioning	A2	16	Air conditioning	A1
6	Air conditioning	B2	17	Fuel injection or Carburettor	B4
7	Radio cassette player	B3	18	Fuel injection or Carburettor	B4
8	Fuel injection or Carburettor	B4	19	Electric mirrors	A4
9	Fuel injection or Carburettor	A2	22	Electric windows	A4
10	Fuel injection	A1	23	Panel illumination dimmer	C2
11	Fuel injection or Carburettor	A1	24	Electric sunroof	A4
			30	Electric windows	C2

Fig. 13.14 Main wiring diagram – 1.6 models (1987 on)

Fig. 13.14 Main wiring diagram – 1.6 models (1987 on) (cont)

Key to Fig. 13.14

No	Description	Grid reference	No	Description	Grid reference
1	Alternator	A1	65	Luggage compartment lamp switch	B4
3	Battery	A1	66	Luggage compartment lamp	B4
4	Starter motor solenoid	A1	75	Automatic inhibitor switch	A1
5	Starter motor	A1	76	Automatic gearbox selection indicator lamp	C3
6	Lighting switch	B2	77	Windscreen washer motor	A3
7	Headlamp dip switch	B2	81	Ashtray illumination lamp	C1
8	Dip headlamp	B1	95	Tachometer	B3
9	Main headlamp	B1	110	Direction indicator repeater lamps	C1
10	Main beam warning lamp	B1	115	Heated rear window switch	A2
11	RH sidelamp	C1	116	Heated rear window	B2
12	LH sidelamp	C1	118	Combined windscreen washer/wiper switch	A4
14	Panel illumination lamps	C1	150	Heated rear screen warning lamp	A2
15	Number plate illumination lamps	C1	152	Hazard warning lamp	C2
16	Stop-lamps	C1	153	Hazard warning lamp switch	C2
17	RH rear lamp	C1	165	Handbrake warning lamp switch	B4
18	Stop-lamp switch	C2	174	Starter solenoid relay	A1
19	Fuses	A2/A3/A4/B1/B2	178	Radiator cooling fan thermostat	A2
20	Interior lamp	B3	179	Radiator cooling fan motor	A2
21	Interior lamp switches	B4	182	Brake fluid level switch	B4
22	LH rear lamp	C1	208	Cigar lighter illumination	C1
23	Horn	B2	211	Heater control illumination	C1
24	Horn switch	B2	240	Heated rear window relay	A2
26	Direction indicator switch	C2	246	Glovebox lamp	B4
27	Direction indicator warning lamps	C1	247	Glovebox lamp switch	B4
28	RH front direction indicator lamp	C1	267	Headlamp washer pump motor	A3
29	LH front direction indicator lamp	C1	286	Rear fog guard lamp switch	B2
30	RH rear direction indicator lamp	C1	287	Rear fog guard warning lamp	B2
31	LH rear direction indicator lamp	C1	288	Rear fog guard lamp	B1
32	Heater/recirculation blower motor switch	B2	297	Brake warning lamp	B4
33	Heater/recirculation blower motor	A2	298	Windscreen wiper delay unit	A4
34	Fuel gauge	B4	305	Auxiliary relay	A3
35	Fuel tank gauge unit	B4	308	Direction indicator/hazard warning flasher unit	C2
37	Windscreen wiper motor	A3	313	Headlamp washer control relay	A3
38	Ignition switch	A1	326	Brake pad wear sensor	B4
39	Ignition coil	A2	381	Knock sensor	A1
42	Oil pressure switch	B4	382	Crankshaft sensor	A1
43	Oil pressure warning lamp	B4	393	Programmed ignition ECU	A1
44	Ignition/no-charge warning lamp	A2	401	Courtesy light delay unit	C4
45	Headlamp flash switch	B2	413	Fusible links	A1
46	Coolant temperature gauge	B4	417	Luggage compartment warning lamp	B4
49	Reversing lamp switch	C2	418	Lighting switch alarm	C4
50	Reverse lamp	C1	493	Dim-dip resistor	B2
56	Clock	C3	494	Dim-dip relay	B2
57	Cigar lighter	A4	495	Instrument illumination dimmer	B2

Connections to supplementary circuit diagrams

No	Description	Grid reference	No	Description	Grid reference
1	Radio cassette player	A4	13	Fuel injection or carburettor	A2
2	Air conditioning	A2	14	Fuel injection or carburettor	A1
3	Air conditioning	A2	15	Fuel injection or carburettor	A2
4	Air conditioning, fuel injection or carburettor	A1	16	Air conditioning	A1
5	Air conditioning	A2	17	Fuel injection or carburettor	B4
6	Air conditioning	B2	18	Fuel injection or carburettor	B4
7	Radio cassette player	B3	19	Electric mirrors	A4
8	Central locking	A2	22	Electric windows	A4
9	Fuel injection or carburettor	A2	23	Panel illumination dimmer	C2
10	Fuel injection or carburettor	A1	24	Electric sunroof	A4
11	Fuel injection or carburettor	A1	25	Fuel injection or carburettor	B4
12	Fuel injection or carburettor	A1	26	Door mirrors	A1
			30	Electric sunroof	C2

Fig. 13.15 Wiring diagram – electric sunroof (August 1986 onwards)

19	Fuse	573	Switch
463	Sunroof motor	574	Change over relay

Connections to main wiring diagram – 24, 30

Fig. 13.16 Wiring diagram – electric exterior rear view mirror (August 1986 onwards)

429a	LH door mirror	429b	RH door mirror	430	Door mirror switch

Connection to main wiring diagram – 19

Fig. 13.17 Wiring diagram – six speaker stereo radio/cassette player (August 1986 onwards)

19	Fuse		336b	Rear LH speaker
60	Radio or radio/cassette player		336c	Front RH speaker
336	Tweeter		336d	Rear RH speaker
336a	Front LH speaker		479	Capacitor

Connections to main wiring diagram – 1, 7

Fig. 13.18 Wiring diagram – two door power-operated windows (August 1986 onwards)

19	Fuses
216	Front RH window lift switch
218	Front LH window lift switch
220	Window lift motors
364	Window power wind relay
386	One-touch window lift unit

Connections to main wiring diagram – 22, 30

Fig. 13.19 Wiring diagram – four door power-operated windows (August 1986 onwards)

19	Fuses	220	Window lift motors
216	Front RH window lift switch	364a	Window power wind relay
217	Rear RH window lift switch	364b	Rear window power wind relay
218	Front LH window lift switch	386	One-touch window lift unit
219	Rear LH window lift switch	387	Isolator

Connections to main wiring diagram – 22, 30

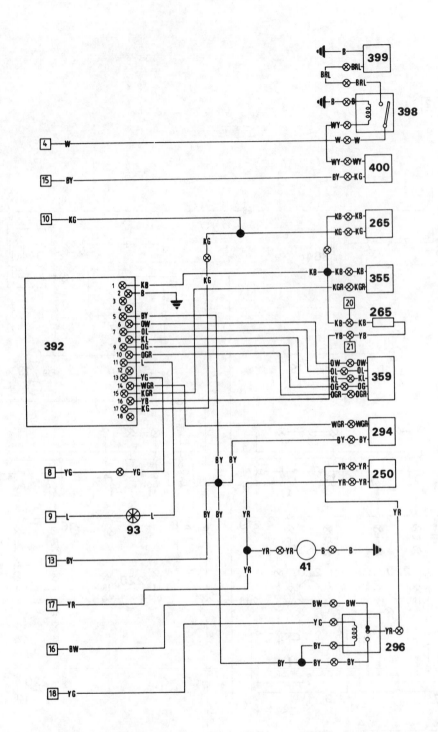

Fig. 13.20 Wiring diagram – fuel management circuit for carburettor models (August 1986 onwards)

41	Fuel pump	355	Throttle switch
93	Inspection socket	359	Stepper motor
250	Inertia switch	392	Fuel ECU
265	Temperature sensor	398	Inlet manifold heater relay
294	Solenoid valve	399	Inlet manifold heater
296	Fuel pump relay	400	Inlet manifold heater switch

Connections to main wiring diagram – 4, 8, 9, 10, 13, 15, 16, 17, 18

Fig. 13.21 Wiring diagram – fuel management circuit for fuel injection models (August 1986 to 1987)

41	Fuel pump	405	Throttle potentiometer
250	Inertia switch	406	Air valve stepper motor
294	Fuel solenoid valve	407	Air flow meter
296	Fuel pump relay	408	Injectors
327	Resistor	409	Main relay
356	Road speed sensor	414	Fuel ECU
404	Hot start (fuel temperature) switch	457	Coolant temperature sender

Connections to main wiring diagram – 4, 8, 9, 10, 11, 12, 13, 14, 17, 18

Fig. 13.22 Wiring diagram – fuel management circuit for fuel injection models without fuel cut-off solenoid (1987 onwards)

41	Fuel pump	404	Fuel temperature switch
47	Coolant thermistor	405	Throttle potentiometer
164	In-line resistor: a) fuel pump (1 ohm) b) engine speed (6.8 K ohm)	406	Air valve stepper motor
		407	Air flow meter
250	Fuel cut-off switch	408	Injectors
296	Pump relay	409	Main relay
356	Speed transducer	414	Fuel electronic control unit (ECU)

Connections to main wiring diagram – 4, 8, 9, 10, 11, 12, 13, 14

Connection to air conditioning circuit (if applicable) – 16

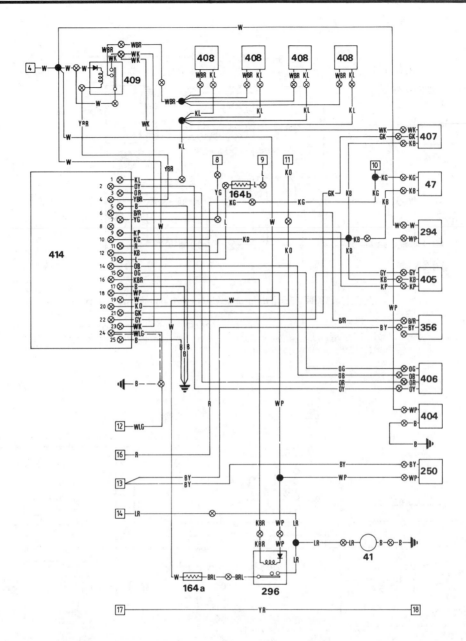

Fig. 13.23 Wiring diagram – fuel management circuit for fuel injection models with fuel cut-off solenoid (1987 onwards)

41	Fuel pump		404	Fuel temperature switch
47	Coolant thermistor sensor		405	Throttle potentiometer
164	In-line resistor: a) fuel pump (1 ohm) b) engine speed (6.8 K ohm)		406	Air valve stepper motor
			407	Air flow meter
250	Inertia switch		408	Injectors
294	Fuel cut-off solenoid		409	Main relay
296	Fuel pump relay		414	Fuel ECU
356	Road speed sensor			

Connections to main wiring diagram – 4, 8, 9, 10, 11, 12, 13, 14

Connections to oil pressure switch and warning lamp – 17, 18

Connection to air conditioning circuit (if applicable) – 16

Fig. 13.24 Wiring diagram – door central locking system

19	Fuse	344B	Door lock motor (rear)
260	Door lock solenoid switch	345	Door lock motor control unit
344A	Door lock motor (front)		

Fig. 13.25 Wiring diagram – 1.3 model air conditioning system

178	Radiator cooling fan thermostat	420	Compressor clutch
179	Radiator cooling fan	421	Air conditioning delay unit
187	Air conditioning relay	422	Evaporator thermostat
353	Air conditioning clutch relay	423	Air conditioning compressor switch
371	Air conditioning fan relay	424	Condenser fan motor
419	Air conditioning switch	425	Idle boost solenoid valve

Connections to main wiring diagram – 2, 3, 4, 5, 6

Fig. 13.26 Wiring diagram – 1.6 model (carburettor version) air conditioning system

164	Ballast resistor		380	Medium pressure switch
178	Radiator cooling fan thermostat		419	Air conditioning switch
179	Radiator cooling fan		420	Compressor clutch
187	Air conditioning relay		421	Ambient temperature relay
265	Ambient air temperature sensor		422	Evaporator thermostat
353	Air conditioning clutch relay		423	Dual pressure switch
371	Air conditioning fan relay		424	Condenser fan motor

Connections to main wiring diagram – 2, 3, 4, 5, 6

Fig. 13.27 Wiring diagram – 1.6 model (fuel injection version) air conditioning system

178	Radiator cooling fan thermostat	380	Medium pressure switch
179	Radiator cooling fan	419	Air conditioning switch
187	Air conditioning relay	420	Compressor clutch
191	Condenser fan switch	422	Evaporator thermostat
353	Air conditioning clutch relay	423	Dual pressure switch
371	Air conditioning fan relay	424	Condenser fan motor

Connections to main wiring diagrams – 2, 3, 4, 5, 6

Fig. 13.28 Wiring diagram – panel lamp dimmer circuit

14	Panel illumination lamps
81	Ashtray illumination lamp
210	Panel illumination dimmer switch
211	Heater control illumination lamp

Connection to main wiring diagram – 23

Fig. 13.29 Wiring diagram – 1.3 model (1987 onward)

Fig. 13.29 Wiring diagram – 1.3 model (1987 onward) (cont)

Key to Fig. 13.29

No	Description	Grid reference	No	Description	Grid reference
1	Alternator	A1	50	Reverse lamp	C1
3	Battery	A1	56	Clock	C3
4	Starter motor solenoid	A1	57	Cigar lighter	A4
5	Starter motor	A1	65	Luggage compartment lamp switch	B4
6	Lighting switch	B2	66	Luggage compartment lamp	B4
7	Headlamp dip/flash switch	B2	75	Automatic gearbox inhibitor switch	A1
8	Dip headlamp	B1	76	Automatic selector illumination	C3
9	Main headlamp	B1	77	Windscreen washer motor	A3
10	Main beam warning lamp	B1	81	Ashtray illumination lamp	C1
11	RH sidelamp	C1	95	Tachometer	B3
12	LH sidelamp	C1	110	Direction indicator repeater lamps, if fitted	C1
14	Panel illumination lamps	C1	115	Heated rear window switch	A2
15	Number plate illumination lamps	C1	116	Heated rear window	B2
16	Stop-lamps	C1	118	Windscreen washer/wiper switch	A4
17	RH rear lamp	C1	150	Heated rear window warning lamp	B2
18	Stop-lamp switch	C2	152	Hazard warning lamp	C2
19	Fuses	A2/A3/A4/B1/B2	153	Hazard warning lamp switch	C2
20	Interior lamp	B3	165	Handbrake warning lamp switch	B4
21	Interior lamp switches	B4/C4	178	Radiator cooling fan thermostat	B2
22	LH rear lamp	C1	179	Radiator cooling fan motor	A2
23	Horn	B2	182	Brake fluid level switch	B4
24	Horn switch	B2	208	Cigar lighter illumination	C1
26	Direction indicator switch	C2	211	Heater control illumination	C1
27	Direction indicator warning lamps	C1	212	Choke warning lamp switch	B4
28	RH front direction indicator lamp	C1	213	Choke warning lamp	B4
29	LH front direction indicator lamp	C1	240	Heated rear window relay	A2
30	RH rear direction indicator lamp	C1	243	Fuel cut-off solenoid	A1
31	LH rear direction indicator lamp	C1	246	Glovebox lamp	B4
32	Heater/recirculation blower motor switch	B2	247	Glovebox lamp switch	B4
33	Heater/recirculation blower motor	A2	286	Rear fog guard lamp switch	B2
34	Fuel gauge	B4	287	Rear fog guard warning lamp	B2
35	Fuel tank gauge unit	B4	288	Rear fog guard lamp	B1
37	Windscreen wiper motor	A3	297	Brake warning lamp	B4
38	Ignition switch	A1	298	Windscreen wiper delay unit	A4
39	Ignition coil	A2	305	Auxiliary relay	A3
40	Distributor	A1	308	Direction indicator/hazard warning flasher unit	C2
42	Oil pressure switch	B4	326	Brake pad wear sensor	B4
43	Oil pressure warning lamp	B4	413	Fusible links	A1
44	Ignition/no-charge warning lamp	A1	417	Luggage compartment warning lamp	B4
45	Headlamp flasher switch	B2	418	Lighting switch alarm	C4
46	Coolant temperature gauge	B4	493	Dim-dip resistor	B2
47	Coolant temperature sender unit	B4	494	Dim-dip relay	B2
49	Reversing lamp switch	C2	495	Instrument illumination dimmer	B2

Connections to supplementary circuit diagrams

No	Description	Grid reference	No	Description	Grid reference
1	Radio cassette player	A4	7	Radio cassette player	B3
2	Air conditioning	A2	19	Electric mirrors	A4
3	Air conditioning	A2	22	Electric windows	A4
4	Air conditioning	A1	24	Electric sunroof	A4
5	Air conditioning	A2	30	Electric sunroof	C1
6	Air conditioning	B2			

Index